Barry was born and raised as the third child in a fa
lived by the river Cam in the heart of the city, attend
college to study Electronics in pursuit of a career in uns up-and-coming industry.
His parents were not affluent and had to take in lodgers and sell "lunch" to local
workers to make ends meet. In fact, Barry's father Jack had to take on two jobs, as a
wireman by day and a waiter at Jesus College in the evenings, meaning Barry barely
saw his father during the week, and only briefly at weekends. After his early years
as an electronic test and eventually design engineer, Barry discovered leak testing
and has dedicated most of his working life to this subject.

Barry has been married to Maureen for nearly 40 years. When they got married, they
moved to the village of Bar Hill near Cambridge and have been active members of
village life as their sons Adam and Nathan have grown up. Barry coached children's
football for over 20 years and ran three youth teams, eventually ending up managing
two adult teams once his children grew up. Barry also ran the village table tennis
club for three years, quadrupling its participants during that time. Not content with
this, Barry also became a member of the local Parish Council but had to give this up
after just over a year due to work and his other sporting commitments.

Barry retired in 2020, and now spends much of his time painting, making models,
and generally doing all sorts of odd jobs around his home, as well as the static
caravan that he secured just an hour and a half from home some six years ago. His
son Nathan and partner Georgia have now presented Barry with his first grandchild,
who he loves spending time and playing games with. They can often be found on a
bridge above a stream playing "Pooh-Sticks".

One of Barry's passions is football, and he was an avid fan of Cambridge United,
also acting as programme seller for the club for many years. Barry's other big passion
is Lego, and as well as a bedroom full of models, he also supports the "First Lego
League", acting as a coach and mentor at local schools, and also refereeing and
supporting the competitions in Peterborough, Cambridge, and Bristol.

Retirement finally gave Barry the opportunity to write this book, which has been
on his "to-do" list for many years but was never completed due to work and other
commitments.

This book is dedicated to my late father, Jack Sidney Dean, whose wealth of knowledge passed with him. (I vowed that I would ensure what I learned would not go with me, but would be passed on.)

And to my boys, Adam and Nathan, who made me so proud and made my life so special, and essentially gave me a reason to write this book.

Barry Dean

LEAK TESTING MADE EASY

Richard 'Spanners' Ready
& the rest of the Radio
Cambridgeshire team

Please do read through this book
- there are some surprising & interesting *
facts about more than Leak Testing.

Thanks for inviting me to discuss
my book live on radio

Barry
#1
"Bubblemeister"

AUSTIN MACAULEY PUBLISHERS™

LONDON • CAMBRIDGE • NEW YORK • SHARJAH

* Pages 47, 53/54/61, 71, 73, 128/9, 210/11, 353

& look at the bubble chart on 549 — Leaks 1 million
time smaller can be found in secs.

A CIP catalogue record for this title is available from the British Library.

ISBN 9781398466159 (Paperback)
ISBN 9781398466166 (ePub e-book)

www.austinmacauley.com

First Published 2022
Austin Macauley Publishers Ltd®
1 Canada Square
Canary Wharf
London
E14 5AA

Just a few of the people I would like to acknowledge from my time as a leak test engineer:

Thanks to the many businesses I have worked for in helping me attain a love of work and helping others: Analytical Instruments, Ai Cambridge, Ion Science and Ion Science Systems, JW Froehlich UK, Fisher Leak Test, Perkins Diesel Engines, Caterpillar.

Thanks to a few people that I have worked with, who have guided and advised me along the way:

The directors of Analytical Instruments (who set me on my way in leak testing), Paul Hickman (electronic education), the people at Ateq (formed out of Analytical Instruments), Steve Hoath (who helped me understand the science of leaks more thoroughly), the team at JW Froehlich (who gave me the opportunity to develop my understanding of engine leak testing), the sales team at Furness Controls, Cliff Harris (who had so much experience in helium leak testing). Last but not least, Perkins Diesel Engines, part of the Caterpillar Group: some of the best people I have worked with, and a great place that I felt proud to be a part of.

Foreword

During Barry's years as a leak test engineer, he honestly felt that leak test companies like to shroud the business as some kind of "mystical" art where only the experts can advise. The intention of this book however, is to show you how to apply basic principles, and look at leak testing in a very simplified way, so that you too can become an "expert".

Barry initially trained as an electronics engineer, but when he began working as an Electronic Test Engineer for a company that made "gas sniffers" for leak testing, It sparked an interest, that he could not contain. Barry soon discovered that leak testing required very basic understanding of the mathematics, physics, and chemistry that he had learned at school, and so it was that he became "hooked" and began to learn all that he could about this enormous (not really, as you will find out from this book) subject.

He soon became aware that he could apply really simple concepts to help him understand how things worked, and has tried to share these in the chapters within.

During Barry's 40 years in the industry, he worked for a number of leak test companies, using his self-taught knowledge to help himself and others with a wide range of leak testing problems and solutions.

He began working as a design engineer, designing the electronic controls and pneumatic circuits for "purpose- built" leak test machines, for a wide range of applications, from fire extinguishers to corned beef cans. Barry then began to get more involved with the customers, by commissioning the machines at their sites, and training their staff on their use and maintenance.

This raised his interest in working with others outside my his organisation, and he then took the step to become a service engineer, to carry out repairs and maintenance both in- house, and at the customers' premises. His success lead him to be promoted to service department manager, covering not only leak testing equipment, but also on security equipment, including explosive and metal detectors, and X-Rray machines.

When the opportunity arose, Barry was asked into acting as product manager for the same company, helping develop the latest range of pressure decay and flow instruments, and he was instrumental in the launch of one of the first R134a gas sniffers (when the old refrigerants were recognised as causing issues with the ozone layer).

But his love of working and advising others soon pushed him into a technical sales role, where he became quite successful, due to the fact that he believed they really appreciated my his simplistic views and willingness to help them to understand the complexities of leak testing. In fact, Barry was so successful, that he considers himself to be very fortunate to travel all over the world, not only selling solutions to potential customers, but also carrying out a large number of training courses (each of which was tailored to the individual customer) around the globe.

Barry continued in this role with a number of companies, until his father-in-law became very ill;, and he was very pleased that when a job opportunity arose that allowed him to be closer to home, working for a more local engine manufacturer, helping them to develop their leak testing. When Barry first started with the engine company, he was being called out to the production line twice daily to resolve problems with the leak test equipment.

In the majority of cases, the equipment was fine, and it was clear that education was needed for the operators, and management staff. Incidentally, after 4 years in this role (and he had handed over to an engineer that he trained), the calls to the production line had receded to less than 1 per week. One of Barry's big successes whilst with the engine manufacturer, was to greatly reduce the number of "leak defects" in the field (at the company's customers). In fact, when he first joined the company, the number of leaks had amounted to over 30% of all defects, but within 4 years, the numbers of leak defects reduced by 70% to less than 19% of all field defects.

Barry's final role before retirement (giving him, at last, the opportunity to write this book), was more general as a "Supplier Development Engineer" (SDE), visiting and assisting suppliers to the company on a wide range of subjects to help them improve their overall quality of products supplied. Of course, Barry never lost his "Subject Matter Expert" (SME) status for leak testing and continued to support both the in- house leak testing as well as advising sister companies, and all suppliers with their own specific leak test needs.

Throughout his career in leak testing, the one overriding factor at top of the mind, was how simple leak testing was, and how educating people, benefitted so many people on so many occasions, so hopefully this book will show "you" how simple it is to understand both what leak testing is all about, and how to make sense of your leak testing equipment.

By no means will this give you all the answers (as for Barry to cover 40 years of experience in a single book would be almost impossible, and probably take him nearly 40 years to write), but if you follow the basic principles enclosed, he is confident that it will help "you" to get the best from your leak test requirements. It is well worth reading through the initial chapter which focuses on basic mathematics, physics, etc. as although these may seem obvious, these will definitely help you (as they did for Barry throughout his long career in leak testing) in the later chapters, and hopefully make all much easier to follow.

It is Barry's sincere wish that you find the content of this book informative, helpful, and useful in getting the best from your leak test requirements.

Table of Contents

Foreword   **9**

1. Skills Required for Leak Test Engineers   **27**

1.1. Mathematics   *28*

1.1.1. Add (or Plus): "+"   *28*

1.1.2. Subtract (or Minus): "-"   *28*

1.1.3. -ve (negative) Numbers   *31*

1.1.4. Multiply (or Times): "x"   *31*

1.1.5. Multiplying (and dividing) -ve numbers   *32*

1.1.6. Division (or Divide by): "÷"   *33*

1.1.7. Concentrations (Parts Per...)   *35*

1.1.8. Indices or Power Notation   *37*

1.1.9. Multiplying Indices   *38*

1.1.10. Rearranging Formulae   *39*

1.1.11. Simultaneous Equations   *41*

1.1.12. Averages   *42*

1.1.13. Medians   *42*

1.1.14. Mathematics Exercises   *43*

For answers: Section 20.1.1   *44*

1.2. Geometry   *44*

1.2.1. Volume   *44*

1.2.2. Geometry Exercises   *49*

1.3. Notation   *49*

1.3.1. Metric Notation   *50*

1.3.2. Leak Rate Notation   *50*

1.3.2.1. Volumetric Leak Rates (Flow)   50

1.3.2.2. Weight Loss as a Leak Rate   52

1.3.2.3. Pressure Decay as a Leak Rate   52

1.3.3. General Conversions   53

1.3.4. Notation Exercises   53

1.4. Sciences - Physics   53

1.4.1. Pressure   53

1.4.2. Temperature   55

1.4.3. Charles Law   55

1.4.4. Boyle's Law   56

1.4.5. Universal Gas Law   57

1.5. Sciences - Chemistry   58

1.5.1. Molecular Sizes/Masses   58

1.5.2. Viscosity   58

1.6. Sciences – Fluid Dynamics(?)   59

1.6.1.1. Hole Size (Diameter and Length)   59

1.6.1.2. Differential Pressure   60

1.6.1.3. Material/Pressure Differential   62

1.6.2. Hagen-Poiseuille's Equation   63

1.6.2.1. For Non-Compressible Fluids (Liquids)   64

1.6.2.2. For Compressible fluids (Gases)   64

1.6.3. Science Exercises   64

2. Understanding Leak Rates/Sizes   **66**

2.1. Why Leak Test?   66

2.2. A Little Bit of History   66

2.2.1. Test as Used   66

2.2.2. Air Under Water   67

2.2.2.1. Bubble to Leak Rate Calculation   68

2.2.3. Dry Leak Testing   69

2.3. Fitness for Purpose   70

2.4. Specifying Leakage Limits (Part 1)   76

2.4.1. Flow (Volume of Gas in Time) Specification 76

2.4.2. Weight Loss Specification 77

2.4.3. Pressure Decay Specification 78

2.5. Leak Rate Conversions Between Units 79

2.5.1.1. Weight Loss to Flow Conversion 79

2.5.1.2. Pressure Decay to Flow Conversion 80

2.6. Specifying Leakage Limits (Part 2) 83

2.6.1. Hagen-Poiseuille Equations (Liquids vs Gas) 83

2.6.1.1. For Non-Compressible Fluids (Liquids) 84

2.6.1.2. For Compressible Fluids (Gases) 84

2.6.2. By Experimentation (The Best Way—Back to Basics) 86

2.6.3. Virtual Leak Diameters (VLDs) 87

2.7. Typical Liquid Leak Specifications 87

2.8. Specifying Leakage Limits (Part 3) Complete Assembly Leak Limits 88

2.8.1. Tolerance Stack Up 89

2.8.2. Leak Limit Refinement 96

2.8.3. Result Review and Limit Refinement for Component Parts 100

2.8.4. Specifying Test Pressure 102

2.8.4.1. Impact on Equipment 103

2.8.4.2. Impact on test cycle time and results 104

2.8.4.3. Impact on Leakage 107

2.9. Specification Summary 110

2.9.1. Leakage Rate Limit 110

2.9.2. Test Pressure 112

2.9.3. Specification for High Pressure Parts/Systems 112

2.9.3.1. Example (Table 2-11) 113

2.9.4. Leakage Rates at Different Pressures 114

3. Choosing the Correct Leak Test Method 115

3.1. Considerations 115

3.1.1. Leak Specification 115

3.1.2. Takt Time 116

3.1.2.1. Multiple Test Machines/Stations   118

3.1.3. Costs   122

3.4.1. Is Gas Present?   126

3.1.5. Detect (Global) or Locate (Pinpoint)   128

3.1.6. Legal, Health, Ergonomic and Safety/Environmental   130

4. Leak Test Equipment   131

4.1.1. Pressure Test Methods   132

4.1.2. Flow Methods   132

4.1.3. Trace Methods   132

4.1.4. Product Deformation Methods   133

4.1.5. Other / Specials   133

4.2. Leak Detection/Measurement Devices   133

4.2.1. Leak Detector Sensitivities   135

4.2.2. Signal to Noise   136

5. Air Testing Methods   138

5.1.1.1. Pressurisation   138

6. Air Leak Test Methods Pressure Decay   140

6.1. How Pressure Decay Works   140

6.1.1. Gauge Transducers   141

6.1.2. Differential Pressure Transducer   144

6.1.2.1. Basic Principals   145

6.2. Pressure Decay Sequence of Operation   147

6.2.1. Stabilisation   148

6.2.1.1. Adiabatic Effects   148

6.2.2. Prefill   151

6.2.3. Standard Test Sequence Summary   154

6.2.4. The Internals of a Differential Pressure Decay Leak Tester   155

6.2.4.1. Prefill (Figure 6-17)   157

6.2.4.2. Fill/pressurise (Figure 6-18)   157

6.2.4.3. Stabilisation (Figure 6-19)   158

6.2.4.4. Measure/Test (Figure 6-20)   158

6.2.4.5. Vent (Figure 6-21)   *159*

6.3. Setting Up a Pressure Decay Sequence   *159*

6.3.1. Further Details of Some of the Parameters   *163*

6.3.1.1. Upper and Lower Pressure Limits (Figure 6-22)   *163*

6.3.1.2. Leak Rate Units   *164*

6.3.1.3. Test Volume Factor   *169*

6.3.1.4. Reference Reject (-ve) Limit   *173*

6.3.1.5. Leak Rate Offset Value   *180*

6.3.2. Setting Up a Pressure Decay Test - Additional Information   *183*

6.3.2.1. Filling Times   *183*

6.3.2.2. Stabilisation Times   *186*

6.3.2.3. Test/Measure Time   *192*

6.4. Special Functions   *193*

6.4.1. Tracking Offset   *194*

6.4.2. Vacuum Testing   *196*

6.4.3. 'N'-Test Function   *197*

6.4.4 Reference Volumes   *199*

6.4.5. Centre Zero (Pairs) Testing   *203*

6.4.6. Sealed Component / Bell Testing   *204*

6.4.6.1. Bell Testing   *205*

6.4.6.2. Sealed Component Testing   *207*

6.4.7. Volume Measurement   *210*

6.4.8. Reclaim Reject Limit   *213*

6.4.9. Fill on Fail   *214*

6.4.10. Remote Exhaust Valve   *215*

6.4.11. Multi-Program Testing   *215*

6.4.12. Temperature Compensation   *217*

6.4.12.1. Basic Temperature Probe   *218*

6.4.12.2. Null Pressure Temp Comp   *219*

6.4.12.3. Stored Temperature Compensation Curves   *221*

6.5. Pressure Decay Summary   *224*

7. Air Leak Test Methods - Air Flow Measurement   **226**

7.1. Pressure Drop Across Laminar Flow Elements   *226*

7.1.1. Basic Principles   *227*

7.1.1.1. Typical Laminar Flow Elements/Tubes (Figure 7-6):   *229*

7.2. Mass Flow Sensors   *230*

7.2.1. Basic Principals   *230*

7.2.1.1. Typical Mass Flow devices   *231*

7.3. Flow Measurement Techniques /Methods for Leak Testing   *231*

7.4. Direct Flow Measurement   *232*

7.4.1. Direct Flow Measurement Test Sequence (Figure 7-9)   *232*

7.4.2. Setting up a Direct Flow Test Sequence   *234*

7.4.3. Continuous Flow Method   *237*

7.5. Reference Tank Flow Measurement   *240*

7.5.1. Reference Volume Flow Measurement Test Sequence   *240*

7.5.2. Setting up a Reference Tank Flow Test Sequence   *243*

7.6. Separated Reference Tank Flow Measurement Test Sequence   *244*

7.6.1. Setting Up a Separate Reference Tank Mass Flow Sequence   *253*

7.6.2. Measure Time   *255*

7.6.3. Ref Tank Pressure   *256*

7.6.3.1. Establishing and Setting the Ref Tank Pressure   *257*

7.6.4. Measure Pressure – Leak Locate   *257*

7.6.5. Leak Rate Offset   *257*

7.6.5.1. Average Value Offset (Figure 7-36)   *258*

7.6.5.2. Minimum Value Offset (Figure 7-37)   *259*

7.6.5.3. Somewhere In-Between (Figure 7-38)   *260*

7.6.6. Volume Factor   *260*

7.6.6.1. Establishing and Setting the Volume Factor   *262*

7.6.7. Smoothing and Smoothing Fraction   *266*

8. Calibration of Air Test Systems   **269**

8.1. Calibration Equipment   *269*

8.1.1. Pressure   *270*

8.1.2. Leakage Rate Measurement 271

8.1.2.1. Known Fixed Leakage Rate (Calibrated Leak Master) 271

8.1.2.2. Adjustable/Variable Master Leaks (Figure 8-6) 273

8.1.2.3. Leakage Rate Measurement 274

8.2. Calibration Checks 276

8.2.1. Simple 1 Point Calibration Checks 277

8.2.1.1. Pressure Check 277

8.2.1.2. Leakage Rate Measurement check 277

8.2.2. Full (Multi-Point) Calibration Checks 283

8.2.2.1. Pressure Calibration Check 283

8.2.2.2. Leak Measurement Calibration Checks 285

8.3. Pressure Decay "In Depth" Calibration 288

Checking the Differential Transducer 291

8.4. Benefits of Calibration Checks 294

9. Summary of Air Testing 297

10. Tracer Gas Leak Detection 299

10.1. General Principles 299

10.2. Trace Gases 299

10.3. Different Detector/Sensor Types 301

10.3.1. Eyes: Air Under Water /Soap Bubbles/Solution 301

10.3.2. Ears (Ultrasound Detectors) 306

10.3.2.1. Background Noise 307

10.3.2.2. Noise Levels from Small Leaks 308

10.3.3. Thermal Conductivity 309

10.3.4. Ion Emission/Detection Sensors 311

10.3.4.1. Heated Filament (Figure 10-7) 311

10.3.4.2. Electron Capture (Figure 10-8) 312

10.3.5. Hydrogen Sniffer 314

10.3.6. Quartz Window Detectors 315

10.3.7. Helium Mass Spectrometer 316

10.3.8. Other Devices 318

10.3.8.1. InfraRed Detectors (Figure 10-11) 318

10.3.8.2. Carona Discharge (Figure 10-12) 319

10.3.8.3. Photo-Ionisation Detector (Figure 10-13) 320

10.3.8.4. Semi-Conductor Sensors (Figure 10-14) 321

10.3.8.5. Quadrupole Mass Spectrometer/Analyser (Figure 10-15) 321

10.3.9. Other Devices 322

10.3.9.1. Cameras 322

10.3.9.2. Liquid Detection Methods 322

10.4. Explaining Detector Sensitivities 322

10.5. Different Detection/Measurement Techniques 325

10.5.1. Direct Sniff 326

10.5.2. Purge Technique 328

10.5.3. CBU (Concentration Build Up) Technique 332

10.5.4. Vacuum Leak Testing with Mass Spectrometer Detector 336

10.5.4.1. Direct Vacuum Testing (Figure 10-32) 337

10.5.4.2. Vacuum Chamber Testing (Figure 10-34) 339

10.5.4.3. Helium Spray Technique (Figure 10-35) 341

11. Considerations for Trace Gas Testing **343**

11.1. Gas Mixtures 343

11.2. Mixing of Gases 347

11.3. Detector Contamination – Gross Leak Protection 350

11.3.1. Sniffing Gross Leak Tests 351

11.3.1.1. Air Gross Leak Test (Figure 11-6) 351

11.3.1.2. Trace Gas Gross Test (Figure 11-7) 352

11.3.2. Spray Test Gross Leak Tests 353

11.3.2.1. Vacuum Part Gross Test (Figure 11-8) 353

11.3.3. Vacuum Chamber Gross Leak Tests 353

11.3.3.1. Pressure Decay Test on Part 354

11.3.3.2. Vacuum Rise Test on Part 355

11.4. Transmission Time 357

11.5. Sealed Component Testing 358

11.6. Trace Gas Costs – Recovery?   *360*

11.7. Helium Testing   *361*

11.8. Atmosphere Monitoring   *363*

11.9. Detector Specificity – for Detection of Other Things...   *364*

12. Calibration of Trace Gas Detectors   **367**

12.1. Calibration Equipment   *367*

12.1.1. Known Leakage Rate (For Direct Detection – Sniffing Mode)   *368*

12.1.2. Internal Calibration Systems   *370*

12.1.3. Known Leakage Rate (Complex Machines)   *370*

12.1.3.1. Fixed onto a Master Part (Figure 12-4)   *370*

12.1.3.2. Introduced into the Air Stream to the Detector   *372*

12.1.3.3. As Part of a Special Calibration Circuit within the System   *373*

12.2. Carrying Out the Calibration Check   *374*

12.2.1. Direct Sniffing   *374*

12.2.2. Within the Complete System   *374*

12.2.2.1. Null Check   *375*

12.2.2.2. Span Check   *375*

13. Other Types of Leak Test   **379**

13.1. Product Deformation   *379*

13.1.1. Linear Transducer Measurement   *379*

13.1.2. Capacitive Measurement   *382*

13.1.3. Burst Testing (Knee Detection)   *385*

13.2. Vibration Detection (Acoustics)   *386*

13.3. High Voltage Detection   *387*

13.4. X-Ray Flaw Detection   *388*

13.5. Other Leak Testing   *389*

14. Leak Test Machines/Systems   **390**

14.1. Connections/Sealing to the Part   *391*

14.1.1. Simple Bolt-On Connections   *391*

14.1.2. Push-On Connections   *392*

14.1.3. Open Port Connections   *393*

14.1.3.1. Mechanically Operated Expanding Bungs   *394*

14.1.3.2. Pneumatically Operated Expanding Bungs   *395*

14.1.4. Screw-In (Screw-On) Connections   *398*

14.1.4.1. Quick Connect Versions   *399*

14.1.5. Seals and Sealing   *401*

14.1.5.1. Seal Application   *401*

14.1.5.2. Seal Design   *403*

14.1.5.3. General Seal Shape/Size   *405*

14.1.5.4. O-Rings   *409*

14.1.5.5. Quad Rings (or X-Rings)   *410*

14.1.6. Seal Design Summary   *411*

14.1.6.1. Seal Materials   *413*

14.2. Automated and Semi-Automated Systems (Connection)   *415*

14.2.1. Controls and Indicators   *418*

14.2.1.1. Typical Controls (Figure 14-34)   *418*

14.2.1.2. Typical Indicators (Figure 14-36)   *421*

14.2.2. H.M.I. (Human/Machine Interface)   *424*

14.2.3. Guarding and Safety   *429*

14.2.4. Electrical Control Systems (Figure 14-53)   *435*

14.2.5. Pneumatic Control Systems (Figure 14-54)   *436*

14.2.6. Fixtures/Fixturing   *436*

14.2.6.1. Interchangeable Fixturing   *437*

14.2.6.2. Clamping   *441*

14.2.6.3. Sensing   *445*

14.2.6.4. Part In Place Sensor (PIP)   *450*

14.2.6.5. Calibration Port (Figure 14-75)   *451*

14.2.7. Other Features of a Complete Turnkey System   *452*

14.2.7.1. Marking   *452*

14.2.7.2. Printers (Figure 14-81)   *454*

14.2.7.3. Scanners (Figure 14-82)   *456*

14.2.7.4. Reject Bins (Figure 14-83)   *458*

14.2.8. Air Pressure Decay and Air Flow Leak Test Machines   461

14.2.8.1. Volume Reduction   461

14.2.9. Trace Gas Test Machines   462

14.2.9.1. Leak Test Chamber   466

14.2.9.2. Volume Reduction   466

14.2.9.3. Test Chamber Materials and Cleanliness   467

14.2.9.4. Vacuum Pump Selection   468

14.2.10. Water Bath Leak Test Machines   470

14.2.10.1. Basic Water Baths/Underwater Testing   471

14.2.10.2. Industrial Water Bath Machines   471

14.3. Test Machines/Systems Summary – Good Practice   483

14.3.1. General Concept   483

14.3.1.1. Just a Leak Test Machine?   484

14.3.1.2. Single or Multiple Parts?   485

14.3.1.3. How Will It Be Operated?   485

14.3.1.4. How will We Control/Meet Our Required Throughput?   486

14.3.1.5. General Layout?   486

14.3.2. Recommended Features and Good Practice   487

14.3.2.1. Calibration Checks   487

14.3.2.2. Clamping and Sealing   488

14.3.2.3. Data Collection   488

15. Limitations of Leak Testing   **490**

15.1. Global Methods - Air Testing (Pressure Decay and Flow)   490

15.1.1. Temperature Variation in Pressure Decay Measurement   490

15.1.2. Temperature Variation in Flow Measurement (Figure 15-1)   492

15.1.3. Volume Variation   493

15.1.3.1. How Do Volume Changes Affect Flow Measurement?   497

15.1.4. False Failures   498

15.1.5. Instability/Adiabatic Effects   498

15.1.6. Tolerance Build Up   500

15.2. Trace Gas Methods   503

15.2.1. *Background Contamination*   *504*

15.2.2. *Clear-Down*   *505*

15.2.3. *Outgassing*   *505*

15.2.4. *Gas Concentration*   *505*

15.2.5. *Homogeneous Gas Mixtures*   *506*

15.2.6. *Transition Times*   *507*

16. Problems and How to Identify/Recognise Them   **509**

16.1. *Failing Everything*   *509*

16.1.1. *Air Testing (Pressure Drop and Flow measurement)*   *509*

16.1.2. *Tracer Gas Testing*   *512*

16.1.3. *Direct Sniffing Method*   *512*

16.1.4. *Trace Gas Systems*   *512*

16.1.4.1. *Leaks in the System*   *512*

16.1.4.2. *Alternative Leak Sources*   *513*

16.2. *Passing Everything*   *514*

16.2.1. *Air Testing (Pressure Drop and Flow measurement)*   *515*

16.2.2. *Tracer Gas Testing*   *519*

16.2.3. *Direct Sniffing Method*   *519*

16.2.4. *Not Detecting Leaking Parts in a Machine Test*   *521*

16.2.4.1. *Master Leak Gives Expected Result*   *521*

16.2.4.2. *Master Leak Gives Low Result (just below expected level)*   *523*

16.2.4.3. *Master Leak Gives High Result (above the expected level)*   *523*

16.2.4.4. *Master Leak Gives No Leak Result*   *524*

16.3. *My Customer Fails Parts that Pass on My Tester*   *524*

16.3.1. *Understand the Problem*   *524*

16.3.2. *Review/Understand the Specification*   *527*

16.3.3. *Review Leak Test Results*   *528*

16.4. *Calibration Check Results Varying*   *531*

16.5. *Occasional Failure for no Apparent Reason
(Part Passes when Retested)*   *531*

16.5.1. *Seems to Get More Failures at a Particular Time of Day
(Or Particular Months During the Year)*   *532*

16.5.1.1. Example 1 – More failures at a particular time of day 532

16.5.1.2. Example 2 – More failures in the summer months 533

16.5.2. Seems to Get More Failures at the Beginning of the Week (Or First Couple of Parts Each Day) 534

16.5.3. Completely Random Failures 535

16.5.3.1. Example 1 – Seal Wear 535

16.5.3.2. Example 2 – Quick Connector Leak 536

16.5.4. Random Failures that Are not Real 537

16.5.4.1. Example 1 - Borderline Leakers 537

16.5.4.2. Example 2 – Operator Error / Missed Rigging (SealingConnection) 538

16.5.5. Other External Effects 539

16.5.5.1. Air Starvation 539

16.5.5.2. Electrical Interference 539

17. Maintenance of Leak Test Equipment **540**

17.1. Rule #1 – Cleanliness 540

17.2. Rule #2 – Calibration Checks 541

17.2.1. Change of Part Fixture 541

17.2.2. Equipment not Used for a Period of Time 541

17.2.3. Regular/Routine Checks 542

17.2.3.1. Every Shift 542

17.2.3.2. Daily 542

17.2.3.3. Weekly 542

17.2.3.4. Monthly 542

17.2.3.5. Annually 542

17.3. Rule #3 – Review Results 543

17.4. Routine Checks (Table 17-1) 543

17.5. Routine Maintenance Checks (Table 17-2) 544

17.6. Manufacturers Recommendations 545

18. Appendix **547**

18.1. Conversion Tables 547

18.1.1. Length Conversions (Table 18-1) 547

18.1.2. Volume Conversions (Table 18-2)   *547*

18.1.3. Pressure Conversions (Table 18-3)   *548*

18.1.4. Bubbles to Leak Rate Conversions (Table 18-4)   *548*

18.1.5. Leak Rate to Bubbles (Table 18-5)   *549*

18.1.6. Weight Loss Conversions (Table 18-6)   *549*

18.1.7. Leak Rate Unit Conversions (Table 18-7)   *550*

18.1.8. Leakage Rate to Pressure Decay Rate (Table 18-8)   *551*

18.1.9. Hole Size to Leakage Rate (Table 18-9)   *553*

18.2. Periodic Table (Figure 18-4)   *555*

18.3. Typical Industry Standard Leakage Rates (Figure 18-4)   *556*

18.4. Fault Finding Charts   *557*

18.4.1. Part Fails Everything – Air Testing (Table 18-10)   *557*

18.4.1.1. Part Fails Everything – Air Testing (Continued) (Table 18-11)   *558*

18.4.2. Part Passes Everything – Air Testing (Table 18-12)   *559*

18.4.2.1. Part Passes Everything – Air Testing (Continued) (Table 18-13)   *560*

19. Seal Examples (Figure 19-1 to Figure 19-4)   **561**

20. Exercise Answers   **565**

20.1.1. Mathematics Exercises   *565*

20.1.2. Geometry Exercises   *569*

20.1.3.. Notation Exercises   *569*

21. Final Summary and Recommendations   **572**

1 Skills Required for Leak Test Engineers

In essence, this is not a simple list of requirements, however as a general guideline, a leak test engineer will generally have:

- An understanding of different measurement units (cm, mL, L, cc, etc.)
- A reasonably good grasp of mathematics (indices, adding, multiplying)
- A basic understanding of science (physics/chemistry)

These are all useful as a background to leak testing, which is very much rooted within these scientific fields, and some of the thought processes/ calculations require a reasonable understanding of geometry and pure mathematics (simultaneous equations, etc.), to enable clear understanding of the variety of calculations and conversions that are required.

In general, however, a logical and simplistic thought process is the overriding requirement for anyone wanting to fully understand this very wide-ranging subject.

As we walk through these pages, you will come to see that the simple ways in which the author views each topic, putting it into a language that makes sense to him (and hopefully you).

Leak testing is a very global term, and as you come to fully understand all of the enclosed, you will find that many leak testing experts are really only experts in their own particular field of leak testing and will themselves need guidance in other aspect of which you will undoubtedly have more experience.

The next few sub-sections will guide you through some of the basic understanding you might/will find extremely useful.

Before I do this however, it is worth just taking a step back to consider what form a leak takes. In simple terms, a leak is a movement of a substance from one area (where the substance is wanted) to another area (where it isn't desirable for it to be). In most of the cases you will come across, this will mean the passage of a fluid (liquid or gas) from inside a container to outside the container. But this is not always the case as sometimes the unwanted substance enters into the place we do not want it to be.

1.1 Mathematics

Before we go into some of the more complex mathematics, let us just refresh our minds on the basic four calculations.

1.1.1 Add (or Plus): "+"

When we see the formula 2 + 3, we know that this is simply the sum of the two numbers 2 and 3. They can be two (2) or three (3) of anything, such as apples:

2 apples	=	🍎🍎
PLUS		
3 apples	=	🍎🍎🍎
EQUALS		
5 apples or	=	🍎🍎🍎🍎🍎
simply		

$$2 + 3 = 5$$

1.1.2 Subtract (or Minus): "-"

Similarly, the formula 5 - 3, this is simply when we take 3 (of something) away from 5 (of something). This "take away from" expression is most helpful way of viewing the minus sign "-".

Again using apples, let us subtract 3 apples from 5 apples (by this I mean let us take 3 apples away from 5 apples):

5 apples MINUS	=	🍎🍎🍎🍎🍎
3 apples EQUALS	=	🍎🍎
2 apples or simply	=	🍎🍎🍎 **5 - 3 = 2**

But what if we see the formula the other way round?

By this I mean, what is the answer to -3 +5

When you first look at this, you may think we simply add 5 to 3, but we must not forget the "-"sign.

In mathematics, the sign ("+" or "-") is always attached to the number it precedes (is in front of). For me, I imagine some brackets wrapping the numbers and the signs, so that I remember which sign is with which number, so if I see:

$$-3 +5$$

I imagine (-3) (+5)

So in this way, I see we have to take away 3 from something, and add the 5 to something. But there is nothing else in our formula, and nothing is zero (0) So, we could write:

+0 -3 +5

Just one thing to notice here is that I have put a "+" sign before the "0"—it is worth remembering that when no sign is written beside a number, then we can automatically put a "+" sign with that number (just as we saw with our early equations, 2 + 3 = 5 which can be written +2 +3 = +5

Clearly using our apples example, we cannot simply take 3 apples from no apples.

But we could first add 5 apples to no apples, and then take the three apples away afterwards.

By this I mean we can rearrange our formula (by imagining the brackets around the numbers with their signs, this allows us to rearrange the formula simply thus

$$(+0) (+5) (-3) \text{ or } +0 +5 -3$$

And we can see that this is the same as our +5 -3 (if we add 0 then the total does not change)

And so

$$-3 +5 = +2$$

This seems very simple, however with subtraction, what if our answer is a minus "-". For example, let us now look at the formula:

3 - 5

As before, we can put the signs in for each number (+3) (-5) = ??

But how can we take away more than we have? In the good old days when I was just a little boy with my 3 pence in my pocket (that was my pocket money), if I went to the shop, then I simply couldn't buy the sweets that cost 5 pence, as I didn't have enough money.

But now I am much older, with a credit card, and with £3 in my bank account. But I want to buy the £5 Lego set, even though I don't have enough money…

Now I can buy that Lego set by paying with my debit card, and my bank account now goes into what is called an overdraft (which simply means I have spent more money than I have).

So, another way to look at numbers is to consider them on a ruler, as below (Figure 1-1). When I add "+", I move that number of spaces to the right, and when I subtract "-", I simply move that number of spaces to the left.

Figure 1-1

So in mathematics, the answer can be a "-" number. These "-" numbers are called negative (-ve) numbers.

But BE WARNED, it is not a good idea to have "-" money in your bank, as this means that I now owe the bank the amount of "-" pounds I have, and I will have to pay it back.

1.1.3 -ve (negative) Numbers

So we have an answer to our previous formula of "-2". But what does this mean?

Another way to view -ve numbers is to see that the 0 line on our ruler (Figure 1-2) is like a mirror, and a "-" (or -ve) number, can be viewed as a mirrored or the opposite of a "+2".

Figure 1-2

1.1.4 Multiply (or Times): "x"

One of the most important mathematics actions we do need to understand is the multiplication of numbers. What does 3 x 2 actually mean? One really simple way of remembering this is to say "lots of" when you see the multiply "x" sign

So 3 x 2 means   3 lots of 2

Let us return to our apples so that I can explain:

We have 2 apples

3 x 2 apples means 3 lots of 2 apples

So in total we can see that we have a total of 6 apples

So 3 x 2 = 6

1.1.5 Multiplying (and dividing) -ve numbers

I think most people understand what a -ve number is, the main difficulty most people have is when multiplying -ve numbers together:

+3 x +2 = +6
+3 x -2 = -6
but -3 x -2 = +6??

Remember, instead of 'times', say the words 'lots of' (shown in Figure 1-3) So:

+3 x +2 is +3 lots of +2, which is +2 and +2 and +2 = +6

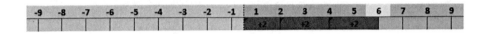

Figure 1-3

Similarly

+3 x -2 is +3 lots of -2, which is -2 and -2 and -2 = -6 (Figure 1-4)

Figure 1-4

As we have just seen 3 lots of -2 is -6 but what is -3 lots of -2 ??
Let us just say this slightly differently by saying it is minus 3 lots of -2, or Effectively moving our brackets around like this "-"(3 x -2).
As minus is the opposite of "+" then we could say it is the opposite of "+3 x -2" (as in Figure 1-5):

Figure 1-5

*In my early years, learning mathematics, I had an excellent teacher who said that unlike the phrase "two wrongs don't make a right"; in math, "two negatives **do** make a positive", which helps me remember how to multiply two -ve numbers.*

1.1.6 Division (or Divide by): "÷"

This is probably the most difficult of all the mathematic symbols, and is not very often written in this way, as we will see shortly, but first a simple formula:

$4 \div 2$

The divide by sign means how many lots of the second number (2) are there in the first number (4). We can do this with our apples as follows:

4 apples   =

How many lots of 2 apples are there? Split them up into groups of 2:

and we can clearly see there are 2 lots of 2 apples. So $4 \div 2 = 2$ (there are 2 lots of 2 in 4).

But what is the answer to $2 \div 4$?

This is much more difficult... how many lots of 4 are there in 2?

This is where we begin by rewriting the divide by "÷" formula in a different way. We put the first number above, and the second number below a line:

$\frac{2}{4}$ The line represents the "÷" sign

When we see numbers above and below a line, this is now called a fraction. Do not worry about this, but it is worth knowing what a fraction is, as it can take many forms. But how does this help?

One of the useful things about fractions is that if we do the same to the top and bottom numbers of the fraction, that it will still mean and be exactly the same. So with our $\frac{2}{4}$ we can do the same to both the top and bottom numbers, and it will still mean exactly the same.

Looking at the fraction, the smallest number is a 2, so what can we do to make this smaller? Well we could start by seeing how many lots of 2 are there in this number…

Quite simply, we can calculate that there is only 1 lot of 2

So we make the 2 smaller by dividing it by 2, but remember we have to do the same to the bottom of the fraction, so we must also divide the 4 by 2…

Our formula then becomes:

$$\frac{\frac{2}{2}}{\frac{4}{2}}$$

I know this seems complicated but bear with me.

As we have already said, there is 1 lot of 2 in 2, so we can now write:

$$\frac{1}{\frac{4}{2}}$$

In the bottom we can see that there are in fact 2 lots of 2 in 4

So we can replace the bottom formula with a single number

$$\frac{1}{2}$$ you might well recognise this as ½ or one half

Dividing -ve numbers

Remember when we're multiplying -ve numbers that two -ve's DO make a +ve Well the same applies when dividing -ve numbers

As we have seen: $\dfrac{+6}{+2}$ = +3

But if the top number is -ve then: $\dfrac{-6}{+2}$ = -3

Or the bottom number is -ve then: $\dfrac{+6}{-2}$ = -3

But if both numbers are -ve we could see how many times -2 goes into each of the numbers and we would see that this would turn both of them +ve, as there are THREE - 2's in -6, and only ONE -2 in -2:

$$\frac{-6}{-2} \quad = \quad \frac{\frac{-6}{-2}}{\frac{-2}{-2}} \quad = \quad \frac{+3}{+1} \quad = \quad +3$$

So dividing two -ve numbers makes a positive result!

Finally, a note on another way to express a fraction. Just as the "x" sign in multiplication means "lots of", in division, the "_" can also be expressed as "per", so $\frac{+3}{+1}$ *can also be expressed as "3 per 1", and* $\frac{+6}{+2}$ *can be expressed as "6 per 2". This will become more useful when we look at leakage rates but it leads our mathematics nicely on to concentrations.*

1.1.7 Concentrations (Parts Per...)

When we later come to look at trace gas testing, we will need to understand Concentrations of one gas within another.

The most common example (and one you will know doubt already know) of this is percent (*which actually means per hundred—as cent means 100—we can see other examples of the use of the word cent in Centimetres, 100 of which equals 1 metre, or Centigrade, where the scale goes from 0o = freezing point to 100o = Boiling point*).

More common in gas concentrations is "ppm" which is parts per million. For example, 4ppm Helium in Air, means 4 particles of helium and 999,996 parts of air, totalling 1,000,000 parts total.

How do we calculate the % value? Let us use examples to explain:

What is 15% of 20?

15% means 15 "per" 100 or another way to write this is $\frac{15}{100}$
100

so 15% of 20 can be written as

$$\frac{15}{100} \text{ lots of 20} \qquad (15 \text{ per } 100 \text{ lots of } 20)$$

Or $\quad \dfrac{15}{100} \qquad$ x $\qquad$ 20

which is 15 lots of 20 divided by 100 (15 x 20 / 100)

Or $\qquad \dfrac{15 \times 20}{100} = \dfrac{300}{100}$

so 15% of 20= $\quad$ **3**

If we have 6 apples and 69 oranges, what %age of all the fruit is apples?

First of all, we need to find out how much fruit there is in total: 6 apples + 69 oranges = 75 pieces of fruit. Now the number of apples as a fraction of all the fruit can simply be written as:

$$\frac{6}{75}$$

But we want to find the percentage, of number of apples per 100 pieces of fruit, so we could find out what we have to do to the "75" to make it into 100, and as with all fractions, do the same to the "6". (In fact this would mean multiplying both halves of the fraction by 1 and $\frac{1}{3}$ which is not quite so simple as you might think—particularly with more complex sums.

However, there is a much simpler way we can do this: simply multiply the fraction by 100.

$$\frac{6}{75} \quad x \quad 100$$

Which becomes $\quad \frac{6x\ 100}{75} \quad = \quad \frac{600}{75} \quad$ *(600 "per" 75)*

We can then work out how many times 75 will go into 600 (=8)
So 8% of the fruit is apples

Note: the act of simply multiplying by 100 comes from simultaneous equations, where we want to find out what 6/75 is when written as per 100. We can write

$\frac{6}{75} \quad = \quad \frac{??}{100} \quad$ *we can then multiple both sides of the equation by 100, and rewrite this as* $\quad \frac{6x\ 100}{75} \quad = ??$

So the ?? represents the per 100 value.

As we will see in our Trace Gas section, we often talk about concentrations in terms of ppm (parts per million). And as you can I am sure appreciate just multiplying the fraction by 1 million (1,000,000 or 1 x 106) is much easier.

1.1.8 Indices or Power Notation

Understanding the meaning of standard power notations will help us later when we need to understand leakage rates/sizes.

103 means 10 to the power of 3, which is 10 multiplied by itself 3 times or "10 x 10 x 10" which is another way of writing 1000.

Combining with our multiplication:

2 x 103 is 2 lots of 103 or 2 lots of 1000 which is 2000

This is a very useful and special way of making big numbers look much simpler by using the "x" sign (or lots of). Take the example of ½ a million pounds. One way we can write this is simply:

500,000

However, we can also write it as a multiplication 5 x 100,000 *(or 5 lots of 100,000).*

Or even simpler:

5 x 105

This is a very helpful notation as we can see that when we write 10"☆" The "☆" tells us how many "0's" (noughts) follow the "1". So 1012 is 1,000,000,000,000 (or a thousand billion). I am sure you will agree it is much easier to write 1012.

As we have seen:

3 x 103　　　　　=　　　　3 x 1000　　　=　　　3000

But what is the meaning of 10-3 ?

The minus in an indices tells us that is actually 1 divided by 10 to the power of the indices.

So 10-3 is in fact:　　　$\dfrac{1}{10 \times 10 \times 10}$

1 x 10-3　　=　　$\dfrac{1}{10^3}$　　=　　$\dfrac{1}{10 \times 10 \times 10}$　　=　　$\dfrac{1}{1000}$　　=

0.001

So as an example: 5 x 10-6

$$5 \times 10\text{-}6 \quad = \quad \frac{5}{10^6} \quad = \quad 5 \times 0.000001 \quad = \quad 0.000005$$

Remember how we found out that in +ve indices of 10 the indices number tells us how many "0's" follow a 1. This is not quite true for -ve indices, so a far better rule to follow is the Moving Point Rule.

This is one of the things I found really helpful at school for "a number times 10 to the power of something", was to look at the power as the number of places to move the decimal point from the start point. If the power is +ve then we move the decimal place to the right, if it is -ve then we move it to the left.

For example, if we have 2×10^3 it means a 2, and then we move the decimal place 3 places:

2.0	move the decimal place to the right once
20.0	now move the decimal place a 2nd time
200.0	and finally a 3rd time (10"3")
2000.0	

And for 2 x 10-3

2	move the decimal place to the left once
0.2	now move the decimal place a 2nd time
0.02	and finally a 3rd time (10"3")
0.002	

1.1.9 Multiplying Indices

One of the best things about multiplying indices is that we can use simple addition when we multiply identical numbers with indices. Let us take 200 x 3000 for example. If we simply multiply these numbers together, we will get 600,000. However, we can also write these two numbers as indices of the base number 10 like this:

2 x 102 x 3 x 103

With indices of the same numbers we can simply add the indices together So the two 10"☆"s become 10(2+3) = 105

And it becomes $2 \times 10^5 \times 3$

We can simply than multiply the 2 and 3 (=6). And it becomes:

$6 \times 10^5 = 600,000$

Remember, -ve indices can be treated in the same way:

$2 \times 10^{-2} \times 3 \times 10^3$ $=$ $2 \times 10^{(-2+3)} \times 3$

                              $=$ $2 \times 10^{+1} \times 3$

$=$ 60

Or in longwinded terms:

2×10^{-2} $=$ 0.02

3×10^3 $=$ 3000

$0.02 \times 3000 =$ 20

As well as understanding basic addition (+), subtraction (-), multiplication (x) and division (i), there are a number of simple mathematic principals which are very helpful to understand.

1.1.10 Rearranging Formulae

Let us use an example where we need to express "a" in terms of everything else:

- **4a**   **=**   **2(a + b) + 4b**

First of all consider the bracket part of the equation. The brackets act like a multiply sign, but meaning that all the items in the brackets are individually multiplied by the bit outside.

So the "2(a + b)" can be transformed to "2a + 2b" giving:

- **4a**   **=**   **2a + 2b + 4b**

Now we can see we have a's on both sides of the equations, and it would be great if we could combine them to simplify things.

To remove the "2a" from the right side of the equation we could simply subtract 2a, but this is an equation and like the top and bottom numbers in a Fraction, we must do the same thing on both top and bottom of the fraction.

This is the main rule to remember for equations and that is to treat both sides the same. So if we subtract 2a from the right hand side of the equation, we must also subtract 2a from the left hand side of the equation.

- 4a – 2a =   2a + 2b + 4b -2a

The 2a's on the right cancel each other out so we get

- 4a – 2a =   2b + 4b

Another trick my school mathematics teacher taught me that was really helpful was to consider that we move the 2a from the right to the left. When we move an item from one side of the equation to the other, we can consider that the bit we are moving crosses a bridge, and when it crosses the bridge, it changes its sign.

By this we mean that if we move the +2a from the right to the left, then on the left it becomes -2a:

- 4a – 2a =   + 2b + 4b

Now "4a" actually means "4 lots of a" (so in fact we could consider that it should be written as "4 x a" (Remember the "x" sign means "lots of".

Bearing this in mind, we can do some basic addition and subtraction and get:

- 2a   =   6b

(4 lots of "a" minus 2 lots of "a" = 2 lots of "a". Similarly 2 lots of "b" plus 4 lots of "b" = 6 lots of "b")

Now if we divide the 2a by 2 to just have "a" we must also divide the right hand side of the equation by 2 so that we get a in terms of all other items:

$$\bullet \quad a = \quad \frac{6b}{2} \quad = \quad \mathbf{3b}$$

1.1.11 Simultaneous Equations

This is an easy to understand principal where we can calculate one missing piece of information when we have similar information in another equation.

For example, if we know that 4 toys cost 36p, then how much would 3 toys cost. Obviously, we could work out how much 1 toy costs from the first statement 36p divided by 4 = 9p. However, we can write these as two statements as equations:

$$4 \text{ toys} \quad = \quad 36\text{p}$$

$$3 \text{ toys} \quad = \quad ??\text{p}$$

Now we can then consider combining these equations as follows:

$$\frac{3 \text{ toys}}{4 \text{ toys}} \quad = \quad \frac{??p}{36\,p} \quad$$ *(This is in fact dividing one equation by the other)*

Now as we saw previously we can rearrange the formula (by multiplying both sides by 36p) to get:

$$??\text{p} \quad = \quad \frac{3 toys \times 36p}{4\ toys}$$

From this we can calculate what 3 toys cost:
(3 lots of 36p = 108p divided by 4 and 108 divided by 4 = 27)

$$??\text{p} \quad = \quad 27\ \text{p}$$

We will see the use simultaneous equations throughout leak testing and especially when we consider the relationships between pressure, volume and temperature.

1.1.12 Averages

To find the average of a set of numbers, simply add the numbers together and divide by the quantity of numbers.

Example: The average of 5 numbers: 12, 9, 7, 14, and 12 is:

$$\frac{12+9+7+14+12}{5} \quad = \quad 10.8$$

1.1.13 Medians

Medians are often confused with average and considered a special type of average that ignore every strange value. In fact the median value is not an average at all but in fact the most popular value.

We will see how this can be useful when looking at leakage rate data, but first an explanation of the difference.

Here is a set of numbers and a chart (Figure 1-6) which shows the actual values, and plots of both the average and the median values. We can see we have one value that is greatly different from the rest (which increases the value of our average).

The median value is the most common value (10).

Which do you think best represents our values? The average is influenced by all of our readings, whilst the median appears to be telling us the typical value we can expect.

There are good reasons to use both/either. So chose carefully.

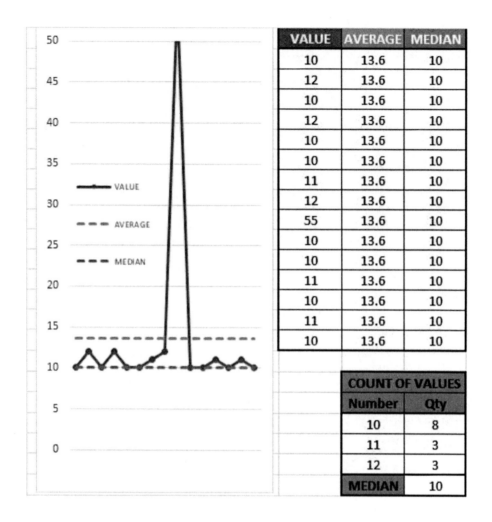

VALUE	AVERAGE	MEDIAN
10	13.6	10
12	13.6	10
10	13.6	10
12	13.6	10
10	13.6	10
10	13.6	10
11	13.6	10
12	13.6	10
55	13.6	10
10	13.6	10
10	13.6	10
11	13.6	10
10	13.6	10
11	13.6	10
10	13.6	10

COUNT OF VALUES	
Number	Qty
10	8
11	3
12	3
MEDIAN	10

Figure 1-6

1.1.14 Mathematics Exercises

1. *Monday, I bought 3 oranges and 4 pears for 66p, Wednesday I paid £1.10 for 10 apples and 3 oranges. Today 6 pears and 4 apples cost me 86p. How much do I need to take with me at the weekend to buy 5 oranges*

2. *Simplify the fraction* $\dfrac{12x10^6}{6 \; x \; 10^{-2}}$ *(into a x 10^b)*

3. *Year 8 at the school has 3 classes as follows:*

- *Class 8A there are 8 girls and 11 boys*
- *Class 8B there are 16 children and 25% of them are girls*
- *Class 8C only five of the 19 children are boys*

Work out the % of boys in the year, and the average class size

In a field there are 3 horses, 197 geese, 2,000 cows, and 7,800 sheep:

Work out the ration of horses to all animals in the field (in terms of parts per million "ppm")

For answers: Section 20.1.1

1.2 Geometry

Geometry is a branch of mathematics that you will have a better knowledge of than you realise, however there are a few items worth mentioning, In this section we simply need to understand that the measurement of leakage is in fact the amount of the leaked substance (from this point on the "substance" will be referred to as the "fluid") in a given time period.

"How much" can be expressed in many ways, as we will see when we look at the basic units of leak measurement, but for our first example let us look at the basic unit used, that of the size, or amount of the fluid.

1.2.1 Volume

By size/amount, we mean how much space does the fluid occupy, and in general terms this is referred to as the VOLUME of the fluid. So, when we talk about leaks, we are talking about a Volume of Fluid escaping.

You will all know what some volumes look like, for example:

- 330 ml is the size of a can of soft drink
- Your car fuel tank may hold 40 or 50 litres

Or considering cooking at home:

1 teaspoon	5 ml
1 tablespoon	15 ml
1 cup	240 ml
1 pint	470 ml

And you will likely also know that volume (Figure 1-7) is measured by calculating the product (by this I mean multiplying together) of the length, depth and height (**Volume = length x depth x height**) of an object).

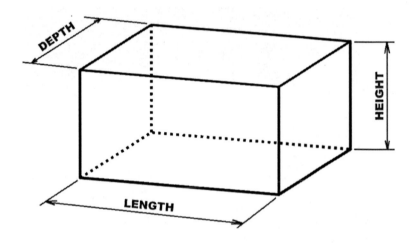

Figure 1-7

Another way to put this is Area x Length (Area = Breadth x Depth). This is particularly useful when considering a tube (which is the most common way to connect to leak test equipment). The tube is in fact a long circle (circle with length). The area of a Circle is given by "π r^2" *(you may recall this from your school days)*.

So the volume of a tube (Figure 1-8) is simply given by:

$$\pi\ r2\ x\ L$$

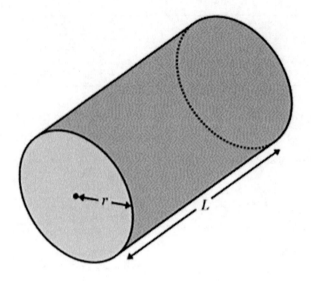

Figure 1-8

But why are volumes of interest in leak testing? We will see how leak rates and volumes relate in some of our calculations later, however one more interesting connections is the relationship of spherical volumes.

Most of us have at one time or another owned a pushbike. And a large majority might well have had a puncture at one time or another. Well the puncture is a leak path, which is letting the fluid (the pressurised gas) escape from the inside of the tyre (container) to the outside world (the atmosphere).

Do you remember how you found the point where the puncture was? Many of you would have held the pressurised tyre under water (Figure 1-9) and looked to see bubbles escaping. You were a leak test engineer, using a trace gas method to locate the leak!

Figure 1-9

But seriously if we wanted to know how fast the tyre would deflate, to see if we could get to school and then pump it up again for our home journey, we could have calculated the Leakage Rate by measuring the size of the bubbles, and how fast they were coming out of the tube.

Each bubble is a specific Volume of the air, so we have our volume in time which is in fact our amount of leaked gas! So how do we measure the size of a bubble? Simple geometry.

A bubble is a sphere (ball shape—as in Figure 1-10) and as such we can calculate the volume if we measure the diameter (distance across) the bubble. (Note the radius "r" of the sphere is one half of the total distance/diameter "d" across the sphere):

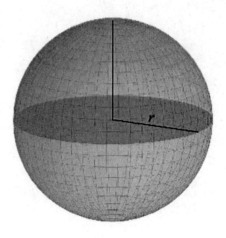

Figure 1-10

The volume of a sphere is given by the following formula:

$$\frac{4}{3}\pi r^3 \quad (\qquad \text{or} \qquad \frac{4}{3}\pi \frac{d^2}{8})$$

> *Note: The appendix contains a bubble conversion chart to enable you to estimate a leakage rate from viewing the bubbles of gas escaping from the part being tested, but let us just have a look at an example:*

For example, if we see 1 bubble every 6 seconds, and each bubble is approximately 5mm in diameter we can calculate the leakage rate as follows:

First calculate the size of each bubble:

$$\frac{4}{3}\pi \frac{d^2}{8} \quad = \quad \frac{4}{3} = \pi \frac{5^2}{8} \quad = \quad 65.48\text{mm}^3$$

Now as we see one bubble in 6 seconds, we will see 10 bubbles in 1 minute, so our volume loss is 10 x 65.48 mm3, or 654.8mm3 per minute.

At this point, I will just explain what is meant by mm3. Simply is means cubic millimetres. This comes about because for a Volume, we multiplied the width (in mm) by the Length (in mm) by the Height (in mm) so we have mm x mm x mm, and as we saw with 103 being 1000 which is 10 x 10 x10 we can similarly write mm x mm x mm as mm3).

Now there are 1000 mm3 in 1 cm3 (because 1cm = 10mm, so it makes sense that 1cm3 = 1cm x 1cm x 1cm = 10mm x 10mm x 10mm or 1000mm3) So our loss will be **0.6548 cm3 min-1**

Again, notice the "min-1" term, and remember that 10-1 was actually $\frac{1}{10}$ and so it is by min^1 we mean $\frac{1}{min}$ which means per minute.

Note: Often you may see mL s^{-1} (ml/sec). It is worth noting that mL, is grammatically more correct than cubic centimetres per minute, because 1mL is 1000th of a litre, and because there are 1000cm3 in a litre 1mL = 1cm3 or 1cc. The s-1 means "per second".

1.2.2 Geometry Exercises

1. Our water bath is 0.5m long, 25 cm wide, and 160mm deep. How many litres of water do we need to fill the bath to the top?
2. Holding our bicycle tyre under water, we see 50 bubbles appear over a period of 85 seconds. Each bubble is 3mm across. How many cm3 of air is escaping every minute to one decimal place?

For answers: Section 20.1.2

1.3 Notation

What do we mean by Notation? By this I mean the way we express different units in leak testing or in other aspects of engineering and life! You may be able to commit a number of basic facts to memory (although I still have to look them up sometimes).

Let us start with basic understanding of metric units and their notation.

1.3.1 Metric Notation

μ	=	micro (1,000,000th of the main unit)
m	=	milli (1000th of the main unit)
c	=	centi (100th of the unit)
k	=	kilo (1000 of the main unit)
M	=	Mega (1,000,000 of the main unit)

etc.

For example for lengths

1 km	=	1000m	=	100,000cm
1m	=	100 cm	=	1000mm
1cm	=	10mm	=	10000μm

etc.

or for Pressure

- 1 kPa=   1000Pa
- 1MPa =   1000 kPa   =   1,000,000Pa (or 106 Pa) etc

1.3.2 Leak Rate Notation

1.3.2.1 Volumetric Leak Rates (Flow)

In most cases we specify leakage rate as a volume in time (amount of the gas/liquid within a given time period, also known as flow rate).

Being able to recognise the different formats of these flow rates is important (here are some examples):

Atm cm3 min-1=cc/min (cubic centimetres per minute)

(This is number of cubic centimetres at atmospheric Pressure per minute)
Also known as "sccm" (Standard Centimetres per minute

Note: cm3   =   cubic centimetres

min^{-1} =   *per minute* $(\frac{1}{min})$

mBL/s=   millibar litres per second
(This is number of Litres at 1mB absolute pressure per second)
Atm L /hr   =litres per hour
(This is number of Litres at Atmospheric pressure per hour)
Note: 1L = 1000cc

One important thing to notice is that ALL flow rate notation has three elements:

- **Pressure:** This the pressure at which the volume is measured. This is particularly important when talking about leak rate of gases, such as air or helium, as gases are compressible fluids.
- **Volume:** This is the amount or quantity of the leaked substance (fluid).
- **Time:** This the duration or period over which this quantity of fluid will leak.

In many cases, people writing specifications get a little lazy, and you will often see leak rate notation without the Pressure part, such as 1cc/min or 1cm3 min-1, but in such cases, where no pressure is identified, then it is automatically assumed that the missing pressure is atmospheric pressure (approximately 1.013 bar, 14.7 psi, etc.) meaning that the volume of gas is the amount of space (or volume) the Gas occupies at normal atmospheric conditions.

This is also known and may be identified as SCCM, which stands for "Standard cc/min".

Just at this point a word about mb L s^{-1} (millibar Litres per second) units. Those of you who come across Vacuum Mass Spectrometer Leak Testing, where the suppliers of this type of equipment invariable specify leak rates in this form. I have already explained that this is in fact the number of Litres of gas leaked in 1 second when measured at a pressure of 1 millibar absolute pressure.

What does this mean in terms of SCCM?

If we consider that 1 Litre is in fact 1000 cubic centimetres then if we multiply our measurement in mB L s^{-1} by 1000, then we will get mB cm^3 s^{-1} (the number of cc of gas leaked in 1 second at 1mB absolute pressure).

We also know that 1mB is 1/1013 atmospheres, so if now divide this mB cm^3 s^{-1} by 1013 we will get atmosphere cm3 sec-1:

So:	atmosphere cm^3 sec^{-1}	=	1.013 x mB L s^{-1}

1.3.2.2 Weight Loss as a Leak Rate

In some industries, where gases inside the part have a larger molecular mass than air (the gas is heavier than air), it is more convenient to express the rate of leakage as a weight loss. For example:

oz yr-1	(oz/yr)	=	Ounces per year
gm yr-1	(gm/yr)	=	grams per year

These units are most often used in aerosol and refrigeration/air conditioning industries, where the gas used is heavier than air, and the introduction or top-up of these gases is also done by measuring the weight of the gas added.

Note that Weight loss units are wholly dependent upon the type of gas/fluid that is leaking, as all gases and fluids have different molecular masses. These can be determined from the periodic table (see appendix).

1.3.2.3 Pressure Decay as a Leak Rate

Similarly, where the engine, component or assembly (such as a car tyre) is filled/topped up to a specific pressure, then leakage rates are often specified as a drop in this pressure. For example:

mB sec-1 (mb/s)	=	millibars per second
Pa Sec-1 (Pa/s)	=	Pascals per second
mm H20 sec-1 (mmWg/s)	=	mm Water gauge per second
psi min-1 (psi/min)	=	pounds per square inch per minute

Pressure loss is wholly dependent on the volume of the part that is being tested (see next section reference PV/T).

As we will establish later, all leak rates can be related to each other by looking at the basic first principals of each unit. In general, the volumetric leak rate (flow) is considered as the primary unit, and other measurements related to this as follows.

1.3.3 General Conversions

It is also worth understanding some of the basic conversions that are often used, such as converting between different units, and measurements, such as length, volume, pressure, weight, etc.

For example, air/gas pressure is specified and talked about in many different units:

- psi/psig *(Pounds per square inch/pounds per square inch gauge)*
- Bar/mBar *(Bar/milli-bar)*
- MPa/kPa *(Mega-Pascal/Kilo-Pascal)*

Understanding the conversions between these units is well worth knowing, although there are numerous conversion charts/calculators available nowadays:

14.504 psi = 1.0 Bar = 100kPa

1.3.4 Notation Exercises

1. *Express 1 x 10-3 cm3sec-1 as mm3min-1*
2. *Three parts are bolted together, they measure 0.217m, 75mm, and 3000µm. How many cm is the total length.*
3. *We want to set our pressure to 5psig, but our gauge is in millibar—what value should we set on the gauge (to the nearest whole number).*

For answers: Section 20.1.3

1.4 Sciences - Physics

1.4.1 Pressure

This is the force that a gas or liquid exerts on the surface it is in contact with. One of my favourite experiments when I was younger was to show how air presses down on a piece of paper. First hang a wooden rule over the edge of a desk, and then without holding the end on the desk down, try and snap the rule with a sharp blow on the open. Not easy to do, but if we now place a sheet of paper on the end on the desk and repeat the experiment, it is surprisingly easy to snap the rule, as the air pressure on the paper acts to hold the desk end down (in a similar way to using your hand to hold it down. (I am sure you can search less destructive experiments of air pressure on the Internet.)

In most cases we talk about the pressure with respect to the atmospheric pressure around us. This is referred to as GAUGE PRESSURE.

The atmospheric pressure around us changes by small amounts depending on the weather. If we look at a typical weather chart on the television, we will see lines on that chart. These are lines of equal atmospheric pressure:

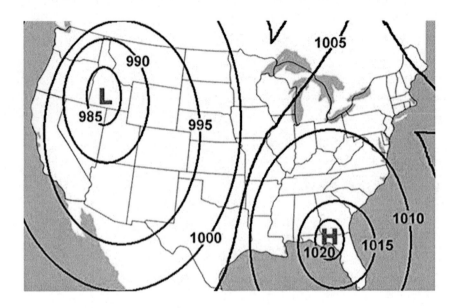

Figure 1-11

In the example here (Figure 1-11) some of the lines have been marked with their barometric pressure—these pressures are in millibar. So the small circular line around the "H" shows that the air is exerting 1020 millibar pressure at these points (1.02 Bar), and the 985 around the "L" indicates an air pressure of only 985 millibar (or 0.95 Bar).

The "H" indicates that this is an area of high pressure, and similarly the "L" represents an area of low pressure. *(Incidentally, how do you think that high and low pressures are created? We will discuss this later.)*

Anyway, in case of gauge pressure, this will clearly vary slightly according to the atmospheric pressure as we can see that the atmospheric pressure is not always the same because of the weather.

In many of our theoretical calculations, we try to remove this variation by measuring pressure in terms of absolute values (i.e., not with respect to the atmospheric pressure) with respect to absolutely zero pressure.

Note: 1 atmosphere is considered to be approximately 14.7 psi, or 1013 millibar.

1.4.2 Temperature

Temperature is just another way of measuring how much energy the molecules of a substance have. But don't worry about this, I think that most people have a good idea of what temperature is.

Just as we have seen with pressure, the temperature of gases and liquids can be measured in many different units (of which 3 are commonly used). See table below (Table 1-1):

	Fahrenheit	Centigrade / Celsius	Kelvins
Boiling Point of Water	212	100	373
Freezing point of Water	32	0	273
Absolute Zero	-459	-273	0

Table 1-1

Like pressure, we generally use absolute units when doing our theoretical calculations so consider the Kelvin scale as most appropriate.

1.4.3 Charles Law

Also known as the law of volumes, Charles Law describes how gases tend to expand when heated; i.e., when the pressure on a dry gas is held constant, the (absolute) Kelvin temperature and the volume will be directly related. This directly proportional relationship can be written as:

- $V \propto T$

or

- $\dfrac{v}{T}$ $=$ k(where k is a constant)
- $\dfrac{v_1}{T_1}$ $=$ $\dfrac{V_2}{T_2}$

One of the best examples of this is when I have a bottle of water in my car when driving around on a warm day. If I close up my bottle and leave it overnight, I can see a remarkable change the next morning, after the cool of the night. The bottle has begun to collapse in on itself. This is because, as the temperature dropped, the volume of the air (in the space above the water) reduces due to the reduction in temperature.

1.4.4 Boyle's Law

In a similar way, Boyle's law describes how the pressure of a gas tends to increase as the volume of the container decreases; i.e., the absolute pressure exerted by a given mass of an ideal gas is inversely proportional to the volume it occupies if the temperature and amount of gas remain unchanged within a closed system.

Note that absolute pressure and absolute temperature values are used for these calculations.

Mathematically, Boyle's law can be stated as:

- $P \propto \dfrac{1}{V}$

or

- P V = k (where k is a constant)
- P1V1 = P2 V2

We can demonstrate this by squeezing a balloon into a smaller and smaller bubble, until it pops because the pressure inside the balloon bubble increases until the balloon cannot hold it back anymore.

1.4.5 Universal Gas Law

Combining Charles' and Boyle's laws we arrive at the Universal Gas law for ideal gases as:

PV =nRT

- *P = Pressure (Absolute)*
- *V = Volume of Gas*
- *n = number of moles*
- *R = universal gas constant = 8.3145 J/mol K*
- *T = Temperature (oK)*

Or, more simply, when looking at changes in any of the variables:

$$\frac{P_1 V_1}{T_1} \quad = \quad Constant \quad = \quad \frac{P_2 V_2}{T_2}$$

Important note: "PV/T = constant" is one of the most important formulas to remember when working with Pressure decay and other air test methods, as it can be used to diagnose many issues. Remember this formula.

This is probably the most useful formula when considering anything to do with air testing (pressure decay or flow) as it can be used to understand the basic conversion theories, and also when diagnosing problems.

Now, remember the weather map? If you recall I posed the question as to how the pressure gets changed from High to low and vice-versa…

Well let me use the Universal Gas Law to explain:

$$\frac{P_1 V_1}{T_1} \quad = \quad \frac{P_2 V_2}{T_2}$$

Now if we consider a fixed amount (or volume) of air, then the volume cannot change so V1 = V2, and if we divide both sides of the equation by this V1 (or V2) We can now see that:

$$\frac{P_2}{T_2} = \frac{P_2}{T_2}$$

And by this we can see that if the sun was to increase the temperature of the air, then the pressure will rise (to keep both sides of the formula equal). And so the "H"igh pressures are generally where the sun is heating the air and we find that it is colder in the "L"ow pressure areas.

1.5 Sciences - Chemistry

Do not worry about these next two sections as they are for information only, but worth understanding.

1.5.1 Molecular Sizes/Masses

As you may or may not know, the properties of gases, and in particular their mass, is useful in determining leakage rates—particularly when the leakage rates are very small (such as when we are trying to detect gas leaks rather than liquid leaks.

At these small leak sizes, the rate at which the gas escapes is generally governed by the physical size of the molecule, and in general terms, the larger the molecule, the greater the mass of the molecule.

So using the periodic table can be useful when relating leak rates of different gases. As a rough guide, the leakage rate is proportional to the inverse square root of the mass of the gas, so *(Q = Leak Rate, M = Mass)*

- $Qg \propto \dfrac{1}{\sqrt{M_g}}$ or

- $Q_{gasA} = \dfrac{Q_{gasBX}\sqrt{M_{gasB}}}{\sqrt{M_{gasA}}}$

1.5.2 Viscosity

Viscosity is the measure of how well the molecules of a substance (gas or liquid) are attached (attracted) to each other. The stronger the bonding between molecules, the more viscous the substance is. This affects the leakage rate by virtue of the fact that the less viscous a substance the easier it can pass through the leakage path. (In common terms, we think of viscosity as how thick the fluid is. For instance, honey is thicker than water = honey has a higher viscosity than water, and water thicker than petrol = water has a higher viscosity than petrol.)

The relationship between leak rates for different gases for viscous leakage, is proportional to the viscosity of those gases *(Q = Leak Rate, η = viscosity):*

- $Q_g \propto \eta_g$ or   or

- Q_A $=$ $\dfrac{Q_B X \eta_A}{\eta_B}$

Some common viscosities are listed below: *(cp = centipoise, and Pa s = Pascal second)*

Air	=	0.1837 cp	=	0.0001837 Pa s	(@ 20oC)
Helium	=	0.196 cp	=	0.000196 Pa s	(@ 20oC)
Water	=	1 cp	=	0.001 Pa s	(@ 20oC)
Motor Oil	~	650 cp	=	0.65 Pa s	(@ 20oC)

Note "~"means approximately

1.6 Sciences – Fluid Dynamics(?)

In this section, we are looking to have some form of common equation that we can use to calculate the leak rate of a fluid (gas or liquid), from the details of the hole size, and the gas/liquid being used etc.

First let as look at all of the different the factors that influence/affect leakage rate. In previous sections of this chapter we have already looked at the effect of different gases/liquids have on how fast the fluid passes through a leak path, but what other thing impact the leak rate?

1.6.1.1 Hole Size (Diameter and Length)

I know this seems very obvious, but in simple terms, the larger the hole the faster the leak rate (or the more gas/liquid that can pass through the hole at any one time).

Not so obvious is the length of the hole, but this is where I personally like to picture gases/liquids as rubberised ball bearings (Figure 1-12) which in effect is what a group of molecules act like.

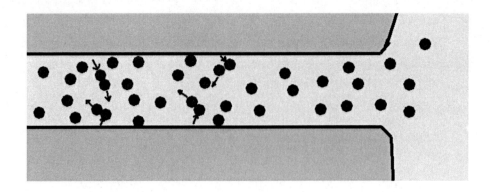

Figure 1-12

These rubber balls will bounce around off the walls of the tube, colliding with other molecules, and slowing down their movement through the tube. The longer the tube, the more collisions, and the slower the flow.

1.6.1.2 Differential Pressure

By differential pressure we mean the driving force that pushes the fluid through the hole/leak path. Again I have simple way of looking at this, by considering the difference in pressure across the leak path as a hill down which the rubberised marbles roll. The steeper the hill the faster the marbles will roll down the hill, and so the higher the pressure differential across the leak, the faster the air/gas flows though and so the greater the leak rate.

One place where we can see this in action is the wind in the air. If we look at the weather maps we see on television (Figure 1-13) we see lines on the maps which show lines linking the points of the same pressure (these are called isobars). When these lines are close together, then the wind is stronger. The further apart they are the breeze become lighter.

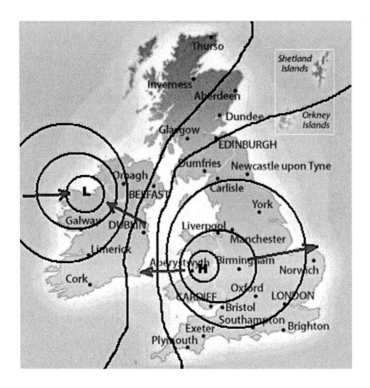

Figure 1-13

Consider looking at this map from the side view (Figure 1-14) and you will hopefully see what I mean and understand how the pressure difference affects the flow/leak rate. (Remember the air molecules are like rubber marbles!)

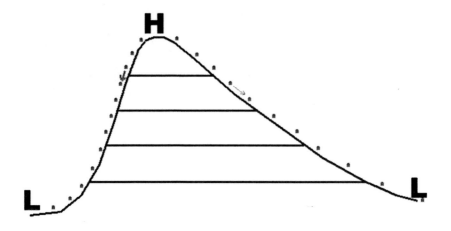

Figure 1-14

Note: In fact the air/wind doesn't travel in straight lines, but actually will travel in a similar way to water as it disappears down our bath plug hole and spirals around.

Figure 1-15

1.6.1.3 Material/Pressure Differential

Whilst not strictly true, one of the biggest mistakes people make when leak testing, is to test a part at inflated pressure differentials across the leak path in an attempt to increase the leakage rate to make it easier to detect.

Whilst this can help in a solid component such as a metal casting, it can also reduce the leakage rate when the material is soft and flexible (Figure 1-16) and as is more often the case when testing assemblies with flexible component parts such as O rings, the increased pressure applied can force the O-Ring into a position where it seals perfectly. When the pressure in normal use is applied, the O-Ring relaxes and the leak will appear.

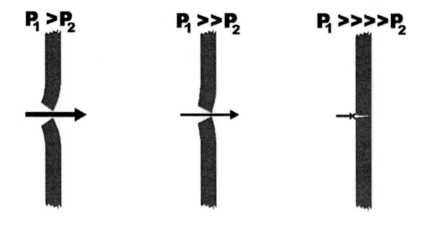

Figure 1-16

But is there any way we can pull all of these factors together into one place so that we can mathematically calculate the leakage rate from the various criteria.

1.6.2 Hagen-Poiseuille's Equation

In the late 1830s-early 1840s, two scientists (G. Hagen and J Poiseuille) independently derived the theoretical equation from their own detailed experimentation.

The equation relates the laminar flow through a straight tube of consistent diameter to the pressures applied, and the type of fluid passing through the tube.

The basic fluid dynamic equation is:

$$\Delta P = \frac{8 \, X \, \mu \, X \, LQ}{\pi \, X \, R^4}$$

Where

- ΔP = pressure Difference (pascal)
- μ = dynamic
- L = length of tube(m)
- Q = volumetric flow Rate(m^3/s)
- π = Pi
- R = radius of tube (m)

Adapting Poiseuille's equation, we can get one of two equations depending on the fluid type:

1.6.2.1 For Non-Compressible Fluids (Liquids)

$$Q = \frac{(P_i - P_O) \times \pi \times R^4}{8 \times \pi \times L}$$

Where

- P_I = Pressure at inlet of tube
- P_O = Pressure at outlet of tube

1.6.2.2 For Compressible fluids (Gases)

$$Q = \frac{\pi x R^4}{8 \times \pi \times L} x \frac{(P_i^2 - P_o^2)}{2 \times P_o}$$

To take into account that the flow rate will not be constant along the length of the tube.

However, be warned—these are all theoretical making a number of assumptions (laminar flow, straight tube, perfectly circular, etc.), none of which are very likely in practice, so these formulae should be used as a guideline only.

1.6.3 Science Exercises

1. For our leak test on an engine fuel circuit, we have pressurised our engine fuel circuit to 1 Bar wrt atmosphere (*assume 2 Bar Absolute*). There is a single fuel filter with a 1 Litre volume, and the fuel circuit pipework is 4mm internal diameter and is 102cm long. All other volumes (pump/ common rail, etc.) add up to a total volume of 15cm^3). Calculate the temperature change that would cause the pressure to drop by 15 Pascals.

2.   During our test on a 1 litre plastic container, we notice that the container swells/expands a little when we apply our 1 Bar Test Pressure. Our test result showed a 22 Pascal drop in pressure. What was the volume change in cubic millimetres caused by the expansion of the container.

For answers: Section 20.1.4

2. Understanding Leak Rates/Sizes

Well, that's basic mathematics and science out of the way, now let's get on with the business of leak testing, but to kick us off first…

2.1 Why Leak Test?

Like other non-destructive tests, leak testing is utilised for a number of reasons, typically:

- Safety.
- Product performance.
- Prevent loss of costly materials.
- Prevent contamination of the environment.
- Product reliability.
- Reduce warranty repairs.
- Reduce liability claims.

All of which serve to reduce costs and most importantly, ensure customer Satisfaction.

2.2 A Little Bit of History

2.2.1 Test as Used

Many, many years ago, people noticed the fluid/liquid coming out of their container (cup) and spilling onto their laps. And so the first leak testing began where they would test the container by filling it with the fluid and visually inspecting the outside of the container for signs of the liquid, before they took the risk of using it as a drinking vessel.

Of course, one thing I always impress on everyone, is that this testing as used is still the acid test for leakage, checking that the fluid (gas or liquid) remains in the container, and this method is still very much in use today in many industries, although generally not where liquids are concerned as follows.

> *For example, aerosol cans, and refrigerators are filled with the gas they use, and then a special detector is employed to inspect the outside of the can/refrigerator for signs of the contents escaping. We can see how this technique is still the best way for a plumber to detect/locate leaks by filling the system with water, and then inspect the joints to determine if there is a leak.*

Of course, this is OK, but it also poses a number of issues such as:

1. It can be very messy, where liquids are concerned (or even dangerous depending on the gas or liquid contained in our product).
2. It can be quite a slow method, when looking for leaks in large, or complex products/structures.
3. When we sell/ship the item tested, the fluid may have to be drained out during transportation.

Similarly, it may also not be the most effective:

1. Was the operator looking properly, or long enough (when looking for very small leaks), for the liquid to escape?
2. Spillages of fluid can lead to false recognition of leakage.
3. Not easy to verify if the product as leak tight to fluid entry (i.e., if we are trying to stop thing getting in).

So people began to look for alternative methods for testing for leakage.

2.2.2 Air Under Water

Then people began inflating things (tyres, balloons etc.) with air Initially by blowing into them). This made the next step fairly simple to take, in that they could hold these air filled/pressurised parts under water and look for bubbles escaping to indicate a leak path. This is everyone's first thought when leak testing is discussed, as I am sure many of you have done this when you had your first bicycle tyre puncture.

Again although very successful, this technique also poses a number of questions/issues.

1. Was the operator looking properly, or long enough for a really small leak to show?
2. Because the part becomes wet, we would most likely need to dry the part before we can sell/ship the part.
3. Water creates a risk of damage, such as rust on metal parts if not properly dried.
4. The problems immersing big items, such as a car engine under water are pretty evident.

But one of the biggest issues (not generally appreciated) is that:

5. This is a very sensitive method, and we might reject/repair, or even scrap parts that are perfectly OK.

This last item definitely needs some explanation, as many leak test equipment suppliers will tell you how insensitive air under water testing is, so let us first look at bubbles to understand the leak rate.

2.2.2.1 Bubble to Leak Rate Calculation

Let's go back to our bubbles. How small is the smallest bubble we can comfortably see with our eyes. If we look at a glass of champagne, we can easily see these bubbles, yet they are probably ½ mm in diameter (or maybe smaller)
Playing safe, let us calculate the volume of a 1mm bubble.

$$\text{Volume of a sphere} = \frac{4}{3}\pi r^3 \quad (\text{or } \frac{4}{3}\pi \frac{d^3}{8})$$

So our 1mm bubble has a volume of $\frac{4}{3}\pi(0.5)^3 mm^3$

$$0.52mm^3 \quad = \quad 0.00052cm^3(\text{mL}) \quad (1000mm^3 = 1cm^3)$$

If we have 1 of these bubbles every second then our leakage rate is

$$= \quad 1 \times 0.00052 \text{ ml/s} \quad = \quad 0.00052 \text{cm3 sec-1}$$
$$= \quad 0.0312 \text{ cm3 min-1 (ml/min)}$$

At this rate, it would take around 22¼ days (nearly 1 month) to lose 1 litre of the air!

As you will see when we discuss limits for liquid leakage, this is a very small leakage rate, rejecting a part with this small a leak rate is often unnecessary.

> *Note: Typical limits for liquid leakage are 1ml/min or greater!*

For a guide to bubbles to leakage rate, please see the bubble chart in the Appendix section of this book.

2.2.3 Dry Leak Testing

So to avoid the messy practices using water and other liquids, people began to look for ways to test parts/products completely dry, and so a wide range of dry testing methods were developed, most of which we still use today.

These can generally be split into the two main categories in use today, although others will be discussed later in this book.

> *Note: There are other (less common) forms of dry testing but these will be discussed later in this book.*

- Dry Air Leak Testing

where we pressurise the part with air, and then monitor the effect of the leakage on that air (either by measuring the drop in pressure caused by the leak, or by measuring the air flow from the leak, by measuring the amount of air required to maintain the pressure).

- Tracer Gas Leak Testing

where we introduce a trace gas (different from air) and then by some technique, and special detecting device, measure how much of the trace gas is escaping.

Both of these methods have distinct advantages over previous methods as follows:

- Dry

No drying or emptying of the assembly is necessary so as soon as the part has passed the test it can be immediately packed for shipment (or moved on to the next part of the assembly process).

- Quantifiable

Because we are able to measure the leakage, we can

o Set limits reducing unnecessary cost for repairs when not required
o Maintain a level of traceability of results against component serial numbers or batch codes/dates
o Monitor results for trends, to highlight process drift etc.
- Semi-automatic

Because these are in the main electronically controlled measurement devices, then we can build these into a machine, releasing the operator to perform other tasks whilst the test is running.

2.3 Fitness for Purpose

As we saw with our air under water tests, leaks can be very small, but why should this matter? Surely any leak is a leak, isn't it?

Let us consider three different items (Figure 2-1)—which of them contains a leak?

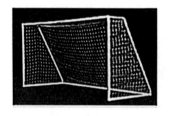  

Soccer Goal?   Colander/Strainer?   Potato Chip Packet?

Figure 2-1

At first glance, and if all were tested to the same criteria, we might consider the soccer goal, and the colander/strainer to leak, and the potato chip pack is not open, so presumably is not leaking. However…

1. The **soccer goal** is correctly strung, and no soccer ball can pass through any of the netting/webbing—does not leak, and is fit for purpose!
2. The **Colander/Strainer** retains all the vegetables whilst they are drained or washed so it also—does not leak, and is fit for purpose!
3. The **Potato Chip** packet however… When opened, the potato chips are found to be soft and inedible—leaking! And definitely not fit for purpose.

So what this tells us is that although air will comfortably pass through both the soccer goal, and the colander/sieve far more easily than it might pass through the potato chip packet. Both the Goal, and the Colander/Sieve are acceptable for the purpose for which they are intended.

The soccer goal and the colander are therefore Fit for Purpose *(this is my favourite phrase when talking about leak testing)*, whilst the potato chip packet is not. What does this mean for us in leak test terms? Simple, it means that we need to specify our criteria for Fit for Purpose of each product.

Even if we only lose 1 cc of the gas in 10 years there is still a measurable leak, so in fact there is really no such thing as no leak (Figure 2-2):

Figure 2-2

But why do I say absolute leak tightness does not exist? This is a little tongue in cheek, as clearly it does relate to, or depend on fitness for purpose as I have previously explained (in the example of the soccer goal… it is absolutely leak tight to soccer balls). However, what I am saying is that we must consider that there are leakages that are very small, even though they do not really concern us.

To help me make some sense of this, I always think about the basic structure of all matter in that all gases, liquids, and solids, are made up of atoms and molecules.

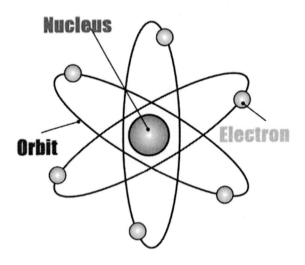

Figure 2-3

An individual atom (Figure 2-3) contains a Nucleus (Made up of Protons and Neutrons), with a number of electrons orbiting around it. Simply looking at this tells me that there is space between the nucleus and the electrons (albeit very small). And (although not strictly true), a space to me indicates the potential for something to pass through.

Let us look at leakage rate in more detail and across a range of leakage rates:

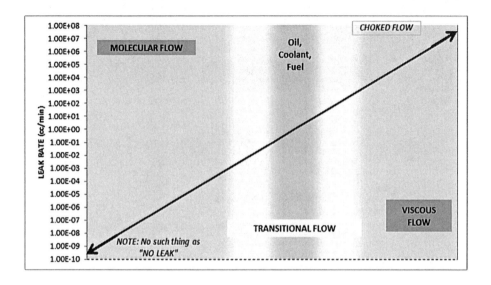

Figure 2-4

The chart (Figure 2-4) above show leakage rates ranging from 0.0000000001 cm3 min-1 to 100000000 cm3 min-1, but it not limited to these boundaries.

Wow! Why on earth would we be concerned with leaks that are as small as 1 x 10-8 cm3 min-1?

Well, let me give you an example that I came across many years ago working with a military application, where they wanted to check that altimeters (these are the devices that tell an aircraft pilot, how high they are above the ground); you will no doubt have heard your pilot announce "we are now cruising at 10,000 meters" when you have been on your flight to your favourite holiday destination.

The higher we go above sea level, the lower the atmospheric pressure becomes (you will likely have heard about rarefied atmosphere at high altitudes meaning that athletes need to get used to this, and why air pilots can be seen wearing breathing apparatus in fighter planes).

Pressure altimeters (like the one in Figure 2-5) contain a very small pressurised cannister/bellows of gas (the red area in the diagram), which are mechanically linked to the altimeter dial.

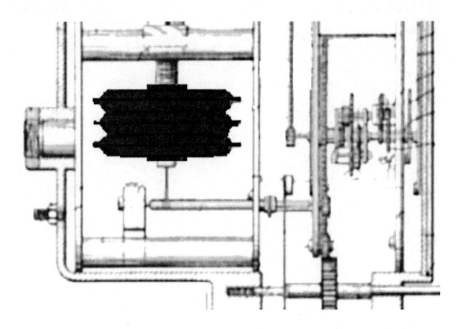

Figure 2-5

As the aeroplane goes higher, the bellows expand as the higher pressure in the bellows tries to get to the lower pressure in the atmosphere. The expansion of the bellows causes the dial to turn and indicate to the pilot how high the plane is. So it is the difference in the pressure between the pressure in the bellows, and the atmosphere which tells the pilot the exact height above ground. Clearly if the bellows leaks some of the pressurised gas/air out, then the pressure inside the bellows will change, and the difference will then changes and the altimeter will not show the correct height of the plane.

Now in the example I worked on these were fitted to fighter planes, which were designed to fly very low (just above the tree tops) to enable them to fly below the area where radar could detect them.

Clearly the altimeter in this case is very important as even a small error could cause the plane to clip the tops of trees, or worse still the tops of buildings! So it is very important that the bellows do not leak!

Now as I said, the bellows is very small, typically as little as only 5cm3 of gas. And as I am sure you can agree they do not want to be changing the altimeter after every flight, maybe change once every 3 months? During routine service periods.

Now if we want to fly at 100meters above the ground, and we need to be accurate to +/- 1 meter, then we can only accept a 1% error. So if we assume there is 5cm3 of gas in the bellows when it is perfect, the maximum amount of gas we can afford to lose between each service, is 1% of the 5cm3, or 0.05cm3

Now if our service period is three months, then this is 60 x 24 x 30 minutes

So our maximum allowable leakage rate is 0.05 cm3 in 129,600 minutes

$$= 7.7 \times 10\text{-}8 \text{ cm3 min-1} \qquad = \qquad 0.000000077 \text{ cm3 min-1}$$

So as you can see for the altimeter to be fit for purpose we need to be able to detect very small leaks indeed!

To help understand the leak sizes on the chart (2-4) a bit more, I have split the graph into regions/areas. (*Please note: these are not accurate or definitive levels, but merely highlighted to give you some idea of the nature of leaks.*)

The lower region of the chart, where the leakage rates at these levels are generally less than 0.01 cc/min (or 1 x 10-2 cm3 min-1 (the leakage rates at this level are very small, are generally considered by me as **molecular** leaks, where the physical size/mass of the molecule has a greater effect than anything else.

To the right side, **viscous** leaks, for leakage rates in excess of 100cc/min (or 1 x 102 cm3 min-1), are governed more by the viscosity (I think of this as thickness) of the fluid (liquid/gas) than the molecular size.

Obviously the transition from one region to the other is not clear cut, and there exists a region in between (which I personally call **transitional leaks**) where the leakage rate is governed by a mixture of both viscosity and molecular size.

For example, when we consider leaks in something like a car engine, we are generally looking at leaks of oil, coolant and fuel (liquid leaks—which I have approximately indicated as the blue region), these will almost certainly have their fitness for purpose points in the upper regions (transitional/viscous) flow regions.

The reason for indicating these different effects (molecular/viscous) is to clear up the misunderstanding that people believe that helium is more searching than air for all leakage rates.

Whilst this is true for molecular leaks where helium is much smaller molecules than those of air, in the larger leak region the viscosities are not greatly different, and air will pass through a leak in very similar quantities to air when under the same conditions. To explain a little further, let us look at the properties of helium and air (Table 2-1):

GAS	FORMULA	MOL MASS (kg kmol)	VISCOSITY (Pa s)
Air	- - -	28.96	18.0×10^{-6}
Helium	He	4	19.4×10^{-6}
Carbon Dioxide	CO_2	44	14.5×10^{-6}
R 134a (Refrigerant Gas)	$CH_2F\text{-}CF_3$	102.03	11.6×10^{-6}

Table 2-1

So we can see that the helium molecule is much smaller than the air molecule, and so for molecular (very small) helium may well be more searching, but we can equally see their viscosities are very similar, so through larger holes the two gases (air and helium) will not behave/pass through the hole with any appreciable difference.

2.4 Specifying Leakage Limits (Part 1)

Now we have discovered the range of leakage rate potentials, and understand that with no leak being virtually impossible, then we must consider how we decide what level of leakage rate will be fit for purpose for our particular product/requirement.

In many cases (as we have seen for our example of the bellows in the altimeter), specifying the maximum amount leakage permissible from a component can be derived from the requirements to remain fit for purpose. Let me give you three such examples, that I came across during my years as a leak test engineer:

2.4.1 Flow (Volume of Gas in Time) Specification

In the switchgear industry, modern switchgear often contains a gas called Sulphur Hexafluoride (SF6) as the quenching agent (quenching sparks). For each product to remain operational for at least 10 years, it can lose no more than 10% of the gas contained within it. If the switchgear has an internal free volume of 17.2 litres and is pressurised to 4.5 Bar (gauge) with the SF6, then we can calculate the maximum permissible leakage rate acceptable.

So at atmospheric pressure (1 Bar absolute) there is 17.2 litres of gas, and when the unit is pressurised to 4.5 Bar (5.5 Bar absolute), we can calculate the total volume of gas inside the unit by ratios as follows:

1 Bar	$\sim$	17.2 Litres
5.5 Bar	$\sim$	?? Litres

$$\frac{1}{5.5} = \frac{17.2}{??}$$

Rearranging this, we can calculate the total volume of SF6 inside the breaker:

$$?? = \frac{5.5 Bar \ x \ 17.2 \ Litres}{10 \ Bar} = 94.6 \ \text{Liters of gas}$$

In order for our circuit breaker to remain fit for purpose, we know that we can only afford to lose 10% of this gas during the circuit breaker's normal lifespan, which could be 10 years. Therefore:

Leak rate	=	10% of 94.6 Litres in 10years
	=	9.46 litres / 10 years
	=	946 cc/yr
	=	2.59 cc/day
	=	0.108 cc/hr
	=	0.0018 cc/min
	=	0.00003 cc/s or **3 x 10-5 cc/s (SF6)**

This is a typical maximum permissible leakage rate value for circuit breakers.

2.4.2 Weight Loss Specification

The simplest example of this type of leak specification is in the refrigeration/air conditioning industry where the amount of refrigerant gas put into the systems is measured as a weight quantity in Kg (kilogram)

For example a quantity of 2 Kg of R134a is placed in a system and the expected life of the system being 20 years. The maximum amount of gas that we can afford to lose (whilst the system remains operational) from this system is 5 % of the total.

So our leak specification will be:

| 5% of 2 Kg in 20 years | = | 100 gm / 20 years |
| | = | **5 gm/yr (gm yr-1) of R134a** |

This level of leakage is quite common in this industry.

2.4.3 Pressure Decay Specification

Quite a common way to specify the maximum permissible leakage is to establish the percentage of the working pressure that can be lost without detriment to the operation of the product.

For example in the fire extinguisher industry, it is often stated that the product must not lose more than 10% of its starting pressure during its working life, where:

| Starting pressure | = | 3 | Bar |
| Working life | = | 5 years | |

So our leak specification will be

3 Bar per 5 years	=	300miliBar / 5 years
	=	600 mB/yr
	=	1.64 mB/day
	=	0.07 mB/hr
	=	0.0011 mB/min
	=	**0.00002 mB/s (mb s-1) or 0.0002 Pa/s (Pa s-1)**

Although this is a typical specification for a fire extinguisher, how would we measure this? (We will see later our pressure decay measurement limit of sensitivity is typically 0.1Pa/s at best.)

So we must now understand the relationship between these different units, and how we can convert between them.

Maximum leakage rate can also be defined in times of the maximum hole size allowed. This is often used in the medical industry where we see the hole size limited to restrict the movement of certain bugs from entering sterile packages. We will look at hole size to leakage rate in Part 2 of Specifying Leakage Limits.

2.5 Leak Rate Conversions Between Units

All leak rates can be related to each other by looking at the basic first principals of each unit. In general, the volumetric leak rate (flow) is considered as the primary unit, and other measurements related to this as we will see.

2.5.1.1 Weight Loss to Flow Conversion

What is meant by the weight of a gas?

In the periodic table (see Appendix), the number above the chemical symbol is the molecular mass of the substance in grams gm).

For example, Hydrogen (H) = 1 gm, Helium (He) = 4 gm, Oxygen (O) = 16gm, Nitrogen (N) = 28gm etc.)

This molecular mass is how much 22.4Litres (known as 1 Mol (mole) at STP [Standard Temperature and Pressure]) of the gas would weigh.

So if our specification is 10 grams per year, and our molecular mass is 102grams (typical for many refrigerant gases), we can easily calculate the volume leakage as follows:

102 grams	$\sim$	22.4 litres
10 grams	$\sim$	?? litres

By simultaneous equations

$$\frac{??litres}{22.4\ litres} = \frac{10grams}{102\ grams}$$

Rearranging this

$$?? \text{ litres} = \frac{10\ grams\ x\ 22.4litres}{102\ grams} = 2.2 \text{ litres}$$

79

This is the leakage in 1 year. But there are 31557600 seconds in 1 year, and 1000 cubic centimetres in a litre, so it is more conventional to write this leak rate in terms of atm cm3 sec-1 as follows:

$$2.2 \text{ litres per year} \quad = \quad \frac{2.2 \times 1000}{31557600} \quad = \quad 0.0000695cc/s$$

Or more conventionally **6.96 x 10-5 atm cm3 sec-1**

So in summary to convert from gm/yr to cc/s you can use the following formula:

$$cc/s \quad = \quad \frac{\frac{gm}{yr} \times 22.4 \times 1000}{Mole\ Mass\ o\ gas \times 31557600}$$

Note: To convert to $cm^3 \ min^{-1}$ simply multiply this by 60.

So we can say that the volumetric leak rate in a given time is equal to the weight loss within that same time period, times the volume of the I Mol, divide by molecular mass of the gas:

$$\frac{\Delta V}{\Delta t} \quad = \quad \frac{\frac{\Delta m}{\Delta t} \times mol\ volume\ (22.4L)}{Mol\ Mass\ of\ the\ Gas}$$

Note: Ensure Volume, Mass and Time units are consistent throughout

2.5.1.2 Pressure Decay to Flow Conversion

Let us consider what happens to cause our pressure decay—which is explained as a drop in pressure within a fixed volume caused by a leakage of gas.

So at the start (Figure 2-6) we have a Volume (V1) which contains our gas at a pressure (P1):

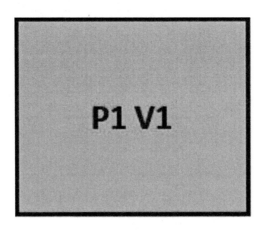

Figure 2-6

After 1 second, some gas will have escaped (Figure 2-7) causing the pressure within the volume (V1) to drop to a lower pressure (P2), the gas that escaped will have a definite volume (V3), at a pressure (P3):

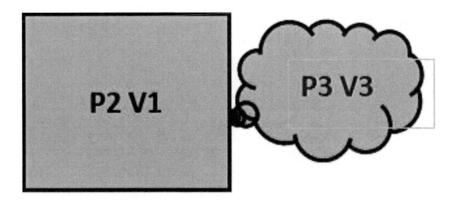

Figure 2-7

Using our universal gas law of PV =nRT, if we assume that the temperature remains constant, then PV = constant.

From this we can say that:

P1 x V1   =   P2 x V2

Now in our case our P2 x V2 is actually all of the gas after 1 second, and so is the total SUM of P2 x V1 PLUS P3 x V3, as clearly, the total amount of gas remains the same in both situations (at the Start, and after 1 second), so:

$$P1 \times V1 \quad = \quad P2 \times V1 \quad + \quad P3 \times V3$$

If we rearrange this equation we can see

$$(P1 - P2) \times V1 \quad = \quad P3 \times V3$$

Rearranging a bit more we get:

$$V_3 \quad = \quad \frac{(P_1 - P_2) \times V_1}{P_8}$$

Now:

$V3 = $ *Leaked volume of gas at atmospheric pressure*

   (in measured time = 1 sec)

P1 – P2	=	*Pressure Drop (in measured time = 1 sec)*
P3	=	*Atmospheric Pressure*

Volumetric leak rate per sec=
(pressure Decay Rate per second x Volume of item under test)
(Atmosphere pressure)

Note: Ensure volume, pressure and time units are consistent throughout. This is the volume of gas at atmospheric pressure.

So we can say that the volumetric leak rate in a given time is equal to the Drop in pressure within that time, times the volume of the part under test, divide by atmospheric pressure:

$$\frac{\Delta V}{\Delta t} \quad = \quad \frac{\frac{\Delta P}{\Delta t} \times v(of\ part)}{Atmosphere\ Pressure}$$

2.6 Specifying Leakage Limits (Part 2)

So far we have considered deriving a specification for leakage rates of gases, which is relatively simple when we are trying to retain the gas inside our part. But what if our component/assembly contains a liquid that we want to keep in.

As we have already discussed, we ideally like to use a dry method (using a gas such as air, or helium), and we know that gases will pass more easily (or at a greater rate) than liquids, so how do we determine maximum allowable gas/air leakages that will effectively retain our liquid?

First of all let us take a small step back to our theory of leakages, and recall there is no such thing as no leak… Is this really true? Clearly it is much more difficult for a liquid to pass through a very small hole than it is for a gas, and other effects such as the meniscus (*A meniscus is a curve in the surface of a molecular substance, such as water,* Figure 2-8, *when it touches another material. With water, you can think of it as when water sticks to the inside of a glass.*), effects, etc. can actually create a point at which liquids will virtually stop leaking in their normal form.

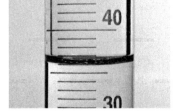

Figure 2-8

But how can we calculate the point at which the water will stop leaking? The only theoretical calculations we have are those of the Hagen-Poiseuille equation (originally established and published in the 1840s).

2.6.1 Hagen-Poiseuille Equations (Liquids vs Gas)

In order to establish an air leakage limit for a fluid containing product let us first consider the standard fluid dynamics equations for fluids, which was developed to describe the relationship between the laminar flow of a non-compressible fluid through a long cylindrical tube with a constant cross section, and the pressure difference across this tube.

2.6.1.1 For Non-Compressible Fluids (Liquids)

$$Q = \frac{(P_i - P_o) \times \pi \times R^4}{8 \times \mu \times L} \text{ib}$$

2.6.1.2 For Compressible Fluids (Gases)

This had to be further developed for compressible fluids (such as gases), but assumes that there are no thermal effects (due to the compression and expansion of the gas in different parts of the tube):

$$Q = \frac{\pi \times R^4}{8 \times \mu \times L} \times \frac{(P_i^2 - P_o^2)}{2 \times P_o} = \frac{\pi \times R^4}{16 \times \mu \times L} \times \frac{P_i^2 - P_o^2}{P_o}$$

Clearly we could combine these to create a relationship between fluid and gas leakage rates as follows. For liquid (non-compressible fluids) flow (QL), we can rearrange the formula as follows:

$$Q = \frac{(P_i - P_o) \times \pi R^4}{8 \times \mu \times L}$$

Or $\dfrac{\pi \times R^4}{8 \times L} = \dfrac{QL \times \mu L}{(P_i^2 - P_o^2)}$ *where μ_L is the viscosity of the liquid

For gas (compressible fluids) flow (QG), we can similarly rearrange the formula as follows:

$$Q_G = \frac{\pi \times R^4}{16 \times \mu \times L} \times \frac{(P_i^2 - P_o^2)}{P_o}$$

Or $\dfrac{\pi x R^4}{16 \times \mu L} = \dfrac{2 \times \mu_G \times Q_G \times P_o}{(P_i^2 - P_o^2)}$

The left hand side of both equations are identical, so therefore the right hand side of the two equations must equal each other:

$$\frac{Q_L \times \mu_L}{(P_i - P_o)} = \frac{2 \times \mu_G \times Q_G \times P_o}{(P_i - P_o)}$$

Rearranging this:

$$Q_G = \frac{Q_L \, x \mu_L}{(P_i - P_o)} \quad x \quad \frac{(P_i^2 - P_o^2)}{2 \, x \, \mu_G \, x \, P_o}$$

If we were now to enter the relevant data for Liquid Leak Rates "QL", plus, μL, μG, Po and Pi, we can develop some form of comparison table (Table 2-2) to give us the corresponding Gas Leak Rates "QG":

Oil Leakage	Air Leakage	Water Leakage	Air Leakage	Fuel Leakage	Air Leakage	Liquid Dia (Mm)
0.000001	0.017	0.000001	0.008	0.000001	0.002	0.12407
0.000002	0.034	0.000002	0.015	0.000002	0.004	0.156319
0.000005	0.086	0.000005	0.036	0.000005	0.011	0.212157
0.00001	0.173	0.00001	0.072	0.00001	0.022	0.267301
0.00002	0.347	0.00002	0.144	0.00002	0.045	0.336778
0.00005	0.867	0.00005	0.359	0.00005	0.112	0.457078
0.0001	1.735	0.0001	0.718	0.0001	0.225	0.575882
0.0002	3.471	0.0002	1.436	0.0002	0.451	0.725566
0.0005	8.679	0.0005	3.589	0.0005	1.129	0.984745
0.000524	9.089	0.000524	3.759	0.000524	1.182	1
0.0006	10.415	0.0006	4.307	0.0006	1.354	1.046448
0.0007	12.151	0.0007	5.025	0.0007	1.58	1.101623
0.0008	13.887	0.0008	5.742	0.0008	1.806	1.151765
0.0009	15.622	0.0009	6.46	0.0009	2.032	1.197884
0.001	17.358	0.001	7.178	0.001	2.258	1.240701
0.002	34.717	0.002	14.355	0.002	4.516	1.563185
0.005	86.794	0.005	35.888	0.005	11.29	2.121569
0.01	173.588	0.01	71.775	0.01	22.58	2.673009

Table 2-2

Note: In this table, different differential pressures were used for the fluids and the viscosities used may vary according to the fluid types, so may vary from other calculations depending on values used.

We could then agree the maximum amount of liquid leak we would consider as a true leak (for example, highlighted in the table, I have shown the fluid leakage as 0.000524 cm3 min-1, as the point at which we assume the point at which we consider the non- compressible fluid to be considered as a true leak) and determine our maximum level of air leakage that would be acceptable to consider the leak path not to leak the liquid. (In my example, this corresponds to 1 cm3 min-1 of air being considered the point at which fuel is considered not to leak, and for no water leak being 3.759 cm3 min-1 of air, and for oil, 9.089 cm3 min-1 of air.)

But of course such calculations are all theoretical, so is there a more accurate/practical way we can establish our leak specifications.

2.6.2 By Experimentation (The Best Way—Back to Basics)

Alternatively, we could do actual experimentation by measuring the air leakage from a component, and then filling the component with the fluid we wish to ensure no leakage of, and then determine the maximum air leakage that would not leak the liquid, and thus establish a true limit for our particular product.

I say this is a true limit, as practice, is always more accurate than theoretical calculations, which do not take into account a number of factors such as:

- Material from which the product is made
- Actual fluid types
- Temperature effects on the liquid (and gas) viscosity
- Shape of the hole
- Length of the hole
- Etc.

A little bit of my own personal history in that, many years ago, when I was just a lad, I spent many months based on a well-known car manufacturers site where they manufactured car radiators to do exactly this. The result was that we established a 4.2 atm cm3 min-1 leakage rate of air would not leak the coolant in the radiator.

I then did exactly the same at a manufacturer of Bathroom Shower units, and in this case we established a maximum allowable leakage rate of 3.8 atm cm3 min-1, that would not allow the hot water to leak from the shower.

So you can see practical experimentation gave different specifications for water (clearly the coolant in the radiator also contained antifreeze, and the structure and materials in a shower unit are not the same as for an automotive radiator assembly).

However, we can see that the specifications were similar if not exactly the same, so are there guidelines out there that may at least give us a starting point?

2.6.3 Virtual Leak Diameters (VLDs)

During more recent times a lot more emphasis was put on leakages (particularly when it was discovered the harm that was being done to the Ozone Layer by refrigerant gases, which were becoming more widely used in the automotive industry). This gave rise to other theoretical calculations that could be used to determine the safe(?) size of hole that could be considered non-leaking. However just defining a simple hole size does not take into account pressure differentials etc. however this term is still applied to some leak specifications today, along with the fluid and pressure differential details.

2.7 Typical Liquid Leak Specifications

Many years ago, a number of automotive engineers got together in the USA, to try and determine a general air leak that would not leak the three main fluids used in the automotive industry.

Now I do not pretend to know how they arrived at their values/conclusions, nor have I ever felt it necessary to fully know how they reached the answers they did. I have heard various explanations such as they carried out physical tests, and some say that they decided that if the amount/size of droplet of fluid/liquid that leaked during a 1 minute period was less than 1 ten thousandth of an inch in diameter, that this would be the determination/classification of no leak. But I have never been able to verify this, or any other theoretical calculation accurately for all relevant automotive fluids.

Rather than trying to justify how or where the specifications came from I have been happy to simple follow the original guidelines, as they have generally worked for me throughout my time as a leak test engineer.

And so, suffice to say, general specifications were developed for engine fluids as follows:

The maximum allowable Air Leakage Rate through a single hole / aperture, that is tight for the liquid specified is:

- *For Engine Oil*   =   *6 to 8 atm cm3 min-1*

  (Depending on the Oil Viscosity)
- *For Engine Coolant*   =   *4 atm cm3 min-1*
- *For Engine Fuels*   =   *1.2 atm cm3 min-1*

However since then many people have tightened up on these limits to further reduce the risk of borderline leaks further, and now use the following leakage rates for automotive fluids as those *just unacceptable.*

For Engine Oil	=	**5.0 atm** $cm^3 min^{-1}$
For Engine Coolant	=	**3.0 atm** $cm^3 min^{-1}$
For Engine Fuels	=	**1.0 atm** $cm^3\ min^{-1}$

The values above relate specifically to the author, when he was the Leak Test SME (Leak Test Subject Matter Expert) for diesel engines at one of his employers.

One important factor to remember is that these air leakages are at the same pressure differential as the liquid leak!

2.8 Specifying Leakage Limits (Part 3) Complete Assembly Leak Limits

So far we have only considered the leakage rate through an individual hole in an individual component. Whilst this is good practice for suppliers of individual component parts, can we use the same limits when testing a complete/complex assembly of parts, such as an automotive/diesel engine?

In an ideal world we would use the standard limit for an individual hole, so that we could detect any single leak path that might leak the fluid/liquid. However the suppliers of each of the components have tested each part with a specific, maximum allowable leak limit, and when these parts are bolted together, we must consider the total amount of leakage for the sum components.

For example, if we consider the coolant circuit of an engine, then each part (radiator, engine block, header tank, coolant hoses, thermostat, water pump, etc.)

will have been tested to our recommended 3 atm cm^3 min^{-1}.), and if we have 10 parts, then they will in effect have been tested to the sum of these... i.e., 10 x 3 or 30 atm cm^3 min^{-1}).

The obvious choice therefore for an assembly (such as the complete engine), would be simply to consider adding up all of the potential total leakage from the various components. This is much like tolerance summation in physical parts bolted together.

Summation of Tolerances
Consider three metal components bolted together. Each part has a dimension of 10mm±0.2 mm. when the three parts are joined together the total dimension of the assembly could be as much as *30.6mm (3 x 10 + 3 x 0.2)*, or as little as 29.4mm (3 x 10 -3 x 0.2), even though our desired dimension is 30mm exactly.

So considering our coolant circuit in an engine, which may have as many (if not more than) as 10 individual component parts (all of which have been tested to the standard 3 atm cm3 min-1), plus as many as 10 separate joints (gaskets/seals), each of which could be allowed to leak at the standard individual hole size rate, whilst remaining fit for purpose.

This is 20 individual parts each of which can have a single hole/aperture that leaks air at 2.99 cm3 min-1—yet all will be fit for purpose.

If we simply add all the tolerances, we would define our leak limit as 20 x 2.99 or 59.8 atm cm3 min-1. (Incidentally this is what some companies do.)

However, this leaves us open to risk of not detecting some leaks (reference *Tolerance Stack Up* as we will explain shortly), when in general most individual parts would have virtually no leak.

Let us explore the risks associated with this method of Summation of Tolerances to determine our leakage rate specification for complex assemblies.

2.8.1 Tolerance Stack Up

Tolerance Stack Up is by far the biggest issue for Global Testing of complex assemblies such as automotive engines.

One of the first things we learned was that there is no such thing as zero leak, and that everything leaks to a lesser, or greater extent, but that this is acceptable, if the leak is small enough to maintain the part's Fitness for Purpose.

This is much the same as the physical dimensions of any object, in that although we specify a dimension, this can never be exact, and we allow a certain amount of tolerance around any dimension, as each item may be slightly smaller or larger than the dimension we have specified.

So let us consider our engine once again. I make no apologies for this as I spent much of my time as a leak test engineer at Perkins Diesel Engines, and working with component suppliers, improving and defining leak testing of complex assemblies and sub components.

Each circuit (fuel, oil, coolant) is made up of a number of component parts. For example, the oil circuit contains a number of component parts including:

- Cylinder Block
- Cylinder Head
- Water Pump
- Sump/Oil Pan
- Oil Cooler
- Timing Case
- Top Cover
- Rear End Oil Seal
- Turbo Oil Feed
- Turbo Oil Drain
- Front End Oil Seal
- Filler Cap
- Oil Temp Sensor
- Numerous Joints

Now each of these individual components is leak tested by the original component manufacturer, according to the specification we have provided (we will use our standard) which means that each one has been tested to ensure it has a total leakage of less than 5 atm cm3 min-1.

When these are installed on the engine, and we leak test this engine, all of the leaks for each component add together (much like tolerances on a group of parts bolted together) so that our resultant leak measured is the total of these, will be as per Table 2-3 below.

Component	Max Leak Spec (cc/min) to meet Fit For Purpose	Actual Leakage Rate (cc/min) = No Leaks - All components Fit
Cylinder Block	5	0.5
Cylinder Head	5	0.3
Water Pump	5	1.4
Sump/Oil Pan	5	0.6
Oil Cooler	5	1.5
Timing Case	5	0.8
Top Cover	5	1.2
REOS	5	0.2
Turbo Oil Feed	5	0.5
Turbo Oil Drain	5	0.2
Filler Cap	5	1.0
Oil Temp Sensor	5	0.1
12 off joints	60	9.3
GLOBAL LEAK TEST RESULT (Total ALL Leaks)		17.6

Table 2-3

All looks OK, but now consider a 2nd engine as below (Table 2-4), where the same suppliers test their parts, but as these are all produced from different batches, these components *just* pass the required 5 atm cm3 min-1 criteria:

Component	Max Leak Spec (cc/min) to meet Fit For Purpose	Actual Leakage Rate (cc/min) = Small amount of air leakage - All components Fit For Purpose
Cylinder Block	5	4.5
Cylinder Head	5	3.7
Water Pump	5	4.6
Sump/Oil Pan	5	4.1
Oil Cooler	5	2.8
Timing Case	5	4.2
Top Cover	5	3.8
REOS	5	3.1
Turbo Oil Feed	5	4.0
Turbo Oil Drain	5	4.5
Filler Cap	5	3.1
Oil Temp Sensor	5	2.7
12 off joints	60	14.4
GLOBAL LEAK TEST RESULT (Total ALL Leaks)		59.5

Table 2-4

We can see that:

- Although all parts are fit for purpose (all suppliers checking parts meet individual leak limit requirements)
- The total leakage when we test the complete assembly is more than 3 times greater than the previous example

So how do we decide the correct limit for our complete assembly?

Obviously if we simply add all the allowable tolerances (as we might do with our bolted together blocks of metal), we could consider this as our leakage limit:

SUM OF ALLOWABLE TOLERANCES	120.0

This seems like a simple solution, but let us now consider another scenario (Table 2-5), very much as above, but where two of our suppliers have decided to save cost by not leak testing, and so two of our components potentially have fairly large leaks that are not fit for purpose, and will potentially leak the fluid (oil).

Component	Max Leak Spec (cc/min) to meet Fit For Purpose	Actual Leakage Rate (cc/min) = Two components are NOT Fit For Purpose
Cylinder Block	5	4.5
Cylinder Head	5	3.7
Water Pump	5	4.6
Sump/Oil Pan	5	12.0
Oil Cooler	5	2.8
Timing Case	5	4.2
Top Cover	5	3.8
REOS	5	15.0
Turbo Oil Feed	5	4.0
Turbo Oil Drain	5	4.5
Filler Cap	5	3.1
Oil Temp Sensor	5	2.7
12 off joints	60	14.4
GLOBAL LEAK TEST RESULT (Total ALL Leaks)		79.3
LEAK TEST LIMIT SET		120.0

Table 2-5

In this case simply having our global limit (limit for the complete assembly) set to the sum of all of the allowable limits, means that our assembly is potentially going to leak oil, even though it passed the leak test.

Clearly trying to make some form of calculation to determine our limit is virtually impossible, as we don't really know how good each component part is.

So let us consider this in a more practical way. We can make some sort of assumptions such as:

- Not all of the parts will be really good
- Not all of the parts will be only just fit for purpose

So let us consider that we expect our supplier to be neither perfect (0.0cc/min) nor at the leak limit (5.0 cc/min) but somewhere in between (Law of

93

averages?), so we might expect all our parts to leak at 50% of the limit (or 2.5cc/min).

Component	Max Leak Spec (cc/min) to meet Fit For Purpose	Actual Leakage Rate (cc/min) = No Leaks - All components Fit For Purpose
Cylinder Block	5	2.5
Cylinder Head	5	2.5
Water Pump	5	2.5
Sump/Oil Pan	5	2.5
Oil Cooler	5	2.5
Timing Case	5	2.5
Top Cover	5	2.5
REOS	5	2.5
Turbo Oil Feed	5	2.5
Turbo Oil Drain	5	2.5
Filler Cap	5	2.5
Oil Temp Sensor	5	2.5
12 off joints	60	30.0
GLOBAL LEAK TEST RESULT (Total ALL		60.0

Table 2-6

Does this make more sense? As we can see (Table 2-6) we have a total leak of 60 cc/min which is half or summation value of 120cc/min.

This is a very useful rough guide, and I myself used this technique for many years when considering complex assemblies, and I recommend setting the limit to around 50% of the total allowable tolerance, i.e., for the oil circuit, we would set our starting limit at 50% of the tolerance summation, or 50% of 120 atm cm3 min-1, or **60 atm cm3 min-1** (or in our previous example of the coolant circuit, 50% of 59.8, or around **30 atm cm3 min-1**).

Using this 50% rule, we can now see that we comfortably detect the in our previous example leaks (Table 2-7):

Component	Max Leak Spec (cc/min) to meet Fit For Purpose	Actual Leakage Rate (cc/min) = Two components are NOT Fit For Purpose
Cylinder Block	5	4.5
Cylinder Head	5	3.7
Water Pump	5	4.6
Sump/Oil Pan	5	12.0
Oil Cooler	5	2.8
Timing Case	5	4.2
Top Cover	5	3.8
REOS	5	15.0
Turbo Oil Feed	5	4.0
Turbo Oil Drain	5	4.5
Filler Cap	5	3.1
Oil Temp Sensor	5	2.7
12 off joints	60	14.4
GLOBAL LEAK TEST RESULT (Total ALL Leaks)		79.3
LEAK TEST LIMIT SET		60.0

Table 2-7

However, I now want to stress now, that I always consider this a starting point limit and not the definitive limit for the assembly. The reason for this is quite simple, in that this still leaves us in an at risk situation, as we can see in the example below (Table 2-8):

95

Component	Max Leak Spec (cc/min) to meet Fit For Purpose	Actual Leakage Rate (cc/min) = Two components are NOT Fit For Purpose
Cylinder Block	5	0.5
Cylinder Head	5	0.3
Water Pump	5	1.4
Sump/Oil Pan	5	0.6
Oil Cooler	5	1.5
Timing Case	5	25.0
Top Cover	5	1.2
REOS	5	0.2
Turbo Oil Feed	5	0.5
Turbo Oil Drain	5	0.2
Filler Cap	5	15.0
Oil Temp Sensor	5	0.1
12 off joints	60	9.3
GLOBAL LEAK TEST RESULT (Total ALL Leaks)		55.8
LEAK TEST LIMIT SET		60.0

Table 2-8

So ideally we would like to achieve a limit much nearer our individual leak path limit to ensure we detect any leak. This is achieved by monitoring our leak test results for the complex assembly, and then refining to get the lowest limit achievable without affecting our production. We will look at this in the following section entitled Leak Limit Refinement.

2.8.2 Leak Limit Refinement

To help you to understand how to review results and consider limit refinements, let us use our example of testing the oil circuit on an engine (again no apologies for this, but the same rules can be applied to any multi component assembly).

So we have decided that our 50% limit point is to be 60atm cm3 min-1 and set our equipment up accordingly.

We now carry out testing and record the resultant leak rates measured. Now this is where I strongly advise the use of graphical representations of the leak test results (by entering the results onto a spreadsheet and plotting an X-Y scatter graph. Below is an example (Figure 2-9) of just such a plot, carried out over 1 day

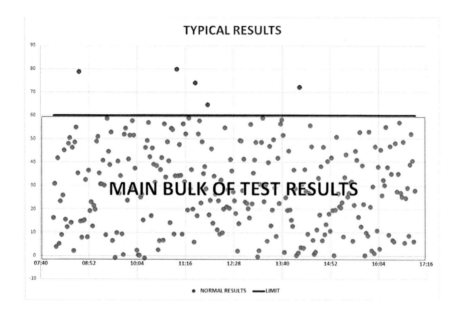

Figure 2-9

In this chart we can see our test results vary considerably. This is due to a number of factors which will be discussed later, but for now let us assume that this variation is the sole result of the variation in leakage from the individual components, and how they combine (add up) in the complete assembly.

As we can see the vast majority of assemblies PASS the test, and lie within what we can see is the normal main bulk of the results. Only around 6 cross the limit and give a leak test FAIL condition. These assemblies would be investigated to find the root cause of the leak test failure.

The number that would require REWORK is minimal, and as such will not impact our production, whilst giving us a reasonable level of protection going forward.

Note: Rework is the act of investigating and finding the leakage, and then repairing to ensure fit for purpose.

At another part of our factory we are testing another version of our complex assembly, and similarly we have recorded the results in graphical form for review to see if there are limit improvements we could make.

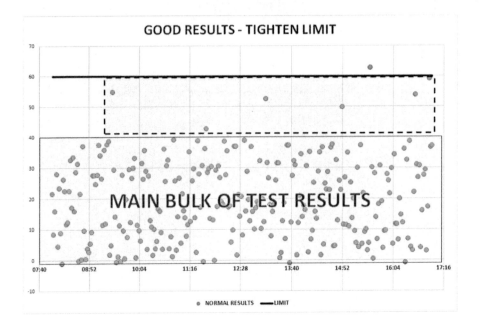

Figure 2-10

Here (Figure 2-10) we see that only one of our assemblies failed the leak test by crossing the limit set at the 50% point ($60cm^3 min^{-1}$).

However looking at the chart we can see that there are a number of results that sit outside/above the main bulk of test results. This is suspicious and tells us that these assemblies do not fall within the normal expectations (pattern). We therefore can suspect that these assemblies may contain 1 or 2 parts that may contain leaks that might make the assembly unfit for its purpose.

In such a case we can identify a possible NEW limit (Figure 2-11) would have captured these outliers and thus ensure a more robust leak test.

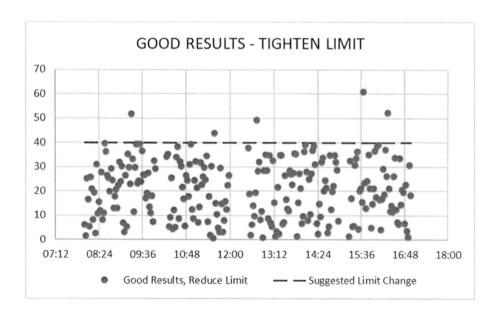

Figure 2-11

Note: Outliers = These are values that lie outside the normal/expected/typical spread of result values.

Similarly we might consider the opposite, where we could open up our limit (Figure 2-12). This at first seems surprising, however consider the recorded results below, where a very large number of assemblies are failing at our 50% limit.

Figure 2-12

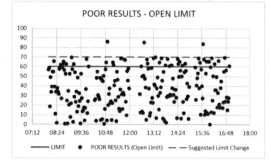

This may be good in some ways as these may all be potential leakers (although this is not necessarily true, as we will see later, because results may vary due to other factors such as temperature effects) however consider the impact on our production schedules...

Each of the assemblies that fail our leak test must be investigated, the leaking part found and replaced. This can often take a considerable amount of time (particularly on complex assemblies), and may cause us to create a major hold up or back log in our process. To alleviate such backlogs companies often incorporate special Rework Areas away from production, to affect the rework without impacting production. This is all very well but it is recommended that each of these assemblies is retested before moving on to ensure it meets our requirements, and as such can cause additional pain to our production process.

I would suggest that initially the limit could be moved up/opened, until the results become more like those seen in our normal example.

So we have reviewed our limit, and adjusted to suit, but of course that is not an end to this process, as it imperative this review is repeated as frequently as possible, as once we have made our adjustments, we may begin to identify common failure modes that can be corrected, and then reviewing again and reducing our limit further, we may possibly identify further improvements and limit reduction allowing us to get nearer our perfect scenario of identifying any single leak path, and thus ensuring Fit For Purpose status for all assemblies.

At this point I would just say that graphical representations are by far the best way to review the results for potential improvements, as looking at a set of leak test results in a long list, is not so easy to identify issues/differences. What do you think?

2.8.3 Result Review and Limit Refinement for Component Parts

So far in this section we have talked about reviewing results, and limits, for complete/complex assemblies, however this process is not solely used for complete assemblies, but can equally be applied to individual components.

Let me give you an example from my own experiences.

A particular supplier was performing leak tests on a small plastic valve for the engine fuel circuit fuel. The component comprised of a number of parts (spring, valve etc.) all housed in two part plastic body which was *spun-welded* together.

> Note: Spin Welding is a method used to join plastic parts by spinning them against each other to create friction and thus heat to effectively melt the plastic at the join and thus fuse them together.

The supplier was adequately dry air leak testing each component to a leak specification of 1 atm cm3 min-1 as advised by their customer, to ensure the effectiveness of the spun welded joint.

However it had been reported that a very few valves began to leak fuel after a short time in service.

So my investigations started with reviewing leak test results from the suppliers equipment (Figure 2-13), and the following was observed:

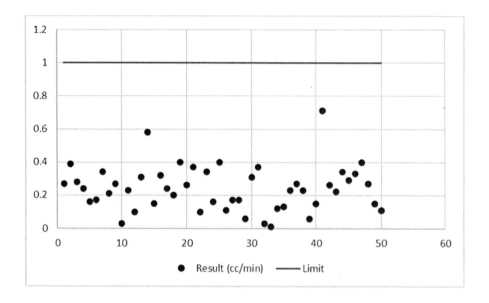

Figure 2-13

Clearly we can see that all parts tested comfortably passed the leak test, however I noticed that two of the parts could easily be considered as outliers away from the typical/bulk of the results.

These two parts were removed, and taken for review to understand why they might be different from the norm.

These two parts were then pressurised and immersed under water, and we saw a very few small bubbles escaping, indicating a gas leak, although clearly they were below the standard limit for fuel and as such should be fit for purpose, and not allow leakage of liquids.

But I considered that when fitted onto the engine, the parts would be vibrated and get warm, so clearly the conditions under which the parts are tested is not the same as the conditions under which they are used on the engine, and I also recalled that the parts were failing after some time in operation, so I believe what might be happening was that when in operation on the engine, the vibration and heat might cause this very tiny leak path to perhaps open as time moved on.

My advice to the supplier was to reduce their limit to 0.5 atm cm3 min-1 in order to catch these outliers (Figure 2-14). This would not create to big an impact on their production, as failures would be small quantities.

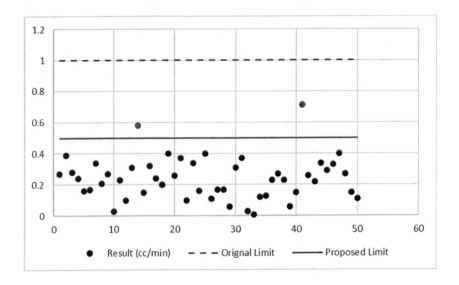

Figure 2-14

Since making this change, there have been no more leaks on engines, and even better, the supplier has further investigated and realised that they could make improvements to their spin weld process, and now they are getting no leaks on their test, so a win/win all round!

2.8.4 Specifying Test Pressure

Up till now we have simply been considering the leakage rate, but as we saw when we discussed flow measurement, the flow (or leak rate) is directly affected by the pressure difference.

In many cases people often think that it is a good idea to increase the leak test pressure above the normal operating pressure in an attempt to identify leaks easier.

Although this seem like a good idea (and it is in some cases), as the increase in pressure will effectively increase the leak rate it is not always the case, and higher leakage rate test pressures also have other impacts as follows:

2.8.4.1 Impact on Equipment

Firstly, let us consider the test equipment and the impact of simply increasing the test pressure when leak testing.

Consider a simple box shape (with 1 face open) of dimensions (10cm x 10cm x 10cm). we want to leak test this box by clamping the open side down onto a table (with a simple rubber seal), and then pressurising the inside of the box.

If the normal operating pressure of this box is 1 bar, then we can reasonably leak test by pressurising this to 1 Bar (or 100kPa [kilopascals]).

We can now calculate the force that the air applies (Figure 2-15) to the top of the box (i.e., trying to push the box upward), from the standard formula.

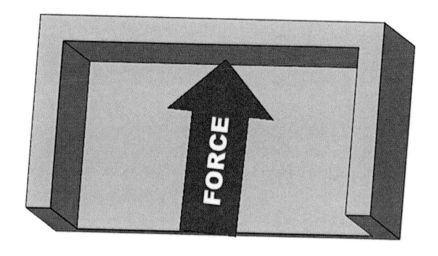

Figure 2-15

Force (kN) =   Pressure (kPa) x   Area (m2)
So the Force applied by 1 Bar Test Pressure will be
Force (kN) =   (kpa)   x   [0.1   x   0.1] (m^3) =1kN

It is clear that if we double our leak test pressure to 2 Bar, then the force trying to lift the box will be doubled also to 2kN.

Now if we are trying to leak test this part we need to be sure to ensure a good seal on the open side, by pressing the part down (Figure 2-16) onto the seal by some form of clamping mechanism. This Clamp will need to not only squash the seal, but also overcome the force being applied by the air pressure.

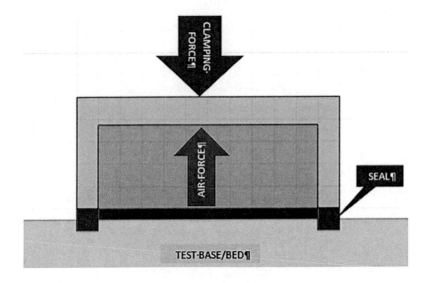

Figure 2-16

So simply if we decide to simply increase the test pressure, then we must consider that our clamping force would also need to be increased just to enable us to continue testing. This will mean clamping devices that will apply an increased clamping force, and it is quite possible that this would increase the cost/complexity of the leak test machine.

2.8.4.2 Impact on test cycle time and results

Do you recall one of the most important things I said to remember about gas laws? That P(ressure) x V(olume) / T(emperature) is a constant:

$$\frac{P_1V_2}{T_1} \quad = \quad Constan \quad = \quad \frac{P_2V_2}{T_2}$$

Well, let us think about what happens when we put our test pressure into the component. Clearly the volume is not changing, so we can remove this from our formula:

$$\frac{P_1}{T_1} \quad = \quad constant \quad = \quad \frac{P_2}{T_2}$$

Now when we initialise our component to 1Bar we are effectively doubling the pressure inside the part, as it already contained air at atmospheric pressure (around 1 Bar also). Now if we double the pressure, then we will double the temperature of the gas from around 293K (20oC) to 586K over 300oC).

This looks crazy, surely the air/gas doesn't get that hot? Well, it won't because the pressure will not change instantaneously, and as the air/gas heats, then this heat will transfer to the body of the component, and subsequently will transfer to the atmosphere from the part. What actually happens is something like the graph below (Figure 2-17)…

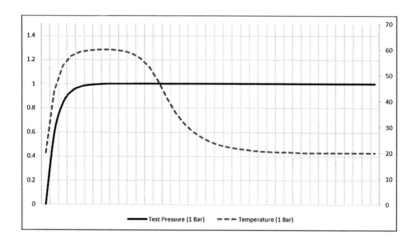

Figure 2-17

Let us now compare the graphs (Figure 2-18) for both the 2 different test pressures:

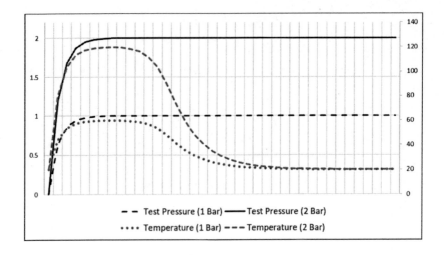

Figure 2-18

This may not seem too much of an issue, but if we look more closely at the shape of the temperature curves, (Figure 2-19), as it approaches the static 20oC level, we can see that the temperature fall of the 2 Bar test is delayed a bit compared to the 1 Bar Test.

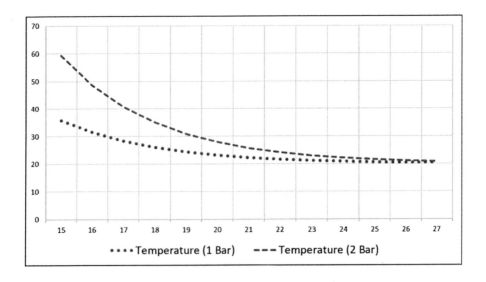

Figure 2-19

Now remember Pressure and Temperature are liked by the important Universal Gas Law, and in a fixed volume.

$$\frac{P_1}{T_1} \quad = \quad constant \quad = \quad \frac{P_2}{T_2}$$

So if our temperature is falling, then it is clear that our pressure will also be falling. So this becomes very important when using air testing methods as the pressure change caused by the temperature change, can give us false results. We will discuss this in much more detail in the sections on pressure decay and flow leak testing.

2.8.4.3 Impact on Leakage

As we previously stated it can be very useful to enhance any leaks to make them easier to detect, and one such way is to increase the test pressure, as this clearly enlarges the leak making it easier to detect... or does it?

In a solid part such as a metal casting like the simple box shape we discussed in the section on air pressure forces this is largely true, and providing it doesn't impact our machine complexity/costs, nor impact our test results/cycle time too greatly, testing at a higher test pressure can be a very useful enhancement.

However, there are cases where this increase in test pressure can be devastating. This is particularly true, where the component is actually an assembly of parts, with some type of flexible component such as an O-ring seal or rubber diaphragm.

Let me explain this with an example again from my own personal experience, working with a supplier of fuel filters—a very poor sketch of which we see here (Figure 2-20), with O-ring joint between the filter bowl and the top housing.

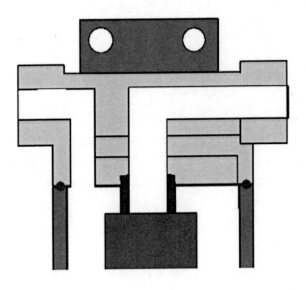

Figure 2-20

The filter assembly supplier had supplied a filter that was later detected as leaking on the finished engine fuel system. Yet when the filter assembly was returned to the manufacturer, the filter passed the leak test with flying colours with virtually no leak measured.

On investigation I discovered that the supplier was leak testing at a much higher test pressure than the filter would encounter during it's normal operation.

They were very happy to pressurise this filter with air and immerse under water, to show me there was no leak. I asked them to reduce the test pressure, and as we neared the normal operating pressure, we saw bubbles emerging at a pretty fast rate from the joint between the bowl and the top housing. They could not understand how this could be possible, as surely with more pressure the leak should be greater.

So I explained that when we apply a higher than required air pressure during the leak test, we have a strong force pressing on the 'o'-ring, causing it to press home into the joint (Figure 2-21) making a good seal, the more we increase the pressure the better the O-ring presses into place.

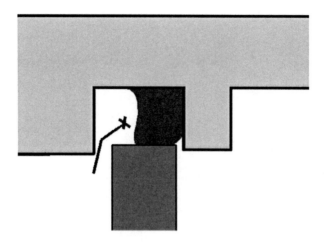

Figure 2-21

If however we relax this pressure back to the working pressure of the filter, the o ring adopted a more natural state (Figure 2-22) allowing the passage of air.

Figure 2-22

So you see the importance of testing at the correct test pressure.

2.9 Specification Summary

In summary, always consider your initial specifications as a starting point, and not a fixed value, as you will find that practical situations differ from theory (as I have found out over the years), and because no leak test solution can be as effective as testing the product in use.

The two items you need to identify are:

2.9.1 Leakage Rate Limit

This being the maximum allowable leakage rate of the trace element you are using to carry out the leak test. This may be calculated from calculations based on your requirements for fitness for purpose (see further example below), or based on one of the many standards applied in industry (see the leak rate standards table) in the appendix of this book.

Spec Calculation example (Table 2-9):

A manufacture of gas suspension units (Figure 2-23) wanted a specification for leakage for a high range automobile suspension unit. The Fitness for purpose statement was that the vehicle should not drop more than 10mm (1cm) in height if left for 24 hours.

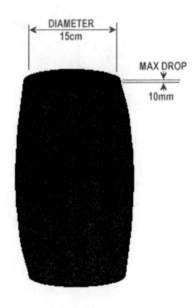

Figure 2-23

1. The gas suspension unit had an approximate internal diameter of around 15cm, and the air inside the suspension unit was 4 Bar gauge pressure (5 Bar Absolute) so we can calculate the maximum volume of gas held in the 15cm diameter and 1 cm depth from the formula for the volume of a cylinder ($\pi r2$)
2. Now this volume as at 4 Bar gauge (or 5 bar absolute, so from PV/T being a constant we can say our maximum allowable leakage is 5 times this volume.
3. Now, this calculated volume of gas loss is in a 24 hour period
4. So, finally, we can divide this volume by the number of seconds in 24 hours to give our leakage specification in cm3 sec-

1	Diameter	15	*cm*
	Max Drop	1	*cm*
	Max Internal Volume loss (At working pressure)	176.79	*cm³*

2	Pressure	4	*Bar*
	Volume at Atmospheric Pressure	35.36	*atm cm³*

3	Max Time	24	*hrs*
		1440	*mins*
		86400	*secs*

4	Max Leak Rate	2.46E-02	*cm³ min⁻¹*
		4.09E-04	*cm³sec⁻¹*

a.	1% Helium	4.09E-06	*mB L sec⁻¹*

Table 2-9

Note in this particular case a helium leak test was introduced due the small leakage rate, and as we used a low percentage of helium [1%], the actual leakage rate of helium would be only 1% of the total gas leakage.

> Note: This will be further discussed in the chapters on trace gas leak testing.

2.9.2 Test Pressure

As we have already seen, it is recommended that wherever possible, any leak test is carried out at the same pressure as the pressure that would be inside the component during it's normal operation. However it is sensible to add a small safety limit of say 5% to 10% above the operating pressure to allow for some variation in the leak test equipment accuracy, and also the actual pressure in operation which may vary slightly.

As an example of this, many years ago, whilst working with an automotive radiator manufacturer.

Test Pressure Calculation example (Table 2-10):

1. The working pressure of the coolant system in their vehicles was around 1 Bar above atmosphere.
2. Now in addition each radiator had a safety pressure relief cap which was set to release coolant if the pressure in the system/radiator rose above 1.1 Bar. This cap was not accurate, and had a possible 0.05 Bar error, so in reality the radiator could reach as much as 1.15 Bar.
3. The manufacturer wanted to be completely safe and so also allowed another 10% safety margin on top of this (allowing for variation and inaccuracies of measurement), and was able to set a test pressure of 1.27 Bar.

1	Working Pressure of cooling system	1	Bar
2	Radiator Cap Max Safety Release Pressure	1.15	Bar
3	Calculated Test Pressure with 10% safety mar	1.27	Bar

Table 2-10

2.9.3 Specification for High Pressure Parts/Systems

Clearly there are some cases where it is not possible to have our test pressure at the working pressure (such as high pressure fuel rails), and in these situations alternatives solutions are sought.

The reason we cannot use high pressures is that, in most cases where under normal operation the high pressure system will contain a liquid (which is not compressible), and so if a leak path occurs, the internal pressure in the system will drop rapidly, and the system itself is less likely to rupture or explode at the weak point (of leakage).

However if we pressurise this with a gas, the gas will compress under the increase in pressure, which means the gas will naturally want to occupy a much larger space, and in the event of a weak joint, the gas has a sort of explosive force as it tries to escape, which could result in parts/projectiles leaving the system at very high velocities, and this be unsafe for anything, or anyone in the surrounding area.

2.9.3.1 Example (Table 2-11)

Let us take the high pressure fuel system as our example.

1. Such fuel systems operate at very high pressures, typically 30000psi (or 2040 Bar) to enable the liquid fuel to be atomised when it is pushed into the piston/cylinders

2. We have decided to use the standard maximum leakage limit for liquid fuel leakage, which is around 1 atm cm3 min-1 at the working pressure

3. But we want to keep our test equipment, and the surrounding area safe by using a much lower test pressure (in this case 2 Bar)

4. SO we calculate the maximum leakage for the gas at this lower pressure by simple ratios

5. Finally we want to reduce the cost of helium usage, so we use a mixture of 10% helium in air, which means our maximum permissible leakage of helium is only 10% of our total gas leakage

1	Working Pressure	30000	psi
		2040	Bar
2	Standard Leak Limit for Liquid Fuel Leakage	1	cc/min
3	Safe Test Pressure for Leak Test	2	Bar
4	Amortise Leak Limit for Leak Test	0.00098	cc/min
		1.63E-05	cc/sec
5	Helium Mixture	10%	
	Max Allowable Helium Leakage	9.80E-05	cc/min
		1.63E-06	cc/sec

Table 2-11

113

2.9.4 Leakage Rates at Different Pressures

Whilst the theory for leakage from Hagen-Poiseuille's equation for compressible fluids (gases) indicates that the leakage rate is a function of the SQUARE of the pressure difference across the leak path:

$$Q \ = \ \frac{\pi \times R^4}{8 \times \mu \times L} \ X \ \frac{(P_i^2 - P_o^2)}{2 \times P_o} \ = \ \frac{\pi \times R^4}{8 \times \mu \times L} \ X \ \frac{(P_i^2 - P_o^2)}{P_o}$$

Remember this assumes that the leak path is straight, perfectly cylindrical etc. however we know this is not the case as leak paths have all manner shapes and forms. In practice, I have personally found that the leak rate to pressure relationship is reasonably linear, as shown in Figure 2-24 (although not exactly, it is close enough to not concern us). So if the pressure difference is halved, then the leak rate will halve, etc.

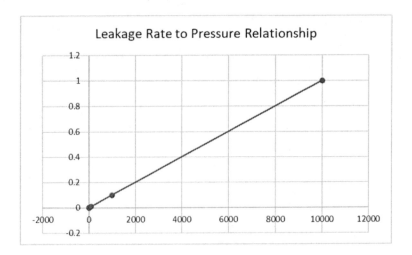

Figure 2-24

So as a general rule, I would recommend that, if the test pressure is half of our working pressure, then we should consider a leakage rate specification of ½ of the fit for purpose specification we are working to (or of our test pressure is one quarter of the working pressure then we should also quarter our leakage rate specification).

3. Choosing the Correct Leak Test Method

Now we understand what level of leakage we are trying to detect we need to decide the most appropriate method of detecting these leaks. This chapter looks at what you should consider and understand when identifying the most appropriate solution, and will hopefully guide you to a reliable method of testing your part/assembly.

3.1 Considerations

So let us first list the main considerations that we might evaluate when determining out test method such as:

- Leak Specification
- Takt Time
- Costs
- Is Gas Present
- Detect or Locate
- Legal/Health and Safety/Environmental

3.1.1 Leak Specification

First and foremost, do we have a leak specification we should work to, i.e., is there a maximum allowable leakage rate:

- To maintain the product in a working condition
- For health and safety reasons (medical or food industry)
- For aesthetic reasons (to maintain to product in good visible condition)

All leak detectors and techniques have specific sensitivity limits, and the size of leak to be detected/measured is highly likely to be the primary criteria in order to determine the best method/detector.

For example, if the part needs to retain a liquid, then we would need to be able to detect leaks in the 0.1cm3 min-1 and above range, whilst if it contains a gas, then it is very likely that the leak to be detected may be much lower (depending on the fitness for purpose) as per the example of the altimeter in the section fitness for purpose where the leakage to be detected was in the 0.0000001cm3 min-1 range.

3.1.2 Takt Time

By this we mean how much time is available to carry out the leak test.

In many cases, the leak test sensitivity can often be increased by taking longer or making an extended test, and of course some leak test methods are naturally slower than others, so choosing the method may be based on how long you can take to make the test.

It is not just the time required to measure the leak, but we must also consider how long it might take to connect the part to our leak test system, and for the part to be picked up/put down etc. In fact we need to consider time required for each and every aspect of our leak test process as per the example below (Table 3-1and Figure 3-1) where the leak measurement time is less than 10% of the total time to complete the leak test, and the total cycle time of the whole leak test itself amounts to only 1/3rd of the total time.

ACTION	Time (s)	% of takt
Pick Up part from rack	2	3.3%
Place part on Leak Test Machine	2	3.3%
Press Start on Leak Test Machine	1	1.7%
Guarding activation	4	6.7%
Part Clamping	3	5.0%
Pressurise Part with gas/air	15	25.0%
Measure Leakage	5	8.3%
Release the pressure/gas	5	8.3%
Etch Mark the part if pass	8	13.3%
Unclamp the part	3	5.0%
Guarding raised	4	6.7%
Lift Part from Test Machine	2	3.3%
Place part in Bag	4	6.7%
Place bagged part in box	2	3.3%
Total Takt	60	100.0%

Table 3-1

OPERATOR TIME	13	21.7%
MACHINE OPERATION	22	36.7%
LEAK TEST CYCLE	20	33.3%
LEAK MEASUREMENT	5	8.3%

Table 3-2

116

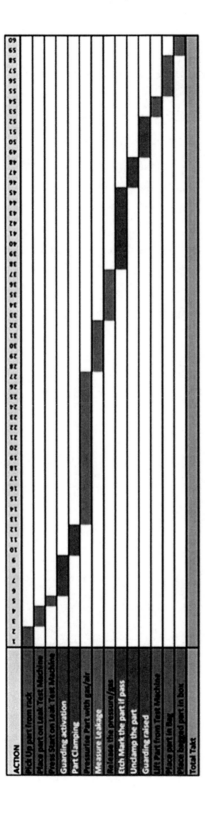

Figure 3-1

As we can see from the above chart, we can effectively only produce ONE tested part every 60 seconds. This may be a problem for us if we want to be able to make more parts than this. There are solutions but beware, we need to consider the implications of these too.

3.1.2.1 Multiple Test Machines/Stations

But we can see that the operator is actually only active for around 1/5th of the total takt time, and idle for a large percentage of the time. So, why not have two or even three leak test machines (both operated by a single operator to keep head count to a minimum).

In the example below (Figure 3-2), we have 3 machines, and by sharing the operator between them, we now have the capability of producing 3 leak tested parts on 76 seconds, or one every 25 seconds, meaning we can produce more than twice (but not 3 times) the number of tested parts than before.

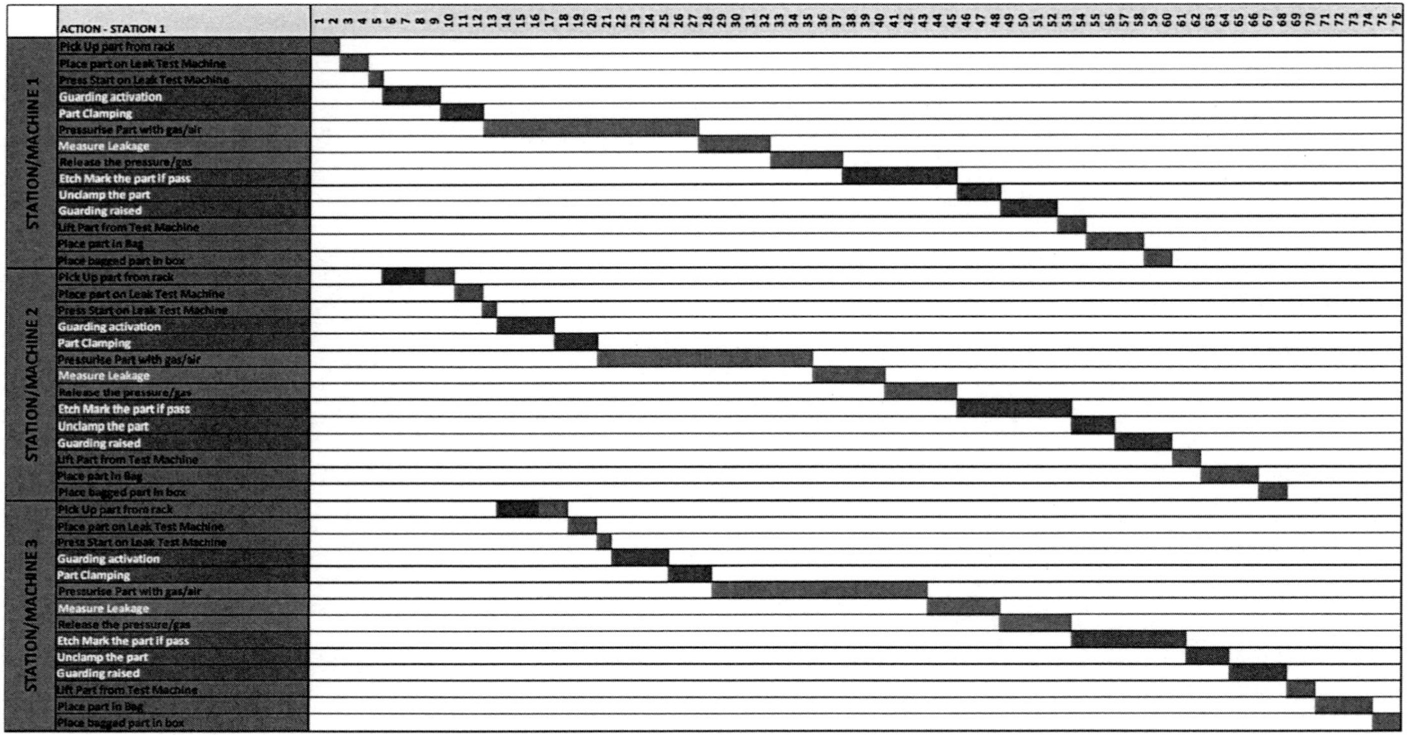
ACTION - STATION 1
STATION/MACHINE 1
Pick Up part from rack
Place part on Leak Test Machine
Press Start on Leak Test Machine
Guarding activation
Part Clamping
Pressurise Part with gas/air
Measure Leakage
Release the pressure/gas
Etch Mark the part if pass
Unclamp the part
Guarding raised
Lift Part from Test Machine
Place part in Bag
Place bagged part in box
STATION/MACHINE 2
Pick Up part from rack
Place part on Leak Test Machine
Press Start on Leak Test Machine
Guarding activation
Part Clamping
Pressurise Part with gas/air
Measure Leakage
Release the pressure/gas
Etch Mark the part if pass
Unclamp the part
Guarding raised
Lift Part from Test Machine
Place part in Bag
Place bagged part in box
STATION/MACHINE 3
Pick Up part from rack
Place part on Leak Test Machine
Press Start on Leak Test Machine
Guarding activation
Part Clamping
Pressurise Part with gas/air
Measure Leakage
Release the pressure/gas
Etch Mark the part if pass
Unclamp the part
Guarding raised
Lift Part from Test Machine
Place part in Bag
Place bagged part in box
1 2 3 4 5 6 7 8 9 10 11 12 13 14 15 16 17 18 19 20 21 22 23 24 25 26 27 28 29 30 31 32 33 34 35 36 37 38 39 40 41 42 43 44 45 46 47 48 49 50 51 52 53 54 55 56 57 58 59 60 61 62 63 64 65 66 67 68 69 70 71 72 73 74 75 76

Figure 3-2

However, this example shows 3 completely independent machines, which means 3 separate leak test devices, and 3 independent control systems etc. This would obviously increase the cost of leak testing dramatically, so are there alternatives?

Why not have one detector shared between three test stations (Figure 3-3), as a potential cost saving. In this way a single detector is used to carry out the actual leak test, whilst other functions for each station are shared between the main control system.

This sounds the same as the above example, however it is not, as we now only have one detector shared and as such it can only test one part at a time, so we would now need to ensure that our Detector times are kept apart, and the chart would look more like this.

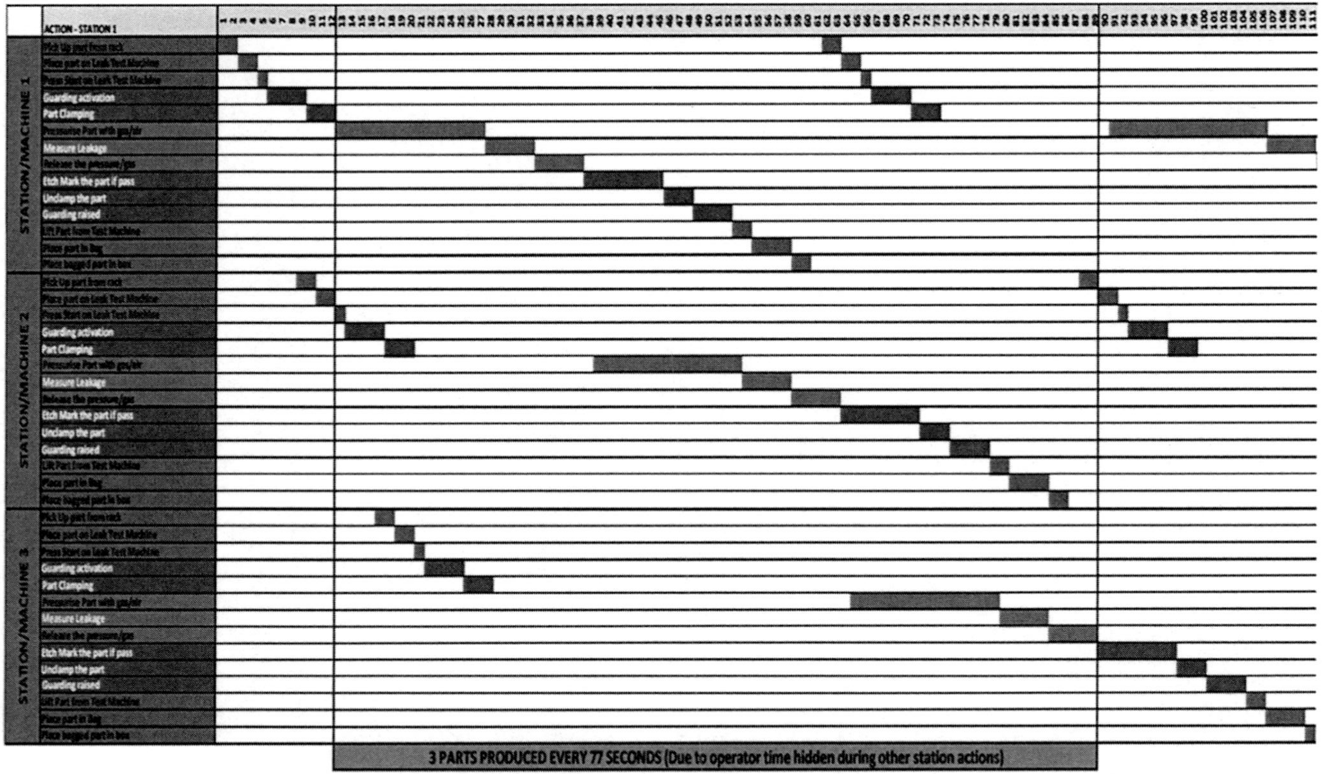
ACTION - STATION 1
STATION/MACHINE 1
STATION/MACHINE 2
STATION/MACHINE 3
Pick Up part from rack
Place part on Leak Test Machine
Press Start on Leak Test Machine
Guarding activation
Part Clamping
Pressurise Part with gas/air
Measure Leakage
Release the pressure/gas
Etch Mark the part if pass
Unclamp the part
Guarding raised
Lift Part from Test Machine
Place part in Bag
Place bagged part in box
3 PARTS PRODUCED EVERY 77 SECONDS (Due to operator time hidden during other station actions)

Figure 3-3

Now although it looks as though we now produce 3 parts in 112 seconds, we actually produce the three parts in 77 seconds (89-12), due to the fact that the operators time now gets hidden within other parts of each stations cycle. We can clearly see this is now almost 3 times faster than our original single test machine, yet cheaper than having the three independent separate leak test machines.

This is JUST one example with specific times for each function/action of the test, if considering multiple stations consider all the different functions of the cycle to completely understand number of stations required to produce the required throughput.

3.1.3 Costs

This has multiple meanings:

- **The cost of the leak test equipment itself** (vary from just a few hundred to many thousands of pounds)

For example a simple pressure measuring device may cost just a few hundred pounds, a Helium Vacuum Mass Spectrometer will be around 100 times that price.

- **Labour costs** associated with leak testing

Mainly the cost of operating the machine, one operator for one or multiple machines/stations, or maybe one operator per machine. But in addition, do not forget cost of technical staff for setup, maintenance staff, etc.

- **Running costs**. There may be many parts to this including:
o *Cost of electricity to run the test machine*
o *Maintenance/service and calibration costs*
o *Gas costs. This is normally only considered when a trace gas such as helium, hydrogen, R34a etc. are used, however do not forget that there are costs associated with pressurising air also (additional loading on compressors etc.)*
  - Where trace gases are used, costs may be able to be reduced by using a gas mixture (e.g., 10% helium in air), or if this not possible, it may be worth considering a reclaim system. Although these can be expensive,

they pump back any gas left in the part to be into the supply system for use on subsequent tests. (Beware though, these are not 100% efficient, and some of the gas will be lost from each test, and the cost of this should be taken into consideration.)

In general compare the cost of having a leak test against the cost of not having one (the cost of quality - field failures, lost business etc.).

At this point it is important to remind ourselves though that leak testing is non value added, so it is well worth looking for opportunities to combine leak test with other facilities such as assembly, other measurements/checks etc.).

One great example of this was the leak testing of the Gas Suspension units, where the cost of leak testing required at least two stations to meet the required production rates, making the leak test machine quite an expensive Non-Value-Added piece of equipment.

In order to make the system more cost effective, it was decided to combine the suspension unit assembly process within the leak test machine.

The suspension unit (Figure 3-4) was made up of three parts (top plate, rubber bellows and a piston) which had to be pressed together (*Note: The rubber bellows incorporate beads on each end, to ensure once fitted would be retained*), which would need to be press fitted onto the top plate and piston.

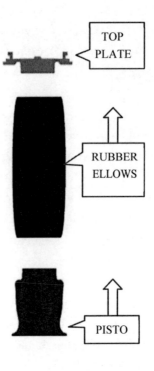

Figure 3-4

The machine was built, so that the three parts could be loaded into the machine, and the safety door closed. This started the automatic sequence as follows:

1. Operator lubricated both ends of the bellows to ensure ease of assembly, and placed this between the top plate and the piston.
2. The piston was then moved/pushed upward, by use of a relatively powerful pneumatic cylinder, until the three component parts popped together (Figure 3-5) and were fully assembled.

Figure 3-5

3. The pneumatic cylinder, supporting the piston, then partially retracted (moved down) until the complete assembly was at its normal operating height.

4. Once static, the complete assembly was then pressurised with a helium mixture to the normal operating pressure

5. A two part chamber was then placed around the complete assembly, with seals isolating it from the outside.

6. After a short time delay, the detector was connected to the chamber to measure the level of Helium within the chamber.

7. This level of helium gas was then compared with pre-set limits to determine if the part leaked more than the fitness for purpose level

8. Once a pass/fail was recorded, and the relevant lamp illuminated, the trace gas was allowed to escape the assembly

9. The assembling pneumatic cylinder then withdrew to its starting position

10. Once completes, the safety door was then released, allowing the operator to remove the fully assembled and leak tested part from the test machine

The system (Figure 3-6) incorporated a shared detector between the two stations to further reduce the overall cost of the machine.

Figure 3-6

3.4.1 Is Gas Present?

This is something that may well be the overriding factor, as in effect it moves our test back to the ideal scenario of testing as it is used.

If the item you are testing contain a gas, and there is a detector available that can detect that gas, then it makes sense to make use of that detector.

A good example of this is a refrigerator (Figure 3-7) which already contains refrigerant gas, for which there are a wide range of detectors available from direct sniffers to complete global test systems (depending on how much you want to spend etc.).

Note: Direct sniffers and other gas detection systems will be discussed in more detail in the section on Tracer Gas Leak Testing.

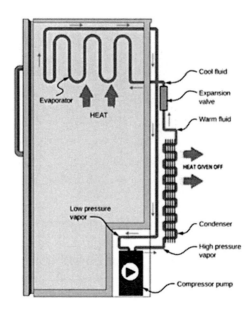

Figure 3-7

Another example might be aerosol cans such as Asthma inhalers.

Note: The author has been asthmatic all his life so has had an additional
interest in leak testing these products.

These cans contain gases (such as HFC134a) which are used to propel the
actual drug out of the cannister in a fine mist format. Similar detectors to those
used in the refrigeration industry can be used to detect any of the propellant gas
leaking.

Note: In practice the use of gas detectors for aerosol cans and medical
inhalers, is not widely used due in the main to time and cost constraints, and
other methods are employed as we will see in subsequent chapters.

Another consideration is the cost of the tracer gas used, and in many cases
manufacturers carry out a coarse/rough global test first to detect larger leaks, so

that when they pressurise with the trace gas, they do not waste large amounts of the costly gas.

3.1.5 Detect (Global) or Locate (Pinpoint)

In previous chapters, we have used the phrase, Global Leak Test. By this we mean a leak test that tests the complete assembly/part, and simply tells you if there is a leak above our fitness for purpose criteria or not. What it doesn't do, is tell us the exact location of the leak, which may be important to us, particularly if we want to carry out rework (effect a repair) so that we can actually use the product.

One such example is in the automotive industry where exhaust systems are manufactured. Each exhaust system requires a considerable amount of operations to manufacture, and to simply throw away a leaking exhaust system is not very cost effective. For this reason such companies want to know the exact location of the leak path, so that they can effect a repair and use/sell the part once the leak path has been eradicated.

But clearly pinpointing the leak path can be more time consuming, so in my experience exhaust system manufacturers carry out a global leak test first to determine if there is a leak or not, and then, if a leak is detected, they immerse the pressurised exhaust under water, so that the escaping bubbles can be identified, allowing the operator to mark the location of the leak, and then remove it for repair.

But there is more than one way to locate a leak path, which takes me back to my very early years in leak testing when the company I worked for produced simple gas sniffers. These gas sniffers were widely used by underground cable/pipeline suppliers/users to locate the leak path.

Let me explain that when a cable/pipeline issue was reported, the exact point of the break/leak wasn't known, so the operating company needed to dig up large amounts of land including roadways etc. until they located the exact leakage point. As you can imagine, this was very costly, and time consuming. With the sniffers however they were able to pinpoint the leakage path within a few feet, and so greatly reduce their costs and time to effect repairs. The way this was carried out was as follows (Figure 3-8):

1. Drill small bore holes in the ground along the route of the cable/pipeline (note you may still see these today as small holes in the tarmac on some roads)
2. Pressurise the pipeline/cable with a trace gas that could be detected by the sniffer

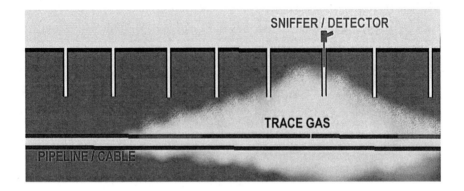

Figure 3-8

3. They would then sniff at each bore hole and record the level of the trace gas they detected
4. Plotting these amounts on a graph (Figure 3-9) enabled them to identify a peak in the gas concentration, and thus more accurately find the exact location of the leak and effect a repair. (The chart below shows a typical example narrowing the distance of digging up required from 100m to just 15 m)

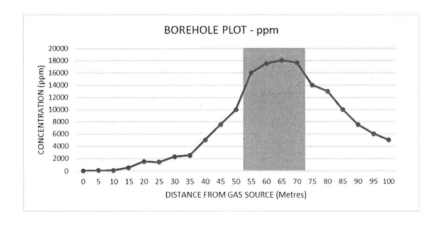

Figure 3-9

These are the core considerations, however there are some important factors that we cannot ignore.

3.1.6 Legal, Health, Ergonomic and Safety/Environmental

Are there any legal or health and safety requirements that dictate the method of leak testing?

Health and wellbeing of operators is essential in all walks of life, and as such we must ensure that our choice of equipment is easy to use and operate, and that there are no risks to operators.

This is another consideration for careful selection of the test pressure to be applied, in that we must ensure no risk to operators from possible projectiles being forced from the part under test.

The list of considerations is exhaustive, and I am sure you will think of, or discover key aspects according to your own products or requirements. But the above, for me, are the main aspects.

4. Leak Test Equipment

There are a very, very large number (almost inexhaustible), methods of leak testing, and many of these methods depend on the detection device being used, which will again largely depend on the criteria discussed in the previous chapter, and/or the various limitations associated with each detection device.

In the following chapters I intend to focus on the main techniques/methods used. The main methods I generally break down into the 5 major categories below (Figure 4-1:)

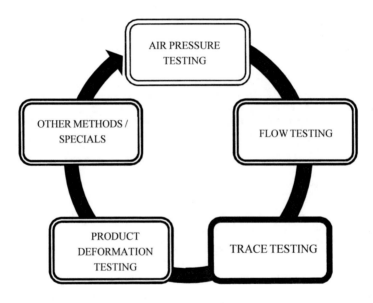

Figure 4-1

I appreciate this is quite general, but I hope all will become clearer on my choice of these as we walk through each in turn, but first, a few bullet points on each technique/method.

4.1.1 Pressure Test Methods

- These are global methods, in that they can detect and measure the total leakage from the assembly/component, but cannot isolate or identify individual leak paths
- Either gauge or differential measuring devices, we pressurise the part, and then monitor/measure this pressure.
- We can record the decay in this pressure over time (or pressure drop) to determine the level of leakage
- Gauge transducers lose sensitivity/resolution at higher pressures
- This method is greatly impacted by volume (larger volumes reduce the sensitivity) and as a general rule, this is generally used for volumes of 2 litres or less

4.1.2 Flow Methods

- Also global methods, so can also only detect and measure the total leakage, but not isolate or identify individual leak paths
- The component is again pressurised, and then we measure the air being used to replace any air that has escaped through leakage
- The top-up air is supplied from a separate, stable pressure source
- Mass flow is most often used for smaller leak rates, whilst laminar flow units are more generally used for higher flows
- Generally used to replace pressure decay on larger volumes

4.1.3 Trace Methods

- The component is pressurised, with air/fluid (or any trace element different from the surrounding air (or substance).
- The air/fluid around the part can be sniffed for traces of the trace element escaping.
- When trace methods are employed within a test machine, they are generally also considered global, and used to detect whether or not there is a leak above our specification.

- Obviously this method can also be utilised to accurately locate a leak path, and as such is often used in repair/rework areas to locate leaks after one of the above global, methods have detected a leak.
- The trace fluid can be air, however in order to be able to sniff the air soap solution, or water baths are used so as to improve the signal to noise by enabling air to be detected in air.

4.1.4 Product Deformation Methods

- In this case we deform the part using pressure or vacuum, and then observe/measure the amount of deformation to determine the presence of a leak.
- This method is often used for packaging of products rather than the product itself, such as food packs, medical packaging etc.
- Some methods in this category do not really act as leak detectors as they are destructive, and really act as a check of our manufacturing process to create a good seal on the packaging.

4.1.5 Other / Specials

- I lump a wide range of methods into this group, some of which can be considered trace methods.
- Some examples include acoustics, light detection, x-rays etc.
- I do not intend to discuss these in detail as they are less common, and specific to particular applications/industries, however I will attempt to give a brief description of some of these in later chapters.

4.2 Leak Detection/Measurement Devices

There is an enormous range of different leak detectors (devices for detecting and/or measuring leaks) available. Below is a long list (but this is by no means a complete list as I am sure many suppliers of alternative devices will be only too pleased to point out). I have tried to categorise them into the different methods that might be used.

METHOD	DETECTOR
AIR TESTING METHODS *(Note: Can use other gases not air)*	• Air Pressure Decay (Gauge) * • Differential Pressure Decay * • Mass Flow Measurement • Laminar Flow Measurement • Anemometers
TRACER GAS DETECTION	• Bubbles Under Water • Helium Mass Spectrometer • Quadrupole Mass Spectrometer • Electron Capture Detector • +ve Ion Emission Detector • Ion Pin Detector • Thermal Conductivity Detector • Quartz Window Ion Gauge • Photo Ionisation Detector • Spectrophotometers • Chromatography • Infrared Detectors • Semi-Conductor Devices • Etc. Etc. - this list is very long indeed
OTHER TRACE ELEMENTS	• Dye Penetrant • Pressure Decay Hydrostatic (Often this is also a pressure measurement)
PRODUCT DEFORMATION	• Capacitive Measurement • Linear Transducers • Compression Sensing • Force Measurement
ACCOUSTIC (SOUND)	• Ultrasound Detectors • Tap Tone
VISIBLE (LIGHT)	• Cameras • Infra-Red Detectors
HIGH VOLTAGE	• Arc Detection • Resistance Measurement
FLAW DETECTION *(Not true Leak detection, more risk reduction)*	• X-Rays • Stress Measurement

BURST TESTING *(Unlike those above, this is a destructive test)*	• Pressure Knee detectors • Burst Pressure Measurement

* = Techniques are similar and cross Method

As you can see from this extract, the list is absolutely huge, and to cover every different detector would require multiple volumes of this book, so in fact I am going to focus on details on how the most common/popular the detectors work.

4.2.1 Leak Detector Sensitivities

As part of our choice of leak test method we would consider the size of leak, and thereby the type of detection method most suitable.

Before we go on, just a quick look at the sensitivity of some of these detectors (Figure 4-2), by which I mean haw small a leak can each detector detect.

Whilst there will be a lot of arguments about the chart below, I have just sketched out (very) roughly how small a leak can be detected under normal operational/manufacturing conditions.

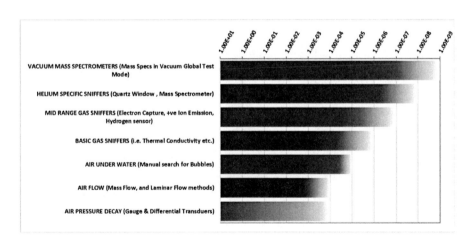

Figure 4-2

- *In general, air testing is less sensitive than other methods*
- *Air under water in the right conditions can do even better, however it suffers from being operator dependent. Please note though, that it is at least two orders better than air pressure decay and flow rate devices (which is not what many air leak test equipment suppliers may infer)*
- *Basic gas sniffers such as thermal conductivity detectors are not discriminatory and are very susceptible to background contaminants giving false readings*
- *Helium mass spectrometers can be used in either sniffer or vacuum chamber modes depending on the sensitivity required*

4.2.2 Signal to Noise

Before we leap into the detectors, I would just like to make specific mention of one factor that effects all detection methods, and one that you need to be aware of when considering leak testing. It is a phrase commonly used in many industries and measurement methods. By Signal to Noise, I mean the effect of background variations on the detection methods.

As an analogy I would liken this to going out and looking at the stars at night.

- ☆ If you go out in the countryside at night, and look up you will see the heavens in all their glory with thousands of stars on view.
- ☆ If however you do the same in the middle of town, there does not appear to be anywhere near the number of stars in the sky.

Why? Simply because of the amount of surrounding background light, the more of this there is, the more difficult it is to see the individual stars.

For leak testing, the background noise may be caused by a number of things. For example we have already learned that Pressure x Volume ÷Temperature is a constant, so if we are measuring pressure, then we must be aware that any changes in volume or temperature may have an effect.

Likewise if we are trying to look for bubbles underwater, if we have a lot of disturbance in the water, causing bubbles or frothing, then it may be difficult to see the bubbles created by the leak itself.

And with gas detectors, any stray gases, present in the area we are trying to detect our trace gas may give us false readings. We will look at each of these effects in more detail when we consider each detection method, and will also look at other conditions/external effects that may impact our leak test method.

5. Air Testing Methods

Whilst there are a wide range of detectors available for air leak testing, they can generally be broken down into three main methods (Figure 5-1) as follows:

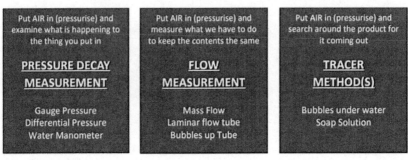

Put AIR in (pressurise) and examine what is happening to the thing you put in	Put AIR in (pressurise) and measure what we have to do to keep the contents the same	Put AIR in (pressurise) and search around the product for it coming out
PRESSURE DECAY MEASUREMENT	**FLOW MEASUREMENT**	**TRACER METHOD(S)**
Gauge Pressure Differential Pressure Water Manometer	Mass Flow Laminar flow tube Bubbles up Tube	Bubbles under water Soap Solution

Figure 5-1

5.1.1.1 Pressurisation

In all cases, you will see we use the term 'pressurise'. Although I am sure you all understand what Pressure means, I think it just worth describing what is meant by pressurising using a bit of a silly analogy, to make some of the effects simpler to understand.

By pressurising I mean that we press, or compress (squash it), air into the part, so that more air molecules are contained in the part, than would normally be present if it contained the normal air in the atmosphere. (Air is a compressible fluid). The increase in the number of molecules can be measured as a pressure.

I personally like to think of these molecules of air as little rubber balloons, that can be squashed down to a smaller size. Let us take a simple box that we can fill to the brim with 100 of these balloons. If we now squeeze another 100 balloons into the box (and firmly close the lid), we now have twice as many as normally fit in the box. These balloons will be pushing on the box, trying to get out and return to their normal size (they are now half the size they normally are). And so they exert a force on the box as they try to escape.

This force is related to the number of balloons, and as such if we put twice as many balloons in as would normally fit, then we have twice the force (or pressure).

And it is the same with our air molecules. Because air is normally at approximately 1 Bar (~100000Pascal / ~14.5 psi), then we put twice as much air as would normally fit into the box, then we have now pressurised the box to 2 Bar (~200000Pascal / ~30psi) or 1 Bar above atmospheric pressure (~100000Pascal / ~14.5 psi).

Now if we allow some of these balloons/air molecules to flow out of the box, then those left in will grow to take up the space left by the balloons/air that have escaped. Those left will grow a little, and subsequently will not put as much force on the walls of the box (hence the pressure inside the box goes down according to the number of balloons/air molecules that have escaped/leaked out in the given time period).

In simple terms this is what is happening when we talk about air leak test methods (pressure decay and flow).

6. Air Leak Test Methods Pressure Decay

Probably the most widely used method of leak testing, it is used as the main source of detecting leaks in individual component parts. It can also be used for complete assemblies, however we must be aware of the limitations that the volume of the part plays, as we will explain later in this chapter.

Although widely used, it is clear from my own experience, that not all the implications, and limitations of this method are understood, so in the following chapters, I hope to make these a little clearer, and help you to understand these factors, and how to recognise them and of course reduce their effect.

Let us first look at how this method actually works.

6.1 How Pressure Decay Works

In this air testing method, as described we pressurise the part we are leak testing to our required test pressure. Once pressurised, we monitor the pressure and look for a decay (or drop) in the pressure. Any pressure drop, would indicate the potential of a leak of air. The amount, or rate of pressure drop/decay, will be a measure of the amount of leakage.

> *Note: Although almost entirely considered an air test method, pressure decay techniques can utilise other gases (for a variety of reasons), but mostly if we wish to locate the actual leak path when using this global method.*

This is something a lot of us regularly do in our cars when we check our tyre pressures. If we see the pressure is a bit lower than it should be, then we pressurise to the correct pressure and monitor it over the coming days. If we see the pressure regularly dropping/reducing, we might conclude that we have a puncture (a leak!), and we will take our car to a service centre to effect a repair.

But the likelihood is that we only check the tyre pressure maybe daily or twice a day at most, which for industry producing multiple parts every hour, isn't practical.

We will shortly examine in more detail the test sequence of the modern leak test devices used in industry, but let me first give you a little detail about the measurement devices/sensors themselves.

6.1.1 Gauge Transducers

The method we use when checking our tyres was the first type of pressure decay developed, and used a simple gauge (Figure 6-1) just as we do with our car tyres.

Figure 6-1

The part would be pressurised, and the gauge observed for any sign of the needle moving towards a lower pressure such that any movement would indicate a pressure drop, potentially caused by a leak.

This was a great start, but the amount of pressure drop that could be reliably detected was limited by the physical size of the gauge, and as such in the 6 Bar pressure gauge example above (where the required test pressure is 4 Bar), it was difficult to reliably detect a movement of less than 1mm, or around 0.2 Bar (Figure 6-2). Of course the longer we wait, the more the pressure will drop, and the smaller leak we can detect.

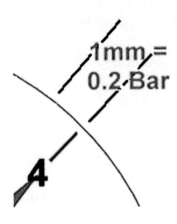

Figure 6-2

But waiting a long time is impractical and so people began making much larger pressure gauges, so that the 1mm distance represented a smaller pressure change (Figure 6-3) but still it could take a long time to detect very small leaks.

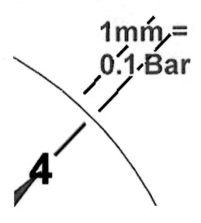

Figure 6-3

However this was eventually resolved by electronic devices/sensors (Figure 6-4), which could reliably detect/measure pressure changes of one 10,000th of the actual total gauge pressure, so in just a few seconds, for our example, we could easily detect a pressure drop of 0.0001 Bar (or just 10 Pascals).

Pressure sensor cross section structure diagram

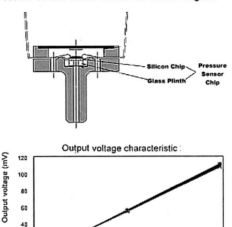

Figure 6-4

These simple electronic versions of our pressure gage are mor commonly known as pressure transmitters, and there are a number of different types, but the most common use electronic strain gauges, which in effect measure the force being applied to the sensing element. Often the strain gauge is attached, or bonded, to a flexible diaphragm which deflects (distorts) depending on the amount of pressure applied to it.

With modern devices and advances in electronics, such devices are capable of resolving down to one 100,000th of the total pressure range (or maybe better) and so we can see in our 5 bar pressure transmitter we can comfortably detect pressure changes as low as 5 Pascals (0.05 milli Bar) (Table 6-1).

Pressure (Bar)	resolution (Bar)	resolution (Pa)
1	0.00001	1
2	0.00002	2
5	0.00005	5
10	0.0001	10
20	0.0002	20
50	0.0005	50
100	0.001	100

Table 6-1

This is all very good, however as we will see shortly we often need to be able to detect pressure changes to an even finer level, and particularly at higher test pressures where the resolution of the sensor is not so good this can be a drawback, as we would again need to wait for sufficient time to achieve a pressure drop large enough to detect.

To overcome this problem a different type of pressure measuring device was needed

6.1.2 Differential Pressure Transducer

This type of sensor was developed to enhance the sensitivity of pressure decay measurement at higher pressures

The transducer itself is in effect two chambers separated by a very thin (typically 15 to 20μm) flexible membrane called a diaphragm in between them (Figure 6-5)

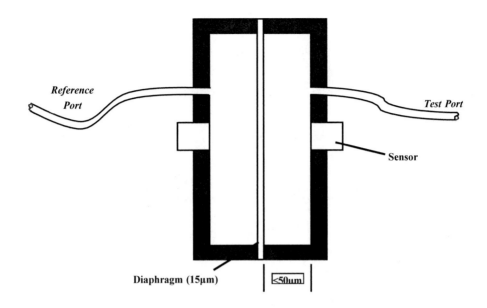

Figure 6-5

The transducer measures the difference in pressure between the two sides of the transducer (Figure 6-6)

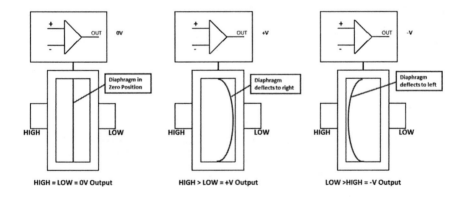

Figure 6-6

6.1.2.1 Basic Principals

In most applications the reference side of the transducer is sealed/connected to a closed reference volume, whilst the test side is connected to the part under test, so that.

6.1.1.1.1   No leak situation (Figure 6-7)

As there is no gas lost from the component under test, the pressure in the test side of the transducer remains constant. As we can see from the diagram, the diaphragm remains central, giving a net zero result.

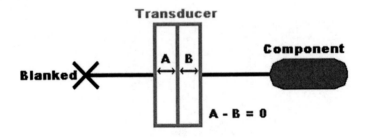

Figure 6-7

6.1.1.1.2   Leaking component

As gas is lost through the leak the pressure in the test side of the transducer drops, causing the diaphragm to deflect (Figure 6-8). A comparison between the measurements on the test and reference sides of the transducer gives us a direct measurement of the pressure decay due to leakage.

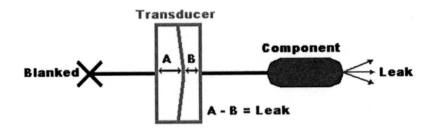

Figure 6-8

In fact the total measuring range of a differential transducer (maximum pressure difference between the two chambers) is typically around 200 Pascals, meaning that we can reliably detect pressure changes of less than 0.01 Pascals.

Comparing this with the gauge transducer we can see the enhanced level of pressure measurement on the chart (Figure 6-9), here.

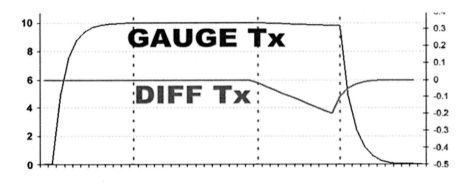

Figure 6-9

In effect the transducer zero point is at the test pressure, and the transducer measurement range can be kept relatively small giving the same high sensitivity at whatever test pressure is selected/used.

6.2 Pressure Decay Sequence of Operation

Now it is time to put these devices into action, but in order to this we need to look at the sequence of events that enable us to leak test using such devices.

In its simplest form, (Figure 6-10) we need to FILL/PRESSURISE the component to the required test pressure with air, TEST/MEASURE the part for leakage by monitoring this pressure (measure the pressure decay), and then get rid of the air, by EXHAUSTing (or VENTing) it to the atmosphere.

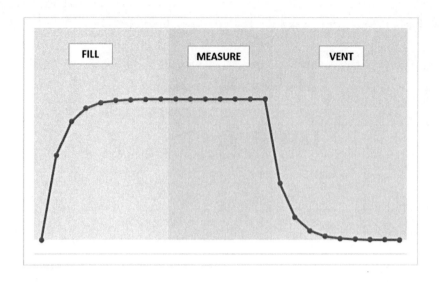

Figure 6-10

In its basic form, this is quite simply what we do, and this was the standard sequence of events for many years.

However when a confined volume (the component under test) is pressurised there are a number of effects, such as temperature increases, and the physical properties of pressurising a confined volume, which can cause false readings in the measuring cycle, so a further stage (STABILISATION) in between the fill and test phases was added to relieve these effects.

6.2.1 Stabilisation

Before we go on a brief explanation of the need for the Stabilisation phase of the test sequence, how it works.

6.2.1.1 Adiabatic Effects

During the fill (pressurising) phase of the sequence, we are forcing more air than would naturally (under normal atmospheric conditions) fit inside the item we are testing.

The 1st thing to remember is Charles' Law which states that in a fixed volume, an increase in the pressure causes an increase in the temperature.

Remember that important universal gas law I mentioned: $\frac{PV}{T}$ = Constant...
(but remember in these gas law calculations, we must use absolute values)

So if we pressurise to 1 Bar gauge pressure, this is in fact 2 Bar absolute, so we are in fact doubling the pressure of the air inside the part, so we will also in theory effectively double the temperature also. So if we consider the temperature of the air inside the part was at standard levels (20oC), then we would in fact increase the temperature of the air from 293K to 586K (313oC).

However whilst this may be true for the air already contained in the part, the actual air we are adding is very likely to come from a mains air pressure line, which will already be at maybe 7 or 8 Bar. for this air, the reduction of the pressure will serve to reduce, or cool the temperature of the supply air.

As the heating and cooling air mix, they will naturally transfer their temperatures to each other. *(the graph Figure 6-11) shows these effect although it is important that this is just a representation and the figures are not meant to be taken literally)*

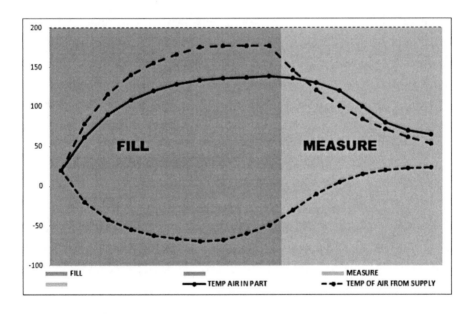

Figure 6-11

The important thing to note is the way the air inside the part is still cooling during the measuring phase (made clearer using a different scale for this air). And as we know if the air inside a fixed volume is cooling, then the pressure of this air will be reducing (which, for our purposes, looks like a leak).

149

Now whilst all of these temperature effects are happening to the air inside the part, we must remember that this air is also is in contact with the part itself, which may be at another temperature all together, and the part is in contact with the ambient air around it. And so we will also get natural transfer of temperature from the part to the air inside the part, and the part to the air outside the part and vice-versa.

Whilst we could try and calculate the time it takes for all these air temperatures to settle to one homogeneous/steady state the maths becomes very complex, and it is not really practical.

Another consideration is the simple movement of the air molecules.

If you recall I like to think of molecules as little rubber balls, so I imagine that when we are pressurising a part, these rubber balls are being fired into the part from the main air supply. As they enter the part they will collide with the air molecules (rubber balls) already in the part, as well as the part itself, so they will bounce around for some time until their energy is fully dispersed, and they settle down to a more relaxed state.

Now as we saw earlier, the transducer membrane is very thin (typically 15 µm)and as such our measurement transducers are very sensitive. And this continual bouncing around will manifest itself as noise on our measurement device

So we need to have a period between our fill and measure/test phases to allow time for these adiabatic effects to dissipate, or settle down. This is known as the stabilise phase.

In the early days of pressure decay testing, people simply extended the fill time long enough for the air to stabilise sufficiently before measurement began, however the idea of separating the stabilisation from the fill had benefits, as during the fill phase, the part remains connected to the supply air, and so adiabatic effects becomes even more complex to ascertain.

Analogy for stabilisation:

I like to explain this as a lift that can hold 20 people, but cannot move safely until the people in the lift (the air in the lift) are standing still (are settled down). There are 100 people urgently wanting to get into the lift (like the main air supply) due to a fire on their floor, or maybe it is time to go home?. Now if we leave the lift doors open the people outside will be pushing those in the lift to try and gain access, and in this way the people in the lift will be unable to remain still, and the lift unable to move safely.

However: *If we close the lift doors once there are 20 people inside, then those inside the lift are isolated, and can settle down to a still state more quickly. And so the lift can begin its travel.*

It was decided therefore that the best and fastest way to stabilise the air inside the part, was to separate it as much as possible from external influences. And so a separate STABILISATION phase was developed, during which the supply air was disconnected (shut off) from the part under test, allowing the air inside the part to settle down/stabilise much more quickly.

And so the standard sequence became that shown (Figure 6-12) below.

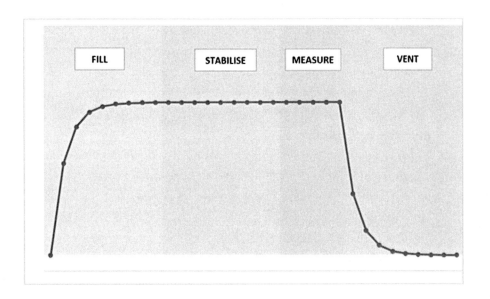

Figure 6-12

6.2.2 Prefill

Before finalising the test sequence, it is worth discussing the additional pressurising phase that is commonly included in modern leak test instruments, that being the prefill.

This is another fill stage, in advance of the standard fill phase, allowing us pressurise the component from a different pressure source (although in many modern devices an automatic, or electronically controlled, pressure regulator is

151

installed as the pressure source, and as such can be programmed to fulfil both the prefill, and the fill phases).

The prefill is generally used to pressurise the part we are testing to a higher pressure than the final desired pressure. But why would we want to do this? This has two main benefits:

1. Faster filling and reduced stabilisation times
a. By aiming for a higher pressure level, the differential between the pressure in the unpressurised part is much greater, and as we have already discussed in the chapter on Leak Rates, this will create a much faster flow of air into the part, allowing it to be pressurised more rapidly.
b. As we have already discussed the pressurising of the part causes temperature increase which must be dissipated before we begin to measure for leakage/pressure decay. And vice-versa, the reduction of pressure will reduce the temperature. By over pressurising, and then dropping the pressure, we can actually create a combined heating/cooling, allowing adiabatic temperature effects to be nullified a little faster.
2. Flexible part pre-stressing:
a. This is specifically aimed at parts that have a flexible component, such as a rubber diaphragm, or thin plastic wall. A good example of this I first encountered in the form of a colostomy bag, which was entirely made of a rubberised material, which had the capacity to stretch. When parts such as these are pressurised, at the point where we stopped pressuring (end of the fill time), during stabilisation the bag was still stretching.

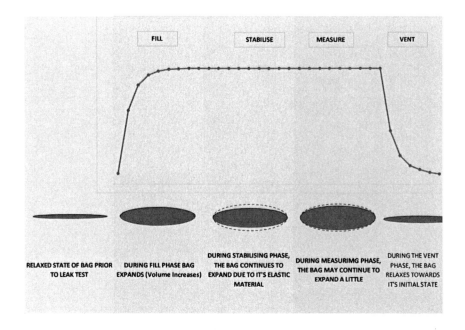

Figure 6-13

b. If the stabilisation phase was not long enough, then the bag may still be expanding during the measure phase (Figure 6-13). This continued expansion, means that the volume of the bag continues to grow, and as we know from PV/T = constant, an increase in the volume will mean a decrease/drop in pressure, which again will look like a leak. Initially the way around this is simply to extend the stabilisation time, until the bag stopped increasing in size, but this created very long test times.

c. By using a prefill pressure higher than the required test pressure, we can expand the bag beyond its expected state when we intend to test, and then as we drop the pressure back to the required level for testing, the bag naturally collapses back (Figure 6-14), allowing the measure period to begin without fear of volume increase.

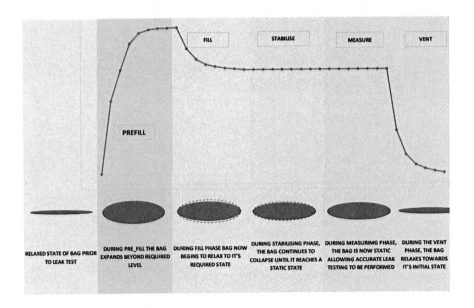

Figure 6-14

6.2.3 Standard Test Sequence Summary

The 5 main stages of our test cycle are therefore as follows (Figure 6-15):

- **Prefill:** Pressurise the system above the required test pressure. Generally used for quicker filling, and/or for flexible components.
- **Fill:** Pressurise the component to the required test pressure.
- **Stabilise:** Allow adiabatic effects to dissipate
- **Test/measure:** Time to measure the leakage rate
- **Exhaust/vent:** Allow test pressure to be safely removed from the part

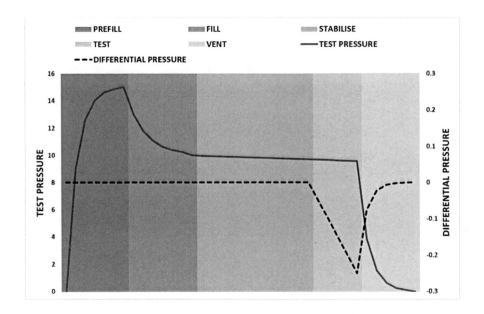

Figure 6-15

This graph shows the sequence of events, together with the response of the differential measuring transducer.

6.2.4 The Internals of a Differential Pressure Decay Leak Tester

Whilst it is not essential to understand the internal workings of a pressure decay leak tester, it is something I like to share, as this additional knowledge may help your deeper understanding, and help you identify the various issues

This diagram (Figure 6-16) shows a typical example of the gas circuits of a typical differential pressure decay system.

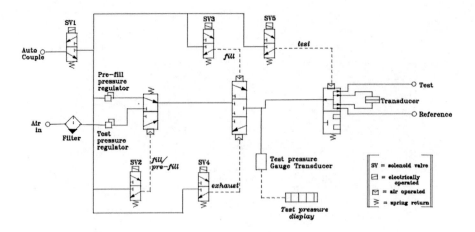

Figure 6-16

Some items to note are:

a) The auto coupling connection, which operates throughout the cycle, and can usually be programmed to begin before the fill time. It can also be programmed to hold on in the event of a leak being detected. This is used to drive clamping, or sealing units for our tester.

b) The gauge transducer mounted in the circuit to enable measurement of the test pressure itself. This allows a comparison to be made against pre-set limits to check this test pressure during the stabilisation phase.

c) The solenoid valves, which are used to operate the main switching valves. A simple way of converting from electronic control circuits to gas switching. The reason this is done is to avoid transfer of heat (temperature as we have seen can cause great issues) from the electrically operated solenoids into the test air circuits.

d) The three position fill/ exhaust valve serves for both filling/ pressurisation and venting of the component. Its centre position is used for the stabilisation phase.

e) The key element of this system is the equalisation valve, which links the differential transducer to the system and the component under test (and the reference port), and is used to separate the stabilisation and measure phases.

The sequence of operation of the various components is as follows.

6.2.4.1 Prefill (Figure 6-17)

During this phase, the fill/vent valve is moved to fill position, whilst the fill valve is maintained in the prefill position, allowing the higher pressure prefill air to travel through and pressurise the transducer and the test and reference ports.

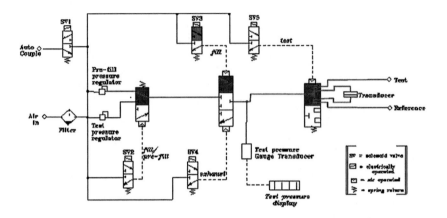

Figure 6-17

6.2.4.2 Fill/pressurise (Figure 6-18)

The fill valve is now switched to the lower pressure fill position allowing the part under test and the rest of the system to achieve the desired test pressure.

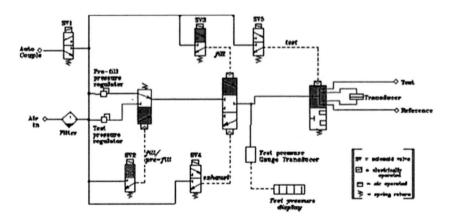

Figure 6-18

157

6.2.4.3 Stabilisation (Figure 6-19)

Now the fill/vent valve is allowed to drop back to the central position, separating the part and transducer from the air supply. The equalisation valve remain in it previous position, allowing the air in the component, and both sides of the transducer to settle down (remaining equal pressure) until the air has stabilised.

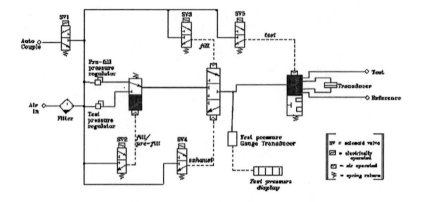

Figure 6-19

6.2.4.4 Measure/Test (Figure 6-20)

The equalisation valve is operated, thus separating the test and reference sides of the differential transducer. With the part under test connected to the test side of the transducer, and the reference side blanked, the system can now measure the difference in pressure between them.

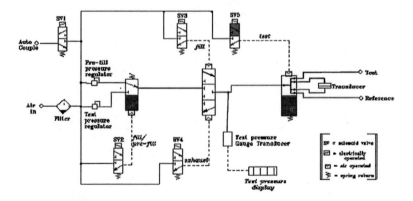

Figure 6-20

158

6.2.4.5 Vent (Figure 6-21)

The final phase allows the air from the test circuits to be simple exhausted away. The equalisation valve returns to its stabilise position ensuring that all air from both test and reference sides can be vented.

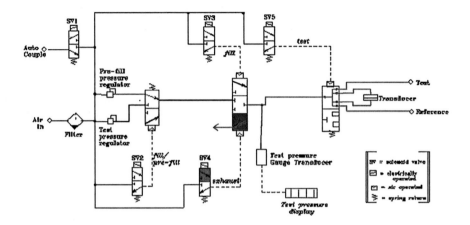

Figure 6-21

6.3 Setting Up a Pressure Decay Sequence

Now we have our test sequence, how do we determine the settings we should use for each phase?

Here (Table 6-2) we can see a typical set of test parameters (these may vary depending on the supplier of the leak test instrument) for a relatively standard pressure decay leak test instrument.

PARAMETER	Units	RANGE
Test Program	Integer number	1 to 32
Pressure Units	Selectable	Bar, kPa, MPa, psi etc.
Prefill Pressure	Bar/kPa etc.	Typically -1.00 to 4.00 Bar *(but dependent on units selected)*
Fill Pressure		
Upper Pressure Limit		
Lower Pressure Limit		
Prefill Time	Seconds	0.0 to 9999
Fill Time		0.0 to 9999
Stabilisation Time		0.0 to 9999
Measure Time		0.1 to 9999
Exhaust Time		0.0 to 9999
Leak Rate Units	Selectable	Cc/min, cc/sec, L/min etc.
Test Volume (Volume Factor)	Typically cm3 *(but could be others)*	0 to 99999
Test Reject Limit	Dependent on which Leak Rate units are selected	0 to 999.99
Reference Reject Limit		0 to 999.99
Offset	Dependent on which Leak Rate units are selected	0 to 999.99
Consecutive Rejects	Integer number	1 to 99

Table 6-2

There are many manufacturers of pressure decay leak test instruments, however they generally all have the same basic parameters. The main differences between different equipment is the different special features available, which we will consider later in this section.

Setting up the various phase times is very much a matter of trial and error, however, like all such things, the more you do the more experience you gain, and soon you will be setting these parameters from a position of knowledge, rather than guesswork.

The following table gives some guidelines to the meaning of each of these parameters, and will hopefully serve help you set up your first leak test programme.

PARAMETER	DETAILS
Test Program (Program Number)	Most manufacturers now offer multiple program units, capable of storing different parameters again a specific program number.
	This parameter is set to select the particular set of test parameters relating to the assembly/part to be tested.
	This is especially useful if you have a range of parts/assemblies (such as we had with different variants of diesel engine) that are similar, but require different parameters due to their size/shape/test requirements. *(Note where parts are <u>very</u> similar, often the same set of parameters can be used for a 'range' of parts).*
	Many suppliers of leak test instruments allow program sets to have names that you can type in yourself. This is a particularly helpful function that allows instant recognition of a parameter set.
Prefill Pressure	This is the pressure required for the prefill phase. **As a general guideline, this is normally around 10% to 30% greater than the fill pressure.**
	It can be higher, but be aware of risks when applying greater pressures, and it is worth seeking advice from your leak test equipment supplier when using this function
Fill Pressure	This is simply the test pressure required to meet the required leak test pressure specification. **My advice is that this would be the normal operating pressure of the part under test, but it is also worth this being set to around 5% to 10% above the normal operating pressure, as a sort of safety margin.**
	Note that on some panels, this is also used for leak location pressure—which is a constant pressure that can be applied to aid leak location (this will be discussed in more detail later)
Lower Pressure Limit	Minimum allowable test pressure—this is a safety factor that will gross fail the test should the pressure drop below this level, thus ensuring the part/assembly is always tested at the correct pressure—**this is usually 5% to 10% below the fill pressure.**
Upper Pressure Limit	Maximum allowable test pressure—this is a safety factor that will gross fail the test should the pressure rise above this level, thus ensuring the assembly/part is always tested at the correct pressure—**this is usually 5% to 10% above the fill pressure.**
Prefill Time	This is set to allow
	a more rapid pressurisation of the assembly/part
	or for a part to attain a higher pressure initially to reduce adiabatic effects more rapidly
	or volume changes caused by flexible part stretching
	Be careful however of the potential to over-pressurise a component which may cause damage.
	The time should be **set sufficiently long enough for the component to completely reach the required pressure.**

PARAMETER	DETAILS
Filling Time	This is the time to fill the part/assembly from the air supply in the unit. Should be **sufficient to comfortably ensure the component under test is fully pressurised to the required test pressure.** It is important to note, that the pressure measuring device (and hence the pressure displayed) is usually located within the leak test panel/instrument, and as such, whilst filling, the pressure will display higher values than are actually in the Component, so always check the pressure after filling, during stabilisation to ensure the correct pressure has been installed in the part.
Stabilising Time	Time to allow the air in the part under test to settle down sufficiently to allow accurate/reliable measurement to take place. **It is recommended to set this at 2 or 3 x the fill time initially, and then to reduce to a level until the test results become unstable. Then increase the time a little more to ensure really good repeatability.** See more detailed explanation earlier in this chapter.
Measuring Time	This is the time for actually measuring the pressure decay (leak). **Ideally this time is kept a short as possible. Generally 2 to 5 seconds.** (If anticipated pressure decay rates are sufficient). The reason to minimise this time wherever possible is simply to reduce the risk of external effects such as temperature changes from cooling fans/heaters etc. Longer times may be required on larger parts or when measuring smaller leaks *(to ensure sufficient pressure decay within the measurement time)*
Venting Time	Time to allow all air to escape or for the pressure in the part under test to reach a safe enough level for disconnection. As a rule of thumb, **it generally takes around 1/3 to ½ of the fill time to vent an assembly to safe levels, but do perform trials to confirm this.** When test pressures are low it is often acceptable to have 0 vent time, and allow disconnection to vent the assembly
Leak Rate Units	This is a selectable parameter allowing the user to have the instrument display the leak rate in a format of his choosing. **however, it is very important to remember at all times that the instrument itself is a pressure measuring device**, and as such the displayed value may be a calculated number and not truly reflective of what is being measured.
Test Volume (Volume Factor)	Volume Factor (also known as Cal Factor) is in effect the volume under test, to make the conversion from pressure decay to leak rate measurement display - **see detailed explanation below.**

PARAMETER	DETAILS
Test Reject Limit	Sometime known as "Limit 1" or "+ Limit", this is simply the reject limit we set for our application. Although it seems sensible to **set this to the required Fail Limit** in the units you have selected i.e.,

	Pascals, cc/min, etc. **However my recommendation is to set this 5% to 10% lower than this, as a safety margin**, to allow for any small variation in our measurement.
Reference Reject Limit	Max –ve value allowed *(effectively maximum pressure rise allowed?).* This is generally used as a safety to ensure –ve values (caused by temp/volume/adiabatic effects) are minimised, **This is generally set to between 10% and 20% of the Fail Limit/Test Reject Limit**—*see further details below.*
Leak Rate Offset	Special value to bring background to zero - see detailed explanation later in this chapter.
Consecutive Rejects	Another useful function to identify repeat failures, which may indicate a manufacturing issue. **This is set (typically to between 3 and 5)** but will bring up an additional alarm to identify if we have a number of consecutive fail results

6.3.1 Further Details of Some of the Parameters

Some of these parameters may not be so obvious, so this section expands on these to hopefully make them easier to understand.

6.3.1.1 Upper and Lower Pressure Limits (Figure 6-22)

These limits are safety limits to ensure the assembly/part is tested at the correct pressure. They are generally active during the stabilisation and measure phases such that should the test pressure go outside of these limits, then the test is usually aborted and a fail result recorded.

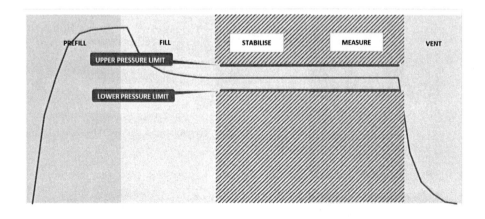

Figure 6-22

163

In general terms, the lower limit acts like a gross leak check as if the pressure drops very rapidly, then this would likely indicate that the part is leaking far more than the normal limit, and it can save wasting time waiting for the complete entire test sequence. (it can also serve a s a check that the test pressure has been correctly set, or that there is no malfunction of the equipment itself.

But what is the upper limit used for? Well clearly it is also a check of your pressure settings, and that the equipment is functioning correctly, however it can also act as a safety stop, by halting the test if the pressure is high, and could cause damage if left to stay high.

These limits are also used in special testing as we will see later in this chapter. But for now let us continue the journey through the various parameters.

6.3.1.2 Leak Rate Units

In general, the leak rate units selectable are split into three categories:

6.3.1.1.1 Pressure decay

= *The total amount of pressure decay measured during the complete measure time. Some of the more typical units are:*

- Pa   =   Pascals
- mB   =   millibar
- psi   =   pounds per square inch (often milli-psi)
- mmWc   =   mm of water column

6.3.1.1.2 Rate of change of pressure/pressure decay

= *The rate per second at which the pressure is decaying. Some of the more typical units are:*

- Pa/s   =   Pascals per second
- mB/s   =   millibar per second
- psi/s   =   pounds per square inch per second
- mmWc/s   =   mm of water column per second

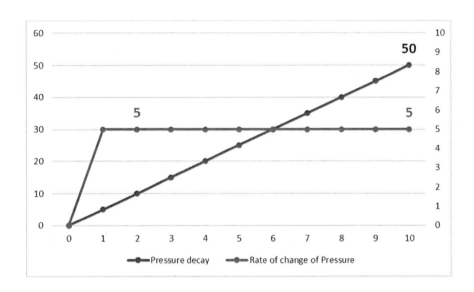

Figure 6-23

This *chart (Figure 6-23) shows* the difference between the two units of pressure measurement (both displaying the same leakage). We can see that after only a couple of seconds, the rate of change of pressure is already showing the same as it would after 10 seconds. This is advantageous, as we can clearly assess the leakage in a very short time. Whilst the pressure decay nit gives us a much larger value, it is also operating for a considerable longer time, and so any external effects (for example: a draft or heater that cause a temperature change) have a greater opportunity to affect our result.

6.3.1.1.3 FLOW UNITS

= *The calculated flow rate of air leakage (calculated from the rate of change of pressure decay. Some of the more typical units are:*

- cc/s   =   cubic centimetres per second (cm3 s-1)
- cc/min   =   cubic centimetres per minute (cm3 min-1)
- L/min   =   Litres per minute (cm3 min-1)

Flow units are calculated inside the electronics of the instrument and not a direct measurement of the pressure decay.

So how is a pressure measuring device able to display the result in flow terms?

6.3.1.1.4 Pressure decay to flow conversion, for flow units

Note: This was previously detailed in the section on Leak Rate Units, and I make no excuses for repeating this, as I hope it will help you to remember this very useful formula.

Let us consider what happens to cause our pressure decay—which is explained as a drop in pressure within a fixed volume caused by a leakage of gas.

So at the start (Figure 6-24) we have a Volume (V1) which contains our gas at a pressure (P1):

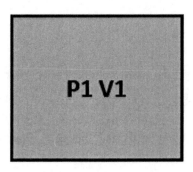

Figure 6-24

After 1 second, some gas will have escaped (Figure 6-25) causing the pressure within the volume (V1) to drop to a lower pressure (P2), the gas that escaped will have a definite volume (V3), at a pressure (P3):

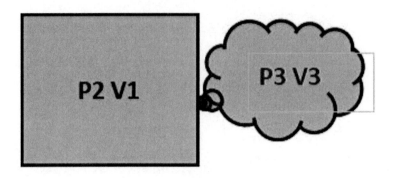

Figure 6-25

Using our universal gas law of PV =nRT, if we assume that the temperature remains constant, then PV = constant. From this we can say that, as the total amount of gas remains the same in both situations (at the Start, and after the leak), so:

P1 x V1 = P2 x V1 + P3 x V3

If we rearrange this equation we can see

(P1 - P2) x V1 = P3 x V3

Rearranging a bit more we get:

$$V_3 = \frac{(P_1 - P_2) \times V_1}{P_3}$$

Now: V3 = Leaked volume of gas at atmospheric pressure
(in measured time = 1 sec)
P1 – P2 = Pressure Drop (in measured time = 1 sec)
P3 = Atmospheric Pressure

So

Volumetric leak rate per sec =
Pressure Decay Rate per second ×Voulme if item under test
Atmospheric Pressure

Now if we measure time in seconds, volume in cubic centimetres, and pressure in Pascals, we can say:

$$cm3\ s\text{-}1 = \frac{Pas^{-1} \times \text{Volume of part under test } (cm^3)}{\text{Atmospheric Pressure}(Pa)}$$

167

> *Note: It is important to remember that this "volume under test" is the entire volume under test, and that will be the volume of the component itself, the volume of any pipework/tubes that connect the part to the leak tester PLUS the internal volume contained within the instrument itself. In many case the pipework and instrument are generally ignored as the part itself, is far greater in volume, however where small parts are being tested, these cannot be ignored.*

Now in our leak tester, we can enter the volume under test, but in the vast majority of cases the Atmospheric pressure is stored as a fixed value inside the instrument (usually the standard value for atmospheric pressure), and so our calculation look s like this:

$$\text{cm3 s-1} = \frac{\text{Pas}^{-1} \times \text{Volume of part under test} \,(\text{cm}^3)}{101325(\text{Pa})}$$

If we want to display our leakage rate in cubic centimetres per minute, we must now add an additional conversion factor, and as there is 60 seconds in every minute, then it makes sense that we would need to multiply the result by 60 and we get:

$$\text{cm3 min-1} = \frac{60 \times \text{Pas}^{-1} \times \text{Volume of part under test} \,(\text{cm}^3)}{101325(\text{Pa})}$$

Similarly if we measure pressure in mB (millibar)

$$\text{cm3 min-1} = \frac{60 \times \text{mBs}^{-1} \times \text{Volume of part under test} \,(\text{cm}^3)}{1013(\text{mB})}$$

Clearly for the correct leakage rate (in flow terms) to be accurate, then the two factors used in the calculation (volume under test, and atmospheric pressure) must be correct but these may not always be true.

a) Part to part variation may also cause some small errors in this calculation, particularly where complex assemblies (such as engine assemblies) are being tested.

168

b) We do know that the atmospheric pressure will vary (as we have seen) due to weather conditions. Although variation is very small (typically lass that 1%) so errors caused only by atmospheric pressure variations are not great.

i.   However, one additional factor not so obvious is that of the test pressure. Although this is not included in our calculation, this will create some variation in the actual pressure decay rate as the amount of leakage is a function of both the test pressure (Pi) and the atmospheric pressure (Po), as described in the Hagen-Poiseuille equation:

$$Q = \frac{\pi \; x \; R^4}{8 \; x \; \mu \; x \; L} \; x \; \frac{(P_i^2 - P_0^2)}{2 \; x \; P_0}$$

So if the atmospheric pressure increases, at the same time the test pressure is low, then the error can be magnified.

All of the above assumes a measure time of 1 second, or that the instrument is set to measure the rate of change of pressure (mb/s or Pa/s etc.), however if our unit is set to measure the total pressure decay over a longer measure time, then we need to adapt our formula accordingly, and it becomes:

$$\text{cm3 min-1} = \frac{60 \times Pa \times \text{Volume of part under test (cm}^3)}{\text{Measure TIme (s) x } 101325 (Pa)}$$

or if measuring in mB (millibar)

$$\text{cm3 min-1} = \frac{60 \times mB \times \text{Volume of part under test (cm}^3)}{\text{Measure TIme (s) x } 1013 (mB)}$$

6.3.1.3 Test Volume Factor

Quite simply this is the volume of the part under test. Internally the leak test unit will use this value in the standard pressure decay to flow rate conversion formula (as previously discussed), to convert the pressure decay it measures into a leak rate (in flow units) that can then be displayed.

$$\text{Volumetric leak rate per minute} = \frac{60 \text{ x Pressure Decay Measured x Volume Factor}}{\text{Measure Time x Atmospheric Pressure}}$$

Important: Unfortunately, when a pressure decay instrument is set up to display leak rate (cc/min etc.), people seem to think that this is what the unit is measuring. Please note, it is important to remember that pressure decay leak test instruments <u>do not</u> measure leak rate. They can only measure pressure (decay).

People often ask "How do I know/measure what volume my component/ assembly/ circuit is, so that I can enter the correct value?"

The best way to calculate the volume factor is by experimentation, rather than trying to calculate the internal volume of an awkward irregular shape (such as a complete engine assembly).

For this you will need a **known leakage**—this is something I very strongly recommend you purchase as this will in the long run, not only help you set up your pressure decay unit, but also enable you to perform regular calibration checks yourselves thus reducing the cost of supplier calibration visits.

In order to determine your volume, first of all set all of the usual test parameters (test pressures, phase times etc. up to get a set of repeatable results). Then follow these steps:

Note: Known leakage, also known as a calibrated master leak this is an essential device in the set up and regular calibration checks that you can perform on your own equipment. This will be discussed later in this book.

---

1. Set the unit to display leakage in pressure, or rate of change of pressure units.
2. Run a test and record the result of the pressure decay test.
3. Repeat this test a number of times (I suggest a minimum of 3 to 5 times) to get an average of the results (and to ensure a reasonable degree of repeatability).
4. Now we will introduce Known Leakage (see later chapters on calibration equipment for further details) and repeat the tests, recording the value of pressure decay for this leakage rate.
5. If we now subtract the value obtained for the part only from the value obtained from the part plus the known leak, then the difference will be the pressure drop/decay caused by the leak.

6. So we now have our leak rate (the known leak), and the pressure decay for that leak, we can use the standard pressure decay formula, to calculate the volume factor from:

If Pressure Decay Units Selected

$$\text{Volume Factor} = \frac{\text{Known Leak Rate (cc per min) x Measure Time(secs)x Atmospheric Pressure}}{60 \text{ x Pressure Decay (Pascals)measured for Leak}}$$

If Rate of Change of Pressure Units selected

$$\text{Volume Factor} = \frac{\text{Known Leak Rate (cc per min) x Atmospheric Pressure}}{60 \text{ x Pressure Decay (Pascals)measured for Leak}}$$

Once entered, always repeat some test to confirm the correct volume factor.
As an example (Figure 6-26):

UNIT SET IN PRESURE DECAY UNITS

Known Leak	6.2	cc/min
Measure Time	3	seconds

Test#	TEST RESULTS		
	Good Part	Part + Leak	difference
1	3	17	14
2	5	19	14
3	5	17	12
4	3	18	15
5	4	18	14
AVERAGES	4	17.8	13.8

Volume Factor =	2275.57971

As a safety Margin, I recommend this is rounded up

2280

UNIT SET IN RATE OF CHANGE OF PRESSURE UNITS

Known Leak	6.2	cc/min
Measure Time	3	seconds

Test#	TEST RESULTS		
	Good Part	Part + Leak	difference
1	1	6	5
2	2	7	5
3	2	6	4
4	1	6	5
5	2	6	4
AVERAGES	1.6	6.2	4.6

Volume Factor =	2275.57971

As a safety Margin, I recommend this is rounded up

2280

Figure 6-26

Now we have seen how to determine our volume factor, what if we already have a volume factor set in our machine, but we now have a very similar part, which we know uses the same parameters, but that the volume factor may need adjustment. Is there a quicker way of determining our new volume factor?

6.3.1.3.1 <u>Adjusting the volume factor</u>

This is very much simpler providing we have our known leak.

1. With the current volume factor set in the machine, run a test on what you believe to be a known good, non-leaking part.
2. Record the leak rate measured.
3. Repeat at least 3 times to get an mean/average.
4. Now introduce the known leakage rate, and repeat the tests, recording the pressure decay for the leak plus engine.
5. Again subtract the value obtained for the component only from the value obtained from the component plus the leak.
6. So we now we use a simple piece of maths based on simultaneous equations, to calculate the new volume factor as follows:

New Volume Factor	*(equates to)*	*Known Leak Rate*
Current Volume Factor	*(equates to)*	*Measured Leak Rate*

From which we can say

$$\text{New Volume Factor} = \frac{\text{Current Volume Factor x Known Leak Value}}{\text{Leak Rate Result Otained with Current Volume Factor}}$$

Here is an example (Figure 6-27):

CORRECTING/ADJUSTING VOLUME FACTOR

Known Leak	6.2	cc/min
CURRENT VOLUME FACTOR	2250	

Test #	TEST RESULTS (cc/min)		
	Good Part	Part + Leak	difference
1	0.23	6.85	6.62
2	0.18	6.88	6.7
3	0.19	6.92	6.73
AVERAGES	0.2	6.883333333	6.683333333

NEW VOLUME FACTOR	2087.281796

Again round up as a safety Margin

2090

Figure 6-27

In this example the volume of the new part is smaller than the previous part. Again, always verify changes by repeating some tests to confirm.

6.3.1.4 Reference Reject (-ve) Limit

In order to minimise the risk of masking leaks, or identifying issues with your equipment or testing, I generally recommend that this limit is generally set to between 10% and 20% of the reject (+ve) leak test limit.

There are exceptions which we will discuss in later chapters, but first a bit more of an explanation of this.

Clearly we would expect the pressure in the part under test to remain constant when there is no leak, or to fall when there is a leak. However as we have seen in previous chapters pressure is easily affected by temperature, and volume variations (which may come from an external source such as a heater located close by (I have even seen people placing their cup of warm coffee on top of an engine during testing, or simply holding onto the part whilst it is being tested, and transferring the heat from their hands into the air under test).

As such our measuring device which simply measures the pressure, could see a small pressure rise, due to a rise in temperature. So let us look at the effect of Temperature in more detail

6.3.1.4.1 Temperature effects

Let me run through a real example of the effect of temperature. In this example, we are testing a component in our factory at a pressure of 1 Bar gauge pressure, and we are trying to detect a 4 atm cm3 min-1 leak. The total volume of the component is 1 litre.

So we have some facts we know already.

P1 = 200000 Pascals (Our Starting Pressure)
–1 Bar Gauge = 2 Bar Absolute = 200000 Pascals)
V1 = 1000 cm3(Or volume under test = starting volume)
Atmospheric Pressure = 100000 Pascal (rounded down for convenience)

We can also calculate (theoretically) our final pressure inside the part from our standard conversion formula

$$\text{cm3 min-1} = \frac{60 \times \text{Volume Under Test (cc)} \times Pressure\ decay\ (Pa/s)}{\text{Atmospheric Pressure}}$$

Rearranging we can see

$$\text{Pa/s} = \frac{\text{Atmospheric Pressure (Pa)} \times cm^3\ min^{-1}}{60 \times \text{Volume Under Test(cc)}}$$

So in our example

$$\text{Pa/s} = \frac{100000\ (Pa) \times 4\ (cm^3\ min^{-1})}{60 \times 1000(cc)}$$

$$= 6.67\ \text{Pa/s}$$

So we are expecting our pressure to drop at a rate of 6.67 Pascals per second if we have a leak of 4 atm cm^3 min^{-1}.

Now we have a heater unit placed above our part (to keep our operator warm during the cold months), and during the measurement time, the heater warms the component (and the air inside it) by 0.005°C per second.

If our starting temperature is 20oC (pretty normal working conditions), then we can say that:

$T1$ =   293K (absolute temp for 20oC)

$T2$ =   293.005 (due to our heater)

As our part is rigid, we know that the volume isn't changing, so our universal gas law equates to Boyle's law.

$$\frac{P1}{T1} = \frac{P2}{T2}$$

From this we can calculate the effect of or temperature

$$P2 = \frac{P1 \times T2}{T1}$$

If we introduce our values

$$P2 = \frac{200000 \times 293.005}{293}$$
$$= 200003.4 \text{ Pa}$$

So we can see that during our measure time the pressure of the air inside our part will rise by 3.4 Pascals. Then following graph (Figure 6-28) shows the various things going on:

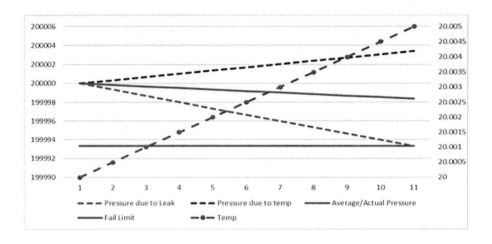

Figure 6-28

1. *The temperature of the air under test rising from 20 to 20.01 °C*
2. *The pressure measured dropping due to our 4 atm cm^3 min^{-1} leak*
3. *The pressure measured rising due to our small temperature increase*
4. *The resultant pressure being measured when these two effects combine*
5. *The reject limit*

We can see clearly that whilst we would expect our 4 atm cm3 min-1 leak to reach our reject limit, and fail, in fact the rise in temperature actually reduces the pressure drop measured and in fact our leaking part will pass the test!

Whilst this appears verry scary, the example uses a temperature change of 0.005°C per second. If we consider our home electric oven and we set our temperature to 180°C, than it can take 15 minutes for this temperature to be reached, so a rise of 0.2°C per second, BUT the amount of power needed to achieve this is quite substantial, and we need a higher rated electrical supply (watch your electric meter).

This shows a number of key things we need to consider

1. Reduce the risk of temperature effects wherever possible.
2. As we see from the chart the longer the test the more the temperature affects our results, so maintaining as short a measurement time as possible is also very important.
3. In addition the careful consideration of test pressure is also important as we can see from the following graph (Figure 6-29), the higher the test pressure, the greater the effect of temperature.

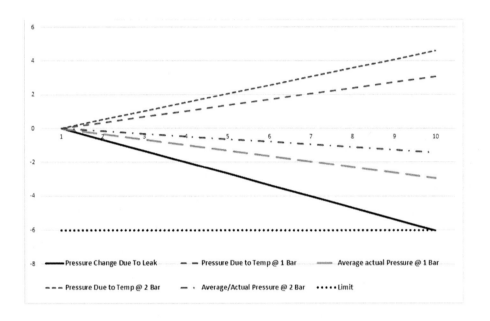

Figure 6-29

The following table (Table 6-3) shows the effect of a 0.01oC temperature drop at different test pressures. As you will clearly see, the greater the test pressure the greater the impact of temperature. One thing to note is the reduced effect of testing at vacuum levels (-ve pressures), which is quite helpful, when temperature problems cannot be avoided.

Starting Temp (deg C)			20		Finishing Temp (deg C)			20.01
Starting Pressure (Bar)	Final Pressure (Bar)	Pressure Change (mB)	Starting Pressure (kPa)	Final Pressure (kPa)	Pressure Change (Pa)	Starting Pressure (psi)	Final Pressure (psi)	Pressure Change (mpsi)
-0.99	-0.990000341	0.000	-99	-99.00003413	0.0	-14.355	-14.35500495	0.00
-0.5	-0.500017065	0.017	-50	-50.00170648	1.7	-7.25	-7.25024744	0.25
0	-3.41297E-05	0.034	0	-0.003412969	3.4	0	0.000494881	0.49
0.5	0.499948805	0.051	50	49.99488055	5.1	7.25	7.249257679	0.74
1	0.999931741	0.068	100	99.99317406	6.8	14.5	14.49901024	0.99
1.5	1.499914676	0.085	150	149.9914676	8.5	21.75	21.7487628	1.24
2	1.999897611	0.102	200	199.9897611	10.2	29	28.99851536	1.48
2.5	2.499880546	0.119	250	249.9880546	11.9	36.25	36.24826792	1.73
3	2.999863481	0.137	300	299.9863481	13.7	43.5	43.49802048	1.98
3.5	3.499846416	0.154	350	349.9846416	15.4	50.75	50.74777304	2.23
4	3.999829352	0.171	400	399.9829352	17.1	58	57.9975256	2.47
4.5	4.499812287	0.188	450	449.9812287	18.8	65.25	65.24727816	2.72
5	4.999795222	0.205	500	499.9795222	20.5	72.5	72.49703072	2.97
5.5	5.499778157	0.222	550	549.9778157	22.2	79.75	79.74678328	3.22
6	5.999761092	0.239	600	599.9761092	23.9	87	86.99653584	3.46
6.5	6.499744027	0.256	650	649.9744027	25.6	94.25	94.2462884	3.71
7	6.999726962	0.273	700	699.9726962	27.3	101.5	101.496041	3.96

7.5	7.499709898	0.290	750	749.9709898	29.0	108.75	108.7457935	4.21
8	7.999692833	0.307	800	799.9692833	30.7	116	115.9955461	4.45
8.5	8.499675768	0.324	850	849.9675768	32.4	123.25	123.2452986	4.70
9	8.999658703	0.341	900	899.9658703	34.1	130.5	130.4950512	4.95
9.5	9.499641638	0.358	950	949.9641638	35.8	137.75	137.7448038	5.20
10	9.999624573	0.375	1000	999.9624573	37.5	145	144.9945563	5.44

Table 6-3

6.3.1.5 Leak Rate Offset Value

This value is used to artificially shift the resultant leak test measured, so that no leak conditions read zero leak rate.

The reason to do this would be because our results are always showing a value above (or below) zero. This could be for a number of reasons:

1. Maybe parts are always warm and then cooling when tested to create a small reading?
2. Maybe there is a small volume change caused by an expanding part, and we do not have prefill function or sufficient time to wait for this to dissipate?
3. Maybe we know that our part has a small leak through a pinhole which is part of the design of the part?

My personal opinion/recommendation is that this function (wherever practical/possible) is not used, as it effectively gives us a calculated (and thus false) reading of the true leakage from our part.

In all cases, I would recommend trying first to eliminate the cause of the repeatably higher than desired values for non-leaking component, however if this does prove impossible, then this function can be very useful.

The way to decide the value to set on the Offset is to run a series of tests on non-leaking parts, recording each test result (Figure 6-30).

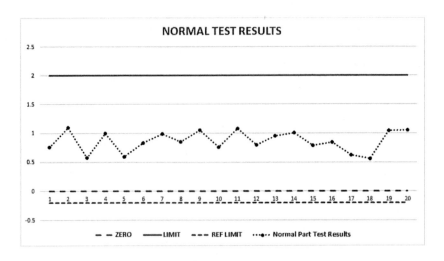

Figure 6-30

Then you can calculate the amount of Offset to introduce from these results.—there are of course a number of options as follows:

6.3.1.4.2 Average value offset (Figure 6-31)

Many suppliers set this value to the average value of these results, which would mean that our average result would be zero leak, however this would mean that some of our non-leaking parts would then read –ve values. In many cases where the offset is relatively small, this is not a problem, however (as shown in the example below) if the values obtained are a significant %age of the leak limit, then this would mean our reference limit would need to be increased, and as such our safety against -ve values will be minimised.

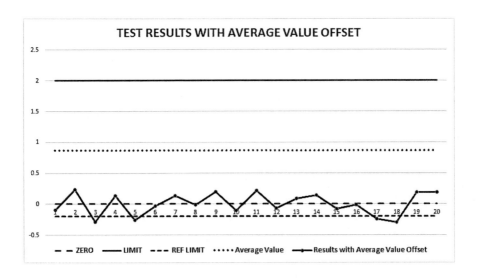

Figure 6-31

6.3.1.4.3 Minimum value offset (Figure 6-32)

In this case the smallest value obtained from our normal test results is used as the offset, resulting in our values with the offset introduced always being +ve, allowing us to keep the reference limit to a minimum, and avoiding the unnecessary questions regarding what is a negative leak.

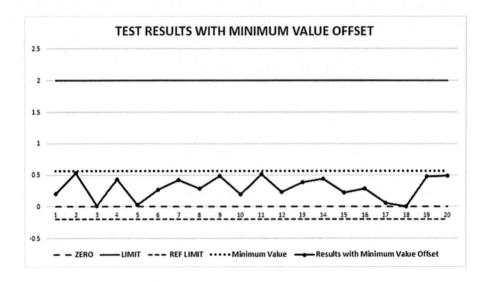

Figure 6-32

If this function is to be used, this is my personal preferred choice of Offset Value, as this means that the smallest value you measure is displayed as a 0.00 (zero) leak rate.

6.3.1.4.4 Somewhere in between (Figure 6-33)

This is to plot the results as I have done here, and then calculate an offset value that will reduce the normal values, but maintain them above our reference reject limit. This is simple to do by subtracting the Reference Reject Limit from the minimum value obtained during normal tests (in our example this was 0.52—(-0.2), so 0.72 becomes our offset value)

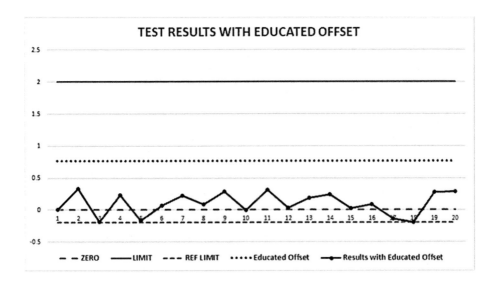

Figure 6-33

6.3.2 Setting Up a Pressure Decay Test - Additional Information

So we have looked at the various parameters, but how do we actually go about it. Some of the parameters such as fill pressure, and leak limits are pre-determined by our requirement and we can check others such as volume factors etc. by completed verification tests.

But how do I know I have set up/optimised the correct phase times, and if I have a practical solution. Some of this comes with experience (so the more times you do it, the better you will get), but there are a few things to look for.

6.3.2.1 Filling Times

Many people have tried to devise calculations/charts, based on test pressures and part volumes, to enable the fill time to be calculated/set, however none of these are perfect, as they cannot take into account the shape of the part, whether it has small apertures, the size of tube connecting the part etc. It is far better to use a practical approach, by observing the pressure displayed on the pressure decay leak tester.

183

It is important to remember that the pressure displayed on the instrument, is measured in the instrument itself, and as such during the Fill phase, the air has to travel from the supply (at the device) into the part.

As we have previously discussed in order to move air requires a pressure differential, and the smaller this differential, the slower the flow of air. So as we begin flowing the air, the pressure in the part is much lower than the pressure in the instrument.

Clearly with small parts, the speed of filling is relatively quick due to the volumes involved, however with larger parts such as complete assemblies (engines and similar), the time it takes for the complete system to reach a uniform pressure can be considerable.

So watch the pressure on the instrument, especially as the part moves into the stabilisation phase.

Although this diagram (Figure 6-34) looks as though our fill time is sufficient, taking a closer look we can see that as the part goes into stabilisation, the pressure begins to drop a little (Figure 6-35).

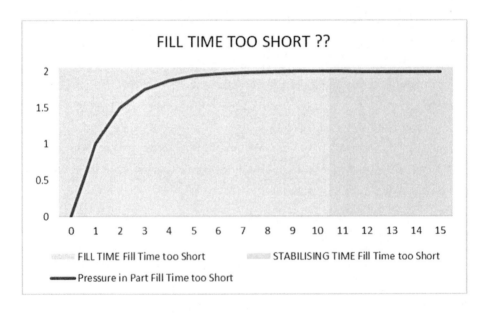

Figure 6-34

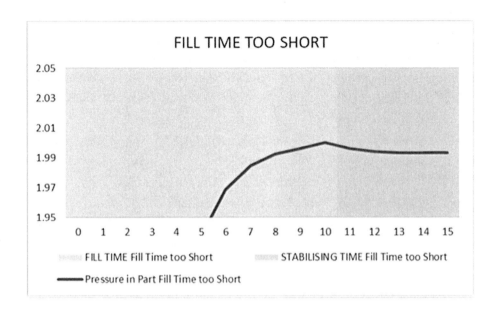

Figure 6-35

By extending the fill time a little (Figure 6-36) we can see that during the stabilising phase, the required test pressure is maintained, so we know that now our filling time is sufficient.

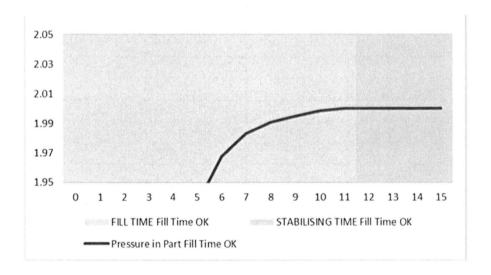

Figure 6-36

185

6.3.2.2 Stabilisation Times

This is more difficult to assess, but once again I take the practical approach by observing the resultant leak measurements of testing a number of parts and observing the repeatability. In very brief terms, the sign of good stabilisation is seen in the test results themselves. The more repeatable the result, the better the stabilisation time set up is.

Ideally, we would like the same result every time for an individual part, and for non-leaking parts, all results would show a zero result. However small variations in atmospheric conditions, air supply repeatability, part handling (warming/cooling of part) will all have a small effect, and so do not expect the results to be ideal!

And so I go back to the aspect of signal to noise ratios to determine what is a good and repeatable result. In most applications (smaller or individual components) we aim for a set of results for non-leaking part of less than 10% of the leak limit.

In order to check this, select a minimum of 5 parts (I recommend 10, as the more the better), and test these parts a minimum of three times each, recording the test results of each test. When testing, ensure:

1. That the sequence of testing is varied something like the Table 6-4: - this is to eliminate any variation that may be caused by a repeatable external effect, or for operators to inadvertently affect the results

Test Sequence	Part # Run 1	Part # Run 2	Part # Run 3
1	1	6	10
2	2	2	9
3	3	8	8
4	4	3	7
5	5	1	6
6	6	10	5
7	7	9	4
8	8	5	3
9	9	7	2
10	10	4	1

Table 6-4

2. Also ensure a minimum of three tests is carried out on other parts between tests on one particular part.-The reason for this is that if we repeatedly test the same part, then temperature effects on the part itself caused by pressurising, will not have time to subside between tests, and so repeated testing of the same part is likely to result in our first test being the correct test value, but subsequent tests are likely to be reduced (Figure 6-37). This is due to the fact that the part is heated during filling, and that the part temperature does not completely recover resulting it warning the air under test during the measurement phase. Over a time of continued testing, we will likely reach a stable level, however when we are testing during normal manufacturing operation, each part only gets one test, so the first test is the only one that reflects the normal use of the equipment.

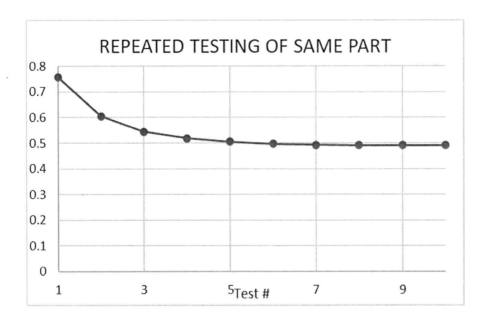

Figure 6-37

Once you have the results, I strongly suggest the use of chart plotting as it makes it much easier to see what our results look like when presented in graphical form rather than trying to decipher a bunch of numbers.

If our test results look like the example in Figure 6-38, we can see two facts quite clearly

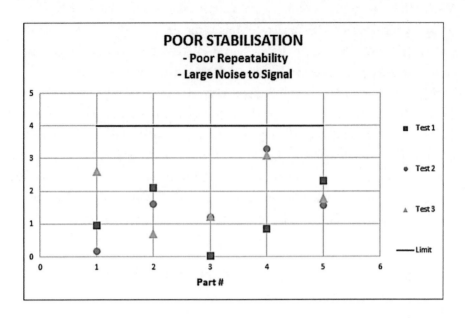

Figure 6-38

1. The variation in results for each part. This indicates that our testing is not repeatable, so how can we trust our leak test machine to give us reliable result data.

2. The results virtually fill the space between 0 and our leak limit. - Assuming these are all good parts, then how can we rely on the results from our leak tester to reliably measure our leakage rate and fail/pass parts in respect of our leak limit.

In this second chart (Figure 6-39) we see a much better set up of Stabilisation time, as we can see that the results for each individual part are all very similar (only minor variation caused by minor variation of things beyond our control.

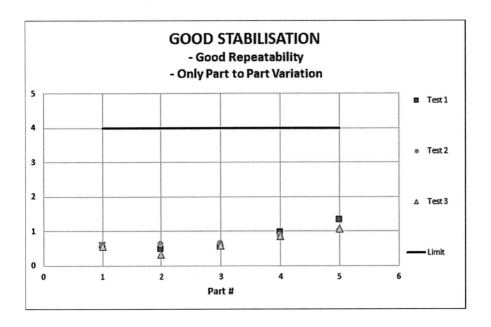

Figure 6-39

But we can see that our results still range between 0 and 50% of our limit—is this a concern? It may be but this really depends on how much we believe we have perfect parts. This type of chart really indicates that the Stabilisation time is good, and that the only variation is caused by variations in the parts themselves (maybe there is an inherent amount of leakage in caused by our manufacturing process, which will vary from one part to another? In any case this may well be perfectly acceptable.

In an ideal scenario, we would see a chart more like that in Figure 6-40, where our good parts are all very much the same (shown by results for all parts being very similar), and we have good stabilisation as can be seen by the minimal difference in each test of each part.

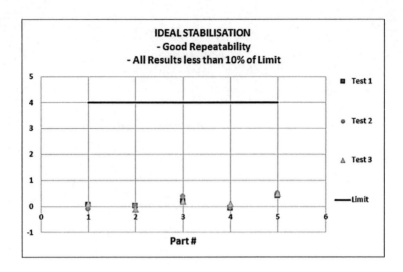

Figure 6-40

This set up is ideal as our results are all less than 10% of our leak limit, so we can be very confident that we can reliably identify parts that leak above our limit, and so confidently separate good and bad parts.

However consider the chart here (Figure 6-41) where the results are in the main -ve values. Would this be satisfactory?

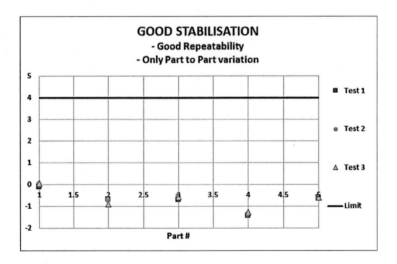

Figure 6-41

Well firstly we can see that the repeatability of the results for each part is minimal, and that the only variation is caused by part to part differences, so this indicated that our Stabilisation time is good.

But there are concerns on being able to identify parts that leak above our limit, as good parts are showing a fairly large -ve value.

In such circumstances there are 2 options:

1. Introduce an offset (of the minimum result achieved) that brings all values into the +ve region (Figure 6-42).

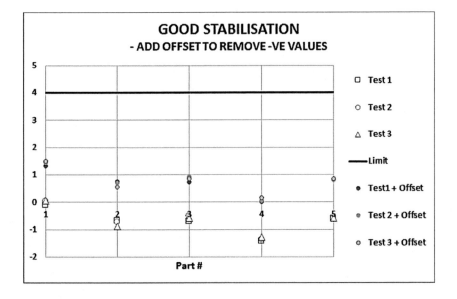

Figure 6-42

191

2. Move our reject limit (down by the minimum value achieved) to account for the - ve value (Figure 6-43).

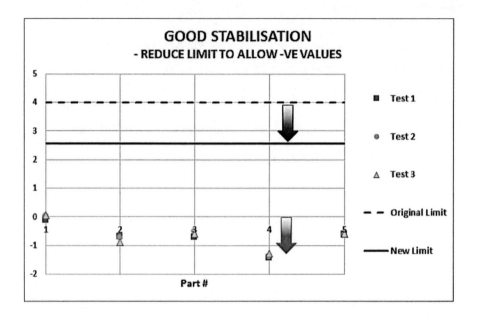

Figure 6-43

6.3.2.3 Test/Measure Time

The correct time for this phase can be determined by considering our leakage rate to pressure decay formula:

$$Pa = \frac{\text{Measure Time(s)} \times \text{Leak Space(cc/min)} \times \text{Atmospheric Pressure (Pa)}}{60 \times \text{Volume Under Test(cc)}}$$

Where: *Pa = Pascal Response to Leak*

Rearranging this:

$$\text{Measure Time(s)} = \frac{Pa \times 60 \times \text{Volume Under Test(cc)}}{\text{Leak Space(cc/min)} \times \text{Atmospheric Pressure (Pa)}}$$

My recommendation is that our leak test limit, given by the formula should be a minimum of 10 times the sensitivity of your equipment, so we can replace our "Pa" in the formula with a value of 10 times the sensitivity as follows:

$$\boxed{\text{Measure Time(s)} = \frac{10 \times Sensitivity\ (Pa) \times 60 \times \text{Volume Under Test(cc)}}{\text{Leak Space(cc/min)} \times \text{Atmospheric Pressure (Pa)}}}$$

Let me explain this with examples

So if our instrument has a resolution of 1 Pascal, then we need to be sure to have a pressure change of at least 10 times this (i.e., 10 pascals) during our measure time, then our Measure time is given by:

$$\text{Measure Time(s)} = \frac{10 \times 60 \times \text{Volume Under Test(cc)}}{\text{Leak Space(cc/min)} \times 100000}$$

If our Part has a volume of 1 Litre (1000 cc) then our formula becomes

$$\text{Measure Time(s)} = \frac{600 \times 1000(cc)}{\text{Leak Space(cc/min)} \times 100000} = \frac{6}{\text{Leak Space(cc/min)}}$$

So if our leak specification is 1 cc/min then we need at least 6 seconds measure time, and if our leak specification is 6 cc/min then 1 second would be just sufficient to give us 10 times our resolution to detect our leak limit. However I would always verge on the side of safety and have 10 seconds for the 1cc/min leak (giving a reading of 16 Pascals, or 16 times our resolution, for our leak), and 2 seconds for our 6cc/min leak (giving 20 pascals, 20 times our resolution, for our leak).

In all cases I personally would always have a minimum of 2-second measurement time (to avoid any noise from initial readings at start of measurement time).

6.4 Special Functions

So far we have only considered the basic functions and test cycle available for pressure decay testing, but there are a number of special options (although these may vary from supplier to supplier) that can be used when our basic functions need a little assistance to overcome some of the issues we encounter.

Below Table 6-5 demonstrates some of these options, aligned with some of the issues that may be encountered.

SPECIAL FUNCTION/ OPTION	ASSOCIATED PROBLEM S(ISSUES)
TRACKING OFFSET	• To adapt for drift in background readings • Reduce Cycle Times
VACUUM TESTING	• Reduce possible Temperature effects
'N'-TEST	• Small Temperature fluctuations • Fine resolution for parts close to limit
REFERENCE VOLUME	• Shorter Cycle Time required • Instability in results
CENTRE ZERO / PAIRS TESTING	• Shorter Cycle Time required • Instability in results • Volume Variation
SEALED COMPONENT/BELL TESTING	• Sealed components • Large Volumes (?)
FILL ON FAIL	• To help Identify Leak Path
RECLAIM REJECT LIMIT)	• Special 2nd reject limit to help identify reclaimable parts
REMOTE EXHAUST VALVE	• Used to avoid potential damage to differential transducer when part are immersed in a water bath
MULTI PROGRAM TESTING	• To make Multiple tests (often used in conjunction with valve operation)
TEMPERATURE COMPENSATION	• For use with warm or cool parts causing response due to temperature

Table 6-5

Whilst these are the main ones I will discuss in this book, these are by no means the only options, and suppliers may offer others.

6.4.1 Tracking Offset

This is also known as transient response, or adaptive offset. In essence it is very similar to the normal offset we have already discussed, however in this case the offset is self-correcting, so that small changes of drift in the general good part results will automatically adjust the offset to adapt for these changes.

So let us look at this tracking/adaptive version of our offset in a little bit more detail.

This graph (Figure 6-44) shows a set of results from our leak test machine, for which we used an offset value to bring our leak readings closer to zero.

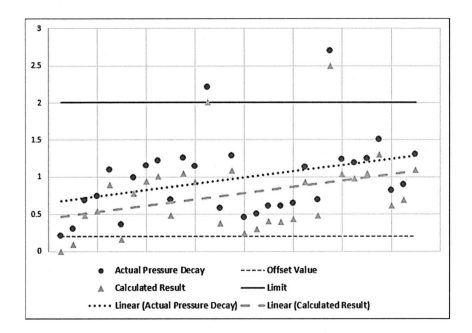

Figure 6-44

However we can clearly see a +ve trend in our results, and as we have a fixed value for our offset, then our calculated results also trend upwards. This trend may be caused by a number of things such as changes to atmospheric conditions, part temperature (from storage) etc.

Because of this we are more likely to fail what are potentially good parts as the background values increase (this will potentially also increase our leak values.

By utilising a Tracking or Adaptive offset (Figure 6-45) the offset value is altered according to each individual result, so as our background values increase, the offset increases to compensate. Thus our trend is now negated and our background good results remain where we would expect, closer to zero.

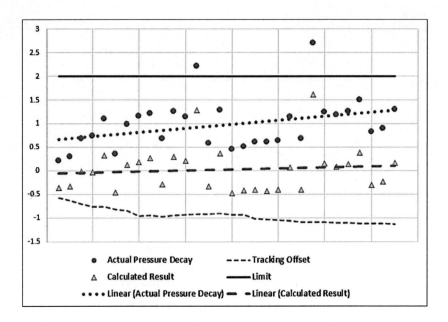

Figure 6-45

We can see how two values that were previously on or above our reject limit have now been reduced by the increased offset, and these parts now pass.

Caution: As I have said before, using an offset creates calculated results, so with a tracking offset, it is even more difficult to know exactly the state of our pressure decay measurement.

Use this function with care as tracking offsets are It is important however that large readings are not used to adjust the offset as a very large leak could make the offset so large that all our test results would begin to go negative, so choose a system where large values are ignored (in the example shown here any actual results greater than 30% of the limit are ignored, and the offset retained at the previous level.

6.4.2 Vacuum Testing

Most often used as an alternative option/solution where temperature variation is very difficult to control.

Referring back to our previous chapter we have seen how a small temperature change of just 0.01°C can make a considerable change to the pressure in our part, and in many cases, this can impact our test results greatly.

Starting Pressure (Bar)	Final Pressure (Bar)	Pressure Change (mB)
-0.99	-0.990000341	0.000
-0.5	-0.500017065	0.017
0	-3.41297E-05	0.034
0.5	0.499948805	0.051
1	0.999931741	0.068
1.5	1.499914676	0.085
2	1.999897611	0.102
2.5	2.499880546	0.119
3	2.999863481	0.137
3.5	3.499846416	0.154
4	3.999829352	0.171

Table 6-6

But as we can see from this table (Table 6-6), the same temperature change in a vacuum has very minimal effect on the actual pressure being measured.

So often people revert to testing under vacuum conditions rather than at the normal test pressure, to avoid the temperature problems.

Caution: As we discussed in very early sections of this book, it is really important, where possible to test the part under the same pressure conditions as it would normally see in its working/operation life, particularly if the part contains flexible components. So my recommendation is to use this as alternative only if absolutely necessary, and ideally never where flexible component parts (such as O-rings, diaphragms etc.) are present.

6.4.3 'N'-Test Function

This is a special function that is used where a small amount of instability is present and is utilised where products often fail the first test due to stresses, and transients, but then pass when another test is performed.

One such example I encountered early on, where this proved very useful was in automotive radiator (heat exchanger) leak testing. Heat exchangers are designed specifically to transfer temperature between the coolant inside the part, and the air outside. So any small changes in the temperature near the core of the radiator, would very quickly transfer to the test air inside, but equally as quickly transfer back out again, as shown in Figure 6-46.

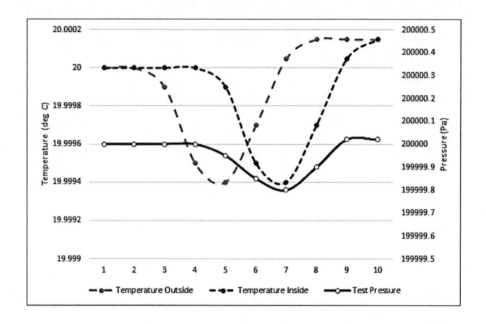

Figure 6-46

The N-Test function operates by viewing the result at the measurement stage, and then making further measurements depending on the result obtained.

If the test result is within +/- 30% of the pre-set reject level, then a second test phase is automatically performed. If the value is outside this range, then the component is passed/failed accordingly.

If during the 2nd measurement phase, the result is within +/-10% of the alarm level, then a third (and final) test/measure phase is initiated. (Again outside these limits the component is passed/failed accordingly.)

During the final measurement phase, the reading is directly compared with the actual limit (as in a normal test). If the product is still showing a reject at this stage, is the component actually failed.

The diagram below (Figure 6-47) shows how this operates. In this case, the part would have failed the test at measure 1, or measure 2 phases—compared to the normal limit. But at the 3rd phase the instability has subsided, and the part passes.

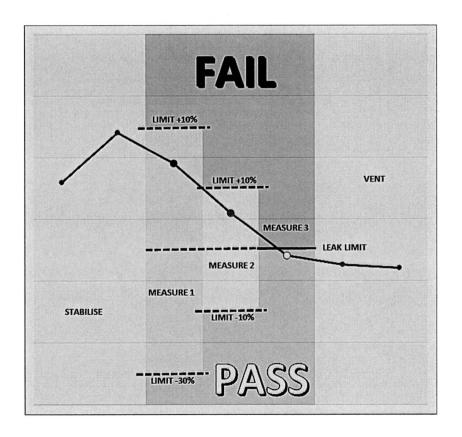

Figure 6-47

In all this option will only add a few seconds maximum to the test cycle, however in some applications it has reduced first time rejects from around 30% to 0.5% resulting in a very large time, and cost saving, that would result in reworking and retesting.

6.4.4 Reference Volumes

This option is really only relevant to differential transducers that have both a test and reference port available at the rear of the leak test instrument, as we now use an actual volume rather than the blanked reference port to be used as the comparison to the component under test.

This is quite useful particularly for larger volumes where stabilisation can take a considerable time.

As we have learned, differential transducers measure the difference in pressure between the component and a sealed reference port. We have also learned that instability is caused by the pressurising of the component, and the temperature effects and unstable air molecules bouncing around.

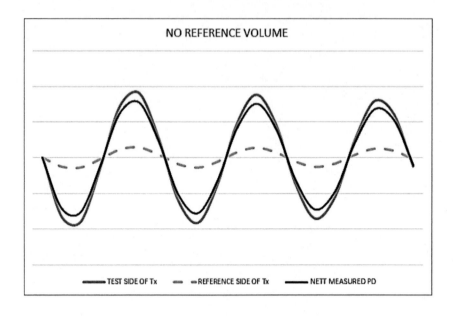

Figure 6-48

Because in normal operation the volume of the part is much greater than the reference side against which it is compared, then it is clear that the instability in each side will be different, and as such the Pressure Difference (PD) will be considerable. (Figure 6-48)

The idea of adding a reference volume is to try and match the instability on each side of the transducer, thus the resultant difference (the value being measured) being zero (Figure 6-49).

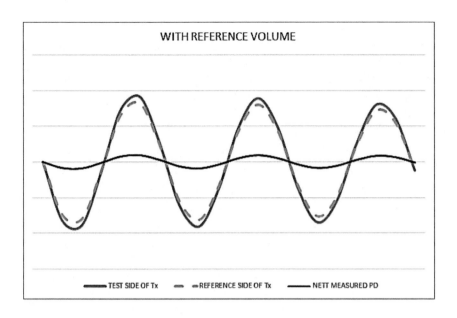

Figure 6-49

Obviously it stands to reason that our reference volume would ideally be identical to the part being tested, thus we would expect the PD to be minimised (zero), however one word of caution in that as we saw from our section on Stabilisation repeated testing of the same part results in reduction in instability due to static temperature differences, so we might expect our reference volume (continuously being repeatedly tested) suffering from this.

I have seen many theories about the reference volume being a percentage (from 25% to 50%) of the part volume to compensate for this, however I have not found this in practice as each part has different shapes/structures, and so each reference volume should be selected according to results obtained.

Reference volumes generally are manufactured to suit and will likely be a basic cylinder or box shape—such as the one shown in Figure 6-50.

Figure 6-50

The problem with such shapes is that the air tends to swirl/bounce around much more (than our shaped part) during the filling phase, and as such the air inside them is more unstable than in our component.

We know that we need the air to be stable in order to make accurate measurement, so we must ensure our reference volume can stabilise as quickly as our part, or our leak test may suffer additional problems.

For this reason it is very important to incorporate some form of BAFFLE system within our reference volume to dampen the instability.

One good way is to fill the volume with something like radiator fins (maintaining a good free volume around the fins), something like the sketch in Figure 6-51, however there are many options, the important thing is to make the free volume within the reference volume into a complex structure/aperture, reducing the amount of air molecule collisions, which create the instability.

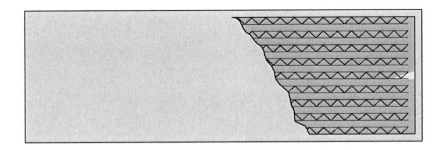

Figure 6-51

One further drawback of this technique, is the increased filling times for pressurising two volumes rather than just one. This does though lead me onto our next special option.

6.4.5 Centre Zero (Pairs) Testing

This technique was originally developed for flexible components (specifically colostomy bags) where even with prefill used, the stabilisation times for such parts became prolonged and not suitable for production testing.

Based on the simple concept of a reference volume it was envisaged that if two identical parts were tested at the same time, one being connected to the test side of the differential transducer, the other on the reference side.

Thus the instability (or in the case of the flexible parts, the increasing volume) on either side of the transducer would be balanced and the resultant pressure difference would be zero.

This appears, on the surface, to be the perfect solution, however there is one important factor to remember: a differential transducer measures the difference in pressure between the two sides of the transducer, and thus in centre zero testing, the difference in pressure between the two components.

So if we have two parts that both leak…

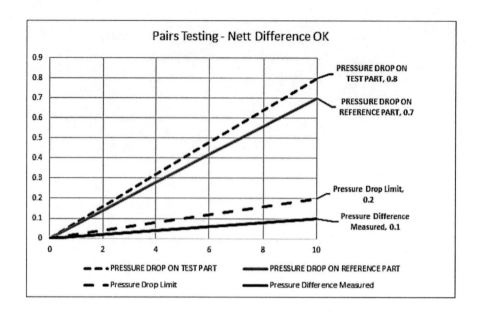

Figure 6-52

Although both parts exhibit leakage rates far greater than the actual allowable leak rate, the nett difference between them is less than limit allowed and thus both parts would pass the test (Figure 6-52).

In some cases a second test can be made on just one of the parts (against another part, or against a blanked reference) but this may well extend our time further, which negates the value of this test.

In general you should consider your production/manufacturing processes, and the likelihood of leaks being produced in a part. If the risks of getting two parts that leak being tested at the same time, are very small then this could be a solution. But I would consider this for simple components, but strongly advise against for complex assemblies which are more likely to be produced with a leak present.

6.4.6 Sealed Component / Bell Testing

This special option is more about the test machine than the use of the instrument. It is used for a wide number of reasons as follows:

- Very high (dangerous) test pressures
- Unable to obtain stability when testing parts normally

- External temperature effects (draughts and heaters) cannot be reduced
- Component to be tested is sealed and cannot be connected to the leak test instrument (such as ping pong balls—my favourite example)

In essence the test instrument is no longer testing the part directly but is actually measuring pressure changes in a sealed container surrounding the part.

6.4.6.1 Bell Testing

The basic concept is to pressurise the component in the normal way, whilst it encased inside a sealed bell or chamber (Figure 6-53). The actual leak test is then performed on the chamber itself.

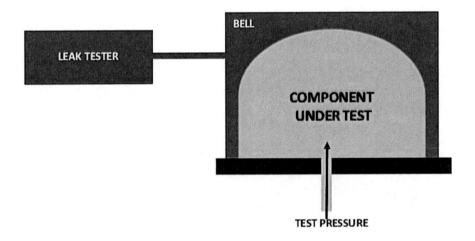

Figure 6-53

Any leak from the part will be trapped within the chamber, so as the pressure decays inside the part, the pressure in the chamber will rise. The rate of pressure rise will be governed by the free volume in the chamber (volume of the empty chamber less the total physical volume of the part), and our calculation for measuring leakage rate in cc/min will be

$$cm^3 min^{-1} \; \frac{60 \times \text{Pressure Rise (Pa)} \times \textit{Free Volume in Chamber}}{\text{Atmospheric Pressure (cc)}}$$

Our calculation for measuring leakage rate in cc/min will be

$$\text{cm}^3\text{min}^{-1}\ \frac{60 \times \text{Pressure Rise (Pa)} \times \textit{Free Volume in Chamber}}{\text{Atmospheric Pressure (Pa)}}$$

Because this is a pressure rise, then in fact in our differential transducer will see this as the opposite to a leak, and so our reference reject limit actually becomes our leak test limit, and our reference limit is then used to check for instability… or is it?

Of course the chamber must be completely sealed or else any air that leaks from the part, could then leak out of the chamber. So to ensure the chamber is sealed, it is very common to introduce a very small pressure (keeping instability to a minimum) inside the chamber and to test for any pressure decay from the chamber. And so our test reject limit now becomes or check on the quality of our sealed chamber (Figure 6-54)

Now our reference reject limit is set as our leak test limit, and our test limit (acting as our check on the chamber leak tightness quality) should be set as 10% to 20% or our reject limit for safety purposes, to ensure our chamber is well sealed).

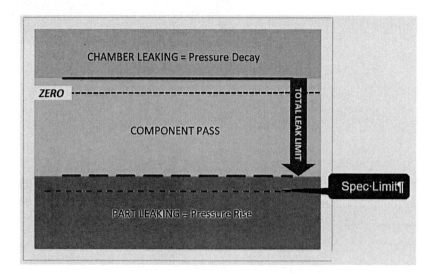

Figure 6-54

It is also worth considering setting our reference limit to this same percentage below our actual (reference) reject limit, as this will ensure that even if our sealed chamber develops a small leak, we will still be sure to fail parts that leak above our specification limit.

6.4.6.2 Sealed Component Testing

In the case of sealed components this bell test is slightly different as we can no longer pressurise the part itself to make the test.

However a similar principal is utilised to test such parts (e.g., ping pong balls) with the component being tested within another sealed chamber (Figure 6-55).

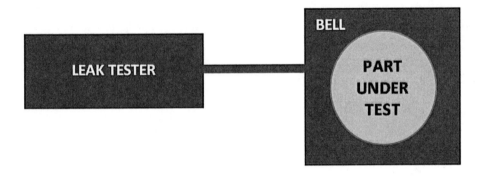

Figure 6-55

However as we are not able to connect to the part itself, then effectively we are only really leak testing the bell itself for leakage. This leakage can therefore be either:

- Out of the bell to atmosphere
- Into the part from the bell

It is therefore much more difficult to determine which of these leaks is the real one, but this is where we can make use of the consecutive rejects can be very useful indeed, in that if we see repeated rejects, we can perform additional checks on the system to ensure our bell is leak-tight. And it is very common for a separate leak test to be performed on the bell only (with no part in place inside the bell), whenever we get this consecutive reject alarm. If this is test passes, then it is clear that the fault lies with the previous parts tested rather than the bell itself.

When this method was first developed, the biggest problem was that if the component internal volume was only a small percentage of the free volume in the bell around the part, then in the event of a gross leak in the part, it was entirely possible to pressurise the part during the fill phase (at the same time as the bell was being pressurised), so that when we came to make the measurement phase, both the bell and the part would be at the same pressure, thus there would be no leak path between the bell and the part (air can only flow if there is a difference in the pressure), and gross leaking parts could possibly pass!

Clearly we could try and limit/control the filling time so that if a gross leak existed, then the required test pressure would not be achieved, and the part would fail as the pressure would be below the lower pressure limit, however with the need for faster testing, fill times could be very short, and so identifying a correct fill time was difficult.

The solution was to perform what is essentially a volume test on the bell. The way this is performed is to pressurise the bell from a separate known volume. The sequence of events becomes:

1. Volume fill
2. Bell fill
3. Stabilise
4. Measure
5. Exhaust

During the volume fill period, the separate volume is pressurised to a known level. Once pressurised, this pressure is then shared with the bell such that the final pressure in the bell, which will be our required test pressure) is given by:

$$Final\ Pressure\ in\ Bell = \frac{Pressure\ in\ Separate\ Volume\ \times volume\ of\ Separate\ Volume}{Total\ Volume\ of\ Bell\ and\ Separate\ Volume}$$

Once this pressure is achieved, then the bell can be isolated from the separate volume, and a leak test performed in the normal way. In the case of a good part with no leak (Figure 6-56) during the Bell fill phase, the pressure reaches the required test pressure, and remains between the upper and lower limits through the stabilise and measure phases.

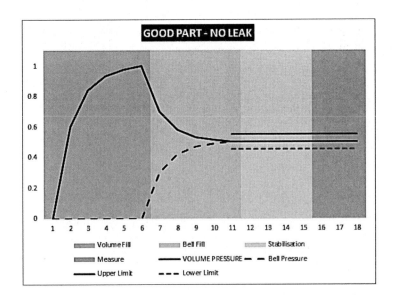

Figure 6-56

In the case of a small leak (Figure 6-57) a normal test is performed, and the leakage rate is small enough that the pressure in the bell remains within the upper and lower limit boundaries, with the leak being detected by our normal test limit.

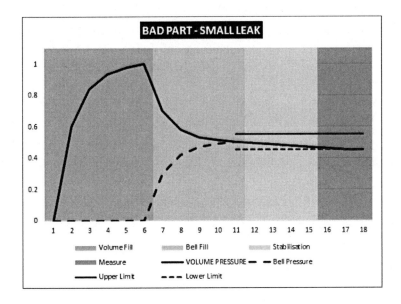

Figure 6-57

In the case of a gross leak (Figure 6-58) in our part, the final pressure in the bell is below the lower pressure limit due to the increased volume being filled, and the test immediately reports a gross leak.

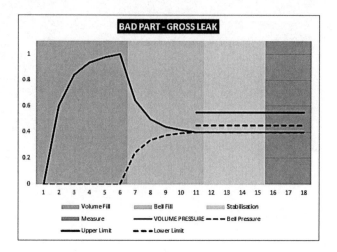

Figure 6-58

Interestingly a very similar technique to this was very successfully employed to make volume measurement checks on volume critical parts. (My example that I personally got deeply involved in was the volume in drinks optics.)

Although not really leak testing and as such not really part of this book, I do think it very interesting and as such I would like to share this with you as it demonstrates, how good pressure is for measuring volume!

6.4.7 Volume Measurement

This special function/option makes use of the pressure to volume relationship by sharing a pressurised volume with another volume, and monitoring the pressure change.

In this case instead of using the pressure transducer to measure the absolute pressure and compare with upper and lower limits we make use of the differential measurement transducer to determine the difference between two volumes and comparing the difference they create when sharing pressure with identical volumes.

The differential transducer can measure very small pressure differences, and so this technique is a very accurate way of assessing the volume of an unknown part compared to a known master.

I first used this technique for a manufacturer of drinks optics (shown here), who needed to be sure that each optic would deliver precisely the correct amount of alcohol, when operated. This method gave the manufacturer a completely dry and accurate way to assess each optic, and so be sure to meet their legislative requirements.

So our set up is as shown below, with two separate identical volumes, used to pressurise one known volume (our master standard), and the second pressurising the component we need to measure the volume of.

The differential transducer is placed between our master standard part and our test part (Figure 6-59).

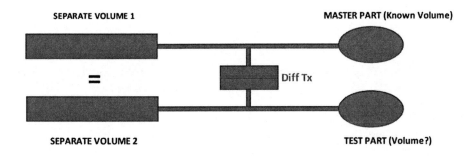

Figure 6-59

Both separate volumes are pressurised, and then the master and test parts are pressurised from these two identical volumes. The difference in final pressure is then measured by our differential transducer to determine if the volume of the test part is correct.

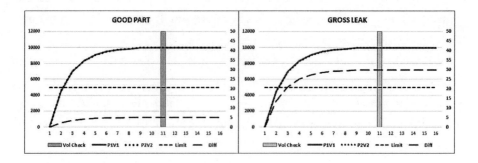

Figure 6-60

As can be seen in the two diagrams (Figure 6-60), it would be virtually impossible to identify an incorrect volume by the test pressure alone, however due to the increased sensitivity of the differential transducer, we can easily discern between good and bad volumes.

This technique can also be combined with the sealed component method where very small sealed component volumes are being tested. Initially to ascertain that a part does not have a large leak (which would look like a volume difference), but if the pressure difference between the master and the part/chamber under test, (Figure 6-61) continues to increase, then a slower leak path is then indicated.

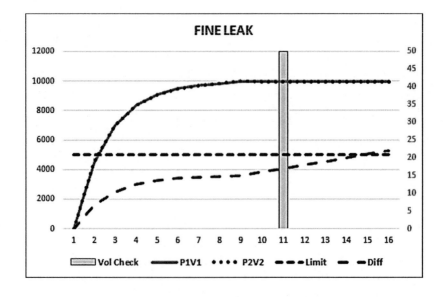

Figure 6-61

6.4.8 Reclaim Reject Limit

This has been shown to be especially useful for cast metal (particularly aluminium) part suppliers, in that it helps identify parts that could be reclaimed by impregnation.

Metal castings are particularly prone to leaks by virtue of inherent porosity (gas bubbles within the metal, created during the liquifying and injection process), within the cast product. It is a common practice to consider Impregnation in such parts to reduce this porosity. However, impregnation is not a perfect process in itself...Let me explain first a typical impregnation process.

6.4.8.1.1 <u>Vacuum Impregnation:</u>

The parts to be impregnated are placed inside a large/sealed chamber
The chamber is then evacuated (vacuum applied) to remove the air from the chamber, and the parts with leak paths.
The impregnation fluid is then introduced into the chamber. The vacuum within the leak paths inside the part then draws the fluid into the leak passage (effectively sealing the leak path).
The parts are then removed and complete a curing process to set the impregnation fluid.

The problem with this process is that is fine for small leak paths, but the impregnation fluid may not always adhere correctly in very large apertures.

So this function allows a 2nd reject limit to be set (Figure 6-62) to identify parts where the leak path passageway may be too large to be effectively impregnated.

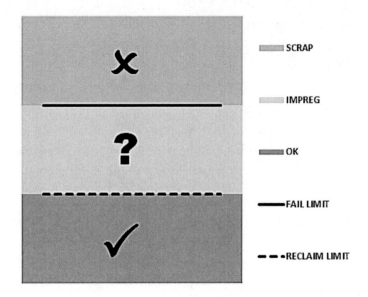

Figure 6-62

✘ Parts that fail above our Normal Reject Limit are not worth risking the impregnation process and it is more cost effective to scrap them.

✔ Parts that are above our Reclaim/2nd reject limit but below our normal limit, have leak paths small enough to benefit from impregnation.

❓ Parts that are below are normal reject level are OK (as we know).

6.4.9 Fill on Fail

Also known as Infinite Fill on fail, this is a function that we can utilise to aid our location of leaks, and thus pinpoint any rectifications that are required.

By selecting this, on any fail result, the component we are testing is then re-pressurised (to the test pressure), and held under pressure until such time as we wish to abort the test.

This means that any leak detected, will still be passing air out, and as such we can employ an alternative search (trace gas) techniques, such as a soap spray solution to help us identify leaks. This is sometimes used in conjunction with tracer gases other than air, and then to use a gas sniffer (see section on trace gas testing) to locate the precise position of the leak path.

Personally, this has proved very useful in my own work by utilising water baths, to immerse the part whilst pressurised to identify the leak location. Using this we make best use of time, as we only pressurise on a fail, and allow good parts to pass through our process simply and efficiently.

6.4.10 Remote Exhaust Valve

This is a separate valve that is fitted between the instrument and the component (Figure 6-63) which in its relaxed state isolates the instrument from the component under test. During the normal test cycle (prefill, fill, stabilisation and measure phases), the valve connects the instrument to the component, but at all other times the valve relaxes, allowing any air within the part to exhaust through this valve, rather than back through the instrument itself.

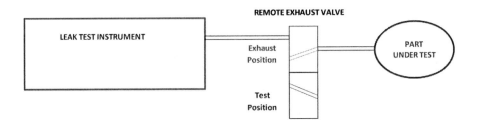

Figure 6-63

This is most often used in conjunction with fill on fail, and parts immersed in a water bath during test (to identify the point of leakage), as it ensures that no moisture can enter the instrument, and cause irreparable damage to the very sensitive differential transducer.

6.4.11 Multi-Program Testing

This is a very basic concept, where the leak tester itself makes one complete test cycle, and then immediately moves onto another test cycle.

This has multiple uses, but is most often used in conjunction with component that contain two separate chambers, such as a mechanically driven water pump on an automotive engine (Figure 6-64). Which has the basic water pump chamber that is driven from gearing within the engine block that contains oil, with a seal between the two chambers.

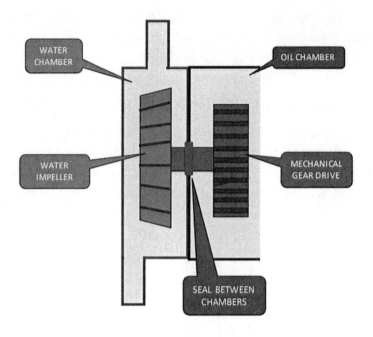

Figure 6-64

Clearly we need to test both the Oil and Water sides of this pump, and both will require different test pressures and different Leakage specifications, so we need to do two tests. One on the water chamber, and a second on the oil chamber.

To make these two tests sequentially, we can use this option, with a **changeover valve** between the test port of the instrument, and the two chambers, which initially connects the water chamber to the instrument on the first test sequence, but then changes over to connect the oil chamber during the second test sequence.

Whilst this is a simple solution it has two major drawbacks:

1) The prolonged test sequence time (two complete test sequences for one pump/part.
2) It can only identify that there is a leak, in each chamber, but if both chambers fail, then could it be that there is a leak between the two chambers that could be repaired (i.e., a missing seal)?

My personal recommendation would be to consider having two leak test instruments, one connected to each chamber, and perform both tests in parallel. Providing both tests are carried out at different test pressures, we can identify the source of the leakage as shown in the following Table 6-7:

RESULT OF WATER CHAMBER TEST	RESULT OF OIL CHAMBER TEST	SUSPECTED LEAK PATH / LOCATION
PASS	PASS	No Leaks
PASS	FAIL (Pressure Decay)	Oil Chamber to Atmosphere
FAIL (Pressure Decay)	PASS	Water Chamber to Atmosphere
FAIL (Pressure Decay)	FAIL (Pressure Rise)	Leak between Water and Oil Chambers
FAIL (Pressure Decay)	FAIL (Pressure Decay)	Leak from both Water and Oil Chambers to atmosphere

Table 6-7

Although the initial cost of the equipment is higher, we will be testing each part in half the time, and also be able to effect repairs much faster, as we now have a pretty good idea of the actual fault/leak path.

6.4.12 Temperature Compensation

I will now attempt to explain just the 3 main versions from the wide range of temperature compensation methods available, but will warn you from the very outset that no compensation method is perfect, and in fact the best method is quite simply to try and eradicate any temperature issues completely rather than look for some compensation systems, that many suppliers will offer at additional cost.

Before I begin, all temperature compensation systems available at time of writing (and I suspect well beyond this) can only really compensate for slow thermal changes in a continuous direction. (such as a part that is warm and cooling over time). I do not believe it will ever be possible to correctly compensate for rapid changes due to draughts, and heaters in the vicinity of the

217

test, particularly where the part under test has a small thermal mass and can transfer heat/cold very quickly, such as automotive heat exchangers etc. (Figure 6-65)

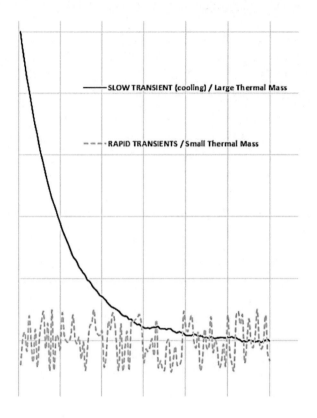

Figure 6-65

In general, therefore, my advice is to only consider this option if you are testing a component of relatively large thermal mass (such as engine blocks, cylinder heads etc.), as this will dampen sharp thermal transients, and allow the temperature compensation to at least give some level of good results.

6.4.12.1 Basic Temperature Probe

The most basic temperature compensation available, a temperature probe is connected to the part, and the temperature recorded at the start (T1) and end (T2) of the measurement phase.

The theory is that if we know the test pressure we have set (P1), then we can calculate the expected pressure change due to temperature change from considering Charles Law where P/T = constant In a confined/constant/fixed volume).

So the change in Pressure is given by:

$$(P1 - P2) = P1 - (\frac{P1 \ x \ T2}{T1})$$

Once we have this change, we can automatically adjust our resultant pressure decay measurement by adding/subtracting (depending on cooling/heating) the calculated change from our result.

This is not so accurate, as the temperature measurement is subject to a number of constraints:

- The location of the probe is pinpoint at one location on the part
- Does not measure the temperature of the test air, only the part itself
- The probe itself is potentially affected by external draughts

6.4.12.2 Null Pressure Temp Comp

This method no longer relies on the use of a temperature probe, but more on the effect of temperature on the air inside the component, and as such is generally more accurate than the basic temperature probe method.

This version of temperature compensation makes an initial measurement of pressure change at Ambient conditions, before pressurising the part, and making the test as normal. The idea behind this, is that if we can measure pressure changed caused by temperature at atmospheric pressure, then we can theoretically calculate the expected pressure change at the test pressure.

The test sequence is therefore altered to include this initial test as follows (Figure 6-66)

Step 1. **Null stabilisation** (a short period of stabilisation, to allow the air inside the part to stabilise at the same temperature, at atmospheric pressure)

Step 2. **Null measure** (a measure time, during which any pressure change is measured at atmospheric pressure, and stored as the ambient PD)

Step 3. **Part fill** (normal pressurising of the part to the required test pressure)

Step 4. **Part stabilisation** (normal stabilisation period))

Step 5. **Part measure** (normal measurement of pressure change at the test pressure)

219

Step 6. **Vent/exhaust** (air is removed from the component)

Now the pressure change measured (Ambient PD) is then multiplied by the ratio of the test pressure to ambient pressure (normal atmospheric pressure (i.e., 1000 mB, or 100,000 Pa).

For example: if our test pressure is 1 Bar above atmospheric, then we will multiply this change by 2000/1000 = 2:

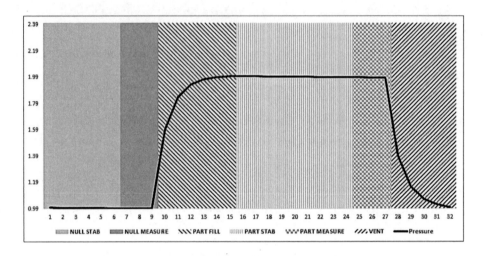

Figure 6-66

This resultant pressure change is then simply used to adjust the pressure change measured at the normal test pressure, to calculate the actual leakage (pressure decay) in the component. Figure 6-67 shows how the temperature effect would have caused this part to fail, but by removing this element (measured during the Null Measurement) of the actual measurement, the part is seen to Pass.

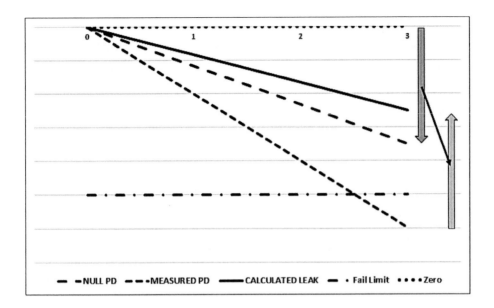

Figure 6-67

Again though this does rely on the temperature curve being very steady and smooth. The main concern with this is the time delay between the null and actual pressure decay measurements, which is likely to mean that the temperature changes may be different at these two points in time.

6.4.12.3 Stored Temperature Compensation Curves

This method involves a considerable amount of work prior to set up of the temperature compensation adjustment factors.

This method requires two temperature probes. One located at, or touching the part itself, and the other located in the surrounding atmosphere, monitoring the temperature of the general room conditions. The system then utilises the difference in temperature between these two points to establish the calibration curve.

Again this only measures temperature at a single point on the part, and in the surrounding air, and is therefore no more accurate than any other temperature compensation method.

The first step in this process is to obtain a known good component (one that is known to be absolutely leak tight) and to retain this as our master part for set up of the temperature compensation curves. Then whilst this part is at ambient conditions (same temperature as the surrounding air, and the leak test machine), make a normal leak test to confirm a good result (as near zero leak as possible)

Once this part is confirmed, we then place it into an oven to enable us to heat the part up to a temperature somewhat higher than the surrounding ambient conditions.

Once at temperature (this can take some time to ensure the complete part is at this higher temperature) the part is transferred to the test machine, and a series of tests performed. During each test, the temperature difference between the two probes, and the resultant pressure decay measurement are recorded, and plotted on a chart. These tests are completed and results recorded, until the difference in temperature is zero (or negligible—by observing the pressure decay being virtually zero).

This process of heating the part and making a series of tests are repeated a number of times, and then ALL of the results are plotted on a graph as in Figure 6-68. (Here I have shown two such plots in both heating and cooling.)

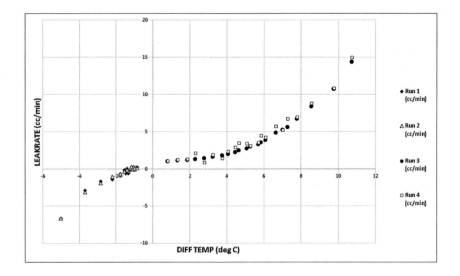

Figure 6-68

For completeness it is also worth repeating with cooling of the part in a refrigerator and recording the temperature differences and pressure changes at the cooled conditions.

Once the trials are completed, you can now add a best fit line for your curves (Figure 6-69) and use this to enter your offset or temperature compensation values into a lookup table within the leak tester. The offset values will be the opposite of the best fit line. You will need to introduce a large number of points along the full shape of the curve, in order to make the required compensation at all parts of the curve (each compensation value will be active at that point only, and gaps between the points calculated assuming a linear transition between the points. So the more points entered, the more accurate your compensation curve).

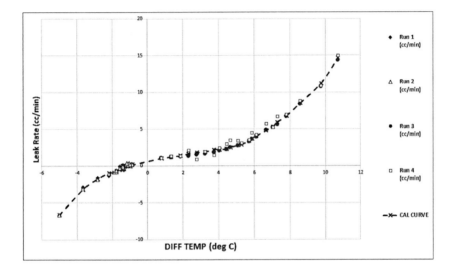

Figure 6-69

Once the values are entered, it is always worth performing the heating and cooling tests once again and reviewing the compensated values achieved, so that you can assess your current temperature compensation curve, and make adjustments as necessary.

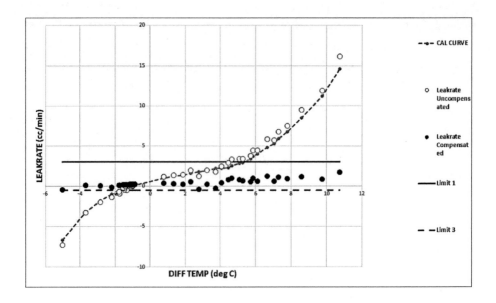

Figure 6-70

Figure 6-70 is a real life example that I personally installed at a major automotive manufacturer testing cylinder heads—hopefully you can see the great improvement in test results to remove the temperature effect.

6.5 Pressure Decay Summary

This completes the section on pressure decay leak testing, and I could have filled twice as many pages, but I believe the details enclosed will give the basic understanding you need. But there is nothing like experience (which how I came to write this book) to fully understand, and I strongly recommend that as a leak test engineer, you should do as much experimentation as you can you gain your own knowledge and understanding of this most common form of leak testing.

In the section entitled Problems with Air Testing, you will find more information to help you understand when you do have issues, and what you might do to identify the root cause and potentially find the solution.

In summary, there are just a few key things that I believe it is important to remember:

1. $$\frac{PRESSURE \times VOLUME}{TEMPERATURE} = CONSTANT \text{ *THIS IS MOST}$$
IMPORTANT

2. Pressure Decay Instruments ONLY measure Pressure and NOT Leak rate

3. Ensure the correct test pressure is used (maybe with a small safety margin)

4. Recommend using a small safety margin (10% or so) when setting up Leak Limit

5. Avoid Temperature Effects wherever Possible

6. Avoid Volume Changes where possible (use Prefill to reduce if necessary

7. Make use of special functions/techniques where appropriate

7 Air Leak Test Methods - Air Flow Measurement

Just as with pressure decay, there is more than one type of measurement device. With flow measurement, there are many types of device, however I will focus on the two devices generally used for leak testing in industry, although there are others:

- Pressure drop across a laminar flow element/tube
- Mass flow sensors

> Note: Many types of device include pressure drop across Laminar tubes, (Venturi tubes, Orifice plates, Variable Area Flow Rotameters, Turbines, Coriolis, Electro-Magnetic, Doppler Flowmeters etc. (the list is almost endless).

Below I have attempted to explain very briefly the principals of operation, but do not worry too much about how they actually work, it is more the application of these sensors that is important.

7.1 Pressure Drop Across Laminar Flow Elements

During our look at how leaks are specified, and our review of the factors that influence leakage, we discovered that a flow of air is created by a difference in pressure. This understanding leads us to realise that as we increase the pressure difference across the leak, then we increase the flow rate. Clearly the same is therefore true, as the flow increases, then the pressure differential will increase.

7.1.1 Basic Principles

So if we consider our leak as a simple tube we can see the following diagrams (Figure 7-1, and Figure 7-2):

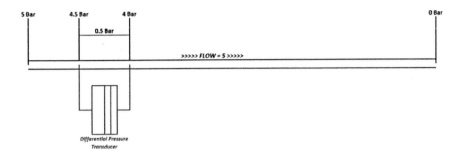

Figure 7-1

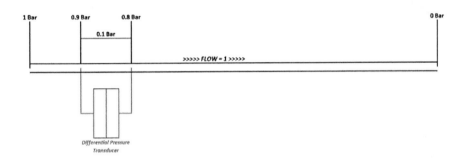

Figure 7-2

This leads us to the conclusion that the pressure difference between the two points in the tube is directly related/proportional to the flow going through it.

So we can measure our leak flow, by measuring the pressure drop between two points of a tube connected to the leaking component as shown in Figure 7-3

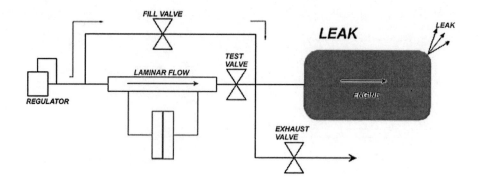

Figure 7-3

But why a laminar flow element/tube?

If we allow air to flow down a simple tube, the molecules of the air will bounce around and sometime even bounce back the way they came from (i.e., the flow goes in the wrong direction). This is called turbulent flow (Figure 7-4) and make flow rates difficult, if not impossible, to accurately measure (as a flow in the opposite direction effectively creates a pressure drop in the wrong direction). Turbulent flow usually occurs at high flow rates and/or in larger diameter pipes.

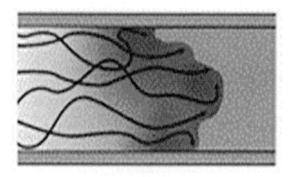

TURBULENT FLOW

Figure 7-4

Laminar flow (Figure 7-5) tends to occur at lower flow rates through smaller pipes. In essence, the fluid particles flow in cylinders. Because the pipe walls exhibit less frictional pull, the flow itself is smoothed out, allowing us to get a far more accurate measurement/relationship between flow and pressure drop.

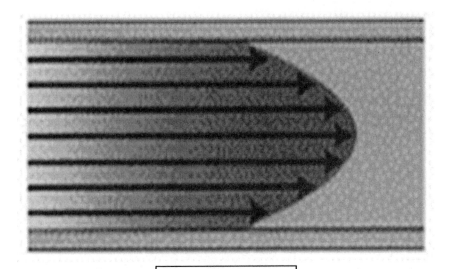

LAMINAR FLOW

Figure 7-5

7.1.1.1 Typical Laminar Flow Elements/Tubes (Figure 7-6):

- Laminar tubes are effectively a bundle of tubes within a large tube
- Note the two pressure connections to make the differential pressure measurement

Figure 7-6

7.2 Mass Flow Sensors

There are a number of variations of mass flow meters, however I will just consider the thermal type for now to explain their operation, as these are the most commonly used Mass Flow Sensor elements in use in leak testing.

7.2.1 Basic Principals

Thermal mass flow meters, measure fluid mass flow rate by means of heat convection from a heated surface to the flowing fluid. They generally comprise a small heated capillary-tube type, which transfers the heat into fluid/air/gas flowing through the tube (Figure 7-7).

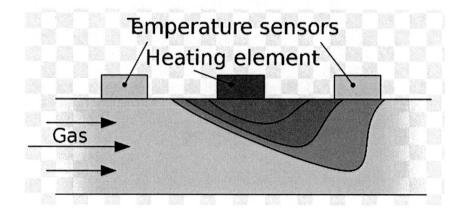

Figure 7-7

The flow rate is proportional to the difference in temperature between the upstream, and downstream temperature sensors. (Note the position of the heated element will vary in different devices).

Mass flow meters have minor dependence on density, pressure, and fluid viscosity, and so the flow meter should be calibrated for the fluid/gas it is measuring.

7.2.1.1 Typical Mass Flow devices

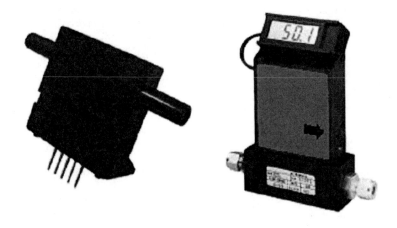

Some are simply sensing elements, with electrical connections requiring power to operate the sensor, and a signal connection to read the flow/volts, whilst others are complete devices incorporating displays etc, that require power only to operate.

7.3 Flow Measurement Techniques /Methods for Leak Testing

Now we have briefly seen the devices, let us consider how these are used. There are generally three main methods of utilising flow sensors:

 ☆ Direct flow measurement
 ☆ Reference tank flow measurement
 ☆ Separated reference tank version

Although both types of sensor can be used in all three techniques, Direct flow is mostly used with laminar flow elements, and to measure higher flows, whilst the reference tank type flow techniques are more applicable to mass flow sensors and lower flow rates. (The reasons will become apparent as we go into more detail on each technique.)

In both cases the flow sensor is generally located between a pressure source, and the component/part under test, so that as the part leaks, it's pressure is maintained/topped up from the pressure source, through the flow sensor. In this

231

way, the flow sensor measures the amount/volume of air required to top-up the part to the required test pressure.

Note: The flow sensor is not always located between the pressure source and the component, as there are some special circumstance where the flow sensor might be connected directly to the part to measure the flow – but these are not usually leak test applications.

7.4 Direct Flow Measurement

In this technique the supply pressure is direct from a continuous supply such as a simple pressure regulator.

Figure 7-8 shows a very basic system for a flow measuring leak test system, where the pressure for the test is taken directly from a pressure regulator. The flow sensor is then placed between the regulator and the part under test, to enable us to measure the flow directly going from the regulator into the part.

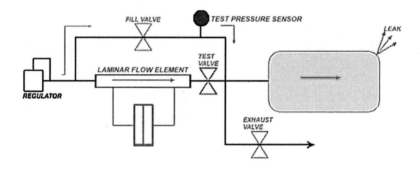

Figure 7-8

Note: The laminar flow tube could be replaced with a mass flow sensor.

7.4.1 Direct Flow Measurement Test Sequence (Figure 7-9)

As with all types off air test, the basic requirements are to fill the component under test to the required test pressure, and then to measure the leak. But just as with pressure decay testing, we also require a stabilisation period to allow for adiabatic effects to reduce. At the end of the test, an exhaust phase is also utilised to allow the air pressure in the part to reduce to a safe level.

1. **Fill:** Fill valve (and test valve) opened to allow test pressure to enter the component and pressurise to the required test pressure level. During this time the majority of air flow is through the fill valve and so virtually no flow goes through the sensor, as the air will take the easiest path to the part.

2. **Prefill:** In some instances such as very large volumes there may also be a prefill valve and regulator set at a higher pressure, so as to reduce fill times etc.

3. **Stabilise:** With the fill valve closed and the test valve open, sufficient time is allowed until all the adiabatic effects have subsided, and the flow through the tube to settle down to a stable level. During the fill time, virtually no flow goes through the flow sensor, so when we shut the fill valve, it will take time for the flow through the sensor to settle down to a stable condition, where the air flowing through the sensor is the same as the air flowing out of the part due to the leak.

4. **Measure:** During this period, no valves change, however the system now compares the flow being measured to that test limit set, and the display shows the amount of air flowing through the flow sensor, as a direct measurement of the leakage rate out of the part under test

5. **Exhaust:** The fill and test valves close, and the exhaust valve opens to allow excess air to safely vent to atmosphere.

Note: The fill valve is also sometimes known as the bypass valve, as it bypasses the flow sensor during the filling phase.

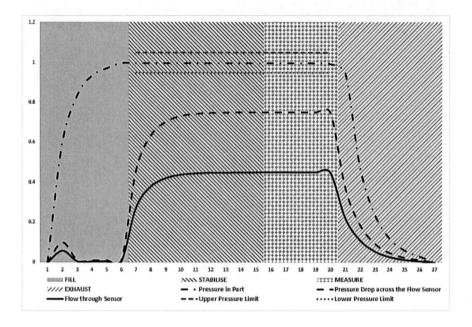

Figure 7-9

A couple of things to notice:

1. In the system we will have the upper and lower pressure limits, just as we had in the pressure decay systems, to ensure we are testing at the correct pressure.
2. You will also notice that the flow sensor may get a small kick as we begin pressurising the part. This is due to the fact that at the point of starting to fill some air will initially rush through the sensor as well as the majority passing through the fill valve.

7.4.2 Setting up a Direct Flow Test Sequence

Here (Table 7-1) we can see a typical set of test parameters for a direct flow measurement system:

Description	Detail
Fill Time	This is set up much in the same way as in the pressure decay method in that the fill time must be long enough to ensure the complete system reaches the required test pressure
Stabilisation Time	This time should be set so that the flow being measured by the flow system is completely stable
Measure Time	Time required for measuring the leakage rate. This will likely be just 1 or 2 seconds, as the flow rate will already be stable at the end of the stabilising time
Vent Time	Time to allow all air to escape from the complete system.
Test Pressure	Simply se to the Test Pressure required to measure our leak (again it is worth adding a safety factor just as we did in our pressure decay to ensure the pressure at the measure stage is at the correct level
Lower Limit	Minimum allowable test pressure—this is a safety factor that will fail the test should the pressure drop below this level, thus ensuring the engine is always tested at the correct pressure
Upper Limit	Maximum allowable test pressure—this is a safety factor that will fail the test should the pressure rise above this level, thus ensuring the engine is always tested at the correct pressure
Reject Limit	Simply set this to the required Fail Limit in cc/min

Table 7-1

In many cases, when the system is at rest, and not making a test, the fill and test valves remain closed and the exhaust valve open, allowing the component to be connected/disconnected safely, however there are special types of flow testers that allow the fill and test valves to remain open, and the test sequence is automatically started by the connection of the part. This method is known as the continuous flow measurement method which I will explain at the end of this section on direct flow techniques.

One of the clear advantages with this technique is that the flow measurement is a direct measurement of the leakage rate, as the air flow passing through the flow sensor (being measured) is the same amount of air that is passing through the leak, and as such no adjustment/volume factor is required (as we will see is necessary with the reference tank technique) to make the instrument read correctly.

However the big disadvantage is the accuracy and stability of the pressure source (regulator). Regulators work by increasing flow when the output pressure drops, so at to maintain pressure at output, then decreasing flow when output pressure goes up, and as such the pressure at the output will go up and down as it tries to maintain the required pressure at a constant level (Figure 7-10). As we already know flow is directly affected by the pressure differential, and as such the flow rate will also vary due to the function/action of the regulator.

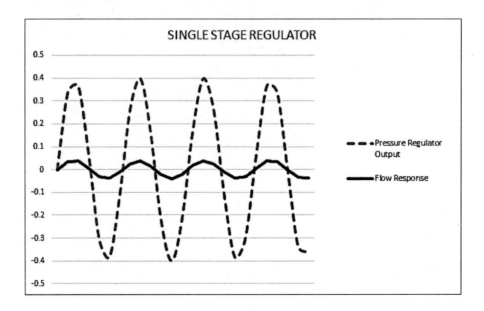

Figure 7-10

One way this can be reduced is to utilise a dual stage regulator which serves to regulate the pressure twice, from the main supply, thus the variation in the second stage pressure is reduced (Figure 7-11) reducing also, the variation in the flow measurement.

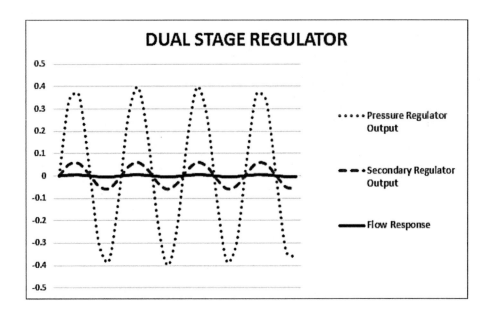

Figure 7-11

Where the flow sensor is measuring larger flows, this is less of an issue as the variation is negligible within the overall flow response. However with smaller flows (smaller leak rates), this variation can be large in comparison with the total flow limit.

Remember signal to noise ratio discussed way back in the chapter on leak limits? So where this noise level is significant, with smaller leak rates, we ideally need a more stable pressure source—a reference tank.

Before we leave direct flow measurement techniques, a brief explanation of **continuous** flow measurement, which is a special type of direct flow measurement.

7.4.3 Continuous Flow Method

This is really just an option as it still uses the direct measurement technique, however it is more correct in this instance to call the fill valve a bypass.

This method (Figure 7-12) allows air flow through the system continuously through the system, and as such there is no requirement for an exhaust valve, as this method is really only employed for low pressure testing. In addition there is no requirement for the test valve as we shall see.

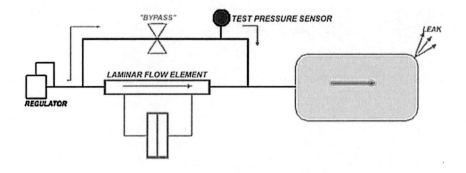

Figure 7-12

In this case, the test is started by simply connecting the part to be tested to the leak tester. Let us briefly return to first the principles of flow and pressure to understand how this works…

(Figure 7-13) With no part connected, like in our simple piece of tube the pressure at the out port on the leak testis is at virtually zero pressure, and a pressure gradient exists in our tube (At this point in time, our pressure sensor see very little pressure and the flow going through our sensor is at maximum level.

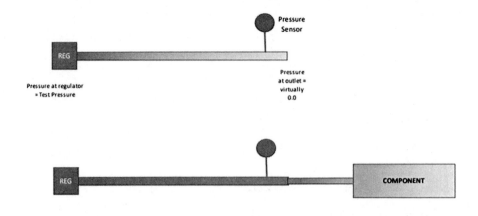

Figure 7-13

As soon as the component is connected, our zero pressure point shifts to the far end of our component (the farthest point from the supply). Suddenly our pressure sensor sees a jump in the pressure (Figure 7-14).

This sudden jump can be used to trigger our test which is now comprises the following test sequence:

1. **Fill:** Triggered by the jump, the fill time is started. This time is set to allow sufficient time for the component to reach the required test pressure.

2. **Stabilise:** At the end of the fill time, the bypass valve is closed, allowing all of the flow to now pass through sensor element. Sufficient time is allowed until flow through the sensor settles down to a stable level.

3. **Measure:** During this period, no valves change, however the system now compares the flow being measured to that test limit set, and the display shows the amount of air flowing through the flow sensor, as a direct measurement of the leakage rate out of the part under test.

4. **Disconnect:** when the part is disconnected, the flow rapidly rises, triggering the end of the sequence, and the bypass valve to reopen.

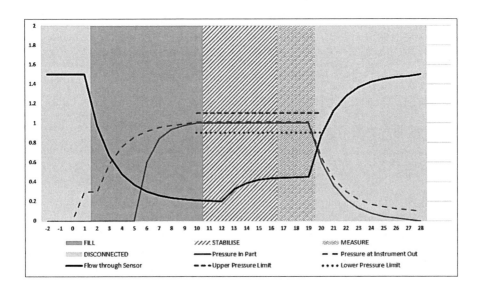

Figure 7-14

As I mentioned earlier, these direct measurement methods are good for larger flow/leaks, however the instability of our pressure source, may have an impact on our flow measurement, so to avoid this we can utilise a different/more stable pressure supply in the form of a reference tank.

7.5 Reference Tank Flow Measurement

This technique replaces the pressure regulator with a fixed reference volume (Figure 7-15) reference tanks and part are shut off from the external pressure source, allowing the pressure throughout the system to become stable, thus the reference tank becomes a stable pressure supply, no longer affected by the variations in pressure caused by the less stable pressure regulator source.

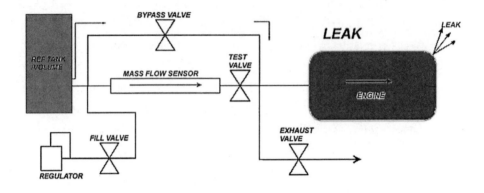

Figure 7-15

7.5.1 Reference Volume Flow Measurement Test Sequence

Just as before we will see, the same fill (pressurise part), stabilise (reduce adiabatic effects), measure (ascertain leakage rate), and exhaust (remove test air) phases of the test sequence, but in this we must also consider the pressurisation of the tank during our fill phase (Figure 7-16).

1. **Fill:** Fill and bypass valves are opened (test valve also) to allow test pressure to enter the tank and component, and pressurise the complete system to the required test pressure level.
2. **Stabilise:** The fill valve is closed and the test valve opened, whilst the bypass valve remains open, whilst the adiabatic effects subside.
3. **Measure:** The bypass valve closes, allowing all air passing from the tank to the part to pass through the flow sensor, and thus measure the leakage rate out of the part under test.
4. **Exhaust:** The fill and test valves close, and the bypass and exhaust valves open to allow all air from the component, and the reference volume to escape/vent to atmosphere.

240

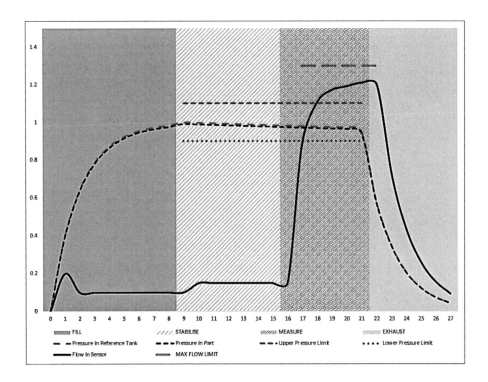

Figure 7-16

Of course it takes longer to fill/pressurise (and exhaust) <u>both</u> the part, and the reference tank than it does to fill/pressurise the part alone, so the separated reference tank version was developed to make the cycle times more similar to those used in the direct flow measurement technique

Now because we have a discreet (fixed) amount of air available for our test, we must bear in mind that as our leak allows air out of the part, the part is being topped up (through our bypass valve and flow sensor) from the reference tank, and so the amount of air in the reference tank is reducing then the pressure in our reference tank is reducing.

This is where I like to use buckets of water to help with the explanation, where the water level is a direct analogy for the pressure. For this the reference tank is one bucket, and our part another, both filled with water. At the start of our stabilisation (Figure 7-17) we have a two buckets, both topped up to our required level (= required test pressure).

241

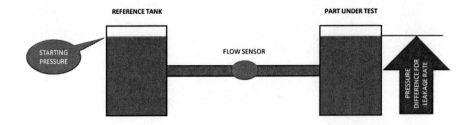

Figure 7-17

As the water (air) leaks out of our part, then the water level (Pressure) will drop, and as this level drops, it is topped up from our reference tank, causing the water level (Pressure) in the reference tank to drop also (Figure 7-18).

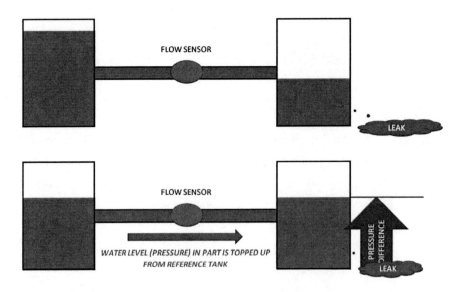

Figure 7-18

This overall drop in level (pressure) reduces the force behind the leak, and the water will begin to leak at a slower rate—as we know leak rate is directly proportional to the pressure difference (Hagen-Poiseuille equation)

In fact, the longer our test cycle (particularly the stabilisation time), the less likely that the pressure will be at the correct (starting) level, and consequently we may not measure the true leakage at the operating pressure.

For this reason in systems where the flow rate that we are trying to measure is significantly large, stabilisation times are minimised, even set to zero, to avoid the issue of the test pressure dropping below our required level.

This isn't a great problem, as with larger flows, the air stabilises much faster, as there is a constant movement of air molecules, and the small amount of instability is insignificant compared to the flow level being measured (again signal to noise ratio). However, this fact must not be ignored, and there are a number of recommendations and/or remedies for this as follows:

1. Ensure our filling pressure is slightly higher than our required test pressure to ensure that at the time of measuring we are nearer our required test pressure
2. Set our reject limit slightly lower than required (safety margin) to ensure we detect all leaks desired =to find
3. Chose a reference tank whose volume is significantly larger than the leak we are trying to measure, in this way our overall pressure does not change due to the overall volume of air (water) being much larger than the leak
4. Minimise the stabilisation time providing flow rate is stable for measurement

7.5.2 Setting up a Reference Tank Flow Test Sequence

Here (Table 7-2) we can see a typical set of test parameters for a separated reference tank mass flow system:

Description	Detail
Fill Time	This is set up much in the same way as in the pressure decay method in that the fill time must be long enough to ensure the complete system (both part and reference Tank) reach the required test pressure
Stabilisation Time	This time should be set so that the flow being measured by the flow system is completely stable, however it should be minimised to ensure test pressure is at the correct level for our measurement phase
Measure Time	Time required for measuring the leakage rate. This will likely be just 1 or 2 seconds, as the flow rate will already be stable at the end of the stabilising time
Vent Time	Time to allow all air to escape from the complete system.
Test Pressure	Simply se to the Test Pressure required to measure our leak (again it is worth adding a safety where stabilisation times might create a lower than required test pressure during the Measure Phase
Lower Limit	Minimum allowable test pressure—this is a safety factor that will fail the test should the pressure drop below this level, thus ensuring the engine is always tested at the correct pressure
Upper Limit	Maximum allowable test pressure—this is a safety factor that will fail the test should the pressure rise above this level, thus ensuring the engine is always tested at the correct pressure
Reject Limit	Simply set this to the required Fail Limit in cc/min

Table 7-2

This reference tank approach has been adapted by one manufacturer which is employed with much larger components (such as engine assemblies). This method, known as the separated reference tank method is very similar, but differs in the way the part is pressurised.

7.6 Separated Reference Tank Flow Measurement Test Sequence

Normal reference tank methods require our fill time sufficiently long to pressurise both the part and the reference tank, which with larger parts, can make our filling times quite long.

This separated reference tank method separates the filling time of the reference tank from the part. In fact the reference tank fill is not part of the normal test cycle, so that during the test sequence, only the part requires pressurising, effectively giving shorter fill times.

When we do pressurise our component, we actually fill our part from the air within our reference tank. This does have additional benefits as it also reduces the amount of adiabatic effects during filling, as the part is now pressurised from an already part stabilised reference supply.

First of all we will review the test sequence for this method which you will see is significantly different from the normal reference tank method. (I will refer to the Reference Tank as Ref Tank.)

1. **Reference tank fill** (Figure 7-19): During this phase, the Ref Tank is pressurised to a pressure level that will allow component we are testing to reach the desired test pressure when the air from the ref tank is shared with the part.

The pressure required in the Ref Tank can be calculated from the formula:

$$Ref\ Tank\ Pressure = \frac{Test\ Pressure \times (Volume\ of\ Ref\ Tank + Volume\ of\ Component)}{Volume\ of\ Ref\ Tank}$$

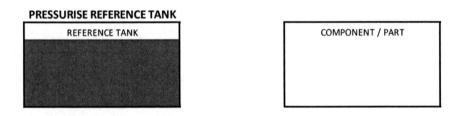

Figure 7-19

2. **Part fill** (Figure 7-20): During this phase, the air within the Ref Tank is shared with the component to be tested, such that the complete system reaches the required test pressure level. Again it is simple to see this with pictures of buckets of water as below.

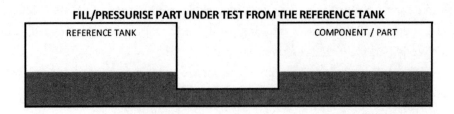

FILL/PRESSURISE PART UNDER TEST FROM THE REFERENCE TANK

Figure 7-20

3. **Stabilise**: This is much the same as our stabilisation time in our other air tests, allowing time for the air in the part and the air in the Ref Tank to settle down/stabilise.

4. **Measure**: this is the period where we measure the flow (leak) through the flow sensor. In fact we are actually measuring the flow from the Ref Tank into the part. More on this later as this is important to understand as we set up the machine.

5. **Exhaust**: The air from the complete system is exhausted/vented to safe levels for disconnection. This includes all air from both the part itself, and the reference tank. (Note: The reference tank should be exhausted in between each test to ensure our starting conditions—particularly air temperature—are always approximately the same.)

First of all here (Figure 7-21) is the overall system showing the different valves:

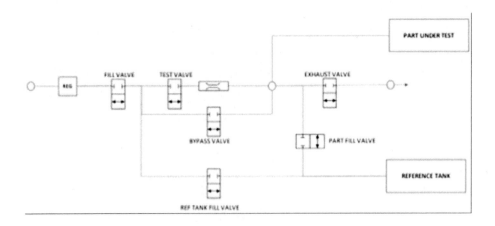

Figure 7-21

246

In order to understand the sequence a little more, follow the steps below, which show the various valves in the system, and the way they operate to control/move air around.

1. **Reference tank fill** (Figure 7-22): The fill valve and reference tank valve open to allow air to flow into the ref tank, until the desired pressure is achieved.

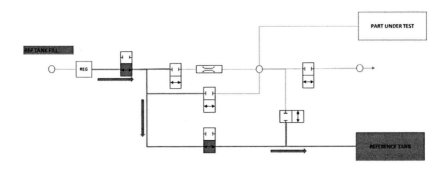

Figure 7-22

2. **Part fill** (Figure 7-23): The fill valve is closed, and the exhaust valve remains shut, whilst all other valves are opened, allowing the air to flow from the Ref Tank into the part and all around the flow measurement system.

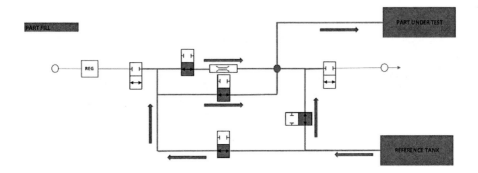

Figure 7-23

3. **Stabilise:** The part fill valve closes, whilst the bypass valve remains open allowing the air in the system to continue stabilising.

4. **Measure** (Figure 7-24): Now the bypass valve closes so that any air required to top up the part (due to a leak in the part) to pass through the flow sensor only.

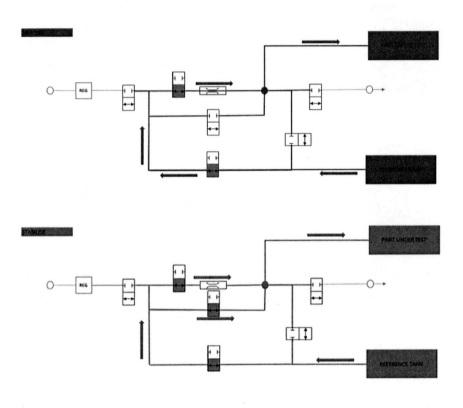

Figure 7-24

5. **EXHUAST** (Figure 7-25): All valves except the Fill Valve are now opened to allow all air from the completes system (Part and Reference Tank) to exhaust to atmosphere.

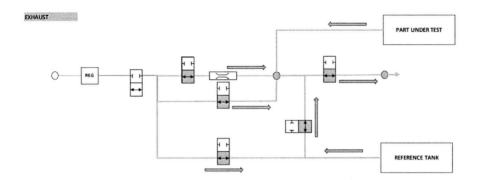

Figure 7-25

Our test sequence (Figure 7-26) therefore can be seen as below:

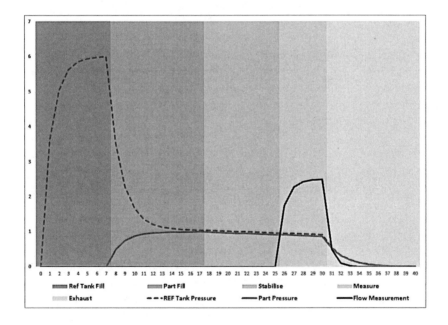

Figure 7-26

But how does this make our test faster? Simply in the fact that the reference tank fill part of the test cycle can happen outside of our standard test sequence (i.e., whilst the component is being connected to the system).

As the Ref Tank will retain its pressure until the part fill is started, then it is not a problem if the part connection takes longer than the Ref Tank fill, as we can afford to delay the part fill for a time until it is completed as below (Figure 7-27):

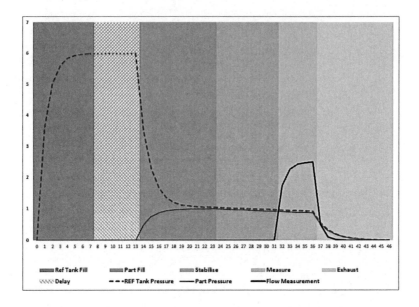

Figure 7-27

This proved very useful for me when leak testing large items such as complete engine assemblies on a production line, as we could effectively lose the Reference Tank Fill Time during operational activities. Let me explain…

The engines moved along a production track with 3 operator stations for leak test as below (Figure 7-28):

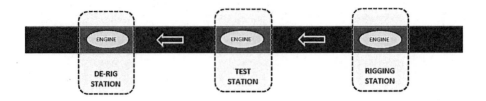

Figure 7-28

250

1. Rigging station: at this station the operator connected all the different sealing bungs to seal off any open ports/apertures
2. Test station: this station was where the actual leak tests were performed
3. De-rig station: after testing, all sealing bungs could be removed

The advantage this method offered was that we could commence the Tank fill during the engine move from the rigging station into the test station as in Figure 7-29 (and after the previous engine test had been completed).

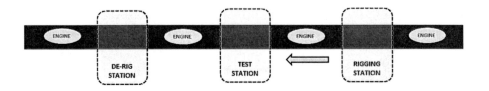

Figure 7-29

So our sequence events was as follows (Figure 7-31)

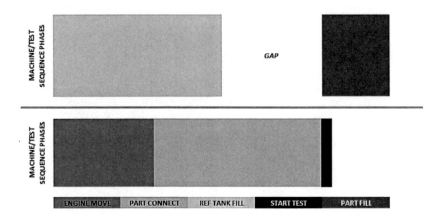

Figure 7-30

Clearly the advantage of this method is that the supply pressure is very stable (no variation), and as such our flow measurement is also more stable, even at low flows.

However the disadvantage is that when we have a leak in our engine, the air topping up our engine pressure comes from the enclosed Reference tank, and so the pressure in our tank drops also. Due to this, the amount of air topping up the engine, is less than the actual leak.

This is best explained by considering once again the Reference Tank and the Part Under Test as buckets of water. Let us examine what happens during the measure phase

At the start of the measure phase, the Reference bucket (Ref Tank) and the Part bucket are both filled to the same level (same pressure) as shown in Figure 7-31

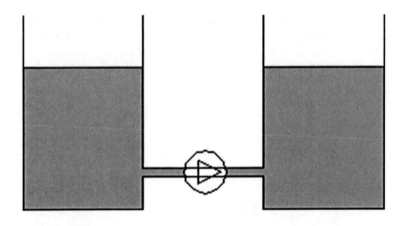

Figure 7-31

Now during our measuring time, our Component bucket loses some of it's fluid (Our Leaked fluid). And the level in this bucket drops by the amount of the leakage) as in Figure 7-32:

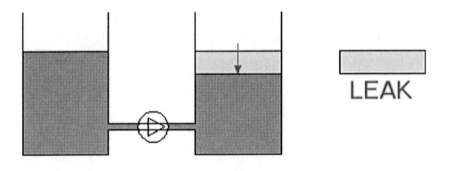

Figure 7-32

To retain the balance in levels, the Reference bucket allows some of it's fluid to travel into the component (Figure 7-33). This is what our sensor (located between the two buckets) actually measures.

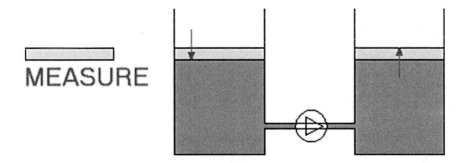

Figure 7-33

As we can see clearly in the diagrams above, the amount of fluid (flow) we measured is less than the actual fluid that leaked.

So we have to introduce a multiplying factor (known as the volume factor) which multiplies the amount of flow measured, in order that we display the actual leakage rate on the instrument.

In the above example, where the buckets are the same size, it is fairly obvious that our volume factor will simply be 2x, and this is because this volume factor is the same as the relationship between the total volume in the test circuit, and the part volume. So clearly, we could calculate the volume factor if we know the part volume and the reference tank volume, however it is far simpler to carry out tests to more accurately assess the volume factor, as part volumes can be very difficult to calculate (particularly in complex assemblies (like engines).

7.6.1 Setting Up a Separate Reference Tank Mass Flow Sequence

Here (Table 7-3) we can see a typical set of test parameters for a reference tank (separated type) mass flow system. You will no doubt notice a few extra parameters not already discussed, but these are the setting employed by the manufacturer who developed this method, and they will be explained in the *further details* section below.

Description	Detail
Ref Tank Fill Time	This is the time required to fill the Reference Tank to the required Pressure (which will be shared with the part under test)
Part Fill Time	Although called Part Fill Time, this is in fact the total time required for the pressure to be shared between the reference tank and the component under test
Stabilisation Time	Time to allow air pressures to stabilise (reducing adiabatic effects to a minimum for good signal to noise)
Measure Time	Time required for measuring the leakage rate
Vent Time	Time to allow all air to escape from the complete system.
Ref Tank Pressure	This is the pressure level required in the Reference Tank to ensure that the part is tested at the correct pressure
Measure Pressure	Test Pressure required (although this parameter does not control the test pressure in the normal cycle, such leak test panels have a LEAK LOCATE feature, which this parameter controls (see detailed explanation below)
Min Measuring pressure	Minimum allowable test pressure—this is a safety factor that will fail the test should the pressure drop below this level, thus ensuring the part is always tested at the correct pressure
Max Measuring Pressure	Maximum allowable test pressure—this is the Upper Pressure Limit to ensure that the part is tested at the correct pressure
Offset	Special value to bring background to zero - see detailed explanation below.
Volume Factor	Volume Factor (Cal Factor) to ensure the leak rate displayed as adjusted to the correct level - see detailed explanation below
Reject Limit (Limit 1)	Simply set this to the required Fail Limit in cc/min
Limit 2	Secondary limit for Reclaim requirements, as explained in the section on special functions for Pressure Decay testing. *(If not required this is usually set to the same level as Limit 1)*

Limit 3	This is in fact the Reference (-ve) reject limit just as we saw in Pressure Decay. This is generally used as a safety to ensure –ve values minimised, This is generally set to between 10% and 20% of the Leak Limit 1
Smoothing and Smoothing Fraction	Enables us to smooth noise in flow sensor signal. The smoothing fraction determines how much of measuring time to carry out smoothing. Set between 0 and 1. Where 1 means smoothing takes place for the entire measurement time, 0.6 means the last 60% of the measurement time etc.)

Table 7-3

Let us look at further details on some of the settings.

7.6.2 Measure Time

This must be sufficient for the flow measurement to stabilise to a steady state. There is a tendency to keep this very short (Figure 7-34) and as such the sensor rate response has not achieved a steady state.

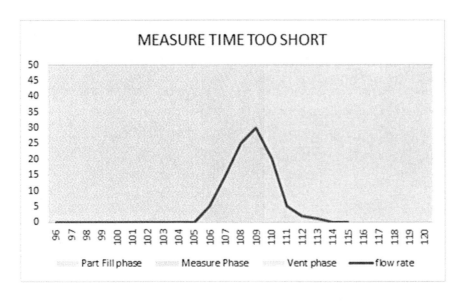

Figure 7-34

When this happens the final value is lower than its true final value, and as such a larger volume factor is likely required to ensure the leak test unit displays the correct flow rate. This causes problems, as the volume factor is simply a multiplying factor and as such multiplies all noise within the system, which can cause poor repeatability.

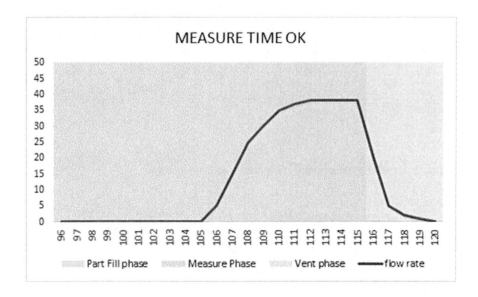

Figure 7-34

7.6.3 Ref Tank Pressure

This is the pressure we will put into the Reference Tank, so that when the air is shared with the part being tested, the final pressure achieved is at the required test pressure. The pressure required in the Reference Tank can be calculated from the formula:

$$Ref\ Tank\ Pressure = \frac{Test\ Pressure\ x\ (Volume\ of\ Ref\ Tank + Volume\ of\ Part)}{Volume\ of\ Ref\ Tank}$$

However this requires knowing the exact volume of your component and all the test connection pipework etc. as this is unlikely to be easy to establish, it is preferred to establish the reference tank pressure by practical experimentation as follows.

7.6.3.1 Establishing and Setting the Ref Tank Pressure

Ideally, in order to accurately set the Ref Tank Pressure, it is ideally essential to have a leak tight component. More about this in the next section on Volume Factors, however a part with a very small leak can be used.

In order to set up the Ref Tank Pressure by this practical method, follow the steps below:

1. Set up the leak test instrument with the ref tank pressure at the same level as the required test pressure. (This we record as Current Ref Pressure.)
2. Run at least 3 tests, and record the final pressure at the end of the part fill phase, and then calculate the average value of these. (This we record as Current Test Pressure.)
3. Calculate the correct new ref tank pressure as follows:

$$NEW\ Ref\ Tank\ Pressure = \frac{Current\ Ref\ Pressure\ x\ Required\ Test\ Pressure}{Current\ Test\ Pressure}$$

4. Enter this new ref tank pressure into the leak test instrument, and confirm that the correct test pressure is achieved during the next test.

7.6.4 Measure Pressure – Leak Locate

As this method is a global method, when we achieve a fail result, we do not know the exact location of the leakage. Many leak test instruments have a leak locate, or constant fill option, which allow the operator to pressurise the component to the required test pressure, and then utilise a soap solution (leak test spray) to search for and locate the precise cause of the failure, and thus allow repairs to be effected.

7.6.5 Leak Rate Offset

Exactly as in the pressure decay systems, this value is used to artificially shift the resultant leak test measured, so that no leak conditions read zero leak rate. The reason to do this would be because our results are always showing a value above (or below) zero. This could be for a number of reasons:

Example:

- Required Test Pressure = 0.5 Bar
- Current Ref Pressure = 0.5 Bar
- Three tests = 0.21, 0.22, 0.22 (Ave = 0.217)

$$NEW\ Ref\ Tank\ Pressure = \frac{0.5\ x\ 0.5}{0.217} = 1.15\ Bar$$

1. Maybe parts are always warm and then cooling when tested to create a small reading?
2. Maybe there is a small volume change caused by an expanding part, and we do not have prefill function or sufficient time to wait for this to dissipate?
3. Maybe we know that our part has a small leak through a pinhole which is part of the design of the part?

In all cases, I would recommend trying first to eliminate the cause of the repeatably higher than desired values for non-leaking component, however if this does prove impossible, then this function can be very useful.

The way to decide the value to set on the offset is to run a series of tests on non-leaking parts, recording each test result. Then you can calculate the amount of offset to introduce from these results. There are of course a number of options as follows.

Just as with pressure decay, my personal opinion/recommendation is that this function (wherever practical/possible) is not used, as it effectively gives us a calculated (and thus false) reading of the true leakage from our part.

7.6.5.1 Average Value Offset (Figure 7-36)

Many suppliers set this value to the average value of these results, which would mean that our average result would be zero leak, however this would mean that some of our non-leaking parts would then read –ve values. In many cases where the offset is relatively small, this is not a problem, however (as shown in the example below) if the values obtained are a significant %age of the Leak Limit, then this would mean our Reference Limit would need to be increased, and as such our safety against -ve values will be minimised.

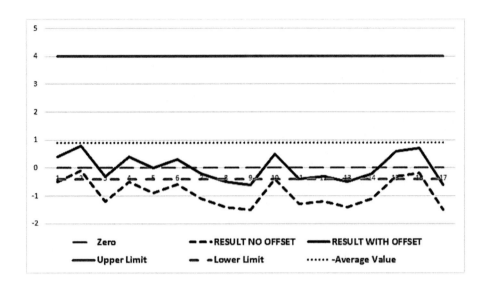

Figure 7-36

7.6.5.2 Minimum Value Offset (Figure 7-37)

In this case the smallest value obtained from our normal test results is used as the offset, resulting in our values with the Offset introduced always being +ve, allowing us to keep the reference limit to a minimum, and avoiding the unnecessary questions regarding what is a negative leak.

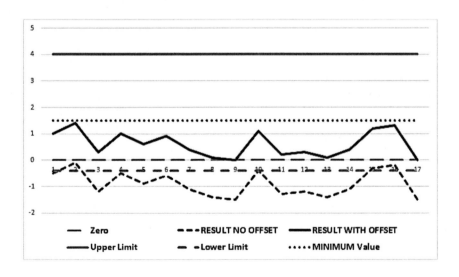

Figure 7-37

259

Again, this would be my preferred choice if this function is used as the smallest value displayed would then be 0.00 (zero) leak rate.

7.6.5.3 Somewhere In-Between (Figure 7-38)

This is to plot the results as I have done here, and then calculate an offset value that will reduce the normal values, but maintain them above our reference reject limit. This is simple to do by subtracting the Reference Reject Limit from the minimum value obtained during normal tests (in our example this was 0.52 – (-0,2), so 0.72 becomes our offset value)

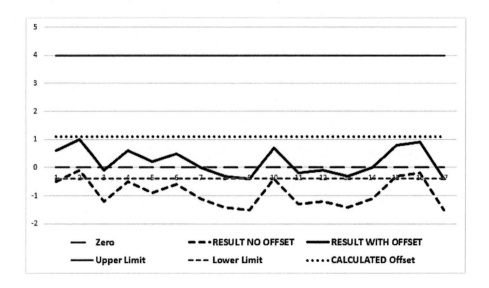

Figure 7-38

7.6.6 Volume Factor

This is the multiplying factor to ensure the leak tester displays the correct leak rate, even though the mass flow sensor is only measuring the flow out of the Reference Tank.

The need for a Volume Factor / Cal Factor is best explained by considering buckets of water. Let us examine what happens during the measure phase in our flow measurement system. At the start of the measure phase, the reference bucket (ref tank) and the part bucket are both filled to the same level (same pressure) as shown in Figure 7-39:

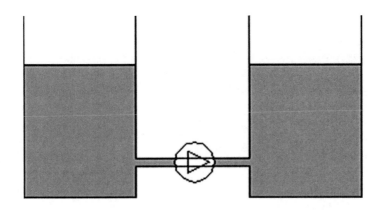

Figure 7-39

Now during our measuring time, our component bucket loses some of it's fluid (our leaked fluid). And the level in this bucket drops by the amount of the leakage) as in Figure 7-40:

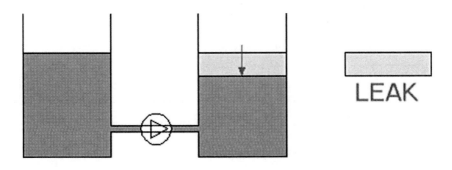

LEAK

Figure 7-40

To retain the balance in levels, the reference bucket allows some of it's fluid to travel into the component (Figure 7-41). This is what our sensor (located between the two buckets) actually measures.

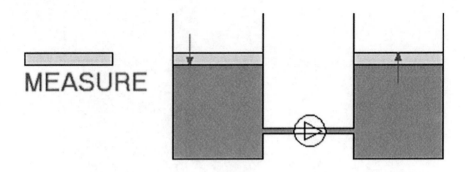

Figure 7-41

As we can see clearly in the diagrams above, the amount of fluid (flow) we measured is less than the actual fluid that leaked. So we have to introduce a multiplying factor (known as the volume factor or cal factor) which multiplies the amount of flow measured, in order that we display the actual leakage rate on the instrument.

As a rough guide, this factor can be calculated from:

$$\textbf{VOLUME FACTOR} = \frac{\text{(Volume of Ref Tank + Volume of Component)}}{\text{Volume of Ref Tank}}$$

However, just as with the reference tank pressure, this requires knowing the exact volumes of your part, test connection pipework, and reference tank. So again, it is preferred to find out the volume factor by practical experimentation as follows.

7.6.6.1 Establishing and Setting the Volume Factor

As we saw before, ideally in order to accurately set the Ref Tank Pressure it is essential to have a leak tight part. In order to establish if the component is leak tight enough, with the volume factor set to 1 (i.e., the leak test instrument will display the amount of leakage from the Reference Tank) observe the results at the very end of the test at initial set up. Multiply these by the ratio of the Ref Tank Pressure to the test pressure:

$$\frac{\textit{Ref Tank Pressure}}{\textit{Test Pressure}}$$

If the result of these is less than 30% of the required leak limit then the part is sufficiently leak-tight. Figure 7-43 is an example in which we establish which of three parts is suitable for our accurate set up of our volume factor. In this example we can see that part 3 will be the ideal component, however if we did not have part 3, then although the calculated result for Part 2 are a little higher than ideal, they are still sufficiently low enough to complete our setup.

TEST #	RESULTS WITH VOL FACTOR SET TO "1"			Limit	CALCULATED RESULT			30% of limit
	Part 1	Part 2	Part 3		Part 1	Part 2	Part 3	
Test 1	0.45	0.18	0.16	6	5.76	2.304	1.984	2
Test 2	0.4	0.2	0.15	6	5.12	2.56	1.92	2
Test 3	0.42	0.19	0.14	6	5.376	2.432	1.792	2

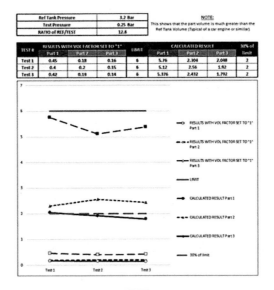

Ref Tank Pressure	3.2 Bar
Test Pressure	0.25 Bar
RATIO OF REF/TEST	12.8

Note:
This shows that the part volume is much greater than the ref tank volume (typical of an engine)

Figure 7-42

In order to set up the Volume Factor by this practical method, follow the steps below:

1. Set up the leak test instrument with the volume factor set at 1.0 *(this will be known as the Current VF)*.

2. Run at least 3 to 5 tests, and record the leakage rate reading at the end of the test period. Calculate the average of these results *(as Current Zero Value)*.

3. Using a known calibrated master leak (see chapter on calibration), introduced into the calibration port of the leak tester, repeat the tests, and again record, and average these leakage rate results *(as Current Span Value)*.

4. Subtract the current zero value from the current span value, to give the current leak rate response.

5. Now calculate the new volume factor as follows:

$$\textbf{NEW VOLUME FACTOR} = \frac{\text{Current VF x Actual Value of Calibrated Master Leak}}{\text{Current Leak rate Response}}$$

6. Enter this new volume factor into the leak tester, and confirm that it is accurate, by repeating steps 2, 3 and 4, and ensure that the difference between, the new span value, and the new zero value is equal to the actual value of the calibrated master leak.

Here (Figure 7-43) is an example:

Calibrated Master Leak Value			6.3 cc/min	
Test #	No Leak Result	+ Leak Result	Difference	Calculated Volume Factor
1	0.17	0.86	0.69	
2	0.19	0.86	0.67	1 x 6.3
3	0.16	0.85	0.69	0.698
4	0.2	0.86	0.66	
5	0.04	0.82	0.78	
Ave	0.152	0.85	0.698	9.03

Figure 7-3

If we were to simply now, multiply our original test results by the calculated volume factor (Figure 7-44) we can see the effect of the Volume Factor.

Calculated Results with NEW VOL FACTOR		Limit
NO LEAK	**+CAL LEAK**	
1.54	7.77	6
1.72	7.77	6
1.45	7.68	6
1.81	7.77	6
0.37	7.41	6

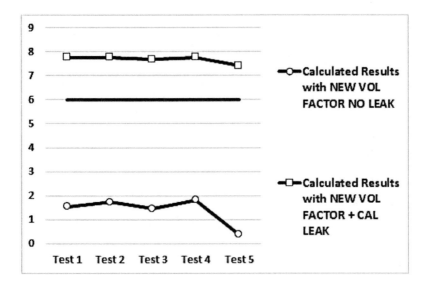

Figure 7-44

It is important to notice that ALL test results are multiplied by the volume factor (not just those with the leak introduced), and we can see that even our no leak results are impacted.

And we can see that our background noise levels are increased as the volume factor increases due to the fact that all values are simply multiplied by this calibration. So it is very important to get the reference tank and part volume ratio correct to reduce the volume factor as much as possible.

As you know, I like to give examples from my own work, and this was never more obvious when I began working as the leak test engineer at an engine manufacturer. One of our plant's producing engines (in China) had been supplied a Reference Tank flow measurement system for testing engines, but they were suffering greatly from false failure (engines failing the test where no leak could be found, and that subsequently passed when retested).

I soon discovered that they had a relatively small Reference Tank compared to the free volume in the engine circuit they were testing, and their Volume Factor was above 20!

The simple solution was to increase the reference tank volume (by a factor of 4) thus reducing their volume factor to just 6.3, and the false failures were no longer an issue.

7.6.7 Smoothing and Smoothing Fraction

Just a brief explanation of this function which is available on a few leak test instruments (including some pressure decay instruments). This function can be used to reduce any small amount of noise seen during our measurement phase of air leak testing.

Before I do just let me briefly explain one key difference between Pressure decay and flow measurement. With pressure decay we are in fact measuring the total pressure lost over a given time period, and as such we are in effect taking an average of a series of individual measurements at discreet time periods throughout the measurement time. In flow measurement, we actually record the final flow reading at the end of the measurement period.

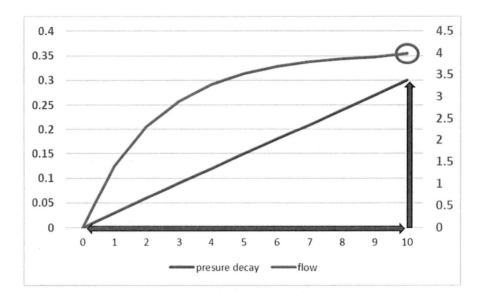

Figure 7-45

Whilst this does not seem greatly different, and indeed isn't if the shape of the measurement curves is nice and straightforward as in the diagram above, (Figure 7-45), it can have potential issues where noise is superimposed on the curves.

The pressure decay reading will be averaged over the time period, and will fall within a range of values, whilst the flow reading will simply be the last reading obtained, and may vary considerably due to the noise (Figure 7-47):

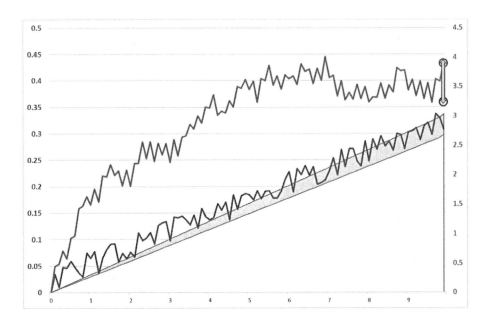

Figure 7-46

For this reason, we introduce a smoothing function.

This smoothing simply averages the readings over a defined time period (Figure 7-46).

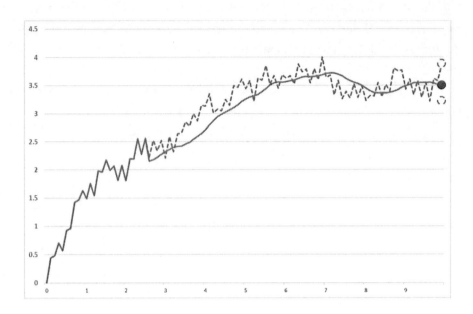

Figure 7-47

The result is that we get a smoother chart, and by averaging the noise, we effectively get a more accurate value for the true flow with the noise removed.

In some leak test instruments, the amount of smoothing can be controlled with the smoothing time setting which can be varied between o and 100% of the measurement period. In the chart above, I have shown a typical setting for 75% of the measurement time.

Of course I cannot cover everything in this book or it would turn into a 10 volume collection, but hopefully the details set out under the flow testing section will give you enough of an understanding to make more informed decisions about the type of equipment, the additional functions, and help you to set up your equipment. However there is nothing better than practical experience to educate you, so if you are a leak test engineer, try and get free time on the equipment whenever possible to experiment and learn more than I can ever hope to impart.

8. Calibration of Air Test Systems

Suppliers of leak test equipment make a large amount of their profits, in offering a yearly calibration service.

For example, I myself worked at one company where we were spending over $20,000 per annum in having the suppliers complete an annual calibration service on our 60 leak testers. But I soon established our own simple to complete in house calibration checks, and instantly began saving this on-cost.

But having worked with this equipment for many years I was clearly aware that the instruments themselves were pretty robust, and as such did not go out of calibration very easily, so I have established a number of simple checks that can be performed to ensure the equipment remained fully operational.

Whilst these calibration checks do not check the calibration of the instruments (and their measurement devices) themselves they do offer a fit for purpose way of ensuring our equipment reliably performed the leak test. (Only if we note severe changes did we ask the supplier to visit and effect a recalibration.)

And so, I will now share these with you as I am certain that you will find the long-term cost savings very worthwhile.

8.1 Calibration Equipment

In order to complete simple calibration checks on air test equipment, we obviously need relevant devices/aids to enable us to perform the checks. So we need to consider exactly what we are asking our instruments to do.

1. Test at the correct test pressure
2. Measure the leakage rate

In fact these are the only two things we really need to check, so if we can establish the equipment required to cover both of these factors, then it would be likely that we can check the performance of our instrument/equipment.

One word of warning is that we need to ensure these checking devices themselves are kept in calibration, but this will be a yearly service that can be offered by suppliers, so instead of having all of your instruments calibrated, simply calibrate one device, and use this to check the calibration of ALL your leak testers.

Obviously if you only have one leak test instrument, then this may not be a cost saving, however, having your own calibration equipment, means you can quickly check your leak testers as often as you wish, and also make checks if you are in any doubt about their performance.

8.1.1 Pressure

To enable us to check our test pressure, we need some form of pressure measurement device.

The actual device required, will very much depend on the pressure you are testing at, but there are a wide range of devices available which range in price from just $100 and upwards. I myself utilised simple battery operated hand held devices, similar to the ones (Figure 8-1) shown here.

Figure 8-1

For differential measurement devices we may also require a secondary differential pressure measurement (these are similar to those above, but can measure very low pressure differences).

8.1.2 Leakage Rate Measurement

There are two aspects to this:

- The Actual Leak
o Master known fixed leak
o Adjustable leaks
- Leak rate measurement

8.1.2.1 Known Fixed Leakage Rate (Calibrated Leak Master)

These come in many formats (Figure 8-2) but essentially they are simple devices that offer a known leakage rate at a specific predefined pressure difference.

They can be introduced into our leak test (most instruments incorporate a self-sealing connection port into which they can be plugged using the connector on the leak itself) at any time to add a known amount of leakage.

Figure 8-2

The most common forms of master leak are sintered disc and laser drilled holes. In either case, the actual leak is housed in a metal body for ease of handling (Figure 8-3). The body will incorporate threaded ends to allow connection of the relevant quick connector required for our leak tester.

Figure 8-3

Most will include a serial number for reference purposes.

8.1.2.1.1 <u>Sintered Disc (Figure 8-4)</u>

These types are manufactured by placing sintered material (in disc format) being placed inside the body. This sinter material is then crushed down until at a given pressure, the lea rate required flows from the leak.

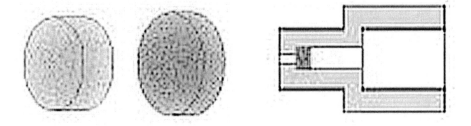

Figure 8-4

8.1.2.1.2 Laser Drilled Holes (Figure 8-5)

In this case holes are drilled into domed discs (usually copper). The disc is then squashed to close the hole, until the required flow passes through at the specified applied pressure.

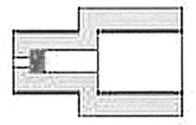  

Figure 8-5

There are many other forms but all essentially offer the same thing, in terms of a known leakage at a set applied pressure.

8.1.2.2 Adjustable/Variable Master Leaks (Figure 8-6)

This version is not a fixed leakage rate, but is effectively an adjustable master, and will/must be used in conjunction with a leakage measurement method, to determine the actual leakage rate set.

Figure 8-6

In essence, these are simply needle valves which create very small flow passages by adjusting the position (Figure 8-7) of the needle (mounted on a very fine thread).

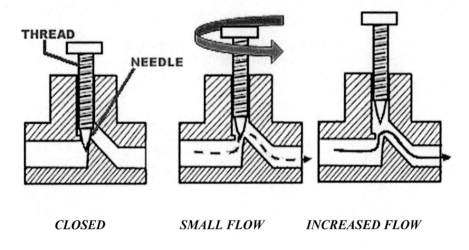

CLOSED   SMALL FLOW   INCREASED FLOW

Figure 8-7

As the needle valve is adjusted, more or less air can pass through valve. These items are available in many different flow ranges dependent on the needle and aperture size, allowing for a range of different applications.

When this type of adjustable leak is used, you will invariably need a way to measure the leakage, and will therefore require leakage rate measurement.

8.1.2.3 Leakage Rate Measurement

Particularly useful (and essential) when employing the adjustable leaks, we require a method of knowing the actual leakage rate set. There are two main versions (although there are others) of measurement employed in leak testing:

- Bubble tube measurement
- Electronic flow measurement devices
- *Mass flow sensor*
- *Pressure drop across a capillary tube (similar to pressure drop across a laminar flow tube)*

8.1.2.1.3 Bubble Flow Measurement (Figure 8-8)

Such devices measure the volumetric flow of the gas, by measuring the time it takes for a soap film bubble to travel up a glass tube of a specific diameter.

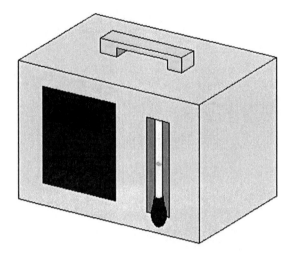

Figure 8-8

A soap film is produced by squeezing a rubber bowl at the base of the tube. This soap film then travels up the tube passing two sensors (the first starts a timer, the second stopping it). The time it takes to travel between the two sensors can then be used to calculate the leakage as volume/time:

$$\frac{\pi \text{ x Diameter of tube (cm)}^2 \text{ x Distance between sensors (cm)}}{4 \text{ x Time for soap film to travel between sensors (s)}}$$

8.1.2.1.4 Electronic Measurement Devices

These electronic devices measure the flow either by use of a mass flow sensor, or by measuring the pressure drop across a small capillary tube (Figure 8-10) in a similar way to pressure drop across a laminar flow tube.

Again these devices are generally calibrated for air, and as such are relevant only to air testing.

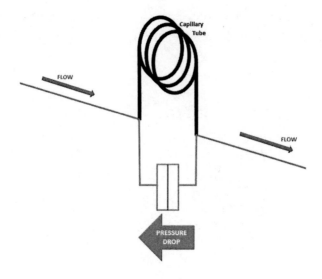

Figure 8-10

8.2 Calibration Checks

There are two levels that we can consider:

- 1 Point calibration check
- Full calibration check

The choice of these depends on the use of our equipment.

Many leak test applications utilise a single set of parameters (i.e., one test pressure, and one leak rate specification), and for these applications it is very simple to carry out simple 1 point calibration checks on our equipment, to ensure they are fit for the purpose we are using them for. These can be carried out more frequently as they require us to carry out only two tests in total to check our system, and are often used in daily or weekly checks of our equipment performance.

For more complex applications, where we may have multiple test programs, with multiple test pressures and leakage rate specifications, or where we might want to confirm the full functionality of our leak test equipment, we would carry out a full calibration check where we will check the functionality of our

276

equipment over a range of values of pressures and leakage rates. These more complex calibration checks are generally carried out annually, as they do take some time and may require additional equipment (which will be explained later in this section).

The frequency of calibration checks is purely a matter of how much confidence we have in the reliability of the equipment. This is a matter for each individual, but I recommend that people start with daily checks on the measurement of the leak, and build confidence, so that the period between checks, may be extended, but I always recommend a maximum of 1 week between leak measurement checks. For test pressure checks, I recommend this is completed at least annually, but maybe monthly you have any concerns.

8.2.1 Simple 1 Point Calibration Checks

8.2.1.1 Pressure Check

To confirm the correct test pressure is being applied, simply introduce the pressure meter into the test circuit during the test, and ensure the test pressure on our calibrated pressure meter matches that displayed as being supplied by our leak test equipment.

Most suppliers of test equipment include a self-sealing port (usually called the calibration port on the instrument to enable rapid connection of the calibration equipment into the test line. Whilst this check can be carried out daily, it most often only carried out on an annual basis, as people have gained a considerable amount of confidence over many years of using pressure supplies, and now trust these systems not to be in error.

8.2.1.2 Leakage Rate Measurement check

This is the most important check to carry out most frequently on your leak test equipment. It is always recommended that this is carried out on the complete test system, and not just the instrument itself, as this checks all of the pipework connecting the leak tester, and the seals connecting to the part as well.

The calibration check is made up of 2 tests, to enable this to be completed reliably, and to help identify any issues:

1. Good Part Test   (Zero Test)
2. Leaking Part Test   (Span Test)

277

8.2.1.2.1 Zero Test - Good Part

For the first test, it is strongly advised to retain a master good part which is known to have no leaks. This should be kept on a safe place and clearly identified as the master. Most people paint the master green (or another identifying colour), and stored so that it cannot get damaged. For more complex applications, it may be preferred to have a known reference volume to simulate a known good part.

Simply test your known good part and record the leak rate displayed. It is suggested that these results are maintained and stored on a single spreadsheet, such that you can review the historical result data, and identify any trends. (For example, you can identify issues such as seal wear, external effects, calibration problems from this simple test—see below.)

8.2.1.2.2 Span Test – Leaking Part

The second test is then made with the same good part plus the introduction of the calibrated master leak (usually connected to the calibration port, but could be connected elsewhere in the system test line).

Note: I have often found people using a master fail part (painted red), however this is usually a part they have simply drilled a hole in, to create a leak. This does NOT check the function/accuracy of the system, as the leak is likely to be very large, and beyond the measuring range of the equipment, so really only checks a gross leak scenario, and not the calibration/measurement of the equipment. Do not do this—but use a known leak.

This result again should be recorded, and maintained, for historic evidence to help identify issues as below. Once you have both results, you can calculate the actual value measured for the master leak by subtracting the zero result from the span result, and this can also be maintained as a record of the accuracy of the instrument measurement.

My advice is to record these results on a spreadsheet, so that you can view the results as follows.

8.2.1.2.3 Good Calibration Check

This is a set of results (Figure 8-11) recorded weekly over a 6-month period:

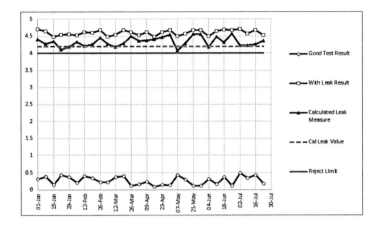

Figure 8-11

On this chart, we can clearly see (at a glance) that the system remains in calibration, with the good and +leak results remaining approximately constant (with some small amount of noise—probably small external draughts, heating etc.)

8.2.1.2.4 Checking the Calibration Accuracy

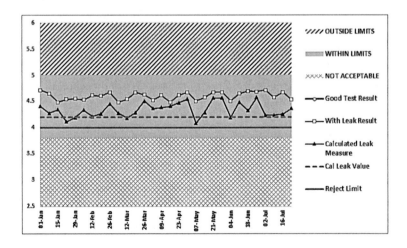

Figure 8-12

279

On this chart (Figure 8-12), I have included our acceptable range/band for our test with the leak (span) to fall within. Provided our results fall within this band, then our check shows a good result.

8.2.1.2.5 Drifting Zero? (Figure 8-13)

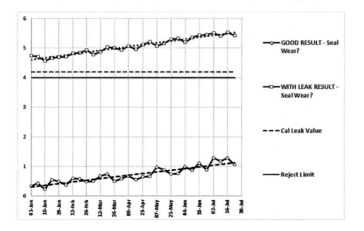

Figure 8-13

This trend upwards in our results suggests an increasing leak on our master good part (zero test). This could indicate possible seal wear or similar?

8.2.1.2.6 Calibration Problems

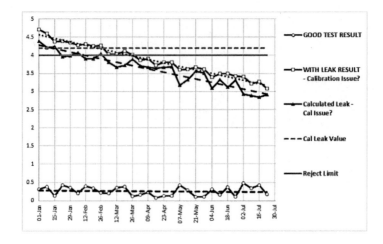

Figure 8-14

In this chart (Figure 8-14), I have shown that although the zero results remain repeatable, the actual result with the leak added is drifting down, suggesting that there may be an issue with the calibration of this equipment.

Although the calibration of the equipment may be an issue, I would strongly recommend that the calibrated master leak is checked first, as in my experience this degradation in calibration is very rare (and I would more likely suspect our master leak, as these can block up over time, if not stored correctly).

Alternatively, the results can be entered onto a simple calibration check certificate (Figure 8-15), which can act as evidence of completion of calibration checks.

You will note that in this case we made a total of three zero and span checks on the leakage rate measurement, for completeness.

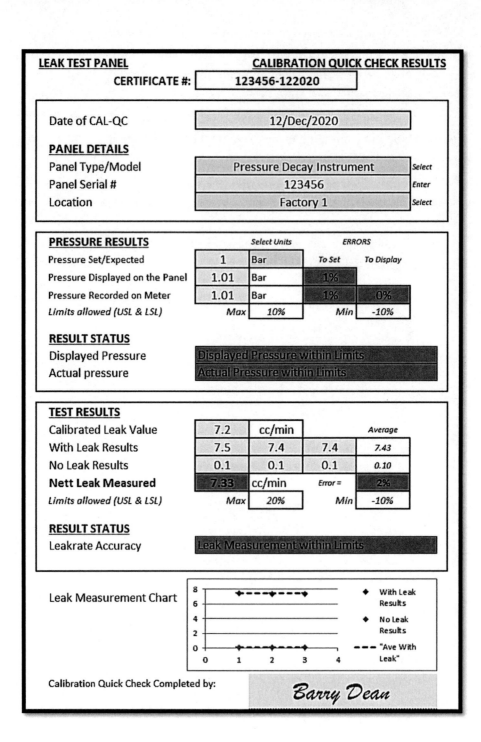

Figure 8-15

8.2.2 Full (Multi-Point) Calibration Checks

This is quite an involved, and lengthy, calibration check and is not used as a daily/weekly check, but more as a once per year full assessment of the equipment.

Again we perform both pressure and leak rate measurement checks, but in this case we perform a minimum of 5 measurements of each across the measuring range of the equipment.

In many cases it is advised to keep at least one program set (on multiple/selectable program units) for this purpose, to avoid leaving the equipment with an incorrect setting, when it is returned for production use.

8.2.2.1 Pressure Calibration Check

To confirm the correct test pressure is being applied, simply introduce the pressure meter into the test circuit during the test, and ensure the test pressure on our calibrated pressure meter matches that displayed as being supplied by our leak test equipment.

In this case we make at least 5 measurements at different test pressures, so that we can assess the accuracy of the pressure supply across the complete range of the instrument. For example on a machine capable of testing up to 4 Bar, I would recommend making checks at 0, 0.4, 1.0, 2.0, and 4.0 bar, although this will depend on what test pressures you are likely to use).

Follow a simple procedure to check each pressure setting such as that below:

1. Set the fill/test pressure to supply one of the pressure levels/settings that you intend to record/check.
2. Run a test and record
a. The pressure displayed on the instrument
b. The pressure displayed on your calibration check pressure meter
3. Repeat these steps (1 and 2) for each pressure you decide to check
4. Record these on your certificate/record sheet
5. Compare the recorded results to the expected accuracy (% error), such that should the equipment be out of calibration, then make adjustments (only if qualified to do so) and repeat all steps to confirm instrument now in calibration

I myself found it very helpful, to develop a simple certificate onto which results could be entered (in my case this was on a spreadsheet, so I could get it to check the error automatically).

On the certificate, I included the serial number and calibration certificate number of the pressure Meter used to measure the pressure, so that I had full traceability to known standards of calibration, thus no longer requiring the supplier to visit and carry out this work.

Here (Figure 8-16) is the example of my certificate (not it is only showing the top section—pressure calibration checks, although the complete certificate had the leak measurement calibration checks on also).

LEAK TEST PANEL CALIBRATION CERTIFICATE

DATE OF CALIBRATION:	18 September 2020	CERTIFICATE No.:	S-12345-9-2020
VALIDITY PERIOD:	Twelve Months.	PANEL SERIAL No.:	12345
MANUFACTURER:	INSTRU MANF	MODEL/TYPE :	MFL 40
MEASUREMENT TYPE:	Mass Flow	CALIBRATED BY:	B DEAN

The instrument has been calibrated at ambient room temperature and at atmospheric pressure.

The calibration has been made with direct reading of the equipment detailed below, which is traceable to International Standards. The relevant procedures and certification are available for inspection if required.

Pressure Measuring Equipment:-	Pressure Meter	Serial no:-	123-9876
Certificate number:-	ABC123	Certificate Date:-	10 May 2020
Flow Measuring Equipment:-		Serial no:-	
Certificate number:-		Certificate Date:-	

We hereby certify that on the day of calibration the instrument performed according to the manufacturer's original sales specification as checked by the calibration procedure, unless otherwise stated.

PRE-CHECKS (Test Plans)

ADJUSTMENTS *(Record any discrepancies/adjustments made)* :

PRESSURE CALIBRATION

Pressure displayed on instrument.		BEFORE				AFTER		
		Pressure Displayed	Pressure Measured	Display Error (%)	Measure Error (%)	Pressure Displayed	Pressure Measured	Display Error (%)	Measure Error (%)
0.00	Bar	0.000	0.000	0.0%	0.0%	0.000	0.000	0.0%	0.0%
0.25	Bar	0.250	0.250	0.0%	0.0%	0.240	0.240	-4.0%	-4.0%
1.00	Bar	1.000	1.000	0.0%	0.0%	1.040	1.040	4.0%	4.0%
2.00	Bar	2.000	1.800	0.0%	-10.0%	2.050	2.050	2.5%	2.5%
4.00	Bar	4.000	3.800	0.0%	-5.0%	4.100	4.100	2.5%	2.5%
Max Error	5%	AVE ERROR %		0.000%	-3.000%	AVE ERROR %		1.000%	1.000%

STATUS:	FAILED - OUT OF CAL	PASSED - IN CALIBRATION

ADJUSTMENTS *(Record any adjustments to the pressure control system made)* :
Adjusted Gain on Auto Regulator

Figure 8-16

You will see that we had very tight limits for pressure of less than 5% error, and even though only one result was outside these limits, we were able to make the adjustments to bring all in calibration.

Also note that we did our first check at 0.25 Bar, as this particular pressure was being used on this instrument for the application.

8.2.2.2 Leak Measurement Calibration Checks

The equipment required for this will vary from machine to machine, however in all cases we do need to have an adjustable calibrated masted leak rate that we can introduce in order to make multiple measurements.

Many people use their master known OK part as the basis for making the measurement and then introduce the known leak on top of this, however this is not always practical (as I found with engine leak testing, and the range of engines being tested), and it may be better to utilise a special known master part of known volume.

This special master invariably take the form of a known reference volume (similar to those used as reference volumes mentioned earlier in the chapters on pressure decay/flow measurement). This volume would be specially constructed (with internal damping), and incorporate a self-sealing connector to which the leak (and if so desired the pressure meter in our pressure checks) can be attached.

Figure 8-17

Figure 8-17 shows a Reference Master that I had produced for my own calibration checks.

We carry out the check in a similar way to the pressure checks as follows:

1. Run a test with no leak (leak rate = 0.00) attached.
2. Run a test and record
a. The value of the master leak rate attached
b. The leakage rate displayed on your instrument
3. Repeat these steps (1 and 2) for a number of different flow rates as required, ensuring it covers at least twice your leak limits
4. Record these on your certificate/record sheet
5. Compare the recorded results to the expected accuracy (% error), such that should the equipment be out of calibration, then make adjustments (only if qualified to do so) and repeat all steps to confirm instrument now in calibration

Below (Figure 8-18), you can see the leak rate measurement section of the same certificate:

FLOW CALIBRATION

Leak Rate/Flow Introduced		BEFORE				AFTER			
		Leak Rate		Display Error (%)	Measure Error (%)	Pressure		Display Error (%)	Measure Error (%)
		Displayed	Measured			Displayed	Measured		
0.00	cc/min	0.020	0.000	0.1%	0.0%	0.000	0.000	0.0%	0.0%
3.00	cc/min	3.100	3.000	3.3%	0.0%				
5.00	cc/min	5.100	5.010	2.0%	0.2%				
10.00	cc/min	10.200	10.050	2.0%	0.5%				
20.00	cc/min	21.000	20.200	5.0%	1.0%				
Max Error	10%	AVE ERROR %		2.487%	0.340%	AVE ERROR %		0.000%	0.000%

STATUS:	PASSED - IN CALIBRATION	PASSED - IN CALIBRATION

ADJUSTMENTS *(Record any adjustments to the pressure control system made)*:

Figure 8-18

In this case, the calibration was OK without adjustment.

Should the calibration not be correct, then it may not be the flow/pressure measuring sensor that is at fault, but actually indicate an incorrect set-up (due to the fact that in most cases we introduce a cal/volume factor into the equipment to ensure it reads the leak correctly).

It is though clear when this incorrect set-up is the root cause of a poor calibration as the results will all be shifted by the same amount.

The example (Figure 8-19) shows a repeatable error in our calibration check.

Pressure Decay Set up

Current Volume Factor

1250 cc

Cal Leak Applied (cc/min)	Leak Measured (cc/min)	% Error
0	0	0
3.5	3.1	-11%
5	4.5	-10%
8	7.1	-11%
15	13.5	-10%

Figure 8-19

It would appear that our error is always around 10% to 11%, so maybe we can simply correct this repeatable error?

But by correcting our volume factor, we can simply attain an OK calibration.

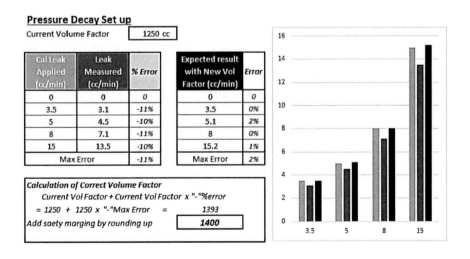

Figure 8-20

287

As we can see the calculation of the correct volume factor is simply using one of 2 formula, either adding the same % error to the volume factor (Figure 8-20), or by ratios of the true leak rate vs the actual leak rate (Figure 8-21):

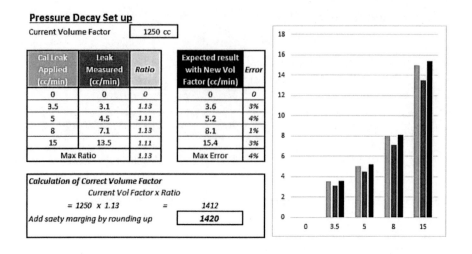

Pressure Decay Set up

Current Volume Factor   1250 cc

Cal Leak Applied (cc/min)	Leak Measured (cc/min)	Ratio	Expected result with New Vol Factor (cc/min)	Error
0	0	0	0	0
3.5	3.1	1.13	3.6	3%
5	4.5	1.11	5.2	4%
8	7.1	1.13	8.1	1%
15	13.5	1.11	15.4	3%
Max Ratio		1.13	Max Error	4%

Calculation of Correct Volume Factor
        Current Vol Factor x Ratio
    = 1250 x 1.13   =   1412
Add saety marging by rounding up   **1420**

Figure 8-21

My personal choice is the easier ratio calculation, as it easier to do, and tends to be a bit more fail-safe.

8.3 Pressure Decay "In Depth" Calibration

So far, I have focussed on the calibration of equipment in relation to supplied test pressure and measured leakage rates. Now in our section on pressure decay, I made it clear that such equipment is only actually measuring pressure and not leakage rates, so in fact our calibration routines previously discussed relating to leakage rate are really only a second level, relying on the correct cal/volume factor being installed, and not the primary calibration of the measurement device itself.

So can we perform a calibration on the pressure decay measurement device. We have a calibrated pressure measurement instrument?

Not quite: although we have a device to measure our supply/test pressure, it is not likely this will be suitable for measuring the pressure decay measurement we expect for our leak.

Let us first examine the amount of pressure change in a simple example of looking for a 4 cc/min leak in a 2 litre volume (our measure time is 5 seconds)

Using our (rearranged) pressure decay to leak rate formula:

$$\text{Pressure Drop (Pa)} = \frac{\text{leak rate (cc/min)} \times \text{Atmos Pressure (Pa)} \times \text{measure time (s)}}{60 \times \text{Volume of Part (cc)}}$$

$$\text{Pressure Drop (Pa)} = \frac{4 \text{ (cc/min)} \times 100{,}000 \text{(Pa)} \times 5\text{(s)}}{60 \times 2000 \text{ (cc)}} = \mathbf{16.7Pa}$$

To measure such a small pressure decay, we are likely to be using a differential transducer type leak test instrument.

Now our test pressure is 2 Bar, so we will likely have a 0 to 4 Bar Pressure Measuring device for our calibration of pressure (this is 400,000 Pascals), so the chances of us being able to see a change of 16 Pascals in 200,000 (0.008% of the display) is virtually impossible.

So we would need another pressure meter capable of measuring such small pressure changes. The way this is achieved is slightly specialised, but can be achieved using the following equipment:

First of all, a calibrated differential pressure measuring device. These are readily available and look very similar to the pressure meters used for our main test pressure supply. (Be careful not to get them mixed up! Or you could severely damage the low pressure meter.)

Next we need to be able to artificially create a very small pressure change. And so a special piece of equipment is required. Based on Boyle's Law which states that there is an inverse relationship between volume and pressure (as the volume increases, the pressure decreases!)

So we can manufacture a special variable volume device to vary our pressure.

I myself designed such a device (Figure 8-22) for use at one of my employers where we wanted to complete a more detailed calibration on differential pressure decay instruments.

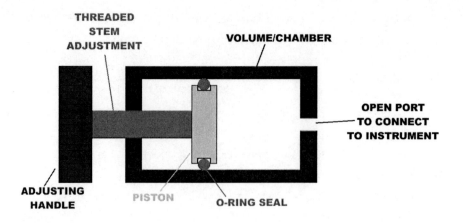

Figure 8-22

As the handle is turned, the threads on the stem move the piston forward and back, and so decrease and increase the volume contained within the chamber (Figure 8-23).

Some important factors to note are:

- *The threaded stem should have very fine threads to ensure adjustment can give fine changes in the actual volume inside the chamber.*
- *The piston/O-rings should be kept greased/lubricated to ensure smooth movement of the piston.*
- *Ensure there are no leaks in the system (likely the chamber will need to be made in two parts for assembly).*

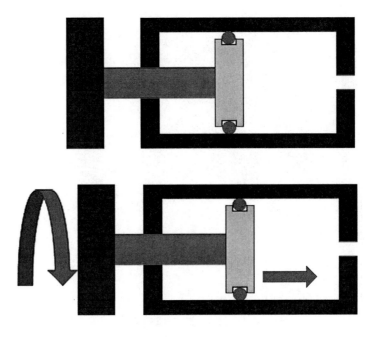

Figure 8-23

Now how do we use such a device to carry out our calibration check on a differential pressure transducer? Here is a simple procedure I developed for one of my employers:

Checking the Differential Transducer

1. *Now select a suitable calibration program as follows:*

TEST PRESSURE   =0.0 *(regulator fully anticlockwise/turned down)*
FILL TIME   =0.0
STAB TIME   =0.0
TEST/MEASURE TIME   =Infinite *(or alternatively maximum 199)*

2. *Fix the variable volume test rig which should also be connected to the differential pressure meter (figure 8-24), to the test port on the rear of the differential pressure leak tester.*

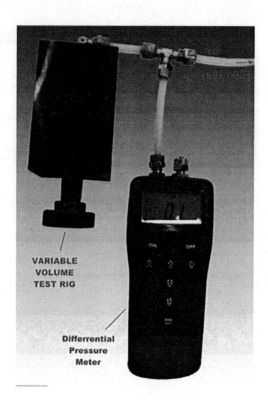

VARIABLE
VOLUME
TEST RIG

Differential
Pressure
Meter

Figure 8-24

3. *Remove the sealing bung (or reference volume) from 'REF' port of the instrument(and leave this port open—in this way both our instrument and our calibration pressure meter are measuring the pressure difference between the test port and atmospheric pressure).*

4. *Ensure the differential pressure meter units are set to display Pascal.*

5. *Press* **START** *button, and ensure the leak tester is in the test/measure phase of the test cycle.*

6. *Check both instrument and pressure meter are at 'ZERO'.*

7. *Now take five readings across the range of the differential transducer (e.g.0 to 200 Pascal), by adjusting the volume to achieve the pressure readings on the pressure meter. It is suggested using the following:*

i.   0.0 to 5.0 Pascal

ii.   20 to 30 Pascal

iii. 50 to 75 Pascal

iv.   100 to 125 Pascal

v. 150 to 175 Pascal

8. *Once all measurements have been taken, STOP/RESET the test on the leak tester.*

9. *Now assess the calibration accuracy of the instrument*

Here (following page) is a typical blank calibration certificate *(Figure 8-25, that I designed for one of my employers to carry out calibration at one of our customers)* for a differential leak tester showing both the Supply/test pressure measurement checks and differential pressure meter checks.

CALIBRATION CERTIFICATE

DATE OF CALIBRATION:	05 May 2021	CERTIFICATE No.:	S-24680-52021
VALIDITY PERIOD:	Twelve Months.	SERIAL No.:	24680
DESCRIPTION:	Leak Detector.	CALIBRATED BY:	Barry Dean
MANUFACTURER:	Supplier	SIGNED:	*Barry Dean*

Measurement standards are derrived from volumetric and time sources, which are traceable to UCAS (NAMAS). The relevant procedures are recorded and are available for inspection if required. The following list indicates the the identification numbers of traceable item of test equipment used in the calibration procedure.

P2000UL	P2000XH							

The instrument has been calibrated at ambient room temperature and at atmospheric pressure.

We hereby certify that on the day of calibration the instrument performed according to the manufacturer's original sales specification as checked by the calibration procedure, unless otherwise stated.

ADJUSTMENTS: Air input filter bowl purged. Visually inspected for damage. Transducer adjustments undertaken if necessary. Readings taken from both transducers are tabulated below. The estimated measurement uncertainty is +/- 2%.

RESULTS

BEFORE					AFTER ADJUSTMENT			
Pressure displayed on instrument.		Actual applied pressure.		Error.	Error. %	Pressure displayed on instrument.		Error.	Error. %
3.00	Bar	2.900	Bar	0.100	3.333%	2.950	Bar	0.050	1.667%
2.00	Bar	1.950	Bar	0.050	2.500%	1.980	Bar	0.020	1.000%
1.38	Bar	1.380	Bar	0.000	0.000%	1.370	Bar	0.010	0.725%
1.00	Bar	1.000	Bar	0.000	0.000%	1.000	Bar	0.000	0.000%
0.50	Bar	0.500	Bar	0.000	0.000%	0.500	Bar	0.000	0.000%
		AVERAGE ERROR %			1.167%	AVERAGE ERROR %			0.678%

BEFORE					AFTER ADJUSTMENT			
Differential display on instrument.		Actual applied pressure.		Error.	Error. %	Pressure displayed on instrument.		Error.	Error. %
150.00	Pa	150.0	Pa	0.000	0.000%				
100.00	Pa	100.0	Pa	0.000	0.000%				
0.00	Pa	0.0	Pa	0.000	0.000%				
-100.00	Pa	-99.0	Pa	1.000	1.000%				
-150.00	Pa	-148.0	Pa	2.000	1.333%				
		AVERAGE ERROR %			0.467%	AVERAGE ERROR %			0.000%

MAXIMUM ERRORS BEFORE CALIBRATION:		MAXIMUM ERROR FOLLOWING CALIBRATION:	
PRESSURE:	3.333%	PRESSURE:	1.667%
DIFF TRANS:	1.333%	DIFF TRANS:	0.000%

Figure 8-25

8.4 Benefits of Calibration Checks

Obviously, as we showed at the beginning of this chapter, one of the biggest benefits of having the ability to carry out calibration checks is simply the cost benefit in not having to have the equipment supplier visit and carry out annual calibration checks.

But by not having to have the OEM carry out annual checks leads on directly to another benefit sometimes overlooked, in that your equipment availability is now completely under your control. One company I worked for had around 40 leak testers, and when they came round to annual calibrations, a supplier visit would be arranged, and this would take place over a two week period, during which time we had to make the equipment available to the supplier to complete their work. This had two effects—downtime of the equipment. And all calibrations expired at the same time each year.

By having our own calibration check facilities, we were able to spread the calibration work and in-house certification throughout the year, and action the work at the most convenient time/date for each piece of equipment. This was included in the duties of our routine maintenance engineers, making the whole process more suitable for our particular needs.

This leads me to the next benefit in that it can help you to identify and root cause problems that you might encounter.

By having calibration check facilities available at all times enables us to carry out checks at times outside normal working times, when the supplier would only be available.

Let me give you a real-life example:

One of the suppliers to one of my employers, was providing parts to assemble to an engine. When we leak tested the engines, we were finding a number of the part supplied were leaking, despite the fact that each of these parts was identified as being leak tested at the supplier.

So we began an investigation as to why these parts had passed the leak test at the supplier, yet were obviously not leak tight.

The supplier arranged for the manufacturer of their leak test equipment to visit and carry out a full calibration check (during normal working hours), only to find that the equipment was correctly identifying leaking parts, which just made this an even greater mystery.

I myself visited the supplier and repeated the test (again in normal working hours), and verified that the equipment was performing as required, and that the equipment appeared fit for purpose.

It soon became clear that something was happening whenever we were not checking the equipment, that would never reveal itself during our routine spot-checks.

So a plan was hatched to repeat the single-point calibration checks on the leakage rate measurements over a full 24 hour period. For this I loaned them a master calibrated leak, so that once an hour, they would add this master leak after a pass result (on the very same part. All results were recorded and then plotted onto a chart (Figure 8-26):

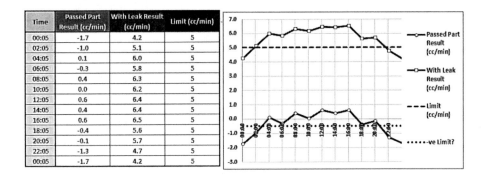

Time	Passed Part Result (cc/min)	With Leak Result (cc/min)	Limit (cc/min)
00:05	-1.7	4.2	5
02:05	-1.0	5.1	5
04:05	0.1	6.0	5
06:05	-0.3	5.8	5
08:05	0.4	6.3	5
10:05	0.0	6.2	5
12:05	0.6	6.4	5
14:05	0.4	6.4	5
16:05	0.6	6.5	5
18:05	-0.4	5.6	5
20:05	-0.1	5.7	5
22:05	-1.3	4.7	5
00:05	-1.7	4.2	5

Figure 8-26

Now we can clearly see the advantage of having the ability to carry out quick calibration checks at any time, as this experiment that revealed a trend related to time of day. This trend shoed that in the middle of the night, the general results were quite strongly -ve, and any leak added to these would not cross the limit set, and the part would pass.

In this particular case it revealed that the root cause was due to the fact that the air supply to the leak test machine was coming through open air from a compressor in the next building. This air was cool at the start of the test (due to lower temperatures outside in the night), and would be warming during the measurement time, causing an additional -ve value to our leak test.

As pressure is proportional to temperature, as the temperature of the air warmed, the air pressure inside the part increased, effectively masking/detracting from any drop in pressure caused by any leaks.

The solution was to include a large air reservoir next to the test machine allowing the air being used in the leak test to be at the same ambient conditions as the room in which the leak test was carried out—result: no more leaking parts.

In addition the supplier did not have a -ve limit set as this may have highlighted the problem earlier as they would have found -ve value failures during the night, stopping leaking parts being passed.

9. Summary of Air Testing

Before we move on to other forms of leak testing just a brief summary of some of the key points for air testing (see chapters 6 to 10 for full details):

1. Specification
a. Ensure all specifications are known including both leak rate and test pressure, which should be at the working pressure to mimic the operation of the part/assembly
2. Global method
a. In general, air testing methods are global
i. They can only detect whether or not the total leakage from our part meets our requirements
ii. Not able to measure individual leaks
iii. Unable to locate the precise position of the leak path
3. Air pressure decay
a. Two types of measurement devices, gauge pressure and differential pressure
b. Test parameters
i. Fill/pressurisation – ensure sufficient to ensure correct test pressure
ii. Stabilisation – Ensure sufficient for repeatable results
iii. Measure/test time – set to ensure good signal to noise ration depending on leakage specification
iv. Other special parameters/features – get advise on their use, but may help reduce cycle times, or improve repeatability
c. Use of reference volumes – ensure correct construction and be aware of increased fill times

d. Main issues for pressure decay

i. Temperature effects – eradicate wherever possible, and use temp comp options with care mas they can mislead

ii. Volume effects – be aware as they are not so obvious

4. Air Flow Testing

a. Two main types – Pressure drop across a laminar flow tube, and mass flow sensors

b. Test parameters- very similar to air pressure decay

i. Volume factor important with reference tanks

c. Main issues for flow measurement

i. Temperature effects and volume effect – suffers exactly same issue as pressure decay

5. Calibration of air testing

a. Must have a master calibrated leak (do not use a part with a drilled hole)

b. Also good to have a pressure meter for full checks

c. Good to carry out single point checks frequently to ensure equipment performance

6. Air testing – good practice

a. Where possible include ability to automatically download/ record results as these can be very useful to identify trends etc.

There will be further information relating to air testing in chapter 15 regarding test machines/systems.

10. Tracer Gas Leak Detection

This section is devoted largely to the use of gases other than air (although as you will discover even air can be used as a trace gas ... more shortly) for the purposes of leak testing.

Most people refer to leak testers using a trace gas as Helium Testers, and whilst this gas and the detectors for this gas are widely used, they are by no means the only trace gas methods employed.

10.1. General Principles

In general terms, a trace gas is used for smaller leaks, that are difficult to detect using normal air testing (in the forms of pressure decay and flow measurement).

The reason is that trace gas leak testing in general offers greater sensitivity, due to the fact that we are reducing our signal to noise ratio, as the level of trace gas in the normal air is (in the main) very low, so any trace gas leaking out is much easier to detect.

Just as with air testing methods, there are many ways to utilise the various detection devices, and this will be dealt with in greater detail in the different techniques.

I will attempt to provide you with all the contributing factors to help you chose the correct trace gas, and test method, but much will depend on your particular component/part, and/or applications as we will see.

10.2. Trace Gases

By trace gas, we really mean any other gas that is not air. There are many options available, but we should consider the choice of trace gas by considering the following factors:

- Is the gas already present?
o If our component/assembly already contains a gas other than air, then it would make sense to use this as our trace gas. For example aerosols contain HFAs, fire extinguishers may contain CO_2, etc.
- Size of leak to be detected
o The smaller the leak, the more sensitive we will likely need to select our trace gas depending on the sensitivity of the different detection devices and techniques available.
- Test method
o This is really just a choice between global testing (where we just want to establish whether we have a leak or not) and leak location testing (where we want to establish the actual location of the leak).
- Cycle time available
o Very much allied to the first two points, we must ensure we chose an appropriate gas for the size of leak we wish to detect, and the time we have to detect it.
- Health and safety
o Last but by no means least! We must always consider our choice of gas and the effect that it can have on operators and the environment.
- Background conditions (signal to noise)
o It may be that there are other gases drifting around the area where we leak test (such as vapours from perfumes/aerosols etc.) and we may need to ensure we chose a gas different to these to avoid falsely detected leaks.
- Part/assembly size and complexity
o This may well have a bearing on our choice of tracer depending on the leak rate we are trying to detect, and the method we wish to employ. (For example, it is not practical to encase a large assembly such as a diesel engine inside a chamber for a helium vacuum system.)

I am sure you can think of other contributing factors, but these are those I have mainly encountered during my time as a leak test engineer in industry

10.3. Different Detector/Sensor Types

Just a brief look at some of the main detectors being used today for trace gas leak testing.

10.3.1. Eyes: Air Under Water /Soap Bubbles/Solution

Yes, we can use our eyes to detect leaks. In most cases this detector is used to detect air escaping. To give us our required signal to noise, we reduce our background (air) by effectively replacing it with another background such as water, or soap solution.

This is the most commonly used method of locating the actual leak path as we can easily see where the bubbles are exiting the part under test, and believe it or not this is a very sensitive method *(although many suppliers of leak testers will have you believe otherwise)*.

In fact it is so sensitive, that it often causes issues when parts that pass an air pressure decay or flow measurement test are immersed under water and bubbles can be seen escaping from the part that we have just passed! I have even seen bubble detection to out-perform some very sensitive trace gas detection devices.

I will explain this with the aid of my very popular bubble charts:

If we think about the bubbles, we can clearly see that they are just simple spheres, and we can easily calculate the volume of a sphere from:

$$V = \frac{4}{3}\pi r^3$$

Now we know that our leakage rate is the volume of the air escaping in a given time period (e.g., cc/min), so if we know the volume of our bubble, and we count the number of bubbles over a given time period, then we can calculate our leakage rate by adding the volumes of all the bubbles (spheres) that escape within that time period.

Now we can create a table (Table 10-1) that shows the total volume of air that escaped during 1 second (i.e., cm3 sec-1) as follows:

301

Number of Bubbles Per Second	Champagne		Fizzy Drink/Straw Under Water			Larger Bubbles (Soap in Hand)		
BUBBLE SIZE/DIAMETER (mm)	0.5	1	2	3	5	10	15	20
single bubble volume (cc)	0.000065	0.000524	0.004189	0.014139	0.065458	0.523667	1.767375	4.189333
1	0.00007	0.0005	0.004	0.014	0.07	0.52	1.77	4.19
2	0.00013	0.0010	0.008	0.028	0.13	1.05	3.53	8.38
3	0.00020	0.0016	0.013	0.042	0.20	1.57	5.30	12.6
4	0.00026	0.0021	0.017	0.057	0.26	2.09	7.07	16.8
5	0.00033	0.0026	0.021	0.071	0.33	2.62	8.84	20.9
6	0.00039	0.0031	0.025	0.085	0.39	3.14	10.6	25.1
7	0.00046	0.0037	0.029	0.10	0.46	3.67	12.4	29.3
8	0.00052	0.0042	0.034	0.11	0.52	4.19	14.1	33.5
9	0.00059	0.0047	0.038	0.13	0.59	4.71	15.9	37.7
10	0.0007	0.0052	0.042	0.14	0.65	5.24	17.7	41.9
20	0.0013	0.010	0.084	0.28	1.31	10.5	35.3	83.8
30	0.002	0.016	0.13	0.42	1.96	15.7	53.0	125.7
40	0.003	0.021	0.17	0.57	2.62	20.9	70.7	167.6
60	0.004	0.031	0.25	0.85	3.93	31.4	106.0	251.4

Table 10-1

Taking this a stage further, we can then calculate the cc/min by multiplying these value by 60. In addition, we can colour code our leakage rates, according to our leak specification (with a 20% margin for error either side) such as is shown on the chart (Table 10-2), where I have colour coded the chart for a 6 atm cm3 min-1 leak of air (corresponding to our specification for oil leaks).

	BUBBLE SIZE/DIAMETER (mm)							
	Champagne		Fizzy Drink/Straw Under Water			Larger Bubbles (Soap in Hand)		
Number of Bubbles Per Second	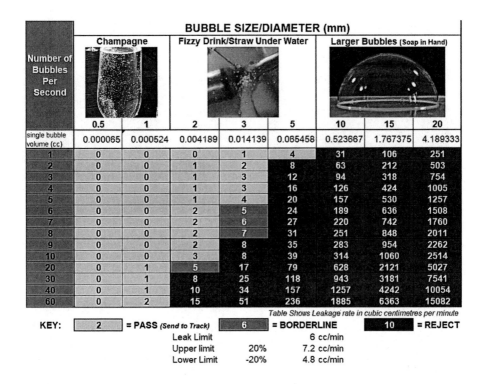							
	0.5	1	2	3	5	10	15	20
single bubble volume (cc)	0.000065	0.000524	0.004189	0.014139	0.065458	0.523667	1.767375	4.189333
1	0	0	0	1	4	31	106	251
2	0	0	1	2	8	63	212	503
3	0	0	1	3	12	94	318	754
4	0	0	1	3	16	126	424	1005
5	0	0	1	4	20	157	530	1257
6	0	0	2	5	24	189	636	1508
7	0	0	2	6	27	220	742	1760
8	0	0	2	7	31	251	848	2011
9	0	0	2	8	35	283	954	2262
10	0	0	3	8	39	314	1060	2514
20	0	1	5	17	79	628	2121	5027
30	0	1	8	25	118	943	3181	7541
40	0	1	10	34	157	1257	4242	10054
60	0	2	15	51	236	1885	6363	15082

Table Shows Leakage rate in cubic centimetres per minute

KEY: 2 = PASS (Send to Track)   6 = BORDERLINE   10 = REJECT

Leak Limit   6 cc/min
Upper limit   20%   7.2 cc/min
Lower Limit   -20%   4.8 cc/min

Table 10-2

Now we can clearly see how although in some cases we may see many tiny (champagne) bubbles emanating from our part they are in fact well below our limit, and as such this part is perfectly fit for purpose. (In fact any bubbles of 1mm or less in diameter is likely to mean a leak below our limit for liquids.)

But remember this method is very much subjective, and left to a judgement call by the operator as to whether or not the leak he sees is actually OK or not and we have no actual leakage rate measurement.

One way this can be overcome is to create a measurement method to determine the leakage rate, by catching the bubbles in a measuring tube over a period of time, and then calculating the leakage rate from the total volume of gas captured by the time it took to capture the bubbles. The following diagrams (Figure 10-1) show this process in a step by step guide.

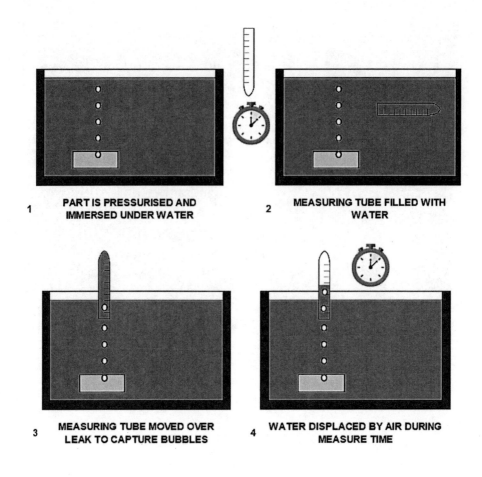

1 PART IS PRESSURISED AND IMMERSED UNDER WATER

2 MEASURING TUBE FILLED WITH WATER

3 MEASURING TUBE MOVED OVER LEAK TO CAPTURE BUBBLES

4 WATER DISPLACED BY AIR DURING MEASURE TIME

Figure 10-1

Once the measurement is completed simply calculate the leakage rate by dividing the volume of water (in cubic centimetres) displaced during the measuring time by the measuring time (in seconds).

This gives you the leakage rate in atmosphere cm3 sec-1 (cc/sec). To convert to cc/min (atmosphere cm3 min-1) simply multiply by 60.

Of course, this method cannot be used when using the soap solution method, where we locate the leak, not by immersing the part under water, but by spraying/applying a soap solution on the outside of the component, and look for bubbles being formed by the escaping gas/air.

The reason we use a soap solution (or a recognised alternative off-the-shelf leak test spray) is that this aids the formation of bubbles much better than water alone.

These photographs (Figure 10-3) show just a couple of examples of the use of soap solution. Because the leakage rate is relatively small, smaller bubbles can form, and the tendency is for a frothing rather than distinct bubbles.

Figure 10-2

Figure 10-3

Now remember how I told you how sensitive this method can be... the best example is from my own experience, when as a young sales engineer, I visited a manufacturer of high-quality polished valves, and I took along a very sensitive tracer gas sniffer, capable of detecting leaks as small as 0.00001 cm3 min-1, to demonstrate.

On arrival the customer provided a part that they knew to be leaking, However I could not detect the leak using my highly sensitive detector despite a number of attempts.

I was then shown their current method which involved pressurising the part with Helium, and immersing under alcohol (the reasons for these choices was that helium is a smaller molecule than air, and alcohol had a much lower surface tension than air, and so bubbles could break free much easier). The operator than placed a very bright light over the part and observed the leak.

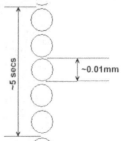

He then showed me the leak which appeared as a very fine line up the side of the part. (the line was very fine and difficult to see, and I liken it to one of the fine lines on a piece of graph paper.

I estimated that the diameter of each bubble was only 0.01 of a mm (0.001cm), and calculated the volume of each bubble:

$$V = \frac{4}{3}\pi r^3 \quad = \quad V = \frac{4}{3}\pi 0.0005^3 \quad = \quad 0.000000004cm^3$$

Even assuming 5 bubbles every second, the leakage rate calculated out to be only 0.000001 cm3 min-1, which was 10 times less than I could find with my leak detector.

Clearly this is an extreme example, but it taught me a very sharp lesson about sensitivity of bubble detection! I suggested they carry on with their Helium under alcohol test!

10.3.2. Ears (Ultrasound Detectors)

Similarly, we can listen for leaks (once again using air as a trace gas). This seems fairly obvious, as many of us will at some time heard a large gushing air sound coming from somewhere, and nearly all of us will no doubt have heard the wind rushing through the trees!

Actually, it is not really the movement of the air molecules we hear, but actually the turbulence they cause as they pass solid objects. And so it is with leaks, we already discovered that we use laminar tubes to reduce this turbulence, but as air passes solid objects, the molecules (the little rubber balls) that the air is made up of will no doubt collide with the walls of the leak passage, and then with each other as they bounce around trying to get from the high to low pressure regions. And as two things hit each other they create a noise.

Well this is OK but the sound we can hear is limited by the frequency range that our hearing can detect (Figure 10-4),and much of the noise made by the turbulence/collisions is in the ultra-high frequency range, what is known as the ultrasound, and beyond our normal hearing abilities

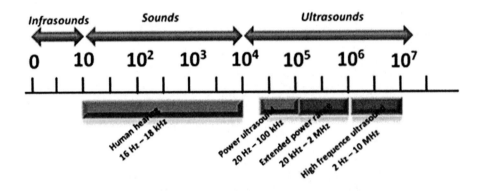

Figure 10-4

So some very clever people (much smarter than I) developed special ultrasound detectors, which effectively take the High frequency noises, and convert them into something we can hear. There is a huge range of devices available, but they are limited by a couple of key points:

1. Background noise
2. Noise level from small leaks

10.3.2.1 Background Noise

Obviously there is movement of air all around, and any two objects hitting each other, parts rubbing together (friction) etc. will create noise, and much of it is in the ultrasonic range.

So it is sometimes very difficult to detect small molecular collisions from a leak in amongst all the general background ultrasonic noise in the world around us. (If you ever get the chance to try an ultrasound detector—try jangling a set of keys in front of it—you will soon understand what I mean about background noise.)

10.3.2.2 Noise Levels from Small Leaks

When a tree is felled, as it hits the ground, you can appreciate the noise level made is very loud, and easily heard. But when a pin is dropped onto a concrete floor (although both objects are relatively hard), the noise level is barely audible.

And thus it is with air turbulence. If the pressure difference is large, and the leak path relatively big, then the amount of ultrasound creative is relatively easy to detect, but low pressure differentials and very small leak paths create far less noise. (Think about the noise created by the wind. A slight breeze Can barely be heard, but a storm wind you can definitely hear. Remember the wind is created by the air passing from high to low pressure...)

To help improve on these two issues, many producers of ultrasound detectors have added focussing devices (Figure 10-5), to help eliminate surrounding background noise, and enhance the noise from our leak path.

Figure 10-5

In all honesty, I have <u>not</u> found such detectors particularly helpful in factory conditions, and prefer to use soap solution to pinpoint leaks.

Where these devices are particularly useful is in identifying costly leaks in mains air supply systems, where the pressure difference is high, and access in not easy (as the mains air supplies are often run inside the roof of our factory). These hand held devices can simply pointed in the direction of the pipework, and leaks identified (as the background noise in the roof area is relatively low).

So now let us look at a few of the detectors developed to detect gases other than air.

10.3.3 Thermal Conductivity

Possibly the most widely used general purpose detection device, as it is capable of detecting a wide range of tracer gases in a large number of applications.

The detector consists of a pair of matched thermal filaments (Figure 10-6) whose conductivity (by which I mean how much electrical current they will pass) responds to their temperature. The temperature of each filament is dependent on the thermal conductivity of the gas(es) surrounding them.

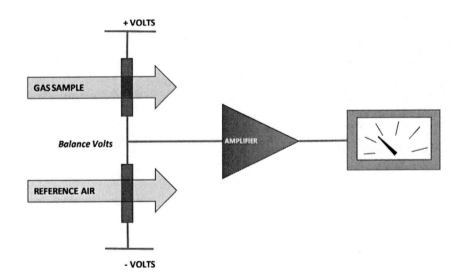

Figure 10-6

A small pump is used to pull a gas sample across each filament with the sample/test filament being in the air stream from the probe, and the reference filament flow from a different area.

Should one of the detectable tracer gases be present in the probe sample, the conductivity of the filament is altered (by the heating, or cooling effect of the gas), which causes an imbalance in the bridge arrangement.

The resultant out of balance current through the filaments is then measured, with the measurement being directly proportional to the amount of gas present in the detection cell. This signal can then be processed to display the actual leakage rate combined with an audible signal.

The advantage of this detector is that it can be used to detect any gas whose thermal conductivity is different to that of air (at this point I am not going to try and bore you with how thermal conductivity is calculated from mean particle speed, molecular heat capacity, Avogadro's number etc., simpler to use a simple look up table available—see Table 10-3).

Gas Name and Chemical Symbol		Thermal Conductivity (@ temp 300K) "mW m^{-1} K^{-1}"	Diff
Air		26.4	0
Argon	Ar	17.7	8.7
Sulfer Hexaflouride	SF$_6$	13	13.4
Hydrogen	H$_2$	186.6	160.2
Ammonia	H$_2$N	25.1	1.3
Helium	He	155.7	129.3
Nitrogen	N	26	0.4
Oxygen	O$_2$	26.5	0.1
Carbon Monoxide	CO	25	1.4
Carbon Dioxide	CO$_2$	16.8	9.6
Methane	CH$_4$	34.4	8
Butane	C$_4$H$_{10}$	16.7	9.7

Table 10-3

The bars give you an idea of how different their thermal conductivities are from air, and so how good the detector will respond to these gases. As we can see Hydrogen and Helium can be easily detected, Ammonia barely at all.

However this ability to detect almost any gas is also one of this detector's disadvantages, in that even breathing near the probe (or the reference side of the air) will cause CO2 (carbon dioxide) to be sampled and thus give us false results.

310

This means that if we do get a response on our detector, we cannot be certain it is the specific trace gas we are searching for. This is known as non-specific or non-selective detection. A problem for many gas detectors, as we will see, although there are exceptions *(and some tricks that have been used as we will also see)*.

Having said that, if we are working in an area, that is well ventilated, and we get a response as we search our component/assembly for leaks, the chances are that it is a leak of the gas we are searching for, and not some random passing gas. And in any case, we can go back to the point of response and confirm the same response. For this reason, it is not worth spending 4 times the amount of money on specific gas detectors over simple thermal conductivity devices.

The sensitivity of thermal conductivity detector is obviously dependent on the gas we are trying to detect, but typically hand held sniffers can detect leaks as small as 0.00001 cm3 sec-1 ($1 \times 10-5$ cc/s) for Helium *(the most commonly used trace gas)*. More typically $1 \times 10- 4$ cc/s in search mode

One point to mention at this point is that the sensitivity of sniffers (see section on techniques/methods) is that their sensitivity depends very much on the sample flow being drawn in through the sniffing probe.

10.3.4 Ion Emission/Detection Sensors

There are a number of different variations of detectors that use this principal, but in essence the sensor operates by ionising the gases that enter the sensor, and then detecting these ions by measuring the current that is formed on the detection pin.

Again these detectors are non-specific, and can detect a wide range of gases. Two examples I have used are:

10.3.4.1 Heated Filament (Figure 10-7)

The heated filament detector, consists of anode (heated ioniser) and cathode (detector pin) elements made from platinum wire.

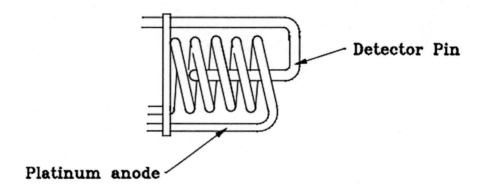

Figure 10-7

The anode takes the form of a coiled platinum tube which is heated to around 800oC which allows a 'standing current' to flow to the detector pin (cathode). The sample is again pumped into the detector cell via the instrument probe. Any detectable tracer gas that enters the cell, reacts with the surface of the heated platinum anode so as to increase the emission of (+ve) ions, thereby increasing the current flow in the cathode (detector pin).

The major drawback with this device is the limited life of the sensor (which itself is relatively expensive) due to the loss of positive ions from the platinum. This results in the need for constant re-calibration to overcome sensor drift, and longer term regular sensor replacement.

Such equipment however is very sensitive, particularly to halogenated gases, and the new HFC's and therefore has been used quite extensively in the air conditioning and refrigeration industries. Typical sensitivities for such gases reach as low as 0.00001 cm3 sec-1 (1 x 10-5 cc/s)

10.3.4.2 Electron Capture (Figure 10-8)

One of the most sensitive hand-held sniffer devices available this device has been used quite extensively for detection of SF6 leaks in High Voltage Switchgear (where this gas is utilised to quench/suppress arcing across the contacts).

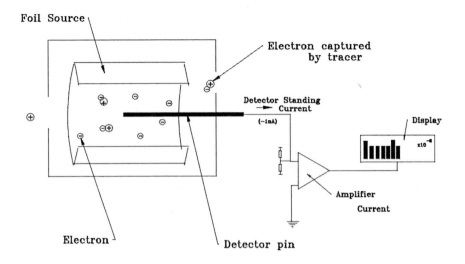

Figure 10-8

The detector cell comprises a central detector pin surrounded by a metallic foil impregnated with a radioactive element, Ni63 (Nickel 63). This foil therefore emits Beta particles (-ve ions), which are collected on the cathode, resulting in a current flow (standing current), in this pin.

Any detectable tracer gas entering the detector cell, react with this ion cloud, serving to reduce the number of ions in the detector pin, so reducing the current flow. The change in current flow is measured, as this change in current is directly proportional to the amount of tracer gas within the cell.

The flow of gases in and out of the chamber is carefully and accurately controlled by a number of restrictors. One of these gas flows is a special inert carrier gas which must be constantly flowing through the detector for it to function.

This type of instrument can be quite expensive and has a limited number of different tracer gases associated with it, the major drawbacks however are that the detector contains a radioactive source, the additional cost of the carrier gas, and that is non-specific.

This detector has been largely superseded by others (particularly Carona Discharge types–detailed in the next section of this book), but when it was more popular could achieve sensitivity to leaks as small as 1 x 10-7 cc/sec (0.0000001).

313

10.3.5 Hydrogen Sniffer

This is a special electro-chemical sensor device used for hydrogen detection. It was developed (and patented to one main manufacturer) some years ago as a potential rival for helium detectors, but has only really established its use in a few market places:

- Pressurised telecom cables, buried or ducted
- Gas pipelines
- Fibre-optic cable ducts
- Gas-filled power cables
- A few automotive applications
- Some refrigeration and air conditioning applications

The sensor consists of a heated electronic amplifier coated with a thin film of metal hydride, which is permeable to Hydrogen atoms only. Hydrogen molecules comprise of two atoms (hence the chemical symbol H2). When the hydrogen molecule strikes the metal surface, the molecule splits into the two individual atoms which are then absorbed by the thin film coating. This creates a small voltage, which is amplified and then displayed as a gas detection measurement.

Because of its design, this sensor is selective (specific) as it primarily only detects hydrogen gas, and due to the fact that the background levels of hydrogen in the normal atmosphere are very low (typically around 0.5ppm – ½ part per million—which means 1 molecule of hydrogen in 2 million parts of air). This means our signal to noise ratio of leakage rates to background is very high, and as such the detector can detect leaks as small as 0.0000001 cm3 sec-1 (1 x 10-7 cc/sec).

The sensor has a couple of drawbacks:

- In the vast majority of cases, the sample is not drawn into the detector (in the case of the only version manufactured commercially) and as such the sensor must be in close proximity to the leakage point to be able to detect very small leaks. *(Obviously as the gas leaks a cloud of the gas will form around the leak site and the detector can detect this cloud at a distance)*—so in search mode the sensitivity is reduced to typically 1 x 10-6 or worse.

- As the hydrogen atoms are absorbed into the sensor, then over time the sensor will become contaminated with the Hydrogen, and it's sensitivity will deteriorate. This is particularly relevant when larger leakage rates are being detected.

One concern for a lot of people is the use of Hydrogen (*everyone has a picture in their mid of Hydrogen balloon falling to earth in flames*), however Hydrogen gas can be safely used in low concentration mixtures with air, and the sensitivity figures quoted assume a 5% Hydrogen in air mixture as the tracer gas (more on this later).

> *Note: The LEL (Lower Explosive Limit – the level below which the combustible gas will not ignite) for Hydrogen is 4% Vol.*

10.3.6 Quartz Window Detectors

I have called these Quartz Window, however they are actually a combination of an ion pump combined with a quartz window. Without going into the details of the Ion Pump, effectively a very low vacuum is created behind the quartz window. The quartz window acts as a filter only allowing gases with a small molecule (such as Helium or Hydrogen) to pass through, so that the vacuum level in the area behind the quartz window changes when these gases pass through, and the pump then draws more current as it re- establishes the vacuum

The big advantage of these detectors is that they are completely specific only detecting the trace gas we are looking for.

The sensitivity of these types of detectors is as low as 0.00000001 cm3 sec-1 (which is 1 x 10-7 cc/sec) in high sensitivity mode or 1 x 10-6 cc/sec in normal search mode.

The difference between these two modes relates to the flow rate of the sample being draw into the detector (which will be explain in the following section on detector sensitivities).

10.3.7 Helium Mass Spectrometer

This device is undoubtedly one of the highest sensitivity tracer gas detectors that is available, by virtue of the fact that it operates in a near complete vacuum (virtually no gas present) and in doing so ensures the maximum signal to noise ratio.

They are also highly specific, and tuned to detect only Helium Gas. This works by ionising the gases, and then bending them through an arc to the sensor, which simply detects the gas molecules landing on it (again I am not going to go into depth on the sensor itself, but just going to explain how this selectivity to Helium is obtained.

I will attempt to make this simple by using different size (weight) marbles being rolled down a slope as in the Figure 10-9.

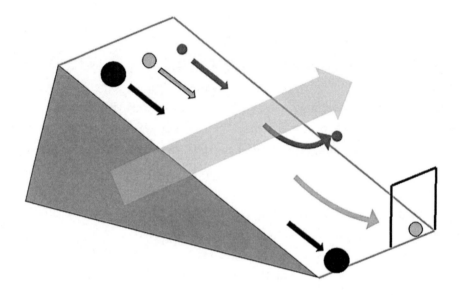

Figure 10-9

If a breeze is blowing consistently across the slope, then the very lightest marbles will be blow off the side, whilst the heavier marbles will travel straight down. Only the right-sized marbles will be bent just the right amount to pass through the goalposts at the bottom of the slope.

So in the Helium Mass Spectrometer, the gases entering the detector cell (Figure 10-10), are ionised which means that they are given an electrical charge by a heated filament as they enter. Like in magnets, where like poles repel, and unlike poles attract (which is how a simple compass works), the same is true of electrical charges. So we place an electronic field across the beam of charged gases going into the chamber.

This causes the gases to bend through an arc, depending on their size (molecular mass) the ionisation and electrical charge around the chamber. Helium Mass Spectrometers are specifically tuned to ensure that only molecules with a mass of 4amu (atomic mass units) will bend at exactly the right amount to reach the sensor at the end of the chamber.

Molecules of higher mass, will not bend enough and are blocked by windows placed in the path, and very light molecules will be bent too much and will similarly be blocked.

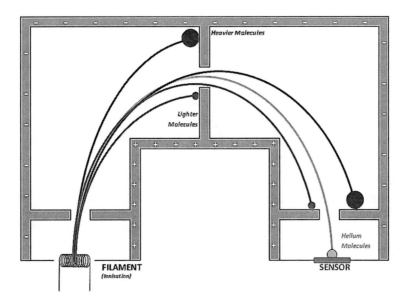

Figure 10-10

So this specific detector will detect only helium gas.

By using a very high vacuum we further enhance the sensitivity by reducing the background levels of helium. As we know, the amount of helium in the normal air is around 4parts per million (4ppm), but by creating a reduced amount of air in the chamber, we also reduce the amount of helium in the chamber. The lower level of vacuum we can achieve, the easier it is to see any additional molecules of helium.

317

Such detectors are therefore capable of detecting very small levels of helium entering the chamber and are capable of achieving leak detection rates as low as 0.000000000001 cc/s (1 x 10-12 cm3 sec-1), depending on the level of vacuum that can be achieved around the part under test.

Note: As these detectors operate in a vacuum, supplier of these devices will discuss leak rates in terms of millibar litres per second ($mb\ L\ sec^{-1}$) – do not be alarmed this simply means that they are measuring the volume (in Litres) of the gas at 1millibar absolute pressure whilst we generally talk in terms of atmosphere $cm^3\ sec^{-1}$ as we are measuring at 1 atmosphere. The two values are virtually the same with only around a 1% difference (as a standard atmosphere is equal to approximately 1013 millibars, and $1cm^3$ is 0.001 Litres.

These detectors can be used in a sniffing mode, but their sensitivity is greatly reduced to typically 1×10^{-6}cc/sec in this mode, as I will explain in the section on detector sensitivities).

That concludes a very brief explanation of the main detectors in common use, however there are others.

10.3.8 Other Devices

Here are just a few other gas sniffers that you may come across.

10.3.8.1 InfraRed Detectors (Figure 10-11)

Less common in leak detection, this type of sensor has been used extensively for atmosphere monitoring, particularly for CO2.

The detection chamber comprises an infra-red light beam travelling to a detector which measures the quantity of the light that reaches it. CO2 entering the detection chamber will absorb some of the light thereby reducing the amount reaching the detector. The sensitivity of such detectors is enhanced by increasing the path length of the beam, and modern instruments utilise waveguides to increase path length whilst maintaining small physical size, as shown here. (Sub ppm levels are detectable with this method.)

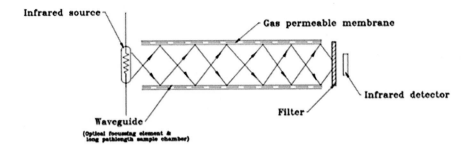

Infrared source

Gas permeable membrane

Infrared detector

Filter

Waveguide
(Optical focussing element &
long pathlength sample chamber)

Figure 10-11

10.3.8.2 Carona Discharge (Figure 10-12)

A very simple device that uses a high voltage charge to ionise the air sample inside the detector cell. The detector itself, consists of a fine platinum wire / pin (anode) and a metal outer tube (cathode).

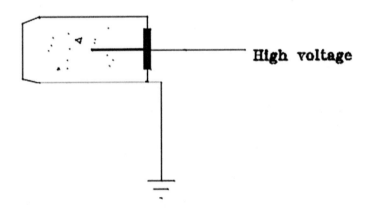

High voltage

Figure 10-12

When a voltage is applied across the detector cell, a ionised cloud is formed between the pin and the detector wall. This cloud supports the 'standing current' from the electrical supply. Detectable tracer gases which enter the chamber react to cause changes in this detector current, and it is this current change which is measured and detected. The amount of current change is proportional to the quantity of tracer gas within the cell.

With a sensitivity of around 1×10^{-4} cc/sec (some modern advances have improved this to 1×10^{-6} cc/sec), its main uses are in the Refrigeration and High Voltage Switchgear industries for locating large leaks of refrigerant and SF6 on gas connections during installation.

10.3.8.3 Photo-Ionisation Detector (Figure 10-13)

Primarily designed to detect volatile organic compounds (VOC's), a sample gas stream is passed through a chamber illuminated by UV light from a lamp.

As the VOC's absorb the light a pair of charged molecular fragments or ions are generated. These ions are then attracted towards a pair of electrodes due to the influence of the electric field generated between them. The electric current required to neutralise the ions at the electrodes is then amplified and measured.

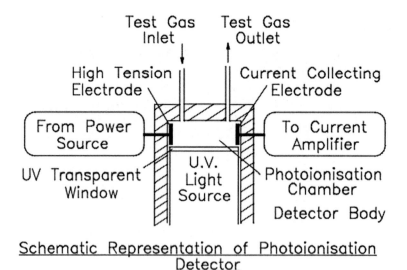

Schematic Representation of Photoionisation Detector

Figure 10-13

Some level of selectivity is achieved by the choice of UV Lamp. However the sensitivity /performance is lost over time, as the amount of detected gas saturation within the detection chamber increases.

Typical sensitivity of these detectors is around 1 x 10-5 cc/sec.

10.3.8.4 Semi-Conductor Sensors (Figure 10-14)

With current advances in sensor technology, many specialised sensing devices have been developed. The majority of these use semiconductors, as the sensor base such that the current flow through the semiconductor changes when the device comes into contact with a detectable gas. In most cases the detection is achieved by chemical reaction at the surface of the semiconductor.

Primarily, this type of sensor has been utilised most effectively for the detection of the new generation of refrigerant gases such as R134a, and butane/propane mixtures, but new types are being continually developed to cover a wide range of gases.

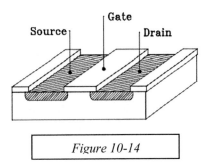

Figure 10-14

10.3.8.5 Quadrupole Mass Spectrometer/Analyser (Figure 10-15)

Effectively, this is a very similar technique to the basic Helium Mass Spectrometer, in that the ionised gases are separated by use of an electric field. In this case however the electric field oscillates around 4 poles.

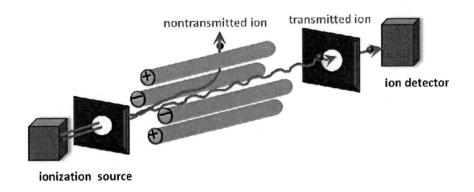

Figure 10-15

Each pair of rods will be successively positive then negative and so forth. In essence, there will always be a pair of positive and negative rods; however, they will alternate at the radio frequency.

As the ionised gas travels between these poles, it is attracted and repelled in accordance with the variation in the electric field. Quadrupole rods (voltage, frequency etc.), may be tuned such that only ions of a certain mass can pass all the way through the system and reach the detector.

Typical commercial quadrupole instruments can achieve unit mass resolution; that is the difference between a gas with mass of 201 can be easily differentiated from a gas of mass 202 etc.

10.3.9 Other Devices

As well as gas sniffers, there are other techniques used for trace detection that you may come across.

10.3.9.1 Cameras

There has been a number of camera systems used to detect leaking gases, but I have never found these to work very well particularly with smaller leak rates, but of course, technology is always advancing so never say never.

10.3.9.2 Liquid Detection Methods

Dye Penetrants can also be used as a trace gas method (using our eyes as the detector). These liquids are painted onto one side of the part we are leak testing, and then we visually inspect the other side for signs of the Dye Penetrant, to indicate the leak path. This can take some time with long leak paths, and of course the Dye must then be removed if we wish to sell the part, so this technique is not widely used other than in investigation, or development, scenarios.

10.4 Explaining Detector Sensitivities

In the above detector descriptions we have highlighted their sensitivity in terms of cubic centimetres per second (cc/sec or cm3 sec-1), as this is how they are often described by the suppliers of the equipment. However this is not strictly true, as in reality we should really define their sensitivity in most cases as their what concentration of the gas they are detecting that they are capable of detecting. Let me explain with a bit of a diagram (Figure 10-16).

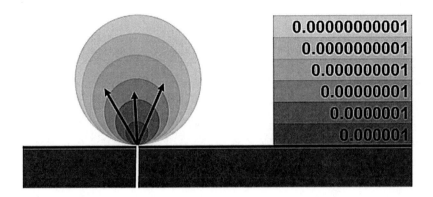

Figure 10-16

If the actual sensor is directly at the end of the probe, then once our probe touches the area of the leaking gas, we will immediately get a response, as we detect our leak. However to be directly in contact with the leak, we either have to know exactly where the leak is, or have to wait until the leaking trace gas, fills a cloud around the area with enough gas for us to detect.

If you imagine our very small leak of trace gas, with the probe of the detector unit (Figure 10-17), we can see how small the amount of gas is in comparison to the physical size of the probe.

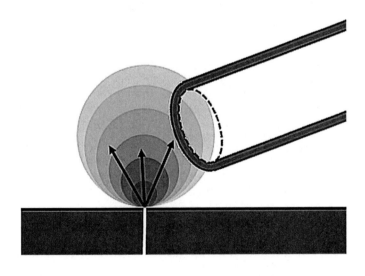

Figure 10-17

If our leak is travelling at 1 x 10-4 cc/sec and the gap between the probe and the sensor envelopes a volume of around 1 centimetre, we can see that to fill this space will take around 1 divided by 1 x 10-4, or 1 x10+4 or 10000seconds which is nearly three hours!. Clearly we do not need the entire 1cc of the probe to be filled with the gas, just long enough for enough gas to travel up the probe for us to be able to detect. However this can take quite a few seconds (depending on the size of the leak) and in a production environment this becomes impractical.

So to help us, it makes sense that we need to draw a sample of the air in, to help the gas travel up the tube quickly enough for us to detect within a second or two.

So most detectors employ a suction pump, to pull a sample of the gas in. So we now need to consider what effect this flow has on our leak. Let me use an example to explain, first of all let us consider that we are releasing 1 sheep every second from a pen, but going past the pen is a very large herd of cows, that go past the pen at a rate of ten (10) cows every second.

Figure 10-18

If we take a picture after 10 seconds, we will have 10 sheep, in amongst 100 cows—believe it or not, there are 10 sheep in this picture (Figure 10-18)—can you count them? Not so easy to see as if we were just looking at a picture of the 10 sheep without the cows.

In fact we can calculate the ratio of sheep to cows as being 1 in 10 or of we want to wait for 1 million cows to pass by it would be 1 x 1,000,000 divided by 10 or 100 thousand ppm. (100,000 sheep per million cows).

So it is with searching for our trace gas in the air flow being drawn into the sample probe. We can count the amount of tracer gas molecules within our air flow stream, and calculate the ppm of tracer gas within the air flow.

Using an example of a leak of 0.000001 cc/sec (1 x 10^{-5} cm^3 sec^{-1}), let us determine the concentration of this trace gas with various flows as per the table below (Table 10-4).

Trace Gas Leak Rate (cc/sec)	Probe flow =drawn sample rate (cc/sec)	Concentration of trace gas (ppm)
0.00001	1	10.0
0.00001	5	2.0
0.00001	10	1.0
0.00001	15	0.67
0.00001	20	0.50
0.00001	30	0.33
0.00001	50	0.20
0.00001	60	0.17
0.00001	100	0.10

Table 10-4

So when we have talked about the sensitivity of some of the detectors, we must remember that the detector itself only responds to the amount of trace gas it sees, in other words it is only capable of detecting a concentration of trace gas, and the leak rates I have quoted are dependent on the actual sampling rate (flow through the detector).

In some cases, you will recall I mentioned the search mode of a detector having reduced sensitivity to leak rates, this is simply because in these modes, a larger sample flow is used to pull the leaking trace gas into the detector to enable us to locate it from a greater distance.

We will look at this concentration issue in more detail when we consider the different techniques of leak testing employed with trace gas detectors.

10.5 Different Detection/Measurement Techniques

Just as we saw with pressure decay and flow measurement, there are a number of different ways of using the basic detection device (in the case of air testing, chamber testing, Vacuum, reference tanks, direct flow etc.), we can employ the trace gas sensors in different ways.

Each of the following methods can be used with most trace gases, dependent on the detector being used, and the size of leakage rate to be detected.

10.5.1 Direct Sniff

The most obvious and simple way to use gas detectors is as a direct sniffer to find the trace gas, a bit like your nose when you can smell your favourite food nearby.

This is known as a location method where we can identify the precise location of the leakage path and measure each leak (where a part may have multiple leakages) independently, as opposed to a global method (which simply tells us whether or not we have a leak or not, and the total amount of leakage from our part).

The component to be tested is simply pressurised with the required trace gas, and then a 'hand-search' is made with the leak detector (Figure 10-19), by slowly moving the sensor/detector probe around the part under test.

Figure 10-19

The speed at which you can move the probe is very dependent on two things (Figure 10-20)

326

- The size of leak we are searching for the larger the leakage rate, the larger gas cloud that is produced by the leak, and so the easier it will be to detect any gas
- The sampling flow rate of the detector the faster the sampling rate the more gas is

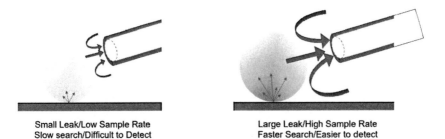

Small Leak/Low Sample Rate
Slow search/Difficult to Detect

Large Leak/High Sample Rate
Faster Search/Easier to detect

Figure 10-20

Now the concentration in parts per million (PPM) of a leakage rate (L/R) of trace gas within the airstream of flowrate "F" (Figure 10-21) will be given by:

$$\text{ppm} = \frac{\text{L/R} \times 10^6}{\text{F}} \quad \text{or} \quad \text{L/R} = \frac{\text{F} \times \text{ppm}}{10^6}$$

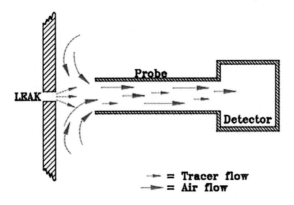

Probe

LEAK

Detector

$\text{-- -- } = \textbf{Tracer flow}$
$\text{----} = \textbf{Air flow}$

Figure 10-21

The clear advantages of this method are simplicity, cost, and the fact that we are able to locate accurately the precise position of the leak path.

The main drawbacks are that it is relatively slow, and that it is operator dependant. This means that leaks can be 'missed' and that the total leakage from the product, must be calculated from the sum of all leaks found. *(Note—some modern instruments are capable of making this calculation for us.)*

To help improve the speed of this method, it is recommended that you only sniff in the suspect areas, for example on a series of tubes and block castings, it is most important to search primarily around the joints rather than along the tubes themselves, or around the body of the castings as they are the most likely areas where a leak might be detected.

10.5.2 Purge Technique

This global method takes away any operator error, by measuring the total leakage from the component. However, it does mean that we are unable to locate the precise location of the leak path.

The idea behind this method is to collect the leaking tracer gas escaping at the leak path and carry this directly to the detector for measurement. With this method, the component to be tested is:

1. Part is pressurised and placed inside a sealed chamber.
2. A high flow of cleaning gas, known as the High Purge, is then used to clear any existing contaminants from the chamber around the component.
3. This is followed by a low carrier gas flow (Low Purge) which passes through the chamber.
a. This Low Purge collects any leaked gas and carries it out of the chamber.
4. After a short time (allowing the tracer gas to be correctly mixed within the carrier, the Low Purge is then diverted to the detector:
a. Where the concentration of the trace gas within the Low Purge can be measured.
5. The High Purge is then reinstated to clear down the chamber, to enable the component to have the trace gas removed, allowing it to be removed from the chamber.

Generally, the cleaning and carrier gases (High and Low Purges) are the same, usually air (but can be an inert gas such as Nitrogen to further reduce background contaminants).

A basic structure/layout and sequence is shown below with the valves that control the flows around the system.

HIGH PURGE (CLEANING) – Figure 10-22

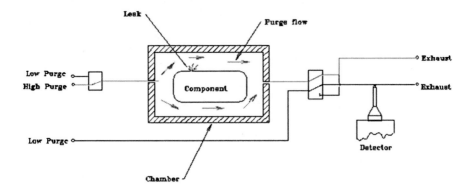

Figure 10-22

LOW PURGE – Figure 10-23

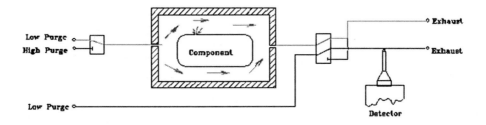

Figure 10-23

DETECTION – Figure 10-24

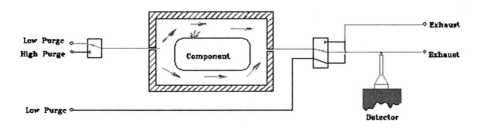

Figure 10-24

The air/purge flow rates required are very simple to calculate as follows:

The cleaning or high purge flow (HP) is easily determined by the fact that to ensure a very low level of background tracer contamination, we need to make at least 10 (ten) air changes within the test chamber.

By free volume, we mean the free volume within the chamber around the part. So it makes sense to minimise this free volume to enable us to make these ten changes as fast as we can. This is normally achieved by making the part be as close a fit within the chamber as practically possible.

The major problem with this method is the sensitivity limits. The limit is made by the fact that the concentration of the tracer gas that reaches the detector is diluted by the carrier gas/low purge flow.

Ideally to ensure that the leak is well mixed within the carrier gas, it is recommended to make at least 2 complete changes of air within the chamber. So our low purge flow (LP) is in general given by the formula:

$$LP = \frac{2 \times \text{Free Volume}}{\text{Time for Low Purge}}$$

Obviously, this is the maximum flow we can allow as this ensures a good leak to carrier mixture within the test time available. However, the minimum low purge is also dependent upon the detection device being employed:

$$HP = \frac{10 \times \text{Free Volume}}{\text{Time for High Purge}}$$

- If the detection device is placed directly within the Low Purge air flow
- If the detection device is drawing a sample into it

Where the detection device is placed directly within the Low purge flow, then the minimum is given as above, however if the detector is pulling a sample of gas from this air flow, then the Low purge must be greater than the Detector Sampling Rate, or we will likely further reduce our gas mixture as we will be pulling some air from the exhaust area (Figure 10-25):

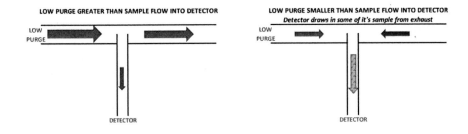

Figure 10-25

So our Minimum Purge flow is given by:

$$LP_{(min)} = \frac{2 \text{ x Free Volume}}{\text{Time for Low Purge}} \text{ or } \mathbf{1.2 \text{ x Detector Sample Flow}}$$

However, we have previously discovered, the detectors themselves actually detect the concentration of trace gas and not leakage rate, so we must be careful to ensure the amount of trace gas within the low purge airflow is sufficient to be able to detect. Now the concentration of our gas mix in ppm is given by:

$$\frac{\text{Leak Rate (x 1,000,000)}}{\text{Purge Flow}}$$

Now this concentration must be greater than the minimum concentration detectable by our sensing device (my recommendation is that the concentration of trace gas should be at least 3 x the minimum level detectable). So we can therefore adjust our formula to be:

$$\text{Minimum ppm Level Detectable} = \frac{3 \text{ x Leak Rate (x 1,000,000)}}{\text{Purge Flow}}$$

Rearranging we can calculate our maximum allowable Low Purge Rate as follows:

This means that if we calculate our LPmin and LPmax, and we find that the minimum low purge is greater than the maximum low purge, then we simply *cannot* use this method.

This method has clear advantages over other methods, as it is relatively low cost, with no requirement for complicated and high maintenance vacuum systems. Its main disadvantages are its limited sensitivity due to Purge flows diluting our sample, and of course it is a global method (meaning we might likely want a sniffer/search method to accompany this to locate the source of the leak.

$$LP(max) = \frac{3,000,000 \times Leak\ Rate}{Minimum\ ppm\ Level\ Detectable}$$

10.5.3 CBU (Concentration Build Up) Technique

When the sensitivity of the purge technique gives us a problem we can utilise an extended test method known as Concentration Build Up. This utilises a similar sealed chamber as for the purge method, however in this method, additional valves are added (Figure 10-26), so that the Low Purge flow is replaced by an additional concentration build up phase, during which no carrier gas flow passes through the chamber, allowing the concentration of gas to build up within the chamber, to a level that is more detectable.

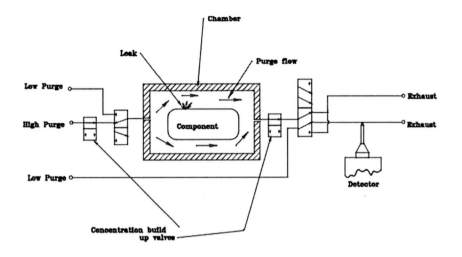

Figure 10-26

The sequence of events thus follows this set by step process:

1. Part is pressurised, and placed inside a sealed chamber.
2. A high flow of cleaning gas, known as the High Purge, is then used to clear any existing contaminants from the chamber around the component.
3. The concentration build up time starts, when there is no air flow through the chamber
a. This CBU time allows the concentration of trace gas to build up inside the chamber to a level that we can easily detect
4. This is followed by a low purge flow being passed through the chamber and carried to the detector
a. Where the concentration of the trace gas can be measured.
5. The High Purge is then reinstated to clear down the chamber, to enable the component to have the trace gas removed, allowing it to be removed from the chamber

Now at this point you may wonder how this is better as we again have our carrier gas carrying our sample to the detector, so how does this help?

What happens is that during the concentration build-up time, the level of trace gas builds up within the chamber. Then when the purge flow is introduced, the higher concentration is pushed through ahead of the carrier gas (Figure 10-27).

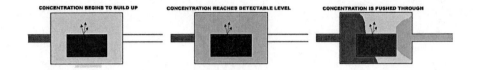

Figure 10-27

And so the tracer gas mixture to be detected acts very much like a slug of gas (Figure 10-28) being pushed through ahead of the carrier gas. The leak rate can be determined by the maximum response from the detector.

Figure 10-28

Of course, another way to reduce the risk of diluting the sample with the carrier gas, and ensure we actually detect the raised concentration levels of trace gas within the chamber (Figure 10-29) at the end of the concentration build up time, is to simply insert the detector into the chamber rather than use a carrier gas flow.

Figure 10-29

In this way the detector actually detects the full true gas concentration within the chamber.

One important factor to bear in mind with this option is that we must ensure the tracer gas mixture is up to the required level where we insert our detector.

We can see that when we use a carrier gas to push the mixture to the detector, the built-up concentration easily gets to the detector.

However, as we have seen in our sniffing mode examples, as the trace gas exits the leak it tends to build up a gas cloud around the leak (Figure 10-30), and may not necessarily reach the area where the detector is inserted/connected.

CONCENTRATION FORMS A CLOUD

Figure 10-30

So to help ensure our trace gas is at the right point, the use of mixing fans is commonly employed (Figure 10-31) to stir-up the gases within the chamber.

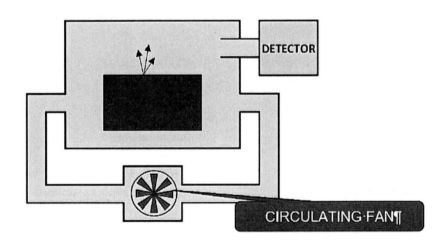

Figure 10-31

335

Clearly the drawback with this method is simply the time consumed waiting for the build- up of tracer to a detectable level. This Concentration Build Up Time is dependent on the free volume of the chamber, the detector sensitivity, and the leakage rate to be detected, and is given by:

$$\text{CBU Time} = \frac{\text{Free Volume x 3 x Minimun Detectable conc. (ppm)}}{\text{Leak Rate x 1,000,000}}$$

(Notice I am recommending that a minimum of 3 x minimum detectable ppm level that the detector can detect, to ensure good signal to noise ratio.)

However, once again this is a relatively low-cost method, but it can be quite slow when trying to detect very low levels of leakage. One of the big advantages of this and the purge technique is the fact that the chamber remains at or above atmospheric pressure. This ensures that any leaks in the chamber itself (although clearly these should be kept to a minimum/zero) do not affect our test, as we will see, can be a serious issue, with vacuum techniques.

This +ve pressure chamber ensures that any leakage will therefore be from inside to outside the chamber. (Remember our understanding of air movement always being from higher to lower pressures.)

This clearly reduces any external effects to zero.

10.5.4 Vacuum Leak Testing with Mass Spectrometer Detector

This method is really dedicated to the use a Helium Mass Spectrometers operating in a vacuum, other than in sniffing mode.

(Again, I am not going into the detail, as the suppliers of this type of equipment can give you far more support, but this is just an indication of how they are used).

The most important thing to know about the Helium Vacuum Mass Spectrometer detection device itself is that it can only operate in a vacuum (due to the susceptibility of the heated ionising element burning out in normal air), and as such we must ensure that the inlet to the sensor is at a vacuum (very low absolute pressure) typically less than 1 millibar absolute pressure (for precise details of this vacuum level please consult with the manufacturers/suppliers of Helium Vacuum Mass Spectrometers).

For this reason when built into leak test machines, to ensure the Mass Spectrometer is provided with the required vacuum a backing pump is included, which effectively serves to reduce the pressure at the inlet to the sensor at the required vacuum level. There are in fact two ways to use the Mass Spectrometer to detect leaks in a global format (identifying if there is/is not a leak).

1. Direct vacuum test
2. Vacuum chamber test

10.5.4.1 Direct Vacuum Testing (Figure 10-32)

With this we connect the detector and Backing Pump directly to the part, and surround the part with Helium Gas (usually within a confined chamber surrounding the part).

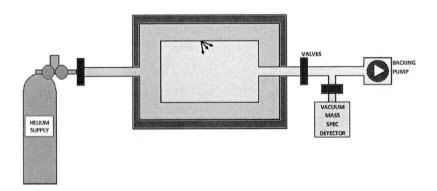

Figure 10-32

In this technique, the part itself is pulled down to the required vacuum, and then helium is used to pressurise the chamber around the part, such that any leak path will allow the helium to enter the part, and be swept off to the helium detector.

Whilst this seems very straightforward and very simple and ensures external background contamination gases cannot affect our test, it suffers from one main drawback in that it is unlikely (?) to MIMIC the normal operation of the part, particularly in the majority of cases, we are leak testing to try and detect leakage

337

out of the part. (Of course, there are exceptions, where the part is normally operated under vacuum, and we are looking for gas ingress into the part.) If you recall I specifically stated that it is ideal to test the component under normal operating conditions as much as possible.

One place where I personally developed a solution for one customer using this technique was in the testing of automotive radiators. This may be confusing for you as Radiators are generally operating at above atmospheric pressure (typically around 1 Bar). However one manufacturer had seen issues at their customer (the vehicle manufacturer) in that they had experience massive leaks of coolant when filling the vehicle with coolant.

On investigation it was discovered that in order to rapidly fill the vehicle with coolant they would create a vacuum in the coolant system using a large vacuum reservoir, and then would allow coolant to be sucked into the system by the vacuum. We then discovered that this was causing some of the tank to header gaskets to be ripped from its position (Figure 10-33), creating a large leak path to form between the core and the header tank.

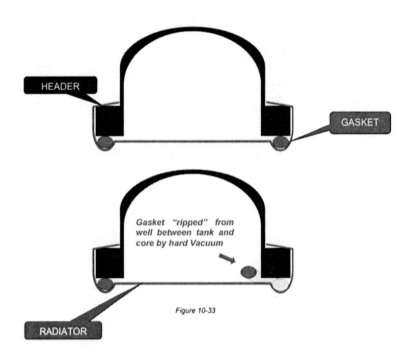

Figure 10-33

Because of this we needed to develop a solution to enable these at risk gaskets could be detected, and so it was decided to introduce a vacuum test.

Clearly we could have completed a simple Vacuum decay test using a pressure measuring device, however due to the increased time that would be incurred, it was agreed that we could make a faster test by using a Helium Mass Spectrometer.

And so we developed a system whereby the initial test on the radiator would be a vacuum test, searching for helium leakage into the radiator. The helium trace gas however was free (no cost) as we made use of the fact that the air around us (normal atmosphere already contained 4 parts of Helium in every million parts of air, so we used this as our trace gas (*more on gas mixtures shortly*).

Here is an extract from the manual for this test system to explain the operation:

- *The component under test is subjected to three tests, a dimensional check, a vacuum test using the Helium Mass-Spectrometer and a pressure test using the pressure decay leak detector.*
- *During the vacuum test, the Mass-Spectrometer detects the helium content of any air leaking into the component and, during the pressure test, the pressure test instrument measures any drop in the pre-set pressure level due to leakage.*
- *Pre-set values used during the vacuum and leak tests depend on the type of component being tested, which is determined by a sensor that measures the thickness of the radiator core.*
- *On completion of a successful test, a Pass label is printed.*
- *The component is rejected if it fails any of the pneumatic or assembly tests, and a fail label is printed.*

10.5.4.2 Vacuum Chamber Testing (Figure 10-34)

This method however solves this problem, as the roles are reversed, with the chamber being connected to the vacuum system, and the part containing the helium trace gas.

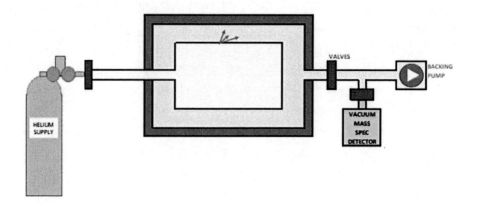

Figure 10-34

In this we can more accurately MIMIC our normal operation by ensuring the correct pressure difference across the potential leak path. Be careful. If our component is normally used in an atmospheric environment (as most components do) our test pressure would be the operating pressure (for example an automatic cooling system component would normally operate at just over 1 Bar gauge Pressure in a normal atmosphere (0 Bar gauge pressure)—which is a 1 Bar differential across the leak path).

In this system our operating environment is a near perfect vacuum, so our environment is at -1 Bar Gauge Pressure (0 Bar Absolute), so we should also subtract 1 Bar from our test pressure, meaning that the pressure of Helium inside our part will be virtually atmospheric pressure to create our 1 Bar differential.

In order to achieve this it is quite often that we might actually evacuate (vacuum) our part initially, and then allow helium in at a very low supply pressure to fill the component under test.

As we have discussed with these methods, we need an additional backing pump to ensure our pressure/vacuum at the inlet to the detector is at the correct level for the system to function/operate correctly.

However Backing Pumps only have limited abilities (due to their pumping speeds—typically up to around 250m3 per hour), and as such if the chamber is very large it may take a very long time to pull the required vacuum. In such cases a further roughing pump is added (which have pumping speeds of up to 15,000 m3 per hour) to the system to gulp as much air out of the chamber (part), as quickly as possible.

I do not intend at this point to bore you with long complicated equations, but the time "t" to evacuate a chamber of volume "V" at a pumping speed of "S", can be calculated using a simple formula:

$$t = \frac{V}{S} \times ln(\frac{P_0}{P_1})$$

- *P0 is the starting Pressure (usually atmospheric Pressure = 1013mB)*
- *P1 is the final Pressure required (for example 1millibar)*

Note: Notice that when we are talking about vacuum systems we always refer to pressures in terms of absolute values (i.e., a perfect vacuum is 0 and normal atmosphere is around 1013millibar).

Whilst this formula gives us a rough guide, it does not take into account a number of additional factors that affect the pumping speed such as:

- *Conductance = the effect of the diameter and length of the connecting pipes between the pump and the vacuum chamber, which will affect the pumping speed capabilities of the pump*
- *Gas Temperature = if we remove the air very quickly, the air remaining will cool (remember P/T = Constant?), which will affect the pumping speed*
- *Degassing = this is one of the biggest issues for high vacuum systems in that liquids, and solids can absorb gas at their surface. When we pull a hard vacuum, these gases begin to release and so will also need to be pumped away. (More on this in the issues affecting tracer gas section of this book.)*

Please seek advice from vacuum system experts when you develop your vacuum leak test solutions.

10.5.4.3 Helium Spray Technique (Figure 10-35)

So far we have looked at the use of vacuum systems in a global testing way, but there is a further option for vacuum systems that is regularly employed to pinpoint the actual leak location. This is known as Helium Spray Technique. This method is used a lot with large assemblies, where chamber testing becomes impractical to use.

This is very similar to the direct vacuum testing method in that we vacuum the component under test and connect this to the detection system, so that we can detect any helium entering the part. However in this case, we do not surround the part with the trace gas, but in fact spray our trace gas at the component from a very basic nozzle arrangement capable of controlling the amount of gas we spray.

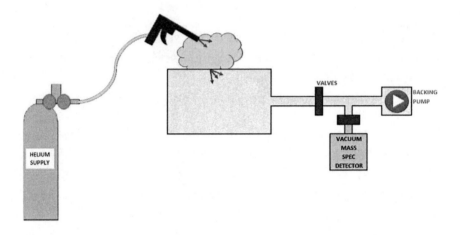

Figure 10-35

The detector will respond only when it detects helium, and as such only when the trace gas being sprayed is directly over the leak path itself.

Of course, it does mean that we are not always correctly applying the pressure in the correct direction, but in some cases this may be the best solution, particularly when surrounding conditions can contain background contamination whilst we are trying to pinpoint the leak path.

11. Considerations for Trace Gas Testing

When considering tracer gas testing there are a number of aspects that should be understood, as they are all very important to the choice of detector, the trace gas, and of course, the method/technique to be used.

11.1 Gas Mixtures

So for in this manual, we have talked about the trace gas, and just considered the trace gas passing through the leak path, and being detected. However unless the specific gas we want to detect is already inside the part (for example refrigerant gases in a refrigerator, or propellants in an aerosol can), the trace gas is an additional item we require to make our leak test (and quite likely we will lose the gas we use for each test, and have to use a new lot for the next test— hence it is considered an additional running cost for our leak test.

Trace gases can be very costly, and even simple gases such as helium are ever increasing in cost. But is there any way in which we can reduce this on-cost?

Using a gas mixture can easily reduce the cost of gases. At the time of writing this book I looked up the costs of different gas mixtures, and discovered that at one supplier, a 10 litre cylinder of virtually 100% Helium cost in excess of £200, whilst the same size cylinder containing 10% Helium and 90% Nitrogen (known as the balance gas), was less than ¼ of the price (less than £50).

But what does using a gas mixture mean to our leak test?

As we have previously discovered all gas sensors have different sensitivities to gases other than air, and where the detectors are specific (only detect the trace gas itself), so it stands to reason that if we are using a mixture of gases, then we are only going to be able to detect the gas for which our sensing device was designed.

343

So if we are using a 10% mixture (trace gas to balance gas) then out of all of the gas passing through our leak, then only 10% of it will be the actual trace gas (the rest will be the balance gas)

Because we can only detect the trace gas (and are unable to detect the balance gas), we will in fact only detect 10% of all of the gas coming out of the leak.

> *At this point I have to make one assumption, that gas mixtures are homogeneously mixed as they pass through the leakage path – by which I mean that if we take a sample of the gas from anywhere, it contains the same concentration of the trace gas within the balance gas.*

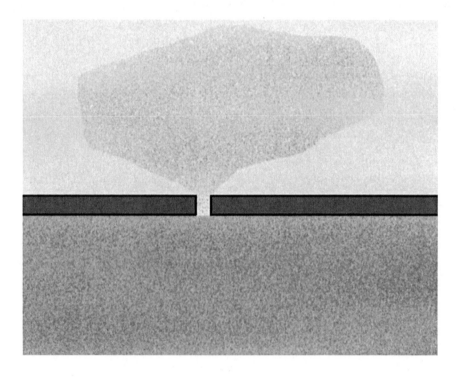

Figure 11-1

The table below (Table 11-1) gives examples of the effect of different mixtures on the leakage rate we are detecting:

TABLE SHOWS ACTUAL LEAK RATE = TOTAL LEAK (cc/min)						
LEAK RATE MEASURED (cc/min)		**GAS MIXTURE**				
		100%	10%	1%	0.1%	Helium in air (4ppm)
1.E-01	0.1	0.1	1	10	100	25000
1.E-02	0.01	0.01	0.1	1	10	2500
1.E-03	0.001	0.001	0.01	0.1	1	250
1.E-04	0.0001	0.0001	0.001	0.01	0.1	25
1.E-05	0.00001	0.00001	0.0001	0.001	0.01	2.5
1.E-06	0.000001	0.000001	0.00001	0.0001	0.001	0.25

Table 11-1

The one I have highlighted is the detection level we used in our radiator test in the previous section.

This is particularly important when using Hydrogen detectors, as high concentrations of Hydrogen can be very dangerous, so safe mixtures (5% Hydrogen in Nitrogen) of Hydrogen are readily available from gas suppliers to ensure safe leak detection can be performed.

Most of the mixtures mentioned in this table are readily available from good gas suppliers (or freely available in the air as per my own experience for radiator) however it is possible to make your own mixture should you wish to (after all 10% costs are not 10% of the price of 100% of the trace gas).

Mixing can be achieved in two ways:

- By Volume
- By Pressure

11.1.1.1.1   Mixing by Volume

To do this we need to understand/calculate how much volume of each gas is introduced into the system. For this we must remember the Universal Gas Law:

$$PV = nRT$$

Now we know that "n" and "R" are constants, and if we assume that the temperature of the gases is the same, then the amount of gas is governed by its pressure and it's volume.

So if we have two chambers of different gases (Gas A and Gas B) both 1 litre in size. If both are pressurised to 1 Bar above Atmospheric pressure we do in fact have 2 Litres of each gas contained within their respective 1 litre volumes. If we now join these together we will therefore have 4 litres of gas in total, 2 litres of Gas A, and 2 Litres of Gas B, this would therefore be a 50% mix of the two gases.

So in order to Mix by volume, we need to work out the pressure/volume of each gas at atmospheric pressure. This table (Table 11-2) shows an example where we have a 1 litre volume of each gas but one gas (air) is at 4 Bar Gauge Pressure with the trace gas only at 1 Bar Gauge Pressure. We can see that mixing these gases gives us a 25% mixture in a 2 litre Volume.

Note the nett Pressure of these two combined volumes will actually be an average of the pressures introduced.

	Volume cc	Pressure mB	Atmospheric Volume	Concentration
Air	1000	5000	6000000	75%
Gas 2	1000	1000	2000000	25%
Mixture	2000	3000	8000000	

Table 11-2

11.1.1.1.2   Mixing by Pressures

Mixing by Pressures, we still need to calculate the Pressure Volume, however in this case our total Volume remains fixed. So we have a fixed volume of gas at one pressure, and then we Add more pressure from a second gas source, into this fixed volume so our total volume remains the same, but we now have a total higher pressure.

Putting this into a simple table (Table 11-3) we can see that mixing by Pressure gives a different concentration of the Trace Gas in the Carrier Air. *(Due to the fact that we are raising the pressure in a fixed volume using the 2nd gas.)*

	Volume cc	Pressure mB	Atmospheric Volume	Concentration
Air	1000	5000	6000000	86%
Gas 2	1000	1000	1000000	14%
Totals	1000	6000	7000000	

Table 11-3

It is strongly recommended to use readily available pre-mixed gases, wherever possible, as mixing your own can be problematic as we will see in the chapter on Limitations for Trace Gas Testing, so my advice is to always seek advice if you are in any doubt.

11.2 Mixing of Gases

As we have seen we can create our own gas mixtures by some simple method, however, our leak test, and the leakage of the tracer gas mix exiting the leakage path, do depend on the fact that trace gas mixtures are homogeneously (thoroughly and evenly) mixed.

Simply mixing by adding a known pressure of the trace gas into our component (which already contains air) does not mean that we will have trace gas coming out of our leak, as the diagram (Figure 11-2) below demonstrates.

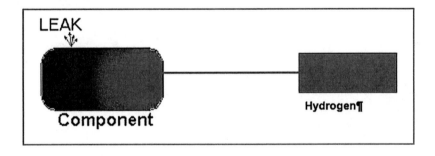

Figure 11-2

As we can see if we simply pressurise the ambient air inside the part we may well simply push the air to the end farthest from the trace gas supply entry, and thus we would not be able to detect this leak, as only Air is passing through the leak path. In reality there will be some mixing that occurs, this method invariably does not give us the correct homogeneous mixture (concentration of trace gas at the leakage path).

There are of course a number of ways around this problem, such as pressurising the component from multiple points with the trace gas, or by introducing mixing fans into our part to stir up the gases and more effectively mix them, however none of these are easy, or practical, so we need to consider other options.

The simplest way to ensure a homogeneous mix is to remove any gas already present in our part (by use of a vacuum system), and then to fill it up (pressurise the part to the required test pressure) using a ready-mixed supply, as in Figure 11-3.

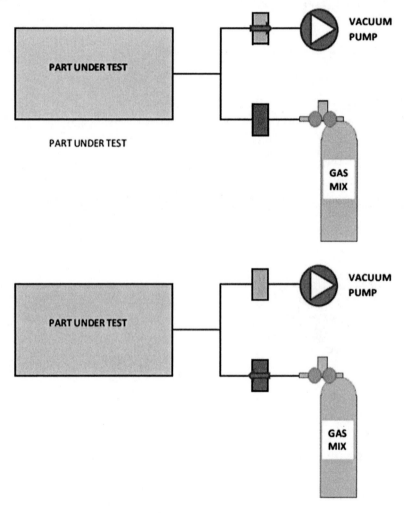

Figure 11-3

Another technique I have employed is to pressurise the part under test with the balance gas (usually air) through a smaller volume containing the trace gas as in Figure 11-4.

Prior to pressurising, both the volume and the part are both evacuated (so as to reduce the risk of pushing the atmospheric air inside the part to one end. Then the small volume is pressurised to a level to control the gas mixture. Once this is pressurised, the balance air is passed through this volume into the part.

In this way, as the air (balance gas) passes through the smaller volume, it collects and mixes with the tracer gas in the volume, carrying this mixture into the part under test as a homogeneous mixture.

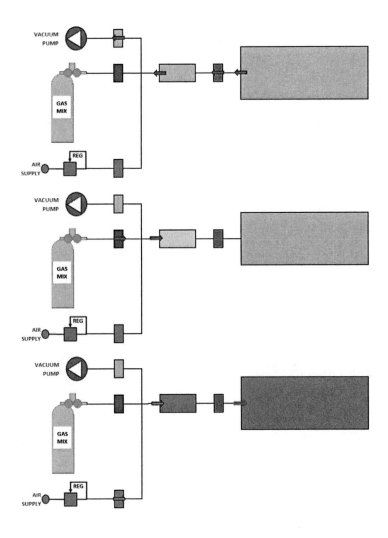

Figure 11-4

349

The concentration of the mixture will depend on the pressures applied and the volume of both the part and the small volume.

$$\text{Concentration} = \frac{\text{PV of Trace Gas}}{\text{PV of All} + \text{PV of Trace Gas}}$$

Where: PV of Trace = Trace Gas Absolute Pressure x Small Volume

PV of All= Balance Pressure x (Part Volume + Small Volume)

(Note Balance Pressure is Absolute pressure of air – Absolute pressure of Trace Gas)

11.3 Detector Contamination – Gross Leak Protection

One of the biggest issues for the majority of trace gas detectors is that they can easily be contaminated, or cease to function of large amounts (caused by large leaks) of the tracer gas enters the detector cell, so we need to protect the detector to a certain degree.

Many detectors available on the market do have a search mode of operation, when used to carry out direct sniffing detection. What this means is that they have a larger flow down the probe in this mode (Figure 11-5), reducing the amount/concentration of trace gas that reaches to detector cell.

$$\text{Concentration} = \frac{\text{Leakrate Gas Flow}}{\text{Total Flow thriugh Probe}}$$

This can give some level of protection for the detector, however it is limited.

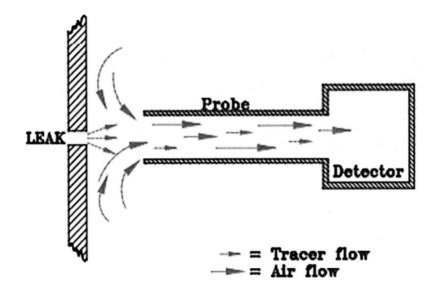

Figure 11-5

Once the search has shown no large leaks, the flow through the probe is reduced, so as to more easily detect the small leaks.

But it is far wiser to carry out some form of gross leak test before employing any form of trace gas detection, so as to reduce the risk of making the detector unusable for a period of time whilst it is able to recover.

This can be completed in a number of ways, depending on the technique being employed. Let us look at these in a little more detail.

11.3.1 Sniffing Gross Leak Tests

Generally used prior to a sniffing leak test. Can also be used in purge and CBU testing.

11.3.1.1 Air Gross Leak Test (Figure 11-6)

The simplest solution is to carry out some form of air test before the detector is introduced to the leak.

Most often this takes the form of a pressure decay leak test, where the part is initially pressurised with air and a simple pressure decay test is completed, with our alarm level set to the minimum detectable level (depending on part volume and time available).

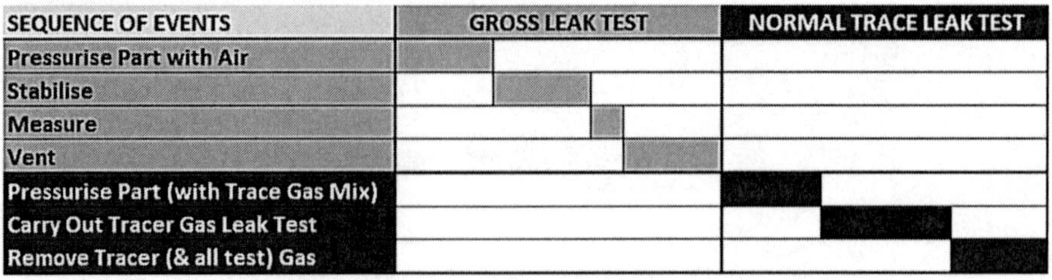

SEQUENCE OF EVENTS	GROSS LEAK TEST		NORMAL TRACE LEAK TEST
Pressurise Part with Air			
Stabilise			
Measure			
Vent			
Pressurise Part (with Trace Gas Mix)			
Carry Out Tracer Gas Leak Test			
Remove Tracer (& all test) Gas			

Figure 11-6

This has one big advantage, in that we do not waste expensive trace gases by allowing them to escape through very large leak paths, however it suffers from one major problem in that it adds a complete test cycle to the overall test (and can often double our total testing times).

If you are not so confident in you processes, and are suspect that you could have very large leaks that may cause contamination problems with your detector, this is still the best solution (as long as time is not an issue).

11.3.1.2 Trace Gas Gross Test (Figure 11-7)

So if we are relatively confident that any leaks we may have are not so great that we would lose a large amount of trace gas, then we could reduce this time delay, by using a pressure decay test, but in this case using the trace gas in place of the air.

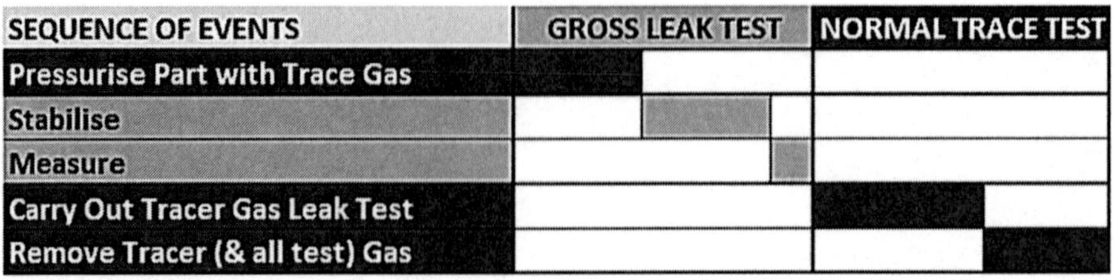

SEQUENCE OF EVENTS	GROSS LEAK TEST		NORMAL TRACE TEST
Pressurise Part with Trace Gas			
Stabilise			
Measure			
Carry Out Tracer Gas Leak Test			
Remove Tracer (& all test) Gas			

Figure 11-7

This dramatically reduces the Cycle time (only really adding the stabilisation and measuring times to our normal trace gas leak test cycle) to something more realistic. However the biggest drawback with this method is that it will allow a large leak of the trace gas, and as such:

- Is a potential waste of expensive trace gas
- Can cause large amounts of background contamination from the trace gas

11.3.2 Spray Test Gross Leak Tests

The above methods are fine when we are looking at simply pressurising the part with trace gas, however as we have seen with some techniques, we are often required to evacuate our part or our chamber prior to leak testing. and we can utilise this Vacuum Phase to complete a gross leak test.

11.3.2.1 Vacuum Part Gross Test (Figure 11-8)

When carrying out a spray leak test, we have to pull a vacuum on the part, so once we have this vacuum, we can perform a pressure decay test (or in fact look for a **pressure rise** using a pressure decay measurement).

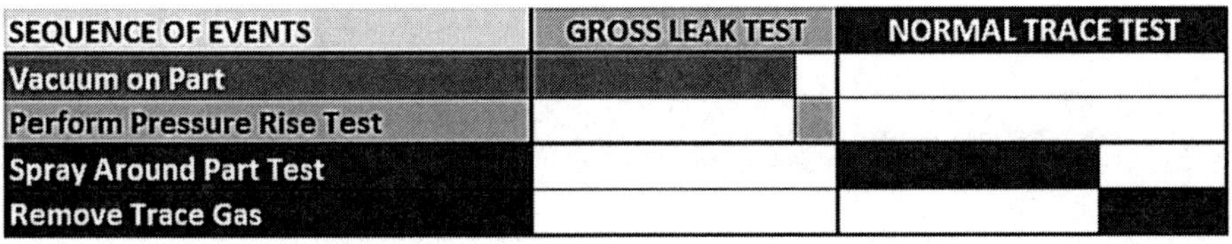

SEQUENCE OF EVENTS	GROSS LEAK TEST	NORMAL TRACE TEST
Vacuum on Part		
Perform Pressure Rise Test		
Spray Around Part Test		
Remove Trace Gas		

Figure 11-8

Any rise in the pressure (vacuum) within the part indicates a gross leak, and as such we can halt the test avoiding unnecessary loss of valuable trace gas.

11.3.3 Vacuum Chamber Gross Leak Tests

When our part is to be tested in a vacuum chamber, there are of course further options, based on those already mentioned above.

11.3.3.1 Pressure Decay Test on Part

In this method, we carry out our gross leak test by measuring/detecting a pressure decay in the part at the time the vacuum chamber is evacuated. The normal sequence of events (Figure 11-9) in a simple vacuum chamber method is likely to be:

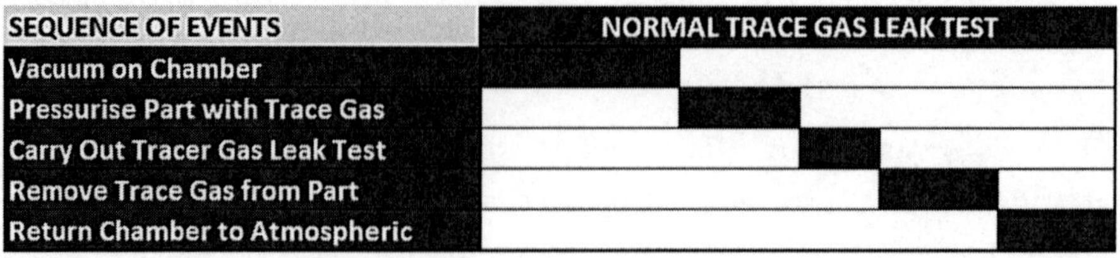

SEQUENCE OF EVENTS	NORMAL TRACE GAS LEAK TEST
Vacuum on Chamber	
Pressurise Part with Trace Gas	
Carry Out Tracer Gas Leak Test	
Remove Trace Gas from Part	
Return Chamber to Atmospheric	

Figure 11-9

However, at the end of our first phase (evacuating the chamber), we could do a short pressure decay test on the part itself (Figure 11-10) as we now have a pressure difference between the part, and its surroundings (approximately 1 Bar), where a leak of the normal atmospheric pressure could leak into the vacuum chamber, so this would be an ideal opportunity to perform out gross leak test.

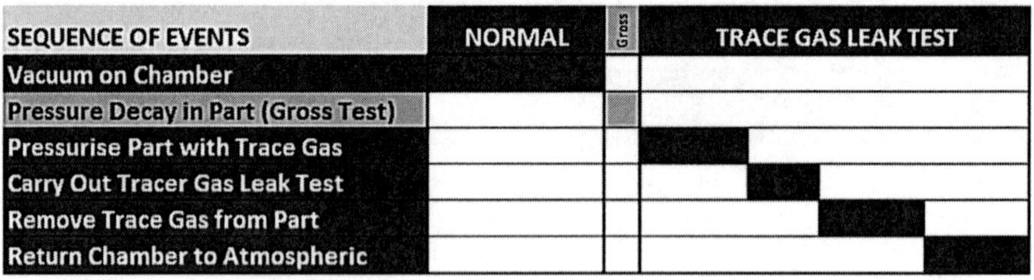

SEQUENCE OF EVENTS	NORMAL	Gross	TRACE GAS LEAK TEST
Vacuum on Chamber			
Pressure Decay in Part (Gross Test)			
Pressurise Part with Trace Gas			
Carry Out Tracer Gas Leak Test			
Remove Trace Gas from Part			
Return Chamber to Atmospheric			

Figure 11-10

This adds a very minimal amount of time to our test sequence.

Let me just show this again, but in a pictorial format (Figure 11-11) which may help to make it clearer. In this, you will notice that I have also included pulling a vacuum on the part as well. This is purely done when using a pre-mixed trace gas supply to avoid the mixing issues previously mentioned.

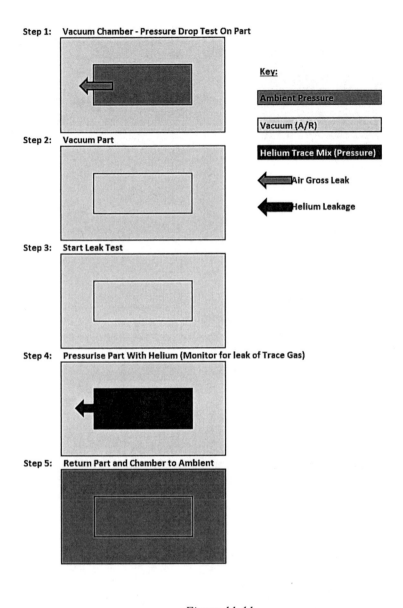

Figure 11-11

11.3.3.2 Vacuum Rise Test on Part

In some chambers where our we need to evacuate the part as well to ensure that our part contains the correct gas mix from a pre-mixed trace gas supply, our sequence (Figure 11-12) is adapted:

SEQUENCE OF EVENTS	NORMAL	Gross	TRACE GAS LEAK TEST			
Vacuum on Part	■					
Pressure Decay in Part (Gross Test)		■				
Vacuum on Chamber			■			
Pressurise Part with Trace Gas				■		
Carry Out Tracer Gas Leak Test					■	
Remove Trace Gas from Part						■
Return Chamber to Atmospheric						■

Figure 11-12

In this case we carry out our gross leak test by looking for a pressure rise in the Part (or alternatively a pressure decay in the chamber), once the part has been evacuated. Again (Figure 11-13) in pictorial form:

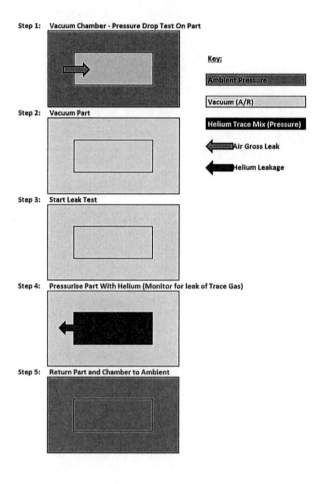

Figure 11-13

356

11.4 Transmission Time

In our tracer gas leak testing, we have rightly understood that these detectors, and methods are much more sensitive than simple air testing methods, however one consideration we have so far overlooked is that of Transmission Time, which is the time it takes for the trace gas to travel through our leak path in order to be detected.

This is a key consideration when deciding on your leak test cycle time.

Let me explain this Transmission time with the help of an example with a diagram (Figure 11-14) and associated calculations:

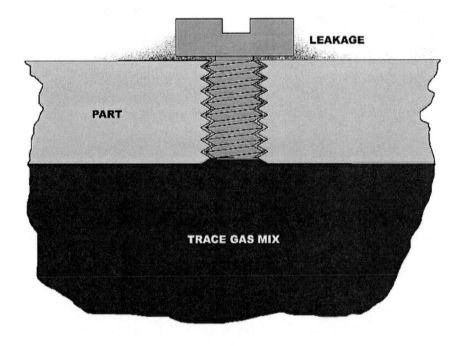

Figure 11-14

Take the simple example of a bolt mounted in the part we are testing. This bolt is not secured/tightened properly, and this means that there is a small pathway up through the threads of the bolt.

We can calculate the length of this path by the circumference of the bolt thread, and the number of threads between the trace gas area, and the outside

For example the average diameter of an M8 bolt is 8mm (Table 11-4), so the circumference is given by:

Circumference = $2 \pi r2$ = = $2 \pi (0.4)2$ cm = 1cm (approximately)

Thread Dia	Pitch (mm)	k (mm)	L (mm)	d (mm)	s (mm)
M8	1. 25	5. 5	100	8	13

Table 11-4

Now if we have 8 threads, then the length of the small gap through which the gas will pass is 8cm. If we estimate the gap between the threads as being around 0.2mm by 0.2mm, then the total volume through which the gas must travel is 0.02 x 0.02 x 8, which is only 0.0004 cubic centimetres.

This does not seem very much, however if the leakage rate through this passage is only 0.00001cm3 sec-1 (1 x 10-5 cc/s) then we can calculate how long it will take for the gas to travel from the inside to the outside, by dividing the volume of the path by the leakage rate:

$$\textbf{TRANSMISSION TIME} = \frac{0.0004}{0.00001} \quad \textbf{40 seconds}$$

As you can see with this very simple example, the transmission time can become a major contributor to deciding leak test cycle times. (this can be very important when considering porosity in castings where the porous chains can be quite long.

11.5 Sealed Component Testing

Until now, we have considered simply pressurising our part to be tested with the trace gas to be detected, which is all very well, but what about our Sealed Components (again I will use the ping-pong ball as our example), where we have no direct connection through which we can insert the trace gas.

How can we pressurise such parts with the trace gas to detect our very small leaks?

The common technique for achieving this is to use a method called bombing, by which we mean that we will prefill the part in advance of the test to be completed, by back-filling it with the trace gas.

The way this is achieved is quite simple, in that we place our component (ideally as many of them at one time as possible) inside a pressure chamber. We than pressurise the chamber with the trace gas and leave it for a period of time.

Any individual part with a leakage path will then allow the trace gas inside (Figure 11-15), until, once sufficient time has been allowed, the part will then effectively contain the trace gas we are trying to detect.

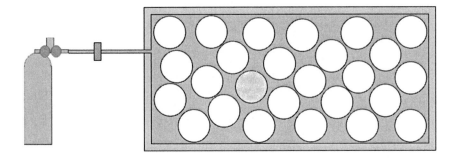

Figure 11-15

The parts can then be removed from the chamber, and then individually tested for signs of the gas re-escaping. Of course, there are a number of factors that must be considered when carrying out bombing, as follows.

11.5.1.1.1   Bombing Time

This must be sufficiently long enough to allow sufficient amounts of the trace gas to enter the component. If we are looking for a small leak for example 1×10^{-5}cc/sec (at 1 Bar differential), then our time must be sufficient to allow the required amount of gas to get through a leak path of this size (this can be a considerable amount of time (for example to get 1cc of the gas through our 1×10^{-5} cc/sec leak path will take nearly 28 hours ($1 \times 10^{+5}$ seconds). In many cases, bombing is carried out for many hours in advance of the leak test, with chambers that can take a large number of components, to make this cost-effective.

11.5.1.1.2   Bombing Pressures

OF course if we were to bomb at 10 times the pressure then the gas will effectively travel through the leakage path at 10 times the speed/rate, so our Bombing time will effectively be reduced by this factor (in our example down to less than 3 hours).

11.5.1.1.3   Trace Gas Concentration

If our sealed part is manufactured at atmospheric pressure, then the pressure inside the part will naturally be at atmospheric pressure, and most likely this will not be the trace gas we are trying to detect. So, it doesn't matter how long we bomb for, we can never achieve 100% trace gas inside the part. In fact our mix will be governed by the ratio of the bombing pressure to the natural pressure inside our sealed component.

Assuming our part contains normal air in its manufactured state, at normal atmospheric pressure (1 Bar Absolute), then we can calculate the maximum concentration that can be achieved as per the following Table 11-5:

Bombing Pressure (Gauge Pressure)	Max Concentration Achievable
1 Bar	50%
2 Bar	66%
5 Bar	83%
10 Bar	90%
20 Bar	95%

Table 11-5

So our detection limit should be adjusted by the same factor. (My advice is to seek support if considering bombing of sealed components.)

11.6 Trace Gas Costs – Recovery?

Early on in this chapter, we highlighted that trace gases can be expensive, and we are likely to throw away the gas used for a leak test once we have completed our test. Not only can this be expensive, but also bear in mind the trace gas we remove from the part should be taken away from the area under test, or we may begin to suffer from high levels of the trac gas in our test area, reducing our signal to noise etc.

However, if this cost is too expensive, we might consider recovering the trace gas from our part once the test is completed, so that we can use it again. This is very possible, and there are suppliers of reclaim systems, however be warned, such equipment is also quite costly, and they are only really capable of reclaiming 90% of the trace gas used in our test, so do calculate the costs of both options (throwing the gas away, or reclaiming it) to understand the best option for you.

11.7 Helium Testing

Whenever I am discussing leak testing and particularly trace gas leak testing, people often jump to the phrase Helium Testing without defining what they mean. So I put together a simple chart (Figure 11-16) that I show to people when they say this to make it clear that there are in fact many different forms of helium testing as we have previously discussed.

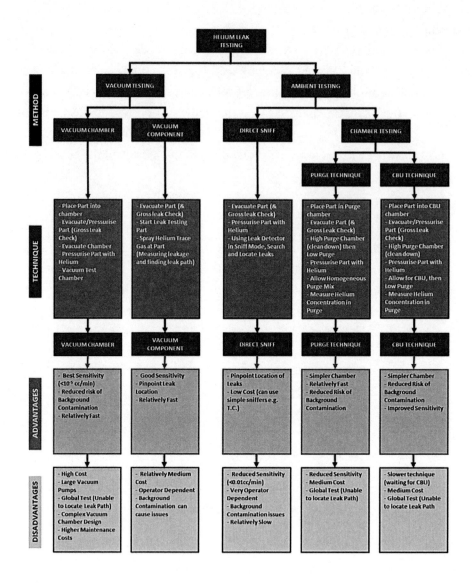

Figure 11-16

Finally, before I leave trace gas leak testing, just a word about the various detectors available and how else they may be employed.

11.8 Atmosphere Monitoring

Clearly many of the detectors mentioned are capable of detecting gases that may be harmful to health, and as such they are often employed in buildings where there may be a potential build-up of a harmful gas, due to the natural processes, or due to unforeseen escape of the gas.

And so I myself became involved in working on a variety of Atmosphere Monitors, used to sample the area in which people lived and/or worked. These ranged from using Infra-Red Detectors to check for the build-up of Carbon Dioxide (CO_2) at an airport (where they utilised the CO_2 to chill the food being taken onto and served on aeroplanes), to detection of refrigerant gases (R12) that was being used to bulk-up cigarette tobacco in a cigarette factory.

The detector in this case is constantly sampling the air, and the instrumentation will alarm if the level of the trace gas it is detecting approaches unsafe levels, alerting the occupants to leave/evacuate the area allowing the emergency services access to resolve the root cause of the issue.

In many cases these detectors are simply sampling in the area, but there are cases where you may want to sample multiple points. Whilst you could install a separate detector at each point of concern, this may become expensive, and so multipoint sampling was developed to enable 1 detector to look at each point in turn.

In these cases the detector would actually sample a much larger air flow that was being drawn from each area in sequence (Figure 11-17), by changeover valves that would divert the flow from each area to/past the detector, which would constantly monitor the flow for levels of the trace gas to be detected.

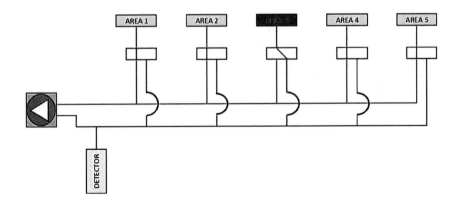

Figure 11-17

In the example above, Area 3 is being sampled by the detector, whilst the samples from other areas remain being sampled by the large pump. This ensures that the detector has the latest/up to date sample from each area as it is selected.

11.9 Detector Specificity – for Detection of Other Things...

Many of these detectors are used in Gas Chromatography, which was developed many years before leak testing, as a way of separating a sample of a fluid etc. out into its constituent parts. This method is still in use today in many laboratories to look at samples of blood, or other biological samples, to determine its make-up.

The way gas chromatography works (Figure 11-18), is that the fluid sample is injected into a tube (known as a column), which is packed full of a substance designed to separate out the various parts of the fluid. This tube is placed in an oven whose temperature can be varied through the process. An inert carrier gas is then used to push the sample through the column onto the detector.

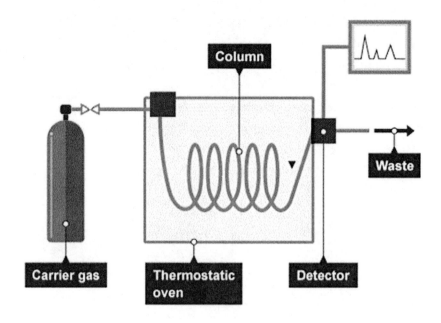

Figure 11-18

The signal from the detector will then trace a graphical representation of the sample, as it's different components are separated (Figure 11-19)

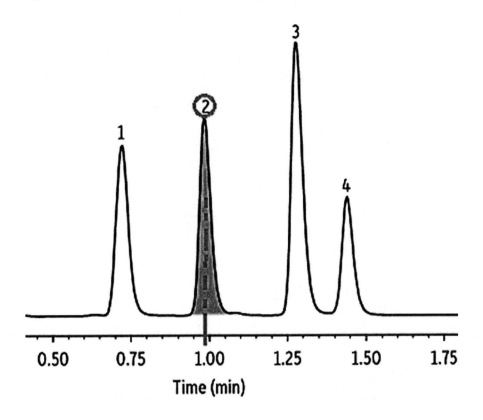

Figure 11-19

The different substances within the sample can be identified by reviewing at what time they are detected, and the amount of each substance can be determined by the area under the peak of that substance.

Whilst the following appears to have nothing to do with leak detection, this separation using heated columns was further utilised at one company I worked for where it was employed as a method to make one particular detector (in fact it was an electron capture detector) gas specific.

In fact the gas we were specifically looking for was the vapours that emanate from explosives, so we used a special dual-column/dual detector principal (Figure 11-20) to separate the explosive vapours from the other gases by the following method.

In fact our special device contained two matched detectors (by matched I mean that we calibrated the detector cells manufactured, so that the two detector cells to be used would have virtually identical response characteristics).

One detection cell was hooked up to one specially packed column which would slow the passage of explosive vapours only, whilst the 2nd column was attached to a null column, that did not slow the travel of the explosives vapours. These columns were heated to a specific level to aid the separation process.

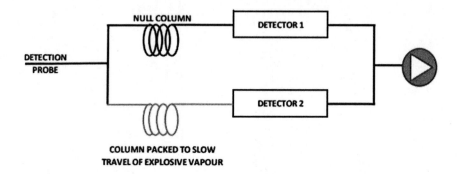

Figure 11-20

The result was that when a non-explosive sample was draw through the two cells (by a common pump), there was no difference in the signals from the two detectors, however when an explosive sample was drawn through Detector 2's response was delayed, and the difference between the two responses alerted that an explosive was present (Figure 11-21).

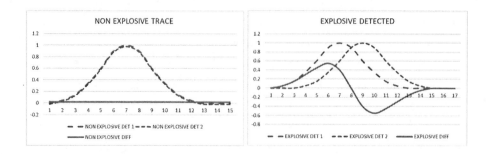

Figure 11-21

12. Calibration of Trace Gas Detectors

Let us now take a brief look at the calibration of trace gas leak testers, which is not too different from pressure decay, but worth going through and identifying the key items for your consideration.

Before we go into detail, I will again say that it is not always possible to calibrate the detector, although some instruments do offer an adjustment to allow you to make the device read correctly. This is often a simple adjustment that converts what the detector measures to the value required, in a similar way to the volume factor in air testing systems, it simply multiplies what is detected by a value/factor to make it read correctly.

We will again focus on calibration checks, where we can monitor the sensitivity of the detector periodically, in order to make adjustments, or complete maintenance to ensure correct performance of our equipment.

12.1 Calibration Equipment

Once again we should consider what items that the trace gas detectors are responding to, or control. In reality, the trace gas detectors themselves do not control any aspect of our leak test (such as the test pressure), but only really measure the amount of trace gas leaking from the part.

So for trace gas leak testing, the key requirement for calibration is to have a known amount of leakage, against which we can test the detector's response. So for trace gas detection, the main piece of calibration equipment required is a known leakage rate of the trace gas we are trying to detect.

However, depending on whether we are using our leak tester in sniffing mode, or as part of a more complex system (such as purge technique, CBU etc.), our known leakage may take different forms.

12.1.1 Known Leakage Rate (For Direct Detection – Sniffing Mode)

When we wish to read our leakage rate directly on our detector, by sniffing the leakage from the part, we ideally need to mimic a part leaking at the required amount.

So for this we would normally employ a fixed calibrate Master Leak, attached directly to a separate gas supply. This normally take the format of a trace gas container (usually a bottle of gas) which is pressure regulated behind one of the fixed Calibrated Master Leaks previously described in the air testing section.

These take a number of forms, with some being simple open pressurised gas containers (Figure 12-3), whilst in some instances they are contained within metal boxes as below (Figure 12-1) to protect the gas cylinder and pressure regulator control.

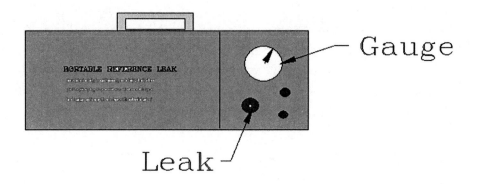

Figure 12-1

As previously described, the actual leak part (Figure 12-2) is manufactured (using sintered discs or laser drilled holes), to allow a specific amount of gas to pass through at a pre-determined pressure applied to the leak.

Figure 12-2

This diagram shows a more informal version with the key component parts indicated.

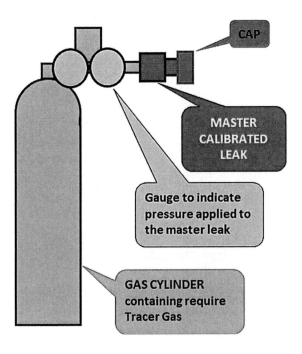

Figure 12-3

As always for more advice on such devices, speak to your supplier of leak test equipment who can give you more accurate details.

12.1.2 Internal Calibration Systems

In many modern leak test instruments, these master leaks are built-in to the instruments, and the instruments themselves have special software programs to complete the calibration check.

But be warned these internal calibrated leaks are simply as described for sniffer leak test calibration, and will require refilling with gas from time to time. More about these special calibration programs in the next section on how to carry out a calibration check.

12.1.3 Known Leakage Rate (Complex Machines)

Obviously with the more complex systems, the trace gas is already present within the machine controls, so in such systems, all that is required is a known master leak (usually in the format described above), that can be introduced periodically to complete a check on the accuracy of the measurement.

These master leaks can be introduced in a number of ways :

- Fixed to a master part
- Introduced into air stream to detector
- As part of a special calibration circuit within the system

The choice is very dependent on the particular leak test being performed, and the frequency of calibration checks required.

12.1.3.1 Fixed onto a Master Part (Figure 12-4)

This is my preferred option, for the simple reason that it directly mimics the thing we are trying to find—a leak in the part itself—and as such directly check the complete operation of the entire machine.

Figure 12-4

This of course requires a known non-leaking part to be located, and then modified to incorporate the master leak into. It also requires that the master leak/or master part itself can be capped (Figure 12-5) to enable a null (or zero leak check to be performed.

Figure 12-5

Many master leaks incorporate a cap (Figure 12-6) to enable this to be carried out.

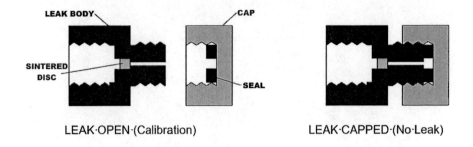

LEAK·OPEN·(Calibration)   LEAK·CAPPED·(No·Leak)

Figure 12-6

12.1.3.2 Introduced into the Air Stream to the Detector

The least popular, and not the most effective, but can be used for calibration checks with those systems where the part is away from the detector, and the sampled air is carried to the detector by an air/carrier gas stream (such as purge flow and concentration build up.

In this case the master calibrated leak remains permanently fixed within the tubes connecting the part being tested to the detector, or into the walls of the chamber into which the part is placed (Figure 12-7):

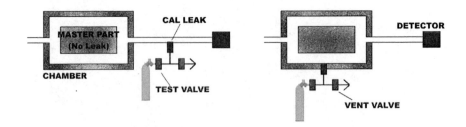

Figure 12-7

(Note: The leak can be introduced into any part of the carrier gas stream either before, in the chamber, or after.)

When a calibration check is required, trace gas is directly applied behind the leak so as to allow the correct leakage of trace gas to enter the chamber/air

372

stream. When not required, the trace gas is simply removed, by reducing the pressure of trace gas behind the leak to zero/atmospheric. This involves the use of valves, to apply and release the pressure from behind the leak as required.

12.1.3.3 As Part of a Special Calibration Circuit within the System

This is generally utilised with the internal calibration systems built into the detector, where the calibration check is carried out routinely by the detector itself. Table 12-1 gives you a guide to the good and bad aspects of different master leak placement positions.

PLACEMENT OF LEAK	ADVANTAGES	DISADVATAGES
IN PART ITSELF	Directly Mimics the requirement of the test Can be performed anytime	Not suitable for frequent calibration checks Check of Leak Master more difficult
INTRODUCED INTO AIR STREAM	Checks more of the system (depends on placement) Easy access to Master Leak for Calibration purposes Checks can be performed more frequently (every test?)	Does not mimic Part Leaking Requires additional valves/circuitry, which could cause problems Special Test Sequence required
AS PART OF A SPECIAL CALIBRATION CIRCUIT	Checks can be performed more frequently (every test?) Likely faster Calibration Checks Built into detector	Only really checks the detector sensitivity, and not the function of the complete system Requires supplier intervention for recalibration of leak

Table 12-1

373

12.2 Carrying Out the Calibration Check

In the previous section, we have already seen how the calibration checks are connected/carried out, but just a little more about the frequency and actual checks to be completed, and records to be kept.

12.2.1 Direct Sniffing

For direct sniffing, it is advised that the calibration check is performed each time the detector is used to sniff for leaks. In this way, we can be sure that the detector is performing correctly at the time we make the test.

This is a two-stage check. First zero the detector in normal atmospheric conditions, then hold the probe of the detector to the leak, and ensure the correct response is achieved.

With many sniffers if this is not correct, then the sensitivity can be adjusted, if this is the case then always repeat the calibration check following adjustment to ensure correct operation.

If not correct, and no adjustment is possible, it may be necessary to calculate the correct value, for any actual response recorded when sniffing our part under test, by performing a simple calculation by multiplying each response/leak detected by an Adjustment Factor to calculate the true leakage result. The Adjustment factor is calculated as follows:

$$\text{Adjustment Factor} = \frac{\text{Value of Master Cal Leak (Expected Response)}}{\text{Value recorded during Calibration Check}}$$

There is no need to record calibration check results in direct sniff mode (unless you do not have any adjustment available), as the calibration check should be performed, and the sensitivity adjusted, prior to every test. If however there is no adjustment available it is worth keeping a record of the Adjustment Factor, to see if this is showing a trend that may require supplier advice on sensor deterioration etc.

In most cases of direct sniff method of leak testing we are generally looking for any response, detected, so that we can rectify any leak issues.

12.2.2 Within the Complete System

In these cases, it is very important to record all calibration check results to determine trends in either/both the null response and the span response. It involves making two tests (in a similar way to that carried out in air test systems), a null (or no leak) test, and then a span test when the master known leakage is added to the previous test.

The frequency of this type of calibration check will depend largely on your confidence with the equipment you are using to measure your leaks (or on advice from the supplier). Whilst the span check could be carried out after every OK test, this will add an additional measure time to each test as below.

12.2.2.1 Null Check

In this test, we place a known good part (non-leaking) into our test machine, and carry out a test. The result should be less than 10% of the reject limit pre-set, to ensure that the master part has not developed a leak, and to ensure that the any background contamination has been successfully cleared from the chamber. Again, my recommendation is to plot your calibration results (Figure 12-8), as this can help identify any issues that may be occurring.

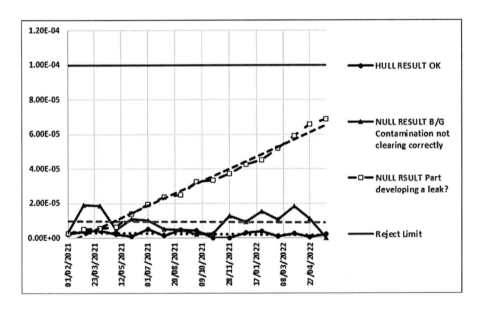

Figure 12-8

12.2.2.2 Span Check

Following the null check, the leak should be introduced (by uncapping the leak on the part), to perform the span check, or response to the leak. Again it is

375

strongly recommended to keep a log of these results (Figure 12-9) for monitoring purposes to ensure the detector is performing/measuring correctly, and to help identify issues.

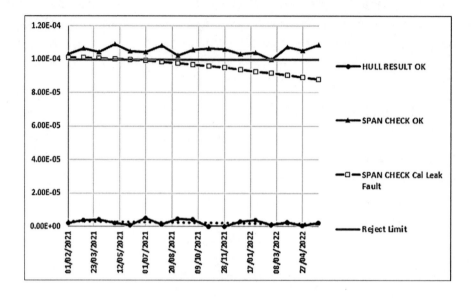

Figure 12-9

As cycle times in tracer gas leak test machines can be extensive, it is often preferred to use any part to complete the calibration checks, providing the result is below the reject limit, and to ensure the difference between null and span checks is in accordance with the added leakage rate. This helps reduce the amount of time in calibration rather than production. (*Note: This was a technique I employed for the engine manufacturer I worked for, as you can imagine, maintaining a master OK engine would involve storing this engine and being able to insert it into a production line as and when needed.*)

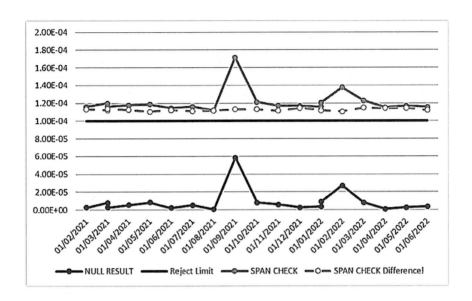

Figure 12-10

This does involve making an additional calculation to plot the difference between the null and span tests on each part (Figure 12-10), however if we maintain our records on a basic spreadsheet, this is relatively simple, and with the time saved can be very beneficia, as we now have a production part that has been tested, whilst we have completed our calibration check!

One word of warning in that you should only use parts that leak below our limit, as large leaks can swamp your additional cal leak value!

One other time saving in this can be in the actual sequence of events when carrying out our calibration check in these types of test machines. And to include a special/selectable calibration sequence to further shorten our test sequence.

In a basic format, we are required to carry out *two* complete tests (Figure 12-11):

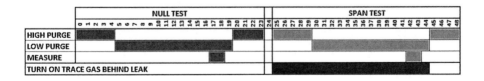

Figure 12-11

However with very simple clever design, we can reduce this two stage calibration check with our special extended test as a special calibration check (Figure 12-12).

In this case we simply make our null check, and then without interruption introduce the trace gas behind the leak, wait a short time for the leak to reach our detector and then make our span measurement.

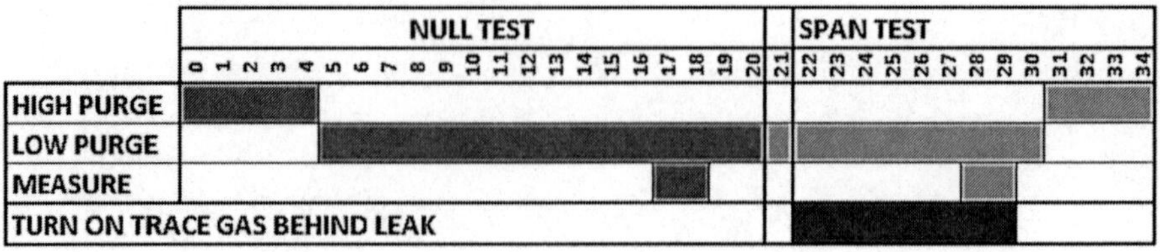

	NULL TEST																					SPAN TEST													
	0	1	2	3	4	5	6	7	8	9	10	11	12	13	14	15	16	17	18	19	20	21	22	23	24	25	26	27	28	29	30	31	32	33	34
HIGH PURGE																																			
LOW PURGE																																			
MEASURE																																			
TURN ON TRACE GAS BEHIND LEAK																																			

Figure 12-12

Of course, it is very important to allow sufficient time for the leaking trace gas to get from the leak point to the detector. If this is of interest, get your supplier to assist in developing a special calibration routine for your equipment. This could simply be called up at the press of a button whenever required.

13. Other Types of Leak Test

We have so far focussed on the main types of leak testing used in industry today, however there are other methods of leak testing, most of which are industry or application specific that I would like to touch on in this chapter.

Again I simply do not have enough space in this volume to cover everything, but I hope the ones covered below, will make up the bulk of those not covered by air and trace gas testing discussed so far.

13.1 Product Deformation

This method of leak detection is primarily devoted to flexible packaging, used to keep the product inside fresh and/or free from contamination. Essentially this type of leak test, stresses the packaging around the product, and measures how the packaging responds.

There are two main versions of product deformation which are detailed below, plus a third which is not so much a leak test, but more a form of process verification.

13.1.1 Linear Transducer Measurement

Most extensively employed for food packaging such as potato chip and peanut packets. The detector itself is a simple linear transducer. A linear transducer is a device that effectively measures distance. There are many variations available that use various methods of measurement but to keep things simple I will just highlight one variant—Resistance Position Measurement.

The detector itself comprises a voltage applied across a resistor coil with a wiper that travels along the resistor (Figure 13-1). The Voltage out (Vout) is the voltage determined by the position of the wiper along the resistor coil.

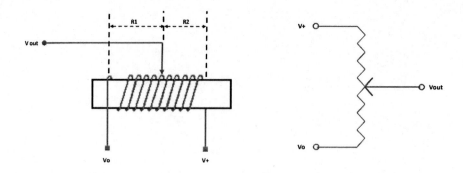

Figure 13-1

These devices can determine changes in distance of less than 100 microns, and as such are relatively sensitive to movement/position.

So now we know how the detector itself works, let us see how we can apply this, and the example I will use will be a simple potato chip packet. We want to ensure that the food pack is leak tight, thus ensuring that the potato chips remain fresh and crisp. *(A bit of background: Food packs like this are flushed with a gas to remove the air/moisture in the pack as they are sealed, and so contain a small amount of gas—at a predetermined pressure—within the packed once sealed.)*

In this case, the potato chip packet is placed inside a sealed chamber, and the linear transducer lowered/sprung loaded onto the outside of the pack (Figure 13-2), causing it to collapse to its lowest height (governed by the amount of gas contained within it).

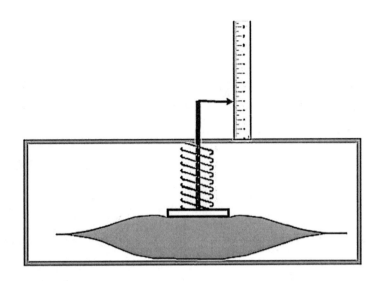

Figure 13-2

A vacuum is then applied around the pack, and due to the difference in pressure between the inside and the outside of the pack, the pack expands against the spring pressure, causing the linear transducer to rise (Figure 13-3). The height it rises to is again governed by the amount of gas within the pack.

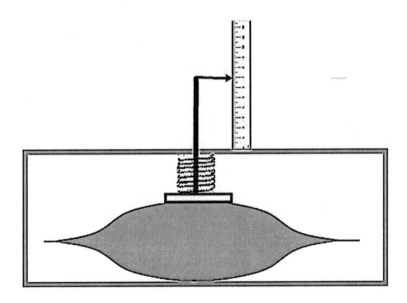

Figure 13-3

Now we wait and begin to measure the voltage from our linear transducer. If the pack seal is good, no gas escapes, and the height of the pack (and hence the position of the linear transducer) is maintained.

Should the pack leak, then the gas escapes from the pack, and the pressure difference between the inside and outside of the pack will be reduced, allowing the sprung loaded linear transducer to fall (Figure 13-4). The rate at which it falls is a direct relationship to the size of the leak.

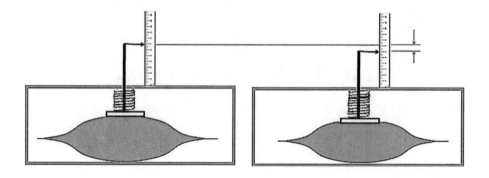

Figure 13-4

This basic principal has been used in many applications from food packs to medical packaging, and is capable of detecting very small leaks in packaging to ensure good shelf life of the product contained within the packaging.

The main use of this technique is to carry out checks on each manufactured batch of products to identify possible manufacturing problems (where the bag is not correctly sealed), and so halt production and rectify the problem reducing the amount of food waste going forward. Of course this also protects the consumer from inadvertently being subjected to risk from incorrectly packed foodstuffs.

13.1.2 Capacitive Measurement

This second form of product deformation is by and large dedicated to tablet/pill packs (Figure 13-5), or similar, which are foil covered.

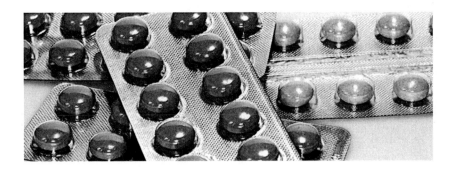

Figure 13-5

It operates in a similar way to the linear transducer however the actual detector itself operates like the differential transducer, in that effectively measures the distance between the sensing electrode and the foil by measuring the impedance/capacitance (similar to resistance). *Note: I do not intend to go deeply into the science behind capacitance, if you want to know more than this is a separate subject you might want to explore yourself.*

Once again, the pill pack is placed into a chamber, and then a number of electrodes or sensing elements are positioned accurately above the foil of each pocket containing a tablet/pill (Figure 13-6).

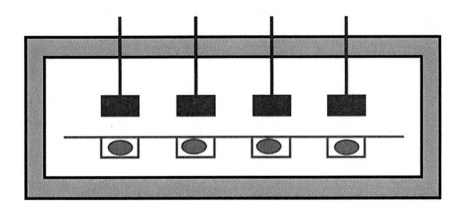

Figure 13-6

A vacuum is then applied above the pack so that all of the individual pockets will rise (Figure 13-7) due to the pressure difference between the pocket and the outside.

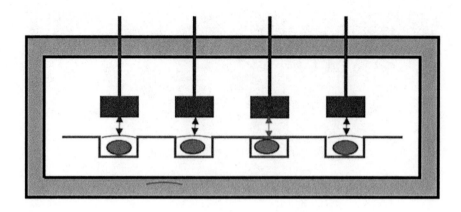

Figure 13-7

This is followed by a positive pressure being applied, such that the foil above each pocket will then fall (again due to the pressure difference)—Figure 13-8.

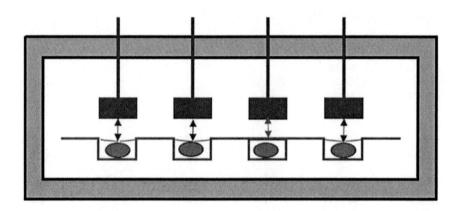

Figure 13-8

The determination of leakage is then a result of the difference between the height of the foil (or in fact how close it is to the sensing element) in each case of Vacuum and Pressure application.

Instruments developed for this type of test are likely to have a display (Figure 13-9) corresponding to the package being tested, such that an individual pocket can be identified as a leaking area.

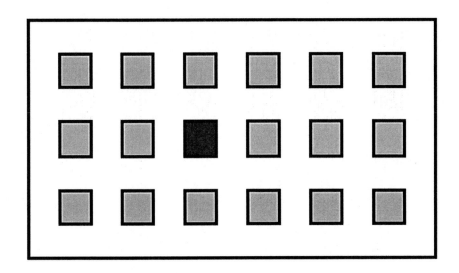

Figure 13-9

This greatly enables operators to identify potential issues in the manufacturing process, and avoid both the risk to the user, and the costly destruction of expensive pharmaceuticals.

13.1.3 Burst Testing (Knee Detection)

Another form of package testing comes in the form of burst testing. However this is not really a leak test as such but more a pack integrity and strength test, alerting the manufacture of the packs that there might be a potential manufacturing issue. This is a totally destructive test and operates by actually pressurising the package until it bursts.

In this the pressure inside the package is raised slowly through a number of steps, until the point at which it bursts, or begins to leak. This pressure can be applied in a number of ways, either directly into the pack, or more likely by squeezing the package with what is in effect a rubber balloon.

The pressure in the pack is monitored throughout the process, and at the point of disruption a small drop in the pressure being applied is identified as a knee point (Figure 13-10) on the pressure measurement, alerting the operator to the pack strength.

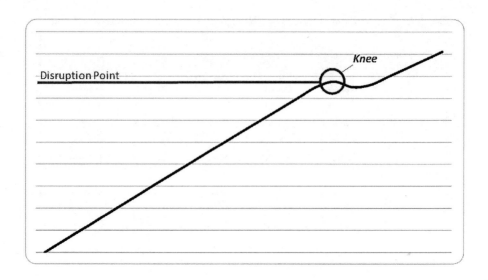

Figure 13-10

13.2 Vibration Detection (Acoustics)

This method of detection effectively listens to the sound made by tapping a metal can, bottle top, or any hard surface that will not deflect under force from air pressure or any other way.

The system works by applying an electromagnetic pulse to the top, which is in effect a tap on the part under test. The can, or top will then resonate (a bit like a musical tuning fork) at a natural frequency depending on its size, thickness, shape etc. but also may depend on the amount of gas space underneath the top, or the presence of any gas at all in the can.

Note: A tuning fork is an acoustic resonator in the form of a two-pronged fork with the prongs formed from a U-shaped bar of elastic metal (usually steel). It resonates at a specific constant pitch when set vibrating by striking it against a surface or with an object and emits a pure musical tone.

These machines will then listen to the sound made by the can/top, and measure the frequency of the tone generated. This tone is compared with pre-set requirements to determine if the can/bottle is sound (or leak tight). If an incorrect tone is detected, this part is automatically rejected.

Such machines can operate at very fast speeds (typically faster than 1 can per second, and in modern machines they can eliminate an individual faulty can/bottle from a stream of product travelling on a conveyer belt at speeds in excess of 1,000 cans/bottles per minute!

13.3 High Voltage Detection

This method was developed originally for testing plastic parts. (However, the principal has been used to leak test rubberised components (such as condoms), rubber sheets, plastic sheet, etc.; anything that is non-conductive, i.e., will not conduct electricity very well.)

For many years, plastic containers were tested for leakage using pressure decay techniques, however due to the speed of producing these containers (and in some cases the large size, reducing the sensitivity of pressure change measurement), they were not very sensitive.

The technique is very simple in that the material to be tested is placed between two electrodes of different voltage, such that the voltage difference is considered very high. In the case of our plastic bottle, a very high voltage electrode and an earthed screen (Figure 13-11).

Should a hole (leak path) be present in the plastic/rubber material, then an arc is created between the two electrodes, and a detectable current flows. *(This is a bit like lightening travelling from the high electrical charge in the storm clouds, to the earth).*

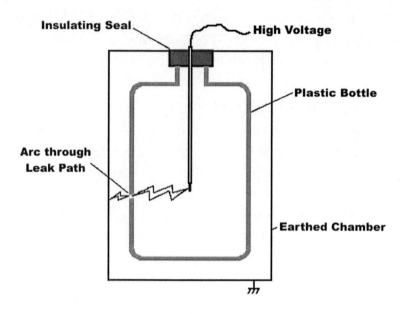

Figure 13-11

Whilst this method is unable to determine the size of the leak path, it nevertheless is a very fast test, and hence it is ideally suited to products like plastic bottles, and condom material, which are produced at very high speeds.

One of this method's distinct advantages is the ability to detect weak spots (where the material is very thin, or damaged) in the material, so it not only detects actual leaks, but also the potential for leakage!

13.4 X-Ray Flaw Detection

The ability to detect the potential for leaks (rather than just actual leak paths) is also important in a number of industries where material strength or soundness is required. This is particularly useful for metal panels (used in aircraft etc.). It works by simply passing X-Ray photons (which are in fact a form of energy that can pass through solid objects), through the object being checked for flaws.

Just like when you have an X-Ray at the hospital, the more dense the material (e.g., your bones), the more the X-Rays are blocked, and do not reach the imaging plate placed the other side of the object being tested.

A basic 2D image is produced on the imaging plate, and this can clearly show areas where a weakness exists (*such as you see on the fractured broken bone*).

13.5 Other Leak Testing

Although I am sure you will find others, it is not my intention to cover every single leak test method, and I have really focussed on the main leak test methods used in industry. Time now to move on and explore the ways in which the two main methods of air testing and trace gas testing are used, in a more practical sense.

14. Leak Test Machines/Systems

So far, we have focussed much on the use of the various air and trace gas instrumentation, with a view to direct connection of these to the part/component to be tested. We have touched on the use of chambers for trace gas testing, and in a small way on fixturing for air testing.

For larger assemblies (such as large engine assemblies), the way the assembly is connected to the leak tester are limited, and the connections are very much manual.

This section is devoted to the employment of air testing and trace gas testing in purpose built automated, or semi-automated machines, and the considerations for their construction. This relates to being able to place a component into/onto a machine, and then letting the machine do the testing for us.

In this section, we will explore the basic structure of machines/systems, including:

- Connecting to the part—including
  o Fixturing
  o Clamping
  o Sealing
- Basic Component Parts/sub sections—including
  o Basic Structure
  o Electronic Control
  o Valving / Pneumatics
  o Pipework etc.
- Guarding/Safety
- Controls and Indicators
- Automation and robotics
- Other useful functions

Whilst I will try and give you some level of detail of the various aspects of leak test systems, again, I am unable to cover details of individual aspects, and so you will find that I may generalise, but I hope that this will give you some thoughts for yourselves to define the equipment that you need to help you get the equipment to ideally suit your own particular needs.

14.1 Connections/Sealing to the Part

Before we launch directly into automatic/semi-automatic machines, let us first look at the different ways we can connect our component/part to our leak test equipment. In the case of trace gas sniffing leak testing, the only real connections we are concerned with are the connections used to apply trace gas to the part.

As these are relatively straightforward, and there are a number of products available for ensuring homogenous gas mixing (please speak to your supplier for this type of equipment).

Let us look at the different types of connection that can be made directly to the part under test, either for the application of the trace gas, or the connection of an air test.

14.1.1 Simple Bolt-On Connections

As an example, here is a basic plate type of connection (Figure 14-1) used to connect the leak tester to the exhaust manifold of an engine:

Figure 14-1

The plate incorporates a number of seals (more on seal design later) on the face in contact with the engine, together with alignment pins to ensure its correct location onto the engine (Figure 14-2). The plate is then simply bolted onto the engine using the 8 bolts built into the plate.

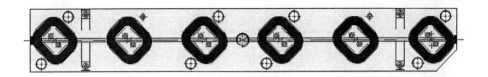

Figure 14-2

In the centre you can clearly see the connection to connect the leak tester to the engine. This is a Quick Connector port, onto which the test line connection is pushed-home, creating a leak tight interface between the leak tester and the connection plate. *(In the diagram, I have tried to show the interconnection, to the 6 engine ports to the air connection port)*.

Due to the physical size of the plate, two handles are provided for ergonomic handling/lifting and placement of the plate.

14.1.2 Push-On Connections

In many instances, we already have a connector on our assembly which might be used to connect fluid feeds (fuel, water, gases, etc.) on the assembly.

Here are a couple of examples (Figure 14-3) of connections that might be employed to connect the leak tester (or trace gas) to such ports. (These particular ones are fuel connections for an engine assembly.)

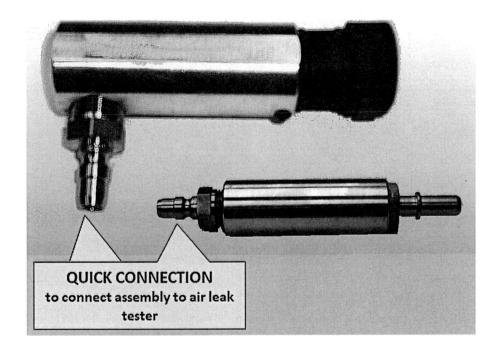

Figure 14-3

The upper connector is a female connection to connect to a male spigot on the assembly to be leak tested, whilst the lower would be used to connect into a female connection on the assembly. The push-on quick connectors on each attachment, are similar to those on the previous example, allowing the rapid connection of the leak tester.

14.1.3 Open Port Connections

If our component connection is through a simple open port or maybe just a simple tube (Figure 14-4) with no bolting places, or special connections then we need to find a secure way we want to test, whilst maintaining a leak tight seal (after all when we are testing our component, we are also testing any connections between the component and the leak tester (or tracer gas supply).

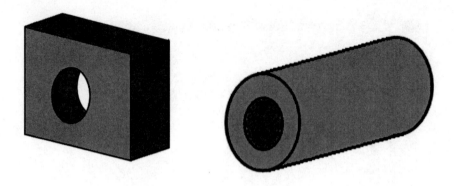

Figure 14-4

To make this sort of connection, we need to utilise a special device known as an expanding bung sealing connectors. These types of connectors are available from a number of manufacturers around the world, as off the shelf items.

These connections are effectively a rubber bung that can be expanded to seal inside the aperture we are trying to connect to. They can be mechanically operated by a lever mechanism, or pneumatically operated.

14.1.3.1 Mechanically Operated Expanding Bungs

The basic function of these is to compress a rubber seal so that it expands to make contact with, and grip onto, the inside of the hole or outside of the tube.

In this mechanically operated male (internal) version (Figure 14-5), as the handle rotates, it presses on the piston section which moves forward to compress the seal so that it expands onto the inside of the hole.

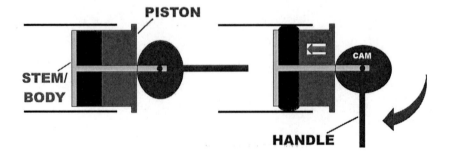

Figure 14-5

This version effectively blanks the hole, however with larger versions we can increase the dimensions of the inner stem, we could introduce a hole through which the test gas (trace or air) could pass through into our part (Figure 14-6).

Figure 14-6

Connectors that allow connection of our component to the test air/gas are called filling connectors. Both blanking and filling types are available in both male and female variants.

14.1.3.2 Pneumatically Operated Expanding Bungs

The example below (Figure 14-7) shows how in the female (external) air operated version this connection between the test gas air and the part is achieved with an aperture right through the centre of the piston itself. Male/internal versions of the pneumatically operated connectors are also available.

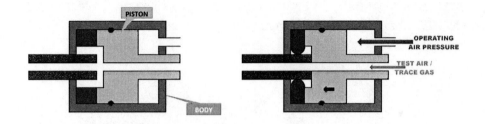

Figure 14-7

In the air operated versions, air pressure is used to push the piston forward to compress the seal, which in this case expands inwards to clamp and affect seal around the outside of the tube.

One thing you may notice is the small O-ring located between the piston and the body. This not only allows the piston to easily slide within the body, but also acts as a barrier to the control air (used to pressurise and move the piston) to ensure that it does not enter the area where the test gas (air/tracer) is fed into the part, or this can create problems for our leak test performance (either diluting the trace gas or it may create a pressure change/rise, in our air test).

Figure 14-8

These O-ring barriers are also found in the male air operated versions of these connectors. Figure 14-9 shows the male air operated version which has a slightly different structure to create the seal expansion.in that the piston actually moves in the opposite direction to the manual version.

The piston is fixed to a nose assembly, which itself then squeezes the rubber seal (In this example, note there are two seals! More about this in a moment.), causing it to expand onto the inside of the aperture/hole in which it is inserted.

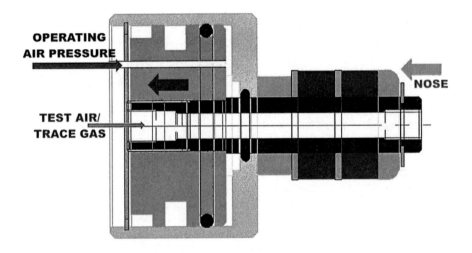

Figure 14-9

The twin seal arrangement has become more common for two purposes:

1. To ensure a better/leak tight seal

    Should, one seal become slightly damaged, then we have a second one to effect a leak tight connection

2. To improve the grip inside the tube

    One of the issues for this type of connector is that it relies on the friction between the rubber seal and the tube/hole onto/into which it is inserted. As the test pressure (Air or trace gas) increases within the part being tested, the force trying to push the expanding bung increases. This force

397

is also dependant on the size of the tube/hole being connected to, as the pressure is measured in force per area (PSI = pounds per square 1 Bar = 10 Newtons per square centimetre). Because of these forces a twin seal type will have twice the frictional force keeping it in place.

(Note: If the connector slips, then remember PV/T = constant so if the connector slips, the volume increases, and so the pressure drops—which would look like a leak on an air test system!)

14.1.4 Screw-In (Screw-On) Connections

The basic versions (both filling and blanking) of these are fairly self-explanatory/obvious in that we can simply connect onto a threaded hole (or threaded stud) by producing a simple threaded connection with an integral seal (Figure 14-10).

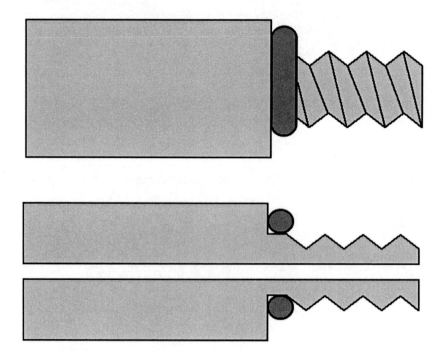

Figure 14-10

Whilst this type of connection is very simple and low cost, it does suffer from a couple of issues:

1. Seal Wear

As the connector get screwed in, then when the seal begins to come into contact with the part under test, friction creates wear on the seal, and so these seals are likely to wear out fairly quickly creating possible leaks.

2. Ergonomics

one of the key issues for operators using these I soon discovered was RSI (Repetitive Strain Injuries) particularly to wrists due to the unnatural action of constant twisting.

14.1.4.1 Quick Connect Versions

A number of companies have developed special manually operated devices (Figure 14-11) to reduce these two main concerns for threaded port connections.

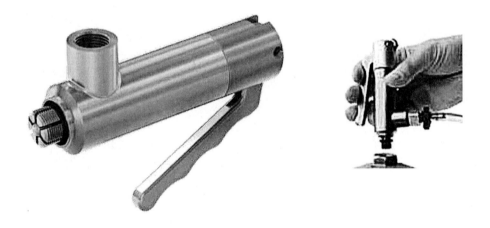

Figure 14-11

By simply squeezing the handle against the main body of the connector allows the threaded end to collapse (Figure 14-12) and the connector can be inserted into the threaded hole. (This happens as a pin down the centre of the SPLIT threaded portion moves out, allowing the split threads to collapse.)

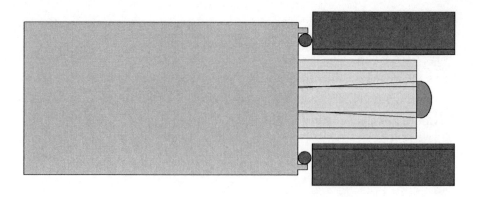

Figure 14-12

Releasing the handle then allows the pin to retract into the body, pushing out the threaded portion to open up, and grip into the threads of the hole (Figure 14-13). Further release, then pushes the seal firmly into position on the face around the hole to be sealed.

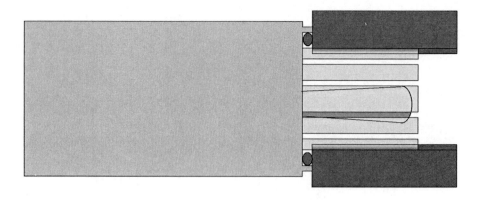

Figure 14-13

By gripping on the threads, there is no risk of movement of the connector due to the forces exerted by the test gas pressure, and by simply pressing the seal into place virtually eliminates wear.

In fact I can highly recommend these connectors, as at one company, where I introduced these in place of simple screw in types, we changed our routine maintenance from twice weekly seal replacement to once every 6 months. So although these can be expensive to purchase, maintenance costs are greatly reduced (not just the cost of seals, but down time to perform the routine maintenance).

These types of connectors are available in many formats to cover a very wide range of thread sizes, and also include push in/pull out versions. I suggest contacting the suppliers of these for more information.

This obviously covers the basic connection to allow introduction of the test air/trace gas into our component, but what if I have more than one port on our assembly where air/gas can escape?

Simple: all of the different connections I have mentioned can also be produced as blanking versions, with no connection to the outside world, and can be used to plug any openings.

Again, there are a myriad of ways to blank or connect to open ports on our component/assembly, and some of these may well be application specific. As always, seek advice and consider what you need to blank off to develop connectors to meet your specific needs.

14.1.5 Seals and Sealing

The principles of making a leak tight seal is evident as we are not only testing the part we want to check for leakage, but also the various connections (blanking or filling) that we make. However, I think it is time we consider the actual seals and their design and application.

14.1.5.1 Seal Application

At this point, I will happily repeat a phase I have continually used during my many years involved in leak testing:

'Mimic the normal operation.'

Just as we explained when we discussed the test pressure, that it should wherever possible reflect the way the part is used, so it is with sealing.

Take the example of connecting to the inlet spout on an engine water pump. Figure 14-14 shows a cross section through the pump, with three options for sealing on/connecting to the pump inlet. Which of these would you recommend/use?

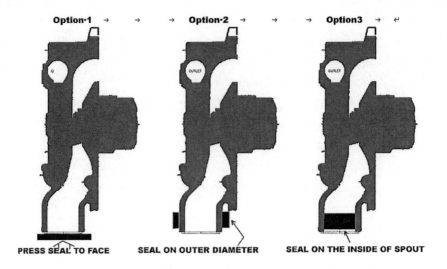

Option·1 → → → Option·2 → → → Option3 → ↵

PRESS SEAL TO FACE   SEAL ON OUTER DIAMETER   SEAL ON THE INSIDE OF SPOUT

Figure 14-14

Let us think of how the water pump is connected on an engine (Figure 14-15), and what we are trying to do with our leak test. The water pump Inlet Port is connected to the return from the coolant radiator, via a large tube which fits around, and is clamped onto the inlet spout of the pump, by use of a band clamp (Jubilee clamp).

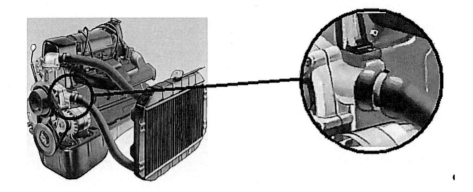

Figure 14-15

This gives us a clue as to the way we should ideally seal on/connect to the water pump inlet—**Option 2** which more accurately mimics the connection in normal operation.

If we want to directly mimic normal operation then it would be correct to use a piece of the hose normally used, and clamp this to the spout (together with a blanking or connecting block/plug clamped into the other end of the hose (Figure 14-16).

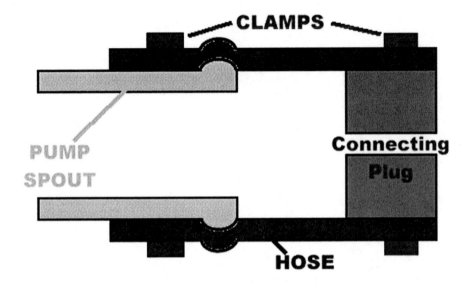

Figure 14-16

However, as you can imagine, to push on the hose and then tighten the clamp around this onto the spout would be somewhat time consuming, so it makes sense to probably utilise one of the external expanding seal type connectors.

Of course, this the ideal solution, but there are some applications where it is simply not possible to directly mimic the normal operation, and in such cases, we just have to utilise the best option we can.

14.1.5.2 Seal Design

This is one of the most critical items in leak testing, in that the actual shape, size, and form of the seal if not correctly designed, can cause several issues in our leak test.

During my many years involved in leak testing, I have, on many occasions, visited customers and suppliers to review their leak test equipment, and on many occasions, all is well, apart from the sealing of the part to the leak test.

As always with leak testing, we should always try to mimic the way the part is used, and this equally applies to seal design as when we test the part, we are also testing the seals that we are using to connect to the part.

Of course, the simplest way to mimic the sealing is to utilise the actual seal or gasket that is used in the part in its normal assembly status/operation. Often, this is a simple O-ring format such as the one shown in Figure 14-17.

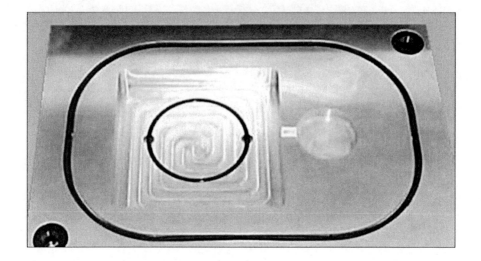

Figure 14-17

Using such O-rings has major benefits in that these seals are relatively low cost and readily available. When it is not possible to use the actual gasket/seal used, or if our gaskets used on our part cannot be employed, then we need to develop specific sealing for our leak test.

Normal operational gaskets may not be useable for a number of reasons, such as:

1. *They are only single use gaskets, and once compressed will not return to original state (such as paper type used in automotive)*
2. *They incorporate a coating which aids our seal (such as some metal gaskets used in manufacturing*
3. *The gasket material may become easily damaged by repeated use*

14.1.5.3 General Seal Shape/Size

When sealing a part onto a flat fixture base, it is often envisaged that just a simple rubber mat (Figure 14-18), will act as a good seal. But in most cases, this does not meet our ideal set up, as it does not really mimic the in operation design.

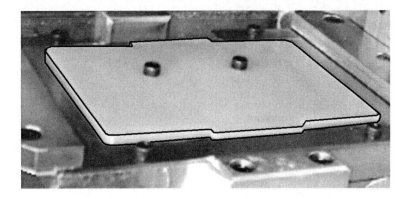

Figure 14-18

One of the biggest problems for this type of seal is that it allows potential volume change, which could give us big problems with our air test solution ($PV/T = constant$). This volume change potential is because the rubber mat can squash and expand, depending on the force applied on it (Figure 14-19) so depending on the clamping arrangement (more about this later) our part may have the potential to float on a cushion of rubber.

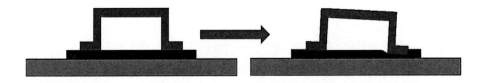

Figure 14-19

So one of the key aspects of seal/fixture design is to ensure that the part remains rigid. This is simply achieved by ensuring a mechanical stop (Figure 14-20) is present to maintain the position of the component being tested remains fixed/rigid.

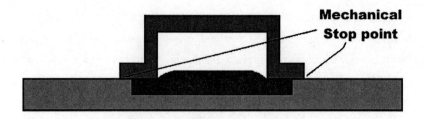

Figure 14-20

Another problem for large flat rubber pad type seals is that they have the potential to mask a leak, that might be present on the part.

Let me take the example of a cast part that is bolted onto a flat surface, with a simple O-ring acting as the seal, in normal operation. (Figure 14-21)

A scratch (or porosity which occurs when machining the face) is present on the base of the cast part, that in normal operation would allow fluid to travel past the O-ring from inside to outside.

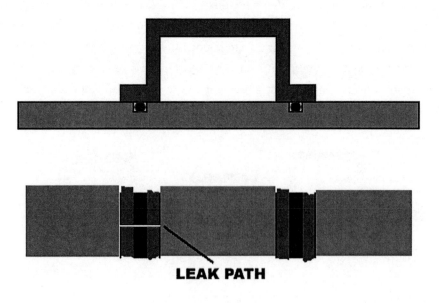

Figure 14-21

If we use a large rubber seal, that completely covers the cast face (Figure 14-22) (right across the scratch), then potentially the seal could mask the leak path (Figure 14-23) during our leak test.

406

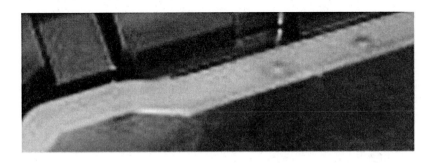

Figure 14-22

Leak Path is MASKED by Seal

Figure 14-23

Another example of masking the leak path is when bolt holes used to fix the part onto a larger assembly get covered by the seal. This is particularly true for castings, which have the fixing (bolt) holes drilled after casting. Again these drilled holes can be a source of porosity, so wherever possible we should ensure that our seal does not block these potential leak paths during our leak test.

Again this shows the benefit of (wherever possible), making our seal directly mimic the seal connection when in normal operation. This is where the use of O-ring seals are particularly useful as they are able to mimic to a large extent some of the special gaskets in use in manufacturing today. One good example of these would be automotive coated metal gaskets (Figure 14-24).

407

Figure 14-24

Many of these have a designs that incorporates raised sections (Figure 14-25) on one or both sides, which compresses and flattens as the gasket is sandwiched between the two parts it is sealing between. The ridges form contact points, which exert additional force into these areas to create a thin bead type seal (with the coating taking up very small surface imperfections).

Figure 14-25

These contact points can most effectively be mimicked by a simple O ring style seal.

14.1.5.4 O-Rings

Having mentioned the use of O-rings, it is important to understand that these seals are normally captivated in our fixture baseplate, so that they remain in position between tests. This is completed by placing the O-ring into a recess, so that only a percentage of the seal is proud of the surface to make the seal.

These are known as half dovetail grooves (Figure 14-26) and are designed specifically to not only retain the O-Ring, but also provide the mechanical stop previously mentioned.

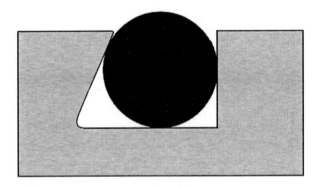

Figure 14-26

The depth of the groove is such that around 15% to 25% of the O-Ring (depending on the size of the O-Ring used), is exposed and the undercut allows the seal to compress into the space (Figure 14-27) unoccupied below the surface.

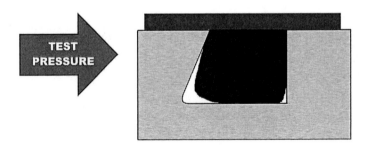

Figure 14-27

The dovetail acts as the retaining part of the groove, so the O-Ring size must be such that the dovetail is on the inside when the O-Ring is stretched slightly to install it into the groove, or on the outside when the O-Ring is slightly larger diameter than the mean diameter of the groove.

The O-Ring groove should also be designed so that the leak test pressure is in the direction shown so that the O-Ring is operating against the flat face rather than the dovetail face.

One last thing to mention with O-Ring Groove design is that it is good practice to provide access points to enable the O-Ring to be easily removed/replaced (Figure 14-28). This is often forgotten, but makes maintenance really efficient.

Figure 14-28

14.1.5.5 Quad Rings (or X-Rings)

When we talk about O-rings we are in the main talking about simple circular rings, with a circular cross section.

However, this type of seal is not limited to simple circular cross section design, and where this basic format is not effective, there are other variants available, that can fit into a standard O-Ring groove. One of the most popular is the Quad-Ring (also known as X-Ring), where the cross-sectional shape takes the form of a cross (Figure 14-29).

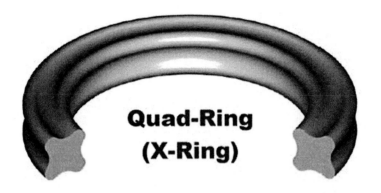

Figure 14-29

The advantages of using these rather than standard O-Rings are:

- Hidden parting lines or flash lines. The flash lines (a line of excess material where the mould tool comes together during manufacture) on an O-ring is always on the outer most diameter, which may be is a sealing surface. On a Quad-Ring™, that flash line is on the inside of the two outer lobes; therefore, it does not affect the sealing lips.
- The Quad-Ring™ is more resistant to rolling as it has a wider footprint and takes up the corners of the hardware groove. So the Quad Ring is less likely to twist or distort.
- Less compression force required to seal. The multi-lobed design provides more sealing surfaces than an O-ring. With these multiple seal points on one ring, less squeeze is required to provide an effective seal. Less friction and wear will ultimately increase service life and reduce downtime.

14.1.6 Seal Design Summary

Just remember these basic rules:

- Should ideally mimic the way the component is assembled to the engine
- Use the actual seal/gasket?
- Where possible use off the shelf seals (e.g., O-Rings)

411

- Follow same seal path
- Do not mask screw holes
- Do not mask machined faces (porosity?)
- Make seal replacement easy

Figure 14-30 is an example of excellent seal design, produced to enable testing of an EGR Assembly, which carries exhaust gas and coolant, that we do not want to leak.

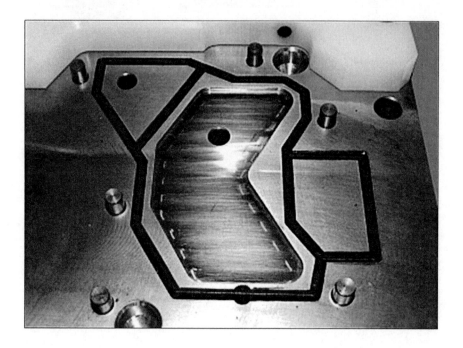

Figure 14-30

This design follows the rules in that it:

1. Mimics the seal used to fit to the engine.
a. Not able to use the single use gasket fitted on engine.
b. Complex seal means not able to use off the shelf seal.
c. Follows the Seal Path of the engine gasket (metallic type).
d. Bolt holes are not masked (used as location points for pins).
e. Thin bead design, so does not mask the machined flange face.
f. Access (at lower end) slot provides ease of replacement.

14.1.6.1 Seal Materials

Seals come in many forms, from simple paper gaskets through to metal gaskets used in the automotive industry.

In general though, we think of rubber materials for use in leak testing, as we think of them as being able to be continually compressed and released, and being able to hold back the fluids (gases) we are using for leak test purposes, however although this is generally true, there are a few aspects of seal materials that we should consider.

14.1.6.1.1   Cost

The cost of seals can be important, particularly in terms of maintenance costs, and there are great variations in the costs of different materials used to manufacture seals.

14.1.6.1.2   Wear/Abrasion Resistance

Obviously, seals are continually coming into contact with different surfaces, and as such are likely to wear out. So the resistance to wear may be an important factor in selecting the seal material. This is especially important when the surfaces of the part we are sealing against are rough in texture.

14.1.6.1.3   Compression Set Resistance

Compression Set is the inability of the material to return to its original shape. All materials will suffer from this in varying degrees (no material will always return to its original shape, particularly if it remains compressed for a period of time, and although this is unlikely with our leak test, the continual compressing and releasing will cause some level of set to occur.

14.1.6.1.4   Permeability/Permeation Resistance

In air testing this is not a great concern (as the leak specification is large compared to the porosity of the seal material), however In our trace gas leak testing the seal will be in contact with the trace gas itself, so the ability to ensure this stays on the trace gas side of the seal is imperative. Some seal materials which have poor permeation resistance can soak up the trace gas (this is particularly true of Helium and Hydrogen—the smaller gas molecules), and so can then release these to our sample when not required, particularly in vacuum testing where the vacuum acts to pull the gases back out of the seal material. For this reason, only a few of the materials are suitable for this type of leak test.

14.1.6.1.5   Chemical/Water Resistance

One of the key elements to leak testing as we will discuss later is the fact that we should ideally test our product (component/part/assembly) in a clean dry condition, however, it is clear that in a water bath, our seals will come into contact with the liquid, so in such cases this factor must be considered.

14.1.6.1.6   Temperature Resistance

Not so important for leak testing, as most of our testing is invariably done at normal ambient conditions, although some underwater testing, where the bath temperature is raised, this may be a consideration.

Let us just take a look at some of the common materials used for leak test seals Table 14-1, and review some of the benefits and drawbacks of each material.

MATERIAL	ADVANTAGES	DISADVANTAGES
Neoprene	Commonly Available and relatively low cost Easy to Cut and Mould	Not very abrasion Resistant Can distort (Compression Set)
Natural Rubber	Soft Grades More Durable Good for rougher surfaces	Difficult to Cut Not very hard wearing
Viton	Good for High Temperature Applications Good Chemical Tolerance Very Good permeation resistance Good Compression Set Resistance	Relatively High Cost
PTFE	Good for High Temperature Applications	Can be permanently distorted (Compression Set) Not good for High Pressure Applications Not Mouldable Expensive
Silicon	Good for High Temperatures Moisture Resistant Medium Cost Permeation Resistant Good Compression Set Resistance	Possible Permanent Distortion
Polyurethane	Excellent Abrasion/cutting resistant Easy to Mould	Relatively Expensive Poor Chemical Resistance

Table 14-1

This is by no means the complete list, so do consult your leak test supplier for the most suitable seals.

14.2 Automated and Semi-Automated Systems (Connection)

In this section, we will look in a bit more detail at the special/purpose-built test machines that we use to carry out our leak test. We will explore the different types of machines for the different types of test (air testing, tracer gas testing and even under water baths), and consider the different parts that make up our machine.

I will also try and give you some ideas on what features can be considered and how they can benefit us. Leak test machines come in many shapes and sizes, depending on our own individual requirements, the part to be tested, the requirements of the test, etc. etc. They can be very simple manual fixtures (Figure 14-31) linked to a leak tester.

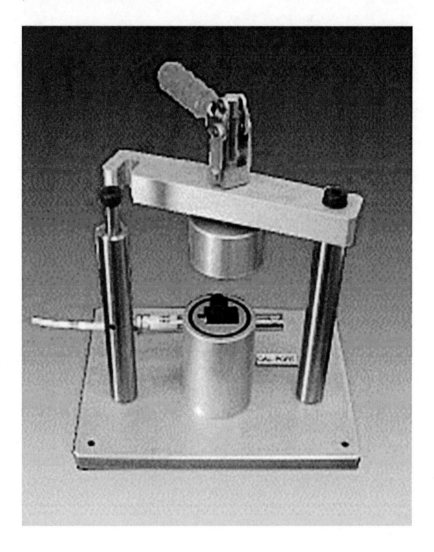

Figure 14-31

Or they may be basic water baths (Figure 14-32).

Figure 14-32

Or indeed they may be far more complex multi station machines, with multiple functions, including sensing, functional checks, part assembly checks, marking, scanning, etc. in fact leak test machine design is almost unlimited.

Let us first have a look at a basic air test machine (Figure 14-33) (this particular one utilises two separate test stations to allow the required production rates to be achieved), to highlight the main component parts/subsections.

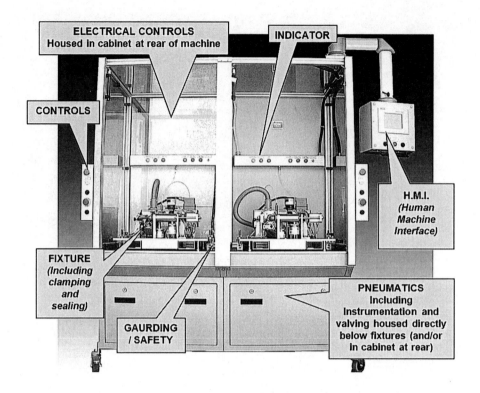

Figure 14-33

Let us take a brief look at some of these various part of the system in a little more detail.

14.2.1 Controls and Indicators

In this type of system, we do need to be able to both have some level of control over the test sequence performed, in the form of push buttons, and selector switches. We also need see the results of the test sequence from simple indicating lamps alerting us to the machine sequence status, and more importantly the part status at the end of the test cycle.

14.2.1.1 Typical Controls (Figure 14-34)

These may vary from application to application, however I suspect that you will likely need most if not all of the following at some time on your test machines.

Figure 14-34

14.2.1.1.1   Emergency Stop

The first consideration for any automatic or semi-automatic machine is safety. The emergency stop control immediately halts the test sequence and reverts our machine back to a safe state, where all test pressure is exhausted, clamping forces removed, and the machine ceases to be operational.

14.2.1.1.2   Control

This button is used to restore the control back to the system after an Emergency Stop or Power off condition. It does not activate any clamping or sealing, but merely makes the machine operational again. In most cases, this pushbutton is illuminated to indicate if control is restored or not.

14.2.1.1.3   Start

Simply used to start the test sequence once the part has been loaded onto the test station. In some semi-automated systems, this control is not required as the test sequence can be initiated by other means such as closing the guard door (or in some very special/rare cases, retracting from beyond the safety curtain).

14.2.1.1.4   Reset

This type of control has multiple functions:

- To reset the machine after Power Off/Emergency Stop, and once control is restored, whereby it positions all clamping and sealing back to its home or starting position.
- To halt a test mid cycle, and return everything to home status.
- To confirm that the operator has recognised the test result. Usually in a fail condition, where we need the operator to acknowledge that a fail has been recorded. This can be very important where fail traps are not provided, to ensure that the operator separates the Bad Parts form those that passed our test.

14.2.1.1.5   Selection Switch (Figure 14-35)

When we have multiple part types to be tested on the same machine, or if we wish to be able to perform different test sequences on our system, this control may be provided to make selection very simple and fast to activate.

Figure 14-35

This example is taken from a water bath machine, which incorporated a dry air flow measurement test. The customer in this case wanted the ability to:

a. DRY = Just perform a dry air flow measurement test.

b. WET = Just perform an underwater test and look for bubbles.

c. WET & DRY = Perform a dry air flow test, and then automatically, on a fail result, immerse the pressurised part under water and locate the source of the leakage path.

14.2.1.2 Typical Indicators (Figure 14-36)

Again these may vary, however the following are most common on most machines:

Figure 14-36

14.2.1.2.1   Part Home

Also known as the part in place, illuminates when the component has been correctly located onto the test machine, and is ready to complete the leak test.

14.2.1.2.2   Test/Testing

This is a simple indicator to alert passers-by that the leak test is currently in progress so that they should not attempt to access the component.

14.2.1.2.3   Pass

This will illuminate to indicate to the operator that the component has successfully passed the required test(s). this will normally only illuminate once the machine has released the test pressure and clamps such that it is safe for the operator to access the part.

14.2.1.2.4   Fail Lamps

In this example (from an automotive radiator leak test machine), there are in fact a number of fail lamps to alert the operator to the precise reason for the failure.

a. Fail Assy – In this example the actual brackets on the radiator assembly were checked for correct orientation and position whilst the leak test was performed.

b. Gross Leak – It is often useful to differentiate between large and small leaks to help with determining the next step to be taken in our manufacturing process (maybe large leaks cannot be repaired, or maybe, as in this case, they indicate that a component part has been missed from the assembly and which can easily be fitted to allow the part to be retested).

c. Fail Leak – Exactly as it sounds that the radiator leaked at a rate greater than the allowable limit.

14.2.1.2.5   Fault

This will illuminate whenever a fault occurs in the operation of the system. This is often combined to work in opposition to the emergency stop, so that it illuminates whenever control has been lost.

14.2.1.2.6   Other Indicators

This panel (Figure 14-37), from an air-spring assembly and leak test machine, shows the range of indicators that might be useful.

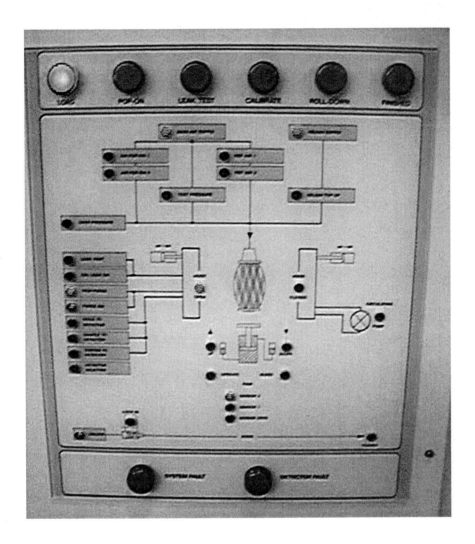

Figure 14-37

In this case, the amber indicators across the top showed the different sequence steps in the assembly and testing process, whilst the small red lamps indicated the different operational functions. (Note the two fault lamps at the bottom—one to indicate an overall system fault, the other to indicate a fault with the helium leak test instrument itself.)

In addition to simple lamps for the operator, some machines also incorporate a traffic light system mounted at the top of the machine (Figure 14-38) to alert others around the area on the machine status.

Figure 14-38

14.2.2 H.M.I. (Human/Machine Interface)

Not always required on more simple systems, but this display touchscreen offers additional features that can be very useful. HMIs can be as simple or complex as required to meet your own individual needs.

In very simple formats (Figure 14-39), the HMI may consist of a simple message display, together with a number of buttons to give you further control.

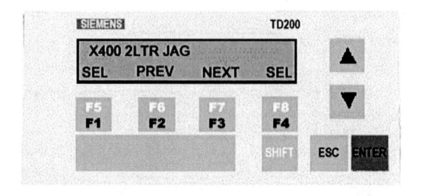

Figure 14-39

In this example the four buttons are designated specific functions, which work in conjunction with the PLC (Programmable Logic Controller—more on these shortly), to give additional control over the test machine.

In more complex HMI's based on PC (Personal Computers) then the display may have a number of options that can be selected, and may be operated by use of a keyboard such as this 3 station leak test machine. (Figure 14-40)

Figure 14-40

In fact HMI options are very flexible with as much or little control and information as you desire. In the main, the HMI offers a number of screens or displays, enabling a wide range of functions to be available to the user. A few of the more popular options for more complex HMIs might include the following:

14.2.2.1.1   Normal Run Screens

This display type is what the operator would normally see during daily use of the system. It may incorporate details of the part number/type being tested, pass and fail counters, test status, leak test information, and selection buttons and controls to access other screens (Figure 14-41). With modern PC type HMIs, a pictorial view of the part under test may also be included.

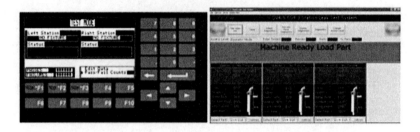

Figure 14-41

14.2.2.1.2   Diagnostics

These screens (Figure 14-42) can be utilised to help resolve issue that may occur with your machine, they may be simple displays of the key elements, or may include a full list of PLC control functions with indicators to identify status.

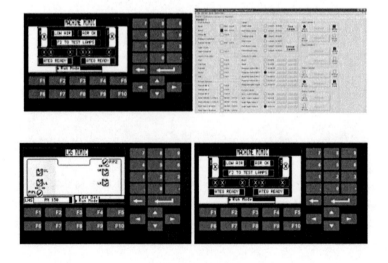

Figure 14-42

426

Some may include list of interruptions to system operation, known as a fault list (Figure 14-43). This can be useful for identifying machine faults.

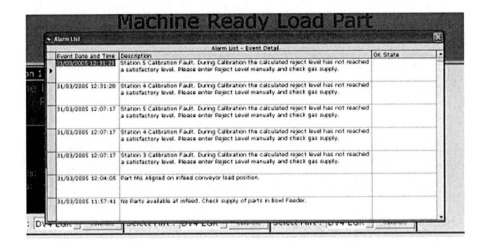

Figure 14-43

14.2.2.1.3   Editing Screens (Figure 14-44)

Many modern machines allow you to add new part numbers to be tested without the need to contact the Original Equipment Manufacturer (OEM), and some even allow super users to edit some of the detail displayed such as adapting alarm messages to better fit with your own operations descriptions.

Figure 14-44

14.2.2.1.4   Calibration Routines

It is quite useful to include special calibration routines that inform the operator when to carry out calibration checks (Figure 14-45).

This function generally allows you to set limits so that if the calibration check does not meet the required standard a warning message is displayed, alerting the user to seek assistance.

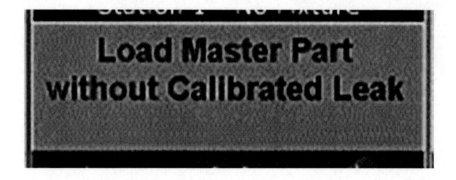

Figure 14-45

This is just a few of the many options available, but as can be seen from this small sample, there are different levels of technical understanding required. After all we do not want our operations to be able to alter key values such calibration limits, part numbers, etc.

14.2.2.1.5   Password Protection (Figure 14-46)

It is therefore imperative that we add some level of protection to many of the screens available. Usually, this involves several levels of password:

- **Operator Level** – to allow operation of the machine (this may include an operator log in, to enable historical information to be stored
- **Maintenance Level** – to access maintenance and diagnostics
- **Manager Level** – to access key features such as message editing, calibration limits, part numbers, etc.

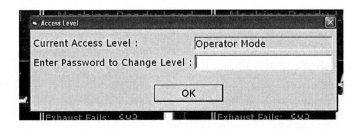

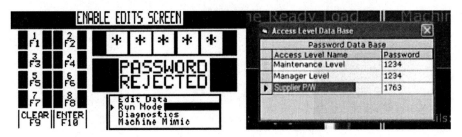

Figure 14-46

Suppliers of the equipment may also have their own password to access more detailed functionality of the system. As I say these are just a few, and my advice is to discuss your own particular requirements with your leak test supplier.

14.2.3 Guarding and Safety

This is one of the most important aspects for automated and semi-automated leak test systems. First of all the safety aspects are paramount, and as such the type of guarding chosen it critical in ensuring protection for the operator from:

- Moving parts of the system – these can be clamping or sealing components, that could trap, bruise or crush the operator's hand, etc.
- Test pressure hazards – High pressures within the component under test have the potential to rupture the part and cause projectiles from exiting the machine and impact with the operator.

But the guarding can have additional benefits in protecting the part under test from external influences.

- Temperature effects – shielding the part from heaters and draughts will greatly improve the repeatability of the leak test (particularly in the case of air test methods)
- Background contamination – for trace systems guarding can also act as a barrier to stray gases causing false failures.

Of course, where test pressure are low, and the part is manually connected to the leak test instrument, guarding may not be required, as can be seen from the open two station automotive radiator leak test machine (Figure 14-47).

Figure 14-47

However, this is not totally unguarded as note the two side guards, which protect people passing the test machine and in addition, protect the radiators themselves from external draughts passing across them.

And in some cases, where the part is contained within a test chamber (such as some trace gas test machines), additional guarding may not be required, as can be seen in the example below (Figure 14-48), where the part was required to be tested at a very high test pressure (around 25 Bar). in fact the test was performed by suppling the very high test pressure from a separate source, whilst the leak test was performed by measuring a pressure rise in the chamber itself.

In this case, the actual chamber in which the test was performed, acted as the guarding to protect the operator. The part was placed inside the chamber, and the chamber lid then lowered onto the chamber seal (note the chamber seal design being a simple O-Ring, as this is being tested at the same time as the part). However, the safety of the operator was still a high priority, and although the lids were not heavy, note the eyebolts on the chamber lid to allow assisted handling.

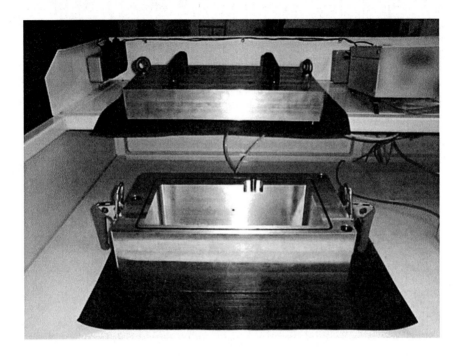

Figure 14-48

Where test pressures do not pose a risk to disrupt the part, then simple open fronted guarding is often used, whilst retaining the overall surrounding of the part to protect it from external effects. This example (Figure 14-49) shows such a machine where the part is loaded/unloaded through an open aperture at the front of the station. However as you can see, many such machines have automatic clamping and sealing, which could cause injury to the operator if a hand is placed inside the machine whilst these operate.

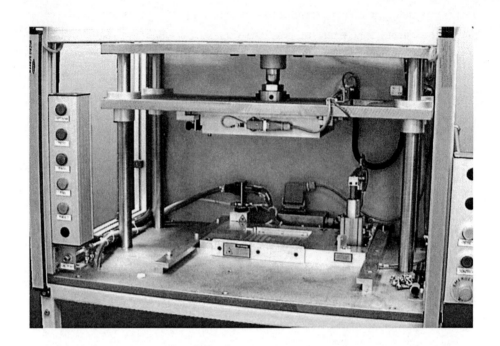

Figure 14-49

To protect the operator, special Light Curtains (The large yellow strips seen either side of the open aperture) which effectively act as an Emergency Stop if something passes through them during the machine operation.

In this example (Figure 14-50) of a completely open machine, note the light curtains completely surround the opening (with the aid of mirrors), halting the test should any interruption of the curtains occur.

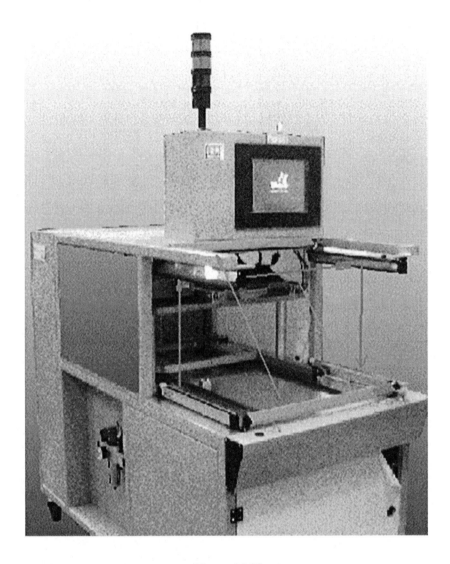

Figure 14-50

When full All-Round Guarding is required then there are also different options. This first example *(*Figure 14-51*)* shows a door on the front of the machine that is manually closed by the operator. Sensors on the door detect when it is fully closed, so that the test can commence.

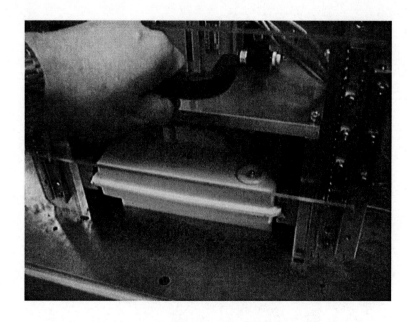

Figure 14-51

Alternatively, the door can be automatically lowered into position, by pressing the start button on the front of the machine *(Figure 14-52)*.

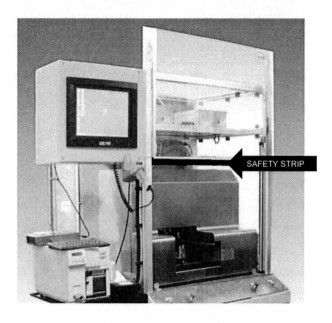

Figure 14-52

But isn't it possible for the operator to place his/her hand under the door closing?—the answer is YES, however note the rubber safety strip at the bottom of the door. This senses any object it comes into contact with, and immediately halts the test, raising the door safely away from the operator.

14.2.4 Electrical Control Systems (Figure 14-53)

These are usually mounted in the electric cabinet and in most cases mounted at the rear (or to one side) of the machine. These cabinets generally contain all of the electronic control systems required to run the machine, including:

- Power supplies (both mains power and DC voltage to power all the system)
- Safety control (light curtains and emergency stop)
- PLC (Programmable Logic Controller – which controls the sequence and functions)

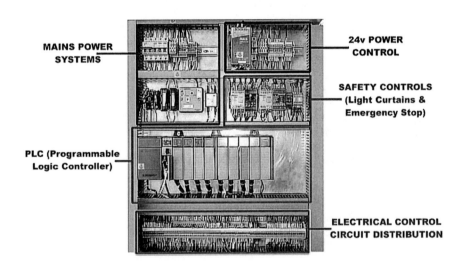

Figure 14-53

14.2.5 Pneumatic Control Systems (Figure 14-54)

Again usually housed in a cabinet at the rear, or side of the machine, these control air pressures etc. to/in/around the machine.

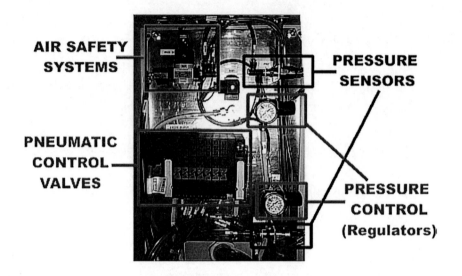

Figure 14-54

14.2.6 Fixtures/Fixturing

The <u>key</u> part of any machine that basically connects the part under test to the leak test device.

In general, fixturing incorporates three key elements:

- Location of the part
- Clamping of the part
- Sealing of the part

But may also include others such as:

- Assembly functions
- Assembly checking

We will deal with each of these separately in a moment, but just a word about the ability to test different variants of part on one machine. If parts are very

436

similar, it may possible to test these parts on a single fixture, which can be permanently fixed in the machine.

14.2.6.1 Interchangeable Fixturing

If the components we wish to test differ in size, shape or are just simply different parts we may wish to consider interchangeable fixtures, as these represent a large cost saving, utilising one machine to test our complete range of parts, with only the additional cost of different fixtures being required for each part type. Here are a few examples (Figure 14-55) of interchangeable fixtures:

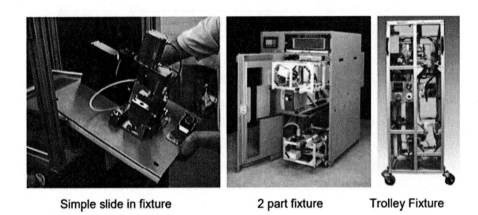

Simple slide in fixture   2 part fixture   Trolley Fixture

Figure 14-55

Each fixture requires to be connected to the machine both pneumatically (to carry the air/test gas to the part on the fixture) and most likely electrically to sense that part is present, or for assembly checks.

In the case of the trolley style fixture the connections are made automatically by pushing the trolley into the machine, however in most cases the connection will be by use of manual plug-in connections (Figure 14-56).

If we are testing completely different variations of part, then it is likely that we would need different parameters for our leak test (such as test pressure, fill time, measure time, reject limits etc. so we need to ensure that we have the correct test parameters selected for the part we intend to test.

Figure 14-56

For me when developing the connections for interchangeable machines, I felt it was always important for the machine to recognise which fixture was installed so that the part selected to be tested could be matched with the fixture, ensuring the correct test parameters were automatically selected. In some cases, we would use the fixture to select the correct parameters when it became connected to the machine. This can be easily achieved by devoting a number of the pins of the electrical connector to fixture identification by hard wiring/connecting (Figure 14-57) these pins to our control voltage (usually 24v dc) in a binary format (Table 14-2) to tell the machine which fixture (and which part = up to 7 with just 3 pins) is to be tested.

Connected to +24V			Binary Code	MEANING
PIN 1	PIN 2	PIN 3		
N	N	N	000*	**No Fixture Connected***
N	N	Y	001	Part Type 1
N	Y	N	010	Part Type 2
N	Y	Y	011	Part Type 3
Y	N	N	100	Part Type 4
Y	N	Y	101	Part Type 5
Y	Y	N	110	Part Type 6
Y	Y	Y	111	Part Type 6

Table 14-2

Note the null or no connections which by default ensure that the fixture is connected.

438

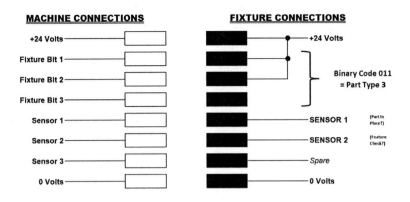

Figure 14-57

In a similar way our pneumatic connections can be plug-in (Figure 14-58), however one essential difference is the pneumatic connection to our part for the test air (or the chamber for our sample air in trace gas systems).

These should be separate quick-connectors that are non-leaking, so as to ensure a leak tight connection, and ensure reliability of our test air/sample.

Figure 14-58

There are a wide range of connectors available, but chose the one that meets your needs, but in many cases these will be the same as the quick connections used on leak test instrumentation.

One word of warning is to consider the different connections required. For example in the case of leak testing two chambers like our EGR components (where we test the gas and coolant sides separately (Figure 14-59) it is worth ensuring that the leak tester connects to the correct chamber to be tested, by keying the connections so that only the correct connection to the chamber can be made.

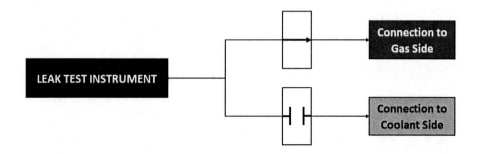

Figure 14-59

This can be achieved simply by using different size quick connectors, or where available utilise special keyed connectors (Figure 14-60) that will only fit into the correct mating part.

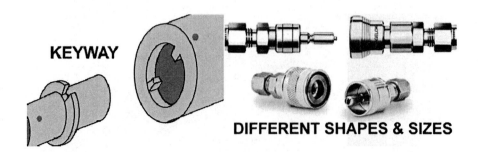

Figure 14-60

One more important point on the test connection is the use of self-sealing quick connectors such as those used on the test instrument.

My advice is to **NEVER** use a self-sealing connector on the connection from the test instrument (Figure 14-61). By this I mean the connection from the instrument should not be of the self-sealing type; although these can be used on the fixture side to avoid getting dust/debris into the fixture test connection.

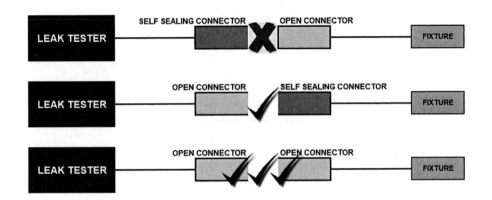

Figure 14-61

This s very important, as if the connection is not made to the fixture, effectively the test connection from the instrument could be sealed, and we would be effectively not testing the part at all but just the self-sealing connector. This could easily result in a pass result even though our part may have a very large leak!

Best advice/solution is to avoid the use of self-sealing quick connectors anywhere in the test connection, to avoid any such risks.

14.2.6.2 Clamping

By clamping, I am referring to the way the part is held on the fixture during the test. This clamping of the part is often overlooked, as being a critical item for the design of a test machine, and the easiest and most simple clamping is used to keep the costs down. However, I would strongly recommend that the way you clamp the part onto the fixture is critical in ensuring you are testing the part correctly.

Once again, as I explained in the section on sealing, I will use the phrase, 'Mimic the way the part is used/clamped' in normal operation.

Take this simple part with a flange (Figure 14-62) that is bolted onto the complete assembly, through the bolt holes in the flange:

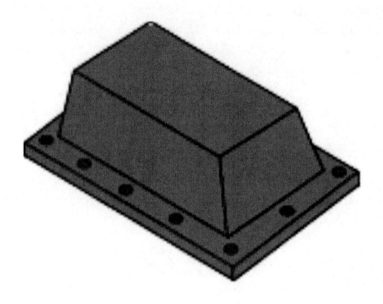

Figure 14-62

Clearly you could clamp the part to the fixture base in many ways, however if we clamp the part with a single clamp pressing down onto the top of the part (Figure 14-63) then we are not really mimicking the fit to the complete assembly.

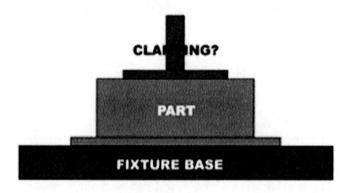

Figure 14-63

And if the part was quite large we would have to exert a considerable amount of downward force in our single clamping system to ensure correct compression of the seal mounted below the flange. This would stress the part itself in an abnormal way.

One example of this type of clamping also served to put the test at risk of volume change where a small variation in the height of the top of the part (less than 0.2mm), caused by the clamping mechanism continuing to compress the part down, actually masked the leak the manufacturer was looking for (more on this later).

By far a better solution would be to mimic the bolts used in normal operation/fit, by clamping at the points where the bolt holes are present on the component as shown (Figure 14-64).

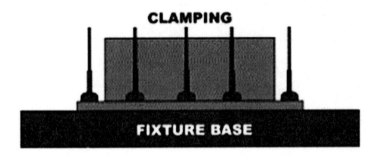

Figure 14-64

The actual force required for each clamp can easily be calculated from the force that the bolt would apply in that location from the following (plus any additional forces required to compress you particular seal):

Where:

- *T* = *Torque applied*
- *K* = *Factor based on Material and size of Bolt*

$$T = K F d \text{ or } F = \frac{Kd}{T}$$

- *F* = *Axial Force applied*
- *d* = *Bolt Diameter*

(Some typical "K" Values for Mild Steel Bolts are: normal dry = 0.2, non-plated black finish = 0.3, zinc-plated = 0.2, slightly lubricated = 0.18)

Please do speak to your supplier for more accurate calculations.

Below are a few examples of good clamping mechanisms that do their best to mimic the part fit onto the complete assembly.

This example (Figure 14-65) was developed to clamp a plastic intercooler header tank which would be held onto the core of the complete assembly by folded over tags on the header plate. The small clamp arms would move forward and then clamp down onto the tank flange.

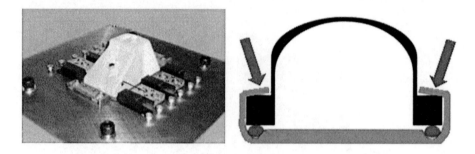

Figure 14-65

Although this does not exactly mimic the part fit, it is as close as was physically possible. Special swing-clamps were used for this oil pan tester (Figure 14-66). The clamps swing over the position of each bolt position *(or at least most of them)*, and then drive down to clamp the part in place exactly as the bolts would on the final engine assembly

Figure 14-66

Again, not every bolt hole point was clamped due to physical constraints, but this nevertheless more accurately mimics the fit to engine.

14.2.6.3 Sensing

Most leak testing of a product is **non value-added,** which means that it is simply an on-cost in the manufacture/production of the product we are producing, and adds nothing to the actual part itself (*other than knowing it does not leak?*).

Wherever possible, we look for ways to add some form of benefit in addition to just a simple 'does it leak or not?'. So during my many years in leak testing, I have constantly sought ways to add to our leak test solution to offer further benefits.

Occasionally, major opportunities present themselves, such as the automotive air spring leak test, where we were able to produce a machine that not only leak tested, but actually performed the assembly process, joining the three sub components of the air spring together prior to leak test.

In most cases, such opportunities are rare, however I have often found opportunities to include other tests, or functional checks within the leak test machines, greatly benefiting the customer by reducing the number of pieces of equipment required to fully check the part being leak tested. Some of these include:

- Functionality of a pressure relief cap (confirming opening pressure is within limits allowed)
- Performing electrical tests on fuel filters to check the WIF (Water In Fuel) sensor to ensure correct type fitted
- Motor operation tests on a windscreen washer system
- Testing of Braze strength on a radiator assembly by a specially developed breathing test

But in most cases there are nearly always opportunities to check some of the physical properties of the part, such as:

- Physical shape of the part (particularly checking automotive radiators for twist and lozenge)

- Bracket positions on our component (are they correctly positioned to ensure fit to full assembly)
- Have all parts been assembled, or are there any missing – or indeed have the correct component parts been fitted?

The list is almost infinite!

In many cases it is possible to carry out mechanical property checks with simple fixture design (Figure 14-67) to include pins, and recesses so that only the correctly shaped component will fit on the fixture

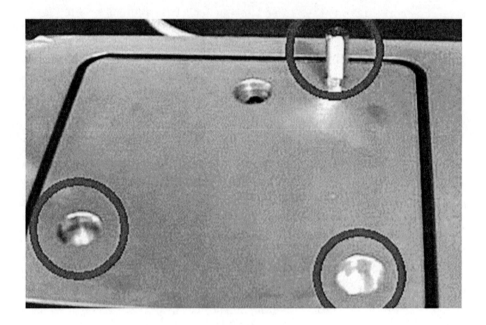

Figure 14-67

But we may need to check more subtle physical properties of a product, and in such cases, these checks are generally performed by some type of electro-mechanical sensor that will meet the requirements of the checks required.

One such example from my early days is to check an automotive radiator (Figure 14-68) for shape (lozenge) and flatness (twist) to ensure it would fit into the vehicle.

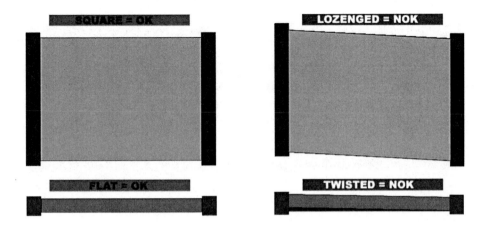

Figure 14-68

For these checks, electro-mechanical sensors were located on parallel bars positioned at the corners of the radiator location on the test fixture, to ensure that the part activated all four sensors in order for the test to be completed.

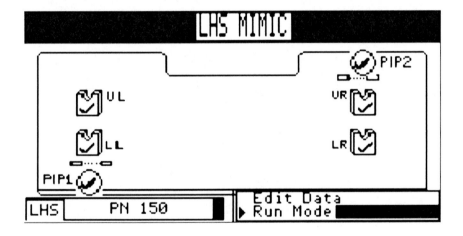

Figure 14-69

The sensors could also be observed/checked on the HMI screen (Figure 14-69), to check functionality.

Figure 14-70

Length of Part Check   **Twist/lozenge check**

An additional part length check (Figure 14-70) was also performed as the left hand parallel bar could be positioned according to the part type to be tested. Of course, the more complex the part requirements, then the more complex the sensing becomes, here are a few examples.

Remember the linear transducer used for package testing? Here is a similar type of sensor to check the height of a bracket on the side of a casting (Figure 14-71):

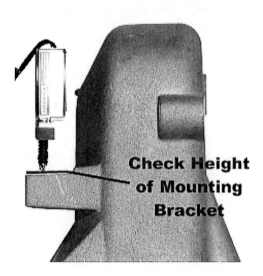

Figure 14-71

Inductive, or capacitive sensors (Figure 14-72) can be used to check for the correct presence of mechanical metal mounting clips fitted onto a plastic part.

Figure 14-72

And optical sensors (Figure 14-73) can be utilised for a wide range of applications, here they are being used to detect the correct cut made in the side support of this radiator assembly.

Figure 14-73

14.2.6.4 Part In Place Sensor (PIP)

But one of the most important sensing elements in a semi-automated leak test machine is the Part Present Sensor, or PIP (Part In Place). This is used to detect that a part is in place within our fixture.

This is very important with semi-automatic machines, as not only does it detect if the part is in the fixture, but also tells us when the part is not in the fixture.

This may seem like a very strange thing to say, but in fact where operators are required to load and unload the parts for testing, it is just as important that at the end of the test that we confirm the part has been removed, as it is to know that the part is in place to enable the test to be started.

Without this it would be very simple for us to continually just start the leak test, testing the same part over and over again. Whilst the PIP does not guarantee that the operator does not simply load the same part over and over again, it does at least force the last part tested to be removed and the PIP to see No Part Present between each test.

The Part In Place is often combined with the safety curtain, or safety door to ensure that the part is fully removed (Figure 14-74). The following flow chart may help explain what I mean.

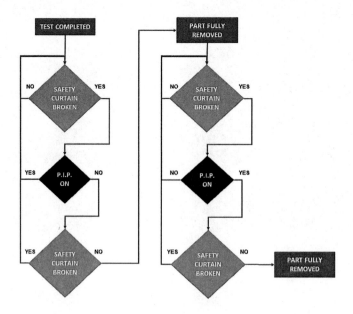

Figure 14-74

450

14.2.6.5 Calibration Port (Figure 14-75)

You may wonder why I have included this under fixturing, as it is not directly part of the actual fixture. Well, you are correct, and calibration ports are more likely to be located on the main machine framework, however I am including it under fixturing as it is important to remember what our calibration port is used for, and that is to check that our complete leak test system is functioning correctly, and accurately measuring leaks.

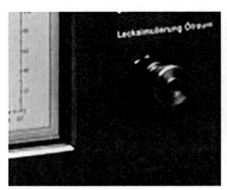

Figure 14-75

Typically suppliers of leak test instruments provide calibration ports on their instruments, however these calibration ports use self-sealing connectors into which the master leaks can be calibrated, and are connected directly to the measuring device, so it does not necessarily mean that we are checking the calibration of the complete system.

It is therefore worthwhile including additional calibration ports on the machine/fixture itself to ensure we are checking all parts of our test circuit. When doing this, it is sensible to use the same type of connectors as used on the instrument, as it enables us to utilise the same calibrated leak master on both the machine and the instrument.

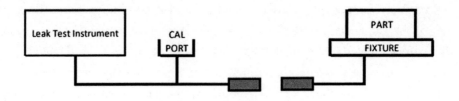

Figure 14-76

Generally, the calibration port is 'Teed' into the test line connection (Figure 14-76), so that introducing the master leak simply adds the leakage into the circuit as required. But a far better solution is to have the calibration ports on the actual fixtures themselves (Figure 14-77), connected to a different point than the test line connection so as to further ensure the part under test is part of the calibration.

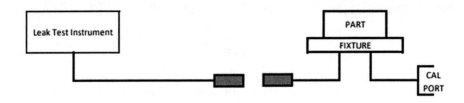

Figure 14-77

14.2.7 Other Features of a Complete Turnkey System

There are just one or two other features often required/incorporated in leak test systems, so just a word about each of these.

14.2.7.1 Marking

Marking parts that have completed a leak test is a very simple way to quickly identify those parts that have been shown to pass our leak test. Just as with everything there are a wide range of marking solutions available from simple Ink Markers (Figure 14-78, or dot punches (Figure 14-79):

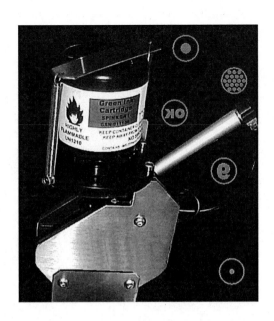

Figure 14-78

Punch Marker (interchangeable Numbering)
Figure 14-79

453

Through to etching (Figure 14-80) part numbers and special logos onto the part with dates of test, and batch numbers etc.

Figure 14-80

14.2.7.2 Printers (Figure 14-81)

An alternative to direct marking of the part is to print a label that can then be attached to the part. Labels can contain numerous details (including bar codes etc.) in a similar way to etch markers.

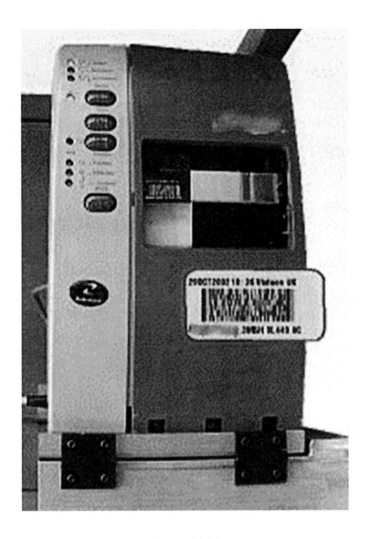

Figure 14-81

One important thing about printers is to have a sensing system built into the printer to confirm that the label has been removed from the printer. Whilst this does not guarantee that the label has been attached to the part it does ensure that the operator has actioned the printed label.

Some modern systems allow for automated removal of the label from the printer, and automatic application onto the part, but these can be expensive.

14.2.7.3 Scanners (Figure 14-82)

These devices allow for a greater amount of control, and enable more detailed records to be kept of the results of our leak test.

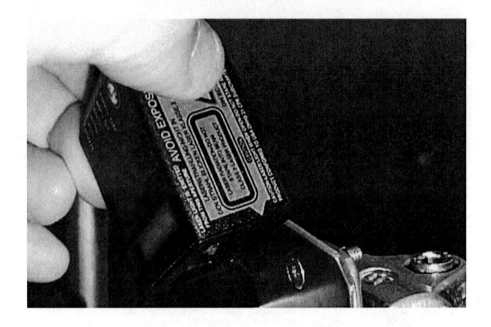

Figure 14-82

Scanners can be hand held, or fixed devices dependent on your requirement.

Hand Held scanners are generally used to scan the bar code already present on the part to be tested, such that the part number, and where applicable the serial number, can be detected. These can be used (Table 14-3) to:

1. Automatically select the correct test parameters for that part type
2. Record the test results against each individual part

PART SERIAL NUMBER	PART TYPE	TEST DATE/TIME	PARAMETER	PASS/FAIL	RESULT
624929	123456	20/01/2014 10:13	COOLANT FILL PRS	P	1.008
624929	123456	20/01/2014 10:13	COOLANT LEAK RATE	P	0.54
692429	123456	20/01/2014 10:13	COOLANT PROGRAM	P	3
624930	135799	20/01/2014 12:32	COOLANT FILL PRS	F	1.024
624930	135799	20/01/2014 12:32	COOLANT LEAK RATE	F	6.34
624930	135799	20/01/2014 12:32	COOLANT PROGRAM	F	1
624931	864200	21/01/2014 10:57	COOLANT FILL PRS	P	1.025
624931	864200	21/01/2014 10:57	COOLANT LEAK RATE	P	0.63
624931	864200	21/01/2014 10:57	COOLANT PROGRAM	P	6
624932	135799	21/01/2014 15:14	COOLANT FILL PRS	P	1.026
624932	135799	21/01/2014 15:14	COOLANT LEAK RATE	P	0.48
624932	135799	21/01/2014 15:14	COOLANT PROGRAM	P	1

Table 14-3

This is particularly useful when reviewing test results, as it enables us to look at results for specific part types, and observe any anomalies or trend for different part numbers.

Fixed scanners can equally be used for the same purpose, however they can also be used in conjunction with a printed label to confirm that the label has been applied to the part following the completion of a successful leak test. Should the label not be scanned, then the part remains locked in place until a scan is completed.

14.2.7.4 Reject Bins (Figure 14-83)

By reject bins, I actually mean a failsafe way of containing /isolating/ quarantining parts that failed our leak test, so that they cannot proceed further in our manufacturing process. This requires some form of sensing to detect that a part has been removed after it failed the leak test.

Quite often, where parts are relatively small, a simple reject chute (or slide) can be built into our leak test machine, down which any failed parts are placed, so that they are retained in a reject bin.

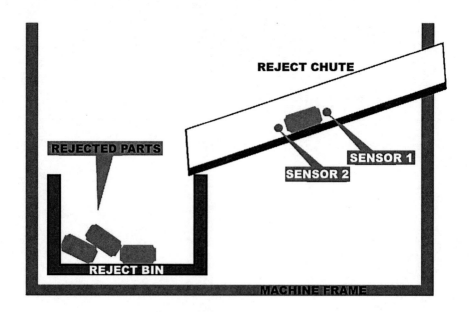

Figure 14-83

To ensure the part is placed in the bin, sensors are positioned on the chute to detect the part passing down the chute.

My advice is to incorporate a two sensor system with the two sensors placed slightly larger spacing than the dimensions of the part, so that to ensure that the part has travelled down the chute, we expect to see the sequence of sensors as in Table 14-4.

ITEM	STAGE IN PROCESS					
	Step 1	Step 2	Step 3	Step 4	Step 5	Step 6
TEST FAIL RESULT	YES				CLEARED	
SENSOR 1 DETECTS PART	NO	YES	NO			
SENSOR 2 DETECTS PART	NO			YES	NO	
READY TO TEST NEXT PART	NOT READY DUE TO FAIL					YES

Table 14-4

If only one sensor is used, then it would be easily possible for this to be interrupted by something other than the rejected part. But reject chutes are not the only way of ensuring failed parts are correctly segregated, and I have seen a wide range of solutions.

One really novel solution I recently came across at one company in Portugal was a reject bin that actually weighed the contents of the reject bin, so that it could easily determine the precise number of failed parts in the bin. If the weight was incorrect for the number of fail results received, then the machine could not be operated to carry out further leak test, without supervisor intervention.

Another really inventive idea, was to use a light curtain entrance (Figure 14-84) to a segregated bay, that recognised when a large assembly was passed through it.

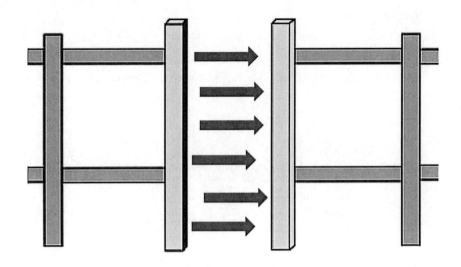

Figure 14-84

Others I have seen include sensed pigeon holes (Figure 14-85 into which parts were placed:

Figure 14-85

Although the details in this section generally apply to all special purpose leak test machines, I think it worth just mentioning some specific items relating to the different leak test methods of Trace Gas and indeed water bath test machines which many of you will also be considering.

14.2.8 Air Pressure Decay and Air Flow Leak Test Machines
14.2.8.1 Volume Reduction

With air testing, we do know that the volume under test can be very important, particularly where air pressure decay is involved, where the smaller the volume we are testing the better the sensitivity (ability to detect smaller leaks).

So whilst we consider our fixturing, is there any way we can reduce the volume to enhance our leak test. I strongly recommend the use of what I call Infills, which are effectively blocks of material that reduce the overall volume under test.

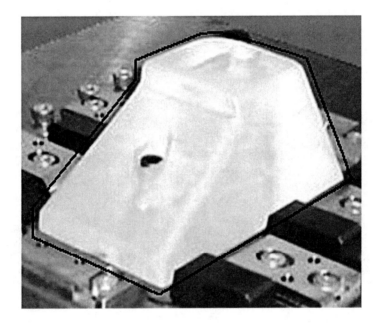

Figure 14-86

As you can see (Figure 14-86) the infill design should as much as possible mimic the inside of the part being clamped down, and should be manufactured from solid materials (in this case plastic). Where larger components are concerned, I have also utilised a number of solid blocks that can be stacked

(Figure 14-87),enabling different variants of part to be tested on the same fixture base, and reducing volume by changing the infill blocks utilised.

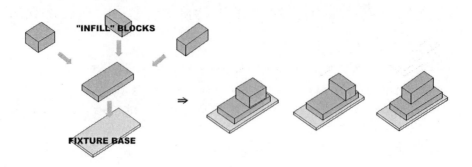

Figure 14-87

Another tip to reduce volume is by keeping pipe connections between the leak test instrument and the fixture as short as possible. This can often be achieved by careful positioning of the leak test instrument as close to the fixture as possible. One orientation I have used is to locate the instrument directly below the fixtures as in this example (Figure 14-88).

Figure 14-88

14.2.9 Trace Gas Test Machines

Just a few words about trace gas machines. These follow similar basic concepts as the air testing machines with the following key elements:

- Controls and indicators
o *Including Pass/Fail, indicators, and Start/Reset and E-Stop controls)*
- PLC or PC control of the test sequence
o *Usually located in electronic cabinet*
- HMI (Human Machine Interface)
o *Plus keyboard for manual input as required)*
- Pneumatic controls (Valves, pressure regulators etc.)
o *Usually located in rear of machine*
- Guarding and safety
- And of course… fixturing (with clamping and sealing)

And may include a number of the additional elements, such as:

- Marking
o Printers, etching, etc.
- Scanners
o Scanning of part type/serial number etc.

Most of these follow the same basic concepts as we have discussed already, but there are additional considerations for trace gas testing that may not be so obvious

First of all here is one such (twin station) trace gas machine (Figure 14-89) that I was personally involved in providing a customer for the testing of automotive air-springs, showing these typical elements

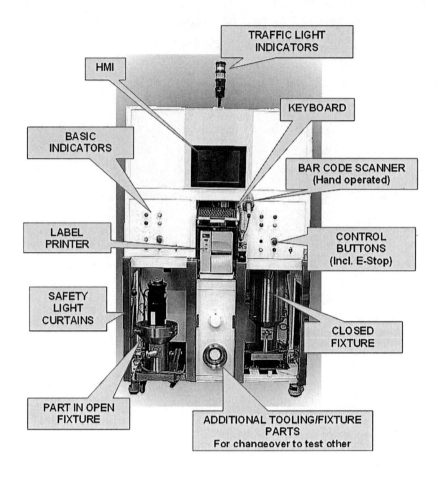

Figure 14-89

The following photographs shows the main components of the trace gas control systems

Electrical Cabinet (Figure 14-90) showing Mains Power distribution for Vacuum Pumps, Detector, HMI, PLC, Safety Relays, etc.

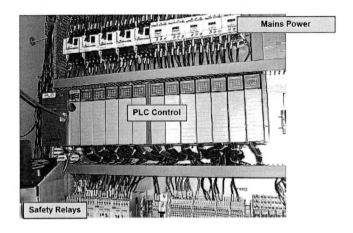

Figure 14-90

Tracer Gas Control Pneumatics (Figure 14-91) showing intensifier (to raise test pressure to required level, Regulators, valves, and gauges etc.

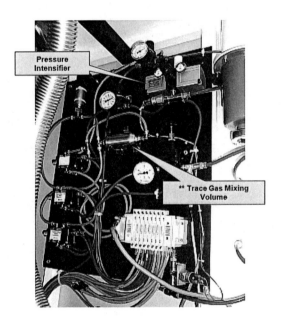

Figure 14-91

Here also we utilised a small volume to enable tracer gas mixing to the required concentration.

14.2.9.1 Leak Test Chamber

Trace gas leak test systems most often employ a chamber in which the part is placed to make the leak test. Consideration should be given to the design of this leak test chamber. The main question to ask is how leak tight it needs to be.

If the chamber will see a vacuum during the test cycle then invariably the chamber needs to be very leak tight, or we are at risk of drawing in a sample of the surrounding air, which may contain a small concentration of our trace gas, which will invariably be detected—causing a false failure.

14.2.9.2 Volume Reduction

This applies to both component under test as well as the test chamber.

14.2.9.1.1   Chamber Volume Reduction

The smaller the free volume the better the test for many reasons, but in the main because the test cycle time will be reduced.

- Shorter time to evacuate in vacuum systems
- Less air/sample to transfer to the detector

Figure 14-92

These pictures (Figure 14-92) show the contoured design of the lower chamber into which this assembly is placed, thus reducing the volume of air to be sampled, effectively increasing sensitivity and/or shortening our test cycle.

14.2.9.1.2   Part Volume Reduction

In the same way as we see from reducing the volume inside the chamber, reducing the volume inside the part can have similar effects (particularly if we are sampling on the inside of our part).

However, what if we are simply filling/pressurising our part with the trace gas? Surely reducing the volume cannot have any benefits? Well, clearly cycle times are reduced if we reduce the amount of trace gas we have to put in. But as we have previously highlighted, trace gases cost money, and so the less we need, the cheaper our test is. Even if we are utilising a Trace Gas Reclaim System, these cannot reclaim 100% of the trace gas, so the less we use for our test, the less we throw away.

14.2.9.3 Test Chamber Materials and Cleanliness

During our brief look at seal materials, we discovered that different materials have the ability to soak up trace gases, which can then be released during our measurement phase, creating potential risk of failing perfectly good parts due the detection of these gases being released.

This releasing of gases is known as outgassing, and should also be a key consideration in the design of our test chambers, particularly where vacuum leak testing is being used.

14.2.9.1.3   Chamber Material

So where we are performing vacuum testing it is important to select a material that is not porous to these small molecule gases, and stainless steel is generally the preferred choice for such systems.

There are also instances with medical products where cleanliness is a key requirement, and as such stainless steel is often the preferred material for our test fixtures/chambers.

14.2.9.1.4   Chamber Cleanliness

Just as materials themselves can soak up the gases and cause issues with outgassing, so it is with general dust/dirt inside our chamber. So it is important to keep our chamber as clean as possible, free from collection of debris/dirt inside the chamber.

We will discuss this keeping our chamber clean later in good practice, but for now one thing we can do to minimise the risk of dust etc. collecting in our chamber, is to make all of our surfaces smooth and easy to clean. I know from my minimal efforts of cleaning around the house, that corners are much more likely to trap dust, making them really difficult to keep clean, whilst smooth/curved surfaces are much easier to be wiped clean to maintain in presentable status.

In our chambers, the same is true, so this is particularly important when we consider the corners of our chambers, where we should minimise the risk of dirt collection (and make cleaning much more effective) by removing sharp corners wherever possible, by creating curved/smooth corners in our chamber (Figure 14-93).

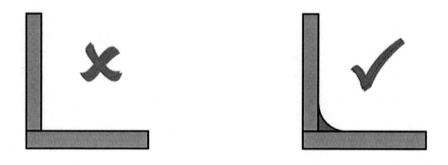

Figure 14-93

14.2.9.4 Vacuum Pump Selection

I do not intend to go into detail about selection of the correct pump for your application, as I feel this is best served with advice from the suppliers of the vacuum leak test equipment/instrument, however just to give you an idea of the complexity, consider the photographs below.

The first photograph (Figure 14-94) shows the detection system (Helium Mass Spectrometer itself, together with the vacuum pumps used for each test chamber:

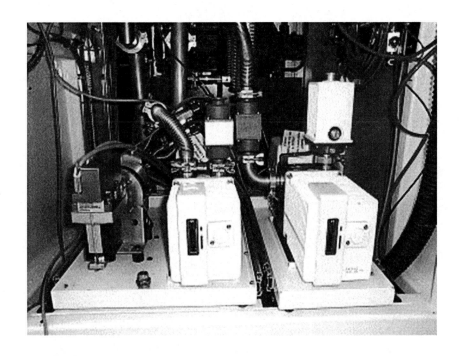

Figure 14-94

These photographs (Figure 14-95) show the complex vacuum circuitry together with large roughing pump used to suck the majority of the air out of the vacuum test chambers.

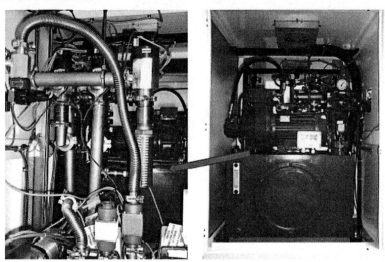

Figure 14-95

14.2.10 Water Bath Leak Test Machines

I have not spent much time looking at these to date, but I think that this is a good opportunity to look at such machines and understand what they are like.

Water baths are most often selected as our choice of leak test, as we want to know the location of our leak path, so that we have an opportunity to rectify/repair the part being tested if it is found to contain a leak.

Many people chose under water testing as a cheap option, however depending on the complexity you put into your machine, this may not be the case, so do look at the section on good practice first to decide if this really is the best solution.

In some cases, people may have a separate bath to locate the leak, after our dry test machine detects that there is a leak, or in some cases I have worked on, we have combined both dry and underwater testing in one machine (with the underwater part being utilised only if a leak is detected by the dry test), as seen in the example of the automotive exhaust component (Figure 14-96).

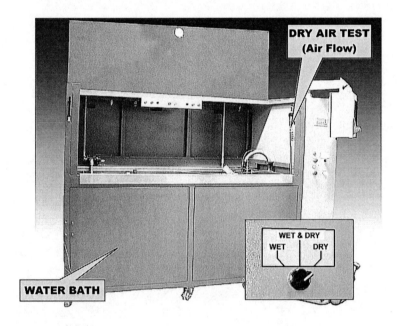

Figure 14-96

Although in this section I focus on water bath and air under water, any liquid can be used as the immersion medium.

470

14.2.10.1 Basic Water Baths/Underwater Testing

This is a simple concept in that a pressurised part can be placed under water, and the operator can then simply look for bubbles. The most basic format is a simple bucket of water, something you may well have used to locate the leak path on your bicycle tyre.

However, in an industrial environment, and with larger parts this immediately becomes a more complex piece of equipment.

14.2.10.2 Industrial Water Bath Machines

In such environments we need to consider the longer term use of a water bath and think about:

- Ease of identifying leak location (and masking of leak path)
- Water cleanliness
- Ensuring operator diligence
- Ease of immersion

Let us consider these in turn and review these factors and consider what options are available.

14.2.10.2.1   Ease of Identifying Leak Location (and Masking of Leak Path)

Despite the use of filtration systems, the water may still take on a slightly cloudy appearance due to the constant immersion of parts that may be coated with grease/oil/dust.

This can make it difficult for the operator to see the leak path properly, so in many systems I have been involved in, we have provided additional underwater lighting (Figure 14-97), to help illuminate the part under test. Bubbles do show up very clearly with good illumination as the light becomes diffracted as it passes between the water and the air in the bubbles.

Figure 14-97

Another consideration for leak location in a water bath is the shape of the part itself. If our part we wish to test has a rather uneven, or some pockets on its surface, then maybe as the air escapes, it becomes trapped underneath the part out of the operators view, and so the leak does not get detected.

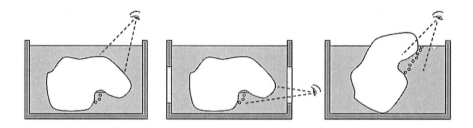

Figure 14-98

Consider the option to include viewing windows in the sides of the bath, or maybe rotate the part (Figure 14-98) whilst under water, so that the bubbles can escape to the surface, making the leak path clearly visible to the operator.

But one of the most important factors of all is to ensure that we **do not allow the water in the bath to mask the leak!** This is something that people do not often realise can happen, however I have seen this occur on more than one occasion during my time visiting leak test facilities around the world.

It happens because the part is immersed in the liquid, before the part is pressurised. This allows a time for the liquid to enter the leak path, so that when the air pressure is applied, it first has to push the fluid out of the leak path before bubbles begin to appear (Figure 14-99).

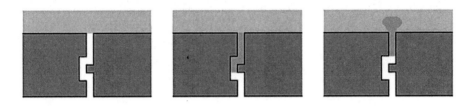

Figure 14-99

The solution is simple enough in that providing we pressurise the part we are testing prior to immersion under water, then our leak path is kept clear, and bubbles will appear instantly on immersion.

I cannot express this strongly enough…

Always pressurise the part prior to immersion in the test fluid, to ensure the leak path is kept clear!

14.2.10.2.2   Water Cleanliness

From a simple health and safety perspective, this is a very critical consideration for us when developing a water bath solution, as we know that dirt/debris can accumulate within the water itself, and make it unsafe for the operator causing potential health risks.

Obviously, the simple solution is to replace the water very frequently, and maintain the bath in a clean state. Whilst this is very easy to do with our bucket, when we have a 2 meter long, 1 meter wide and ½ meter deep water bath this is not quite so easy to do.

In such large baths, it is possible that the water bath can be emptied and cleaned out from time to time, but ideally we would prefer to minimise such downtime (when the system is not in use) and so we look for alternative ways to keep our water in a healthy state. Let us look at some techniques we can use.

14.2.10.2.2.1 Water Pumps and Filtration

One way in which we can continuously clean the water itself is to circulate it through a filtration system. Any of you who have kept tropical fish tanks will be fully aware of such systems, that draw in the water from the tank and then pull it through special filter pads that remove any unwanted contaminants caused by uneaten food, and fish faeces etc. (Figure 14-100)

The filter medium that removed the harmful chemicals is placed just before the pump itself, so that the pump is only moving clean water, and a simple foam barrier is placed ahead of the active filter, to stop large particles from clogging up the filter and reducing its effectiveness.

Figure 14-100

Similar principles can be used in large industrial baths, as can be seen (Figure 14-101) with the water being drawn through the filters from the bottom of the tank (where all the debris would settle), and then the pumps the clean water back into the top of the water bath.

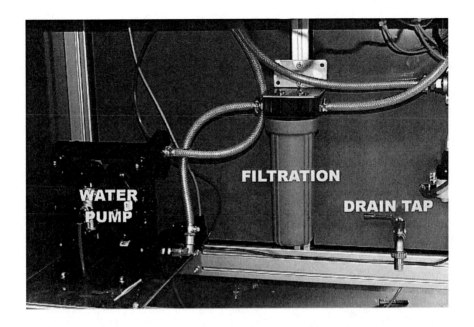

Figure 14-101

Note at the bottom that there has been a drain tap provided on the bath to enable complete draining and replenishment of the water from time to time whilst the bath itself is cleaned out. (The particular water pump provided on this machine was an air operated piston pump to provide large volume of water movement.)

14.2.10.2.2.2 <u>Weir Systems (Figure 14-102)</u>

An additional feature that I myself have employed is the use of a Weir system.

The weir is a section of the tank, partitioned from the main bath, which acts as an overflow, so that the surface (top) of the water in the bath falls into the weir. From here it is pumped through the filters to clean it thoroughly, before it is pumped back into the main bath.

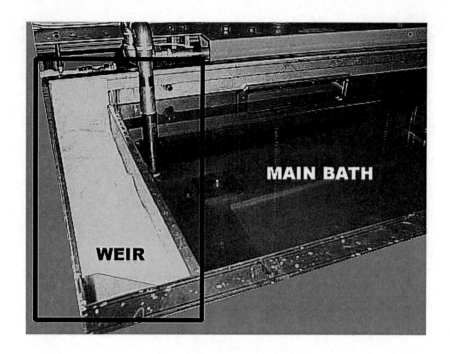

Figure 14-102

This weir includes the replaceable foam barrier to catch large particles of debris

14.2.10.2.3 Ensuring Operator Diligence

One of the biggest problems with the water bath immersion (bubbles under water) method is that it is a very subjective test, in that it is highly dependent on the operator to identify/detect a leak. It is only too easy for an operator to immerse the part, and then get distracted taking focus off of the bath. (I know—I have done it!)

So keeping the operator's attention on searching for bubbles is very important. I have seen a number of different methods employed, but one of the most successful, was the two-handed control method.

This technique is where the operator must keep their hands holding down control buttons on the machine, so that they are positioned correctly to observe the tank and search for signs of leakage. They must remain holding the buttons down for a specific time period, failure to do so, brings up an audible alarm and locks the parts in place, until the operator can repeat for the required time period.

14.2.10.2.4   Ease of Immersion

Of course, all of these fineries assume that the part is immersed, but precisely how do we immerse the component we are testing?

There are many methods, too many to mention, from simply holding the part under water in a fixed bath by hand to raising and lowering the entire bath on a scissor jack ... yes, I've done most of them at some time or other. Here are a few examples of the techniques I have used.

14.2.10.2.4.1 Small Parts on a Tray (Figure 14-103)

In this semi-automatic machine, the components were simply connected to the manifold for pressurising, and then the whole tray was automatically lowered into the fixed bath.

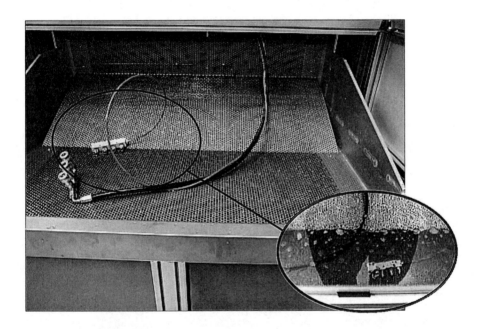

14.2.10.2.4.2 Larger Parts on a fixture

Another semi-automatic machine (Figure 14-104) however this one incorporates a full fixture, onto which the component to be tested is clamped and sealed for leak testing.

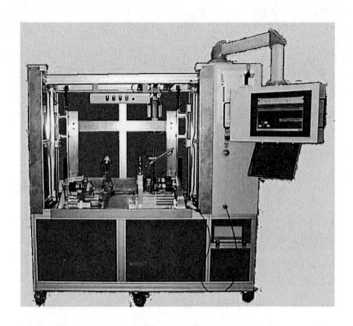

Figure 14-104

Again the bath is fixed in position, and when we wish to test the part it is placed onto the fixture and the clamps applied. On pressing the start button, a dry air leak test is carried out. If the part fails this dry air test, then it is pressurised, and automatically lowered into the bath, by use of a geared pully system (Figure 14-105).

Figure 14-105

478

This system also incorporated a Weir System to keep the water clean, and as with all water baths, the weir (and the main bath) incorporated water level sensors, to ensure the water is kept at the optimum level. In the case of the weir, the sensor (Figure 14-106) was used to trigger the pump to operate only when sufficient water was present in the overflow section of the bath.

Figure 14-106

14.2.10.2.4.3 Raising Bath Type System

So far we have seen different part variants being lowered into the fixed bath, but there are machines where the part remains fixed and the bath itself is raised on a scissor lift, to surround and immerse the part.

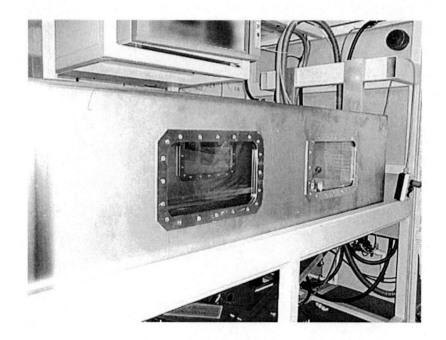

Figure 14-107

Here (Figure 14-107) we can see the bath in the raised position (showing the scissor lift below the bath - Figure 14-108). The bath itself includes windows, to enable the operator to view the part.

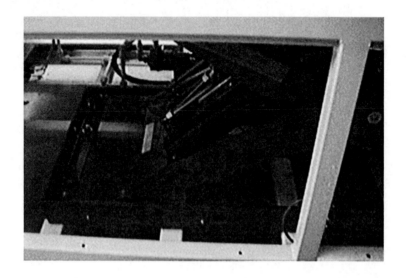

Figure 14-108

Such machines can be complex, and expensive, and most of all safety becomes more complicated requiring light curtains spaced away from the front of the machine, inhibiting the movement of the bath whilst the light curtains are interrupted.

The raising and lowering of the fixtures, or even the bath itself, does create additional safety risks from moving parts, which is never the ideal scenario. So how can we complete an underwater test, without moving the fixture or bath?

One technique I have employed very successfully is to use water displacement by air.

14.2.10.2.4.4 <u>Water Displacement</u>

In this method our fixture (these can be interchangeable just as with any other leak test system) remains inside the fixed bath, mounted on top of an inverted tank within the Main Water Bath (Figure 14-109).

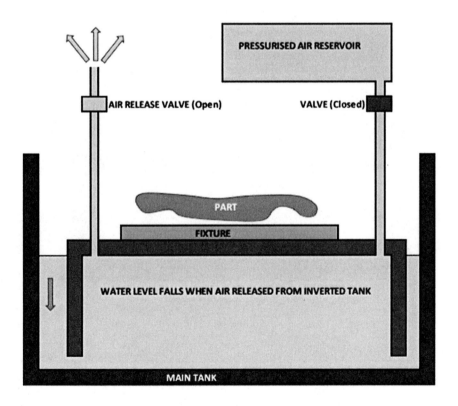

Figure 14-109

A reservoir (fig 14-110) is pressurised to a level so that when this air reservoir is connected to the inverted tank, the pressure drop to normal atmospheric pressure. the volume of air in the reservoir is thus shared between the reservoir and the inverted tank, so as to occupy the volumes of the two combined.

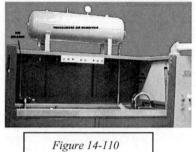

Figure 14-110

When it is required to immerse the part (Figure 14-111), then a fixed amount of air is allowed into the upturned bath. This air displaces the water in the upturned section, forcing the water level to rise above the part. In this way there are no moving parts to act as a safety hazard.

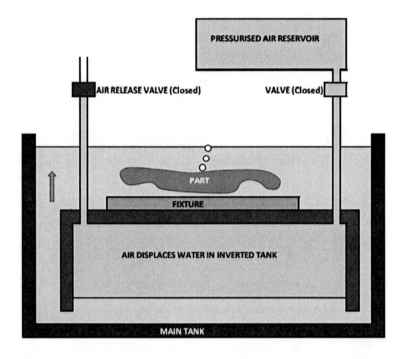

Figure 14-111

Of course, the flow of air from the reservoir to the inverted tank should be controlled, so as not to cause too much turbulence (Figure 14-112) in the water which might make bubble identification difficult.

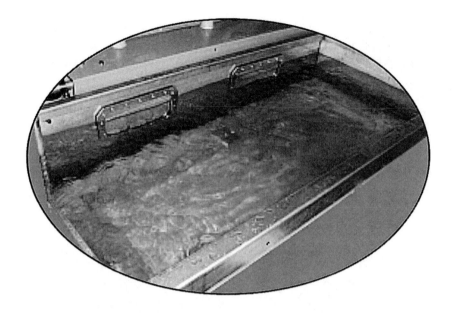

Figure 14-112

This method was preferred by many of my customers, as it had no moving parts, so the safety risks were minimised.

14.3 Test Machines/Systems Summary – Good Practice

Effectively, this section is a summary of special purpose leak test machines, with a view to highlighting some of the considerations you should consider when developing your own leak test solution.

14.3.1 General Concept

By this I mean we should initially think carefully about precisely what we would like our leak test machine to do for us.

- Is it just a leak tester, or do we want it to carry out additional checks?
- How will it be operated?
- How will we control/meet our required our throughput?
- General layout?

14.3.1.1 Just a Leak Test Machine?

Remember, leak testing is effectively non-value-added, so my advice is to look for opportunities to investigate what else could we get our machine to do for us. Maybe there are opportunities for us to include assembly, or can we carry out other physical checks on our part to ensure it has been correctly assembled.

In some cases, I have helped define and develop leak test machines that not only carry out the leak test, but also complete other functional checks.

One of the companies I worked for even operated a windscreen washer pump, whilst the leak test was performed to really mimic in use leak checks. (However, we did have to add some special smoothing software to reduce the noise effect on the leak test, whist the pump rotated.)

Figure 14-113

Note that this relatively simple machine (Figure 14-113) incorporated many of the items we have discussed including indicators and simple HMI, interchangeable tooling/fixtures, marking unit and E-Stop.

14.3.1.2 Single or Multiple Parts?

Do we want our machine to be dedicated to one part or to we want to maximise the useable time of our leak test facility by testing multiple parts or variations of parts using interchangeable fixtures where necessary.

With multiple parts, or part variation, do consider the opportunity to make the test fail safe with automated program parameter selection (for each part type/variant) to optimise our test. This can be achieved by bar code scanners, or part shape sensing, combined with fixture identification by electrical control pins.

14.3.1.3 How Will It Be Operated?

Do we want our machine to be fully automatic, semi-automatic, or just a simple fixture and leak test?

If we are considering full automation, then the feed and part removal systems must be considered as part of the machine design to ensure effective and accurate loading of the part onto the fixture.

Automated feeding bowls (Figure 14-114) could be an option, but we must ensure correct orientation of the part for loading onto the fixture.

Figure 14-114

Of course, we could load/unload our parts with the aid of a robot arm, which gives greater flexibility (but likely at greater cost). Semi-automatic machines are most common, with the operator taking responsibility for loading and unloading of the part, but in these machines, do consider the ease of loading accurately with the use of location pins or part nests.

And when unloading, how can we be sure that failed parts are not simply passed through. So do consider marking and or reject chutes/bins as a way of separating the good from the bad.

14.3.1.4 How will We Control/Meet Our Required Throughput?

With leak test machines, the instrument used to measure the leaks has specific requirements in terms of when it is required to be connected to the part/chamber under test. For air systems this is virtually the complete test cycle, whilst with tracer gas type systems, all of the filling and stabilising etc. can be completed in isolation from the actual detection device.

Although in the overall price of our machine, the detection device may not be a large portion of the cost, it can be beneficial to use one detector shared between multiple fixtures. After all the part still has to be loaded and unloaded, and one part could be being tested whilst the operator accesses the part.

The advantage of sharing one detection device is in the cost of maintenance, and the fact that one calibration check ensures our instrument good for all.

My advice is to do some work in advance looking at takt times, and assessing the requirements. I have found in many cases that multiple machines can have great benefits. This is particularly true where multiple variants/parts are to be tested. Consider having the same base machine able to take all of the different fixtures. This can offer great benefits in the event of one machine not being operational, as it enables you to test any part on any machine. (I am sure you will have seen from most of the examples, that we have often incorporated wheels on the base machines, enabling them to be located, and moved if necessary, to the required point of use for a particular part type.

14.3.1.5 General Layout?

A simple case of good ergonomics, and reducing movement is essential when developing your leak test machine. A good example of this is where I had one customer who wished to complete assembly, leak test, and then part number etching on a single assembly. The leak test incorporated a water bath, so it was not ideal to develop a single machine to perform all!

So we ended up with three separate machines (Figure 14-115) laid out specifically to make it easy for all three machines to be operated by 2 operators.

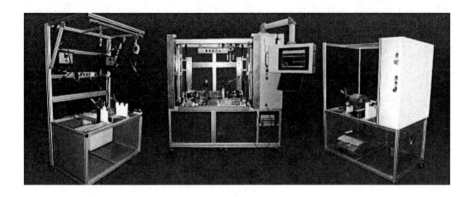

Figure 14-115

In order to ensure that the leak test could only test parts that had been correctly assembled, and for the etcher to only be able to mark parts that had passed the leak test, we incorporated hand scanners to record the serial numbers of each part on each station, and the result of the actions on that station. Bluetooth communications between the three stations then ensured that only properly assembled and leak tested parts could be finally marked and used for sale.

14.3.2 Recommended Features and Good Practice

In this section, my intention is to summarise my personal recommendations for specific leak test machine features. Whilst none of these are mandatory, I do believe they will offer great advantages to you as I will explain.

14.3.2.1 Calibration Checks

This is my simple MUST HAVE feature for any leak test facility, whether it be a simple leak tester or a complete system. However, for a bespoke leak test machine, this offers more than just a check that the leak tester is correctly calibrated and set up, as it also checks all of your fixturing and sealing for continued reliable operation.

By maintaining records of your calibration checks you can soon identify any form of drift, caused by seal wear, clamping effectiveness, pipework integrity, etc.

Please refer to calibration details in air and tracer testing sections for more details.

14.3.2.2 Clamping and Sealing

Please follow my guidelines on the best practice for clamping and particularly sealing of your part, to ensure it mimics the operational methods applied to the part, and wherever possible utilise the actual seals, and clamping points used on the part in normal operation.

14.3.2.3 Data Collection

You will by now have seen the number of charts I use to explain leak testing, most of these are simple test results plotted on graphs using a simple spreadsheet.

This is one feature that I almost insist on. In the main, it is simple storage of the leak test results, although where possible if you do have serial numbered parts, storage of the result against the serial number has even further benefits, as this enables you to have evidence to your customer (in the event of them suspecting you supplied a leaking part) that that particular part had been leak tested and that it was within their specifications!

On so many occasions, I have been asked to assist people with their leak test, none more so than suppliers to the Diesel Engine Plant that I worked for, particularly when we discovered leaks in their components during our leak testing of the complete engine assembly.

My first question to these suppliers was always do you have a set of leak test results that I can look at, and in many cases the answer was "no", which meant an additional need to collate some information about their leak test, which not only took time, but was in addition to their normal workloads, causing pain for all of us!

One great example was when we were finding the occasional component from a particular supplier would exhibit a leak. In discussions with the supplier they had correctly set up their leak test to the correct limit of 4 atm cm3 min-1 at the required operating pressure. I asked them then to run a number of tests and record the leak test results. In fact to get a good overall picture of the performance of their Leak Test, they had to complete 100 tests. They were not so happy about doing this as they did not have automatic result storage/collection, and had to manually write down the result of each test. (If they had automated data collection they could have just sent me their last 100, or even 1000, results from their stored data.)

When we reviewed the results (Figure 14-116), we could see that their leak test was performing really well showing repeatable results with a good gap between the test results and the leak limit, showing stable test conditions.

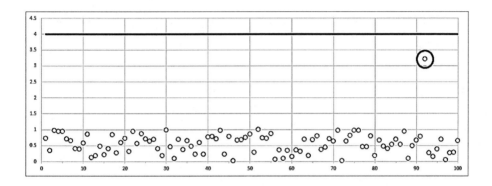

Figure 14-116

But we saw just a single result that was outside of the normal/bulk of the distribution, and although this was still comfortably inside of the leak limit, it made us think... Could parts with this leak value be the leaking parts we have been finding?

With the supplier's full understanding of what we found, we agreed to lower the limit set on the machine to just 3 atm cm3 min-1. This they did, and from that point on there was no further reports of leaking parts at our engine test.

Hopefully, this demonstrates that the ability to have results available to you personally give you the opportunity to review your testing at any time, so as to help you identify calibration issues, seal wear, or even just identify improvements that you can make to your own leak test (or even better to your part manufacture).

Having a date/time stamp against each leak test result can also benefit further in the identification of any patterns caused by shift change, seal wear and even the effect of ambient condition changes, etc.

15. Limitations of Leak Testing

Much of this has already been discussed in other sections, but it is worth just reviewing these once more before we go on to identification of problems that you might encounter.

15.1 Global Methods - Air Testing (Pressure Decay and Flow)

In general <u>all</u> air testing suffers primarily from the laws of physics (the Basic Gas Law states that $PV = nRT$ which (as n and R are both constants), is translated into

$$\frac{P_1 V_2}{T_1} = \frac{P_2 V_2}{T_2}$$

Or in other words pressure is directly affected by volume and temperature changes. The vast majority of issues for pressure decay and flow testing, are as a result of one of these two effects; however the root causes of these changes may not be so obvious, but do keep in mind that the root cause will no doubt be causing one of these.

15.1.1 Temperature Variation in Pressure Decay Measurement

One of the biggest issues surrounding air testing is the effect of temperature on the measurement.

If we consider the part under test as being a fixed volume, then:

$$\frac{P_1}{T_1} = \frac{P_2}{T_2} \quad or \quad P_2 = \frac{P_1 T_2}{T_1}$$

So as the temperature increases, then the pressure increases, and vice-versa, and because our pressure decay and flow systems rely on a leakage causing a pressure change within our component, clearly a change in pressure caused by a change in temperature can affect the value of leakage measured. The simplest way to view the effect of temperature change is by examples.

Example 1

Test pressure is 1 bar, and the leak we have causes a drop in pressure of 40 Pascals. (*Note: Our reject limit is set at 30 Pascals.*) What happens to the pressure inside the part if, during the measure phase, the temperature of air in the part increases by 0.05oC:

P_1 =   1 Bar   =   2 Bar absolute =   200000 Pascals

T_1 =   20oC   =   293 Kelvin

T_2 = 20.05oC   =   293.05 Kelvin

P_2 $= \dfrac{200000 \times 293.05}{293}$ =   200034   - this is an increase of 34 Pascals

Now our leak causes a drop in pressure of 40 Pascals, so our net result measured will be:

6 Pascal = PASS

So an increase in temperature could in fact mask our leak!

Example 2

Test pressure is 1 bar, and our component is very good, and only has a slight leak, causing a drop in pressure of only 10 Pascals (our reject limit is set at 30 Pascals). What would happen if, during the measure phase, the temperature of air in the part this time decreases by 0.05 oC:

P_1 =   1 Bar   = 2 Bar absolute = 200000 Pascals

T_1 =   20oC   = 293 Kelvin

T_2 =   19.95oC   = 292.95 Kelvin

P_2 $= \dfrac{200000 \times 292.95}{293}$ =   = 199966 A decrease of 34 Pascals

Now our leak causes a drop in pressure of 10 Pascals, so our net result measured will be:

44 Pascals = FAIL

So a decrease in temperature could in fact make a good part fail (false failure)!

15.1.2 Temperature Variation in Flow Measurement (Figure 15-1)

It is equally and really important to understand that temperature changes can equally cause problems with flow measurement just as much as air pressure decay testing. As we know from the Hagen-Poiseuille equation, flow is directly proportional to the pressure difference, as is most often demonstrable in the wind speed on our weather charts.

$$Q \ (flow) \quad = \quad \frac{\pi \ x \ R^4}{16 \ x \ \mu \ x \ L} \ x \ \left(\frac{P_i^2 - P_0^2}{P_0}\right)$$

To take into account that the flow rate will not be constant along the length of the tube

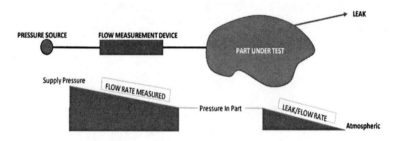

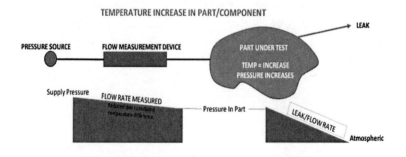

Figure 15-1

Many modern test machines incorporate an option to include temperature compensation, which can be really helpful in eliminating temperature effects from the likes of a heater washer system used on a component part such as a cylinder block or cylinder head. In such cases the cooling curve is generally quite predictable due to the thermal mass of the component itself.

However, temperature compensation is far less useful when the effect is created when heaters or cooling fans are directly in the location of the component under test (*or if someone puts their hot cup of coffee on top of an engine being tested—yep I have seen this happen!*), as these are less predictable and cannot be so easily adjusted for.

My advice: Avoid or fix any temperature effects wherever possible!

The table below (Table 15-1) gives a guide to expected effect of temperature changes for different test pressures assuming a starting temperature is 20oC (293Kelvin):

CHANGE IN PASCAL		TEMP CHANGE (deg C)						
		0.001	0.002	0.005	0.01	0.02	0.05	0.1
	-0.99	0.003	0.007	0.017	0.034	0.068	0.17	0.34
	-0.5	0.17	0.34	0.85	1.71	3.41	8.53	17.1
	-0.1	0.31	0.61	1.54	3.07	6.14	15.4	30.7
	0.1	0.38	0.75	1.88	3.75	7.51	18.8	37.5
	0.25	0.43	0.85	2.13	4.27	8.53	21.3	42.7
TEST PRESSURE (BAR)	0.5	0.51	1.02	2.56	5.12	10.2	25.6	51.2
	0.75	0.60	1.19	2.99	5.97	11.9	29.9	59.7
	1	0.68	1.37	3.41	6.83	13.7	34.1	68.3
	2	1.02	2.05	5.12	10.2	20.5	51.2	102
	5	2.05	4.10	10.2	20.5	41.0	102	205
	10	3.75	7.51	18.8	37.5	75.1	188	375

Table 15-1

15.1.3 Volume Variation

In a similar way, variation in volumes can also create problems when air testing. In solid components this is not such a big issue but where component parts contain flexible membranes, such as diaphragms or the part itself is made of a flexible material, slow creep of these items can alter the volume.

The biggest volume problems encountered on component parts (Solid or Flexible) though are caused by poor fixturing. In essence the component under test is not firmly restrained and can move of flex during the test phase. The main problem is parts not correctly clamped down to a hard/metal stop point (due to poor seal design—big squidgy seals), and allowed to sit on a cushion of rubber, but equally as devastating is a thin-walled component, that is not correctly supported allowing it to flex during the test.

Volume changes can also be caused by incorrectly fitted seals or sealing bungs, used to blank off open apertures. If any of these are not correctly engaged, then they can potentially slip during testing, causing a slight increase in the total volume under test, which will look like an additional leak.

Calculating the effect of volume change is similar to calculating the effect of temperature, but this time we assume the temperature remains constant in our universal gas laws.

$$P_1 \; x \; V_1 = P_1 \; x \; V_1 \quad or \quad P_2 \;\; = \;\; \frac{P_1 V_1}{V_2}$$

So as the Volume increases, then the pressure decreases, and vice-versa. Let me use an example from my own experience to demonstrate.

Again let me use a real life example, in this case, a large oil pan that is 500 x 500 x 100mm, which is correctly clamped down onto a test base (with correct sealing methods employed). The fixture also has an infill block reducing the actual volume under test to just 1000cc. However the large surface of the oil pan remains unsupported during the test so that it has the potential to flex due to the test pressure applied onto the inside of the part it begins to raise (Figure 15-2).

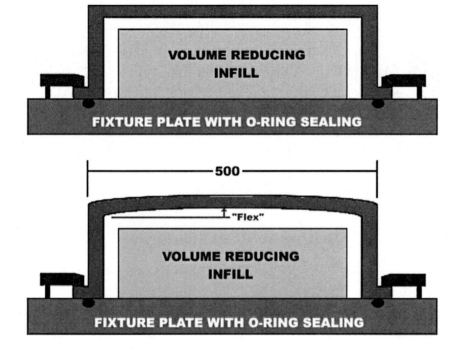

Figure 15-2

Our leak specification is 6 atm cm3 min-1 which gives us a pressure drop of 10Pa/s at a test pressure of 0.5 Bar (150000 Pa absolute). If our part expands, as shown, then the volume will increase.

Assuming our part normally gives a leakage rate of 0.0 Pa/s then we can calculate the height increase that would equate to a pressure change of 10Pa/s (or leak rate limit—and hence a false fail. Calculating the volume change that would relate to a change of 10Pascals, our values known are:

- P1   =   0.5 Bar (150000 Pascals absolute) – our test pressure
- P2   =   149990 Pascals (150000 – 10)
- V1   =   1000 cm3 (the free volume under test inside our oil pan)

So our Volume change can be calculated:

$$P_2 = \frac{P_1 V_1}{V_2} = \frac{1000 \times 150000}{149990} = 1000.07 \text{cm3}$$

So a volume change of only 0.07cm3 (70mm3) will create a pressure drop of 10Pascals in our test pressure; i.e., will look like a leak! To estimate the actual amount of movement of the top surface of the oil pan, we will assume it takes the shape of a pyramid (although not absolutely correct, it will suffice to give us an idea of how high the top face will move.

The volume of a pyramid is given by **Volume = 1/3 x W x L x H** (Figure 15-3).

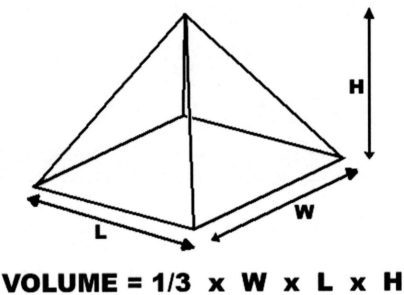

VOLUME = 1/3 x W x L x H

Figure 15-3

Now our W and L are both 50cm (500mm)
So we can calculate our height (H) from

$$H = \frac{3 \, x \, Vol \, Change \, (0.07cm3)}{W \, (50cm) \, x \, L(50cm)} = 0.00084cm$$

This is just 8.4 microns!

This clearly demonstrates the need to ensure no movement during the test/measurement phase/period of our test. The chart below (Table 15-2) give a guide to the volume effects at different test pressures assuming an initial test volume of 2 Litres (2000cm^3):

CHANGE IN PASCAL	VOLUME CHANGE (mm3) I n a volume of 2 LITRES						
	0.1	0.2	0.5	1	2	5	10
-0.99	0.0005	0.001	0.003	0.005	0.010	0.025	0.050
-0.5	0.025	0.05	0.13	0.25	0.50	1.25	2.5
-0.1	0.045	0.09	0.23	0.45	0.90	2.3	4.5
0.1	0.05	0.11	0.27	0.55	1.10	2.8	5.5
0.25	0.06	0.13	0.31	0.63	1.25	3.1	6.3
0.5	0.08	0.15	0.38	0.75	1.50	3.8	7.5
0.75	0.09	0.17	0.44	0.88	1.75	4.4	8.8
1	0.10	0.20	0.50	1.00	2.0	5.0	10.0
2	0.15	0.30	0.75	1.50	3.0	7.5	15.0
5	0.30	0.60	1.50	3.0	6.0	15.0	30.0
10	0.55	1.10	2.8	5.5	11.0	27.5	55.0

(TEST PRESSURE (BAR))

Table 15-2

Examining the effects of Temperature and volume on pressures, it would appear that the smallest of changes will have large effects on the leak rate measurement, however do not be too alarmed, as these temperature changes, would have to change the temperature of ALL the air throughout the volume under test, which as you can imagine, with thermal losses through the walls of the component, is much more difficult. But that's not to say there are no effects!

15.1.3.1 How Do Volume Changes Affect Flow Measurement?

Just like with temperature changes, changes in volume, whilst the flow measurements are taking place, will have an effect on these measurements, as the volume change alters the pressure in the part as we saw with temperature.

As before, the volume change will effectively change the pressure within the component under test. This pressure change alters the differential pressure between the supply and the part pressure, and so directly affects the flow rate through the flow measuring device as this pressure difference is directly proportional to the flow rate.

So a reduction in the volume of the part, will cause the pressure in the part to rise, effectively masking leakage, or if the volume expands, and the pressure falls we effectively measure a larger leakage rate than is actually present in the part.

15.1.4 False Failures

One of the major issues around leak testing is false failures, by which is meant, the component/assembly fails the leak test, but no leak can be found, and when the part is retested, is passes. There are a number of reasons for this.

Temperature and Volume Variation: As we have already seen changes in temperature or volume can create additional components to our leak test reading. But what else can cause such false failures to occur?

- Adiabatic effects
- Tolerance stack-up

15.1.5 Instability/Adiabatic Effects

Instability and adiabatic effects are more difficult to demonstrate. However let us again consider the Basic Gas Law, which shows the relationship between pressure and temperature and volume:

$$\frac{P_1 V_1}{T_1} = \frac{P_2 V_2}{T_2}$$

Adiabatic effects refer to the effect created when pressurising a fixed volume. As we can see the temperature of the air will increase dramatically.

But as we have already mentioned heat transfer between the test air and the physical part material itself, and then between the part material and the atmosphere, serves to cool the air inside the part. If left long enough, the air inside the component under test, and the component itself, will reach the same temperature as the surrounding air (Figure 15-4).

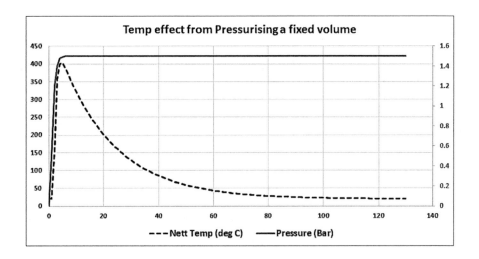

Figure 15-4

As we have already discussed if we were to measure during the period when the temperature is dropping rapidly, then this temperature drop would cause the pressure to change, and would look like a leak.

Clearly, we could wait until all the temperatures (air in part, and part itself) have reached an equilibrium with the surrounding air. But this might take an incredibly long time (particularly with large assemblies such as an engine).

So we have to accept some level of compromise, and wait sufficiently long enough for the rate of change of temperature to be small enough so that during our short measurement phase the pressure change caused by adiabatic effects, is insignificant compared to the level of pressure drop expected for our leak limit (typically below 5%?).

But adiabatic effects are not just combined to temperature effects, but also the physical properties of the air itself, as I mentioned before, I like to try and think of the air itself as being made up of a load of small rubber balls, which bounce around, and collide with each other, and so the effect on sensitive devices can be quite dramatic. In the case of differential transducers (Figure 15-5) they bounce on the thin membrane, causing it to vibrate, and in the flow systems (Figure 15-6), the collisions with other air molecules cause the air molecules to travel backwards looking like a flow in the wrong direction.

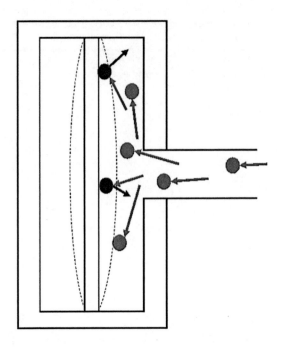

Figure 15-5

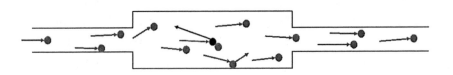

Figure 15-6

In general, most adiabatic effects are caused mainly as a result of allowing insufficient time to carry out the test (as a result of ever reducing "tackt" times on engine assembly lines).

15.1.6 Tolerance Build Up

This is by far the biggest issue for global testing of large assemblies such as automotive engines (*using air or even with trace gas in a global method*).

One of the first things we learned was that there is no such thing as zero leak, and that everything leaks to a lesser, or greater extent, but that this is acceptable, if the leak is small enough to maintain the part's fitness for purpose.

So let us consider an automotive engine. Each circuit (fuel, oil, coolant) is made up of a number of component parts. For example, the oil circuit contains a number of component parts including:

- Cylinder block
- Cylinder head
- Water pump
- Sump
- Oil cooler
- Timing case
- Top cover
- Rear end oil seal
- Front end oil seal
- Numerous joints

Now each of these individual components is leak tested by the original manufacturer, according to the specification we have provided (calculated earlier from our conversion from liquid to air leakage) which means that each one has been tested to ensure it has a total leakage of less than 5 atm cm3 min^{-1}-.

When these are installed on the engine, and we leak test this engine, all of the leaks for each component add together (much like tolerances on a group of parts bolted together) so that our resultant leak measured is the total of these, as below (Table 15-3).

CONSIDER OUR ENGINE		
Component	Max Leak Spec (cc/min) to meet "Fit For Purpose"	Engine 1 (No Component Leaks - ALL Fit For Purpose
Cylinder Block	5	0.5
Water Pump	5	0.4
Sump/Oil Pan	5	1.4
Oil Cooler	5	1.1
Timing Case	5	1.5
Top Cover	5	1.0
REOS	5	1.4
FEOS	5	0.1
10 off joints	60	9.3
GLOBAL LEAK TEST RESULT (Total ALL Leaks)		16.7
RESULT FOR TOTAL ENGINE		
Limit Set	45	PASS

Table 15-3

As we can see, we set out limit not to the sum of these tolerances but somewhat lower—as previously discussed in fitness for purpose on a complete engine. All looks OK, but now consider a 2nd engine as below (Table 15-4):

CONSIDER A 2nd ENGINE			
Component	Max Leak Spec (cc/min) to meet "Fit For Purpose"	Engine 1 (No Component Leaks - ALL Fit For Purpose	Engine 2 (Small Component Leaks - ALL Fit For Purpose)
Cylinder Block	5	0.5	4.3
Water Pump	5	0.4	3.7
Sump/Oil Pan	5	1.4	4.6
Oil Cooler	5	1.1	4.1
Timing Case	5	1.5	4.8
Top Cover	5	1.0	4.7
REOS	5	1.4	4.3
FEOS	5	0.1	3.8
10 off joints	60	9.3	14.4
GLOBAL LEAK TEST RESULT (Total ALL Leaks)		16.7	48.7
RESULT FOR TOTAL ENGINE			
Limit Set	45	PASS	FAIL

Table 15-4

We can see that:

- Although all parts are fit for purpose (all suppliers checking parts meet individual leak limit requirements)
- The total leakage crosses our leak test limit, and the engine fails

Whilst this is not a major issue, and acts in a fail-safe way, this is a false fail and operators may be searching for a leak path that will not leak our liquid. Far more worrying is this 3rd Engine (Table 15-5):

NOW CONSIDER A 3rd ENGINE				
Component	Max Leak Spec (cc/min) to meet "Fit For Purpose"	Engine 1 (No Component Leaks - ALL Fit For Purpose	Engine 2 (Small Component Leaks - ALL Fit For Purpose)	Engine 3 (TWO REAL Component Leaks - NOT Fit For Purpose)
Cylinder Block	5	0.5	4.3	1.5
Water Pump	5	0.4	3.7	1.9
Sump/Oil Pan	5	1.4	4.6	5.2
Oil Cooler	5	1.1	4.1	1.1
Timing Case	5	1.5	4.8	12.7
Top Cover	5	1.0	4.7	1.2
REOS	5	1.4	4.3	1.2
FEOS	5	0.1	3.8	2.0
10 off joints	60	9.3	14.4	3.4
GLOBAL LEAK TEST RESULT (Total ALL Leaks)		16.7	48.7	30.2
RESULT FOR TOTAL ENGINE				
Limit Set	45	PASS	FAIL	PASS

Table 15-5

As we can see that:

- Although there are 2 components *not fit for purpose*, and likely to leak our liquid
- The engine *passes* our leak test and potentially these leaks reach our customer

15.2 Trace Gas Methods

Tracer gas methods are not adversely affected by the general laws of physics; however, they are subject to issues that will serve to give false fails and passes just as air systems.

15.2.1 Background Contamination

Most common issue with sniffer methods (but can also impact sealed tracer systems). If gas dispersal into the atmosphere is not efficient, then some of the trace gas may hang around and create gas clouds/raised background levels of trace gas, which can then be drawn into the sniffer/sampling tube causing false readings, that may look like a leak.

Although Helium and Hydrogen are significantly less mass than air, and they have a tendency to travel upwards, activity around the area will 'stir up' the air and trace gas, causing it to mix and remain in the area. For this reason, it is important that any unused trace gas is effectively removed from the area of the test. this can be achieved in a number of ways.

With direct sniffing the problem can be controlled in a number of ways, such as extraction hoods (Figure 15-7) located above the work are, where the leak testing is carried out.

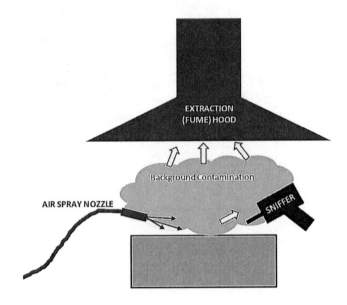

Figure 15-7

And often operators will utilise a small air flow that can be directed, so that in the event of trace gas being detected, the operator can clear any potential background contamination by clearing the area from a remote air supply.

Background contamination however can also be caused by outgassing from dirty areas, so it is essential to keep our work area as clean as possible.

15.2.2 Clear-Down

A similar effect is found more commonly with sealed trace gas systems, particularly after a large leak on a part, causes large amounts of the trace gas to remain in the test chamber, or detector itself. This results in wasted time allowing all of this gas to disperse, but can also cause false reading from residual gas.

In the enclosed systems, the part of the cycle that clears residual gases should be sufficiently long enough to remove as much residual gas as possible.

- In the case of purge and CBU systems this will be the High Purge part of the cycle. (suggested a minimum of ten air changes within our test chamber). It is recommended that a minimum of 10 air changes occur in the chamber to effectively reduce any background, although this will vary depending on the machine design.
- For vacuum systems, this will likely be the evacuation time for the chamber being sufficiently long enough to rid the area of stray gas concentrations (including and background gas from outgassing!).

15.2.3 Outgassing

With vacuum chamber helium systems in particular any corners, or dirt collection will serve to absorb, or hang on to trace gases allowing them to leech out over time causing false readings (hence the need for high levels of cleanliness, and smoothed corners in chambers for this type of equipment)—this is known as outgassing.

This is a particular problem in vacuum systems as they require on the vacuum level achieved, and any outgassing (e.g., caused by moisture or dirt in rubber seals, the corners of our test chamber etc.) can cause issues with the system and it's repeatability/accuracy.

In summary: Keep all leak test areas—fixtures, test chambers, etc.—as clean as possible and set up a regular routine for cleaning between tests.

15.2.4 Gas Concentration

Clearly, the gas mix will have a large bearing on the amount of helium being measured, as we should multiply any reading we get by the inverse of the trace gas concentration, to give us our approximate total leakage.

Total Leak ≈Measured Leak x % concentration of trace gas

For Example: If we are using a 1% Helium in Air mixture as our trace gas, and our detector gives a reading of 1 x 10^{-3}cc/sec (0.001 cc/s), as our leak Then our total leak is really 100 times this (1 x 10^{-1}cc/s = 0.1cc/s), = 6 cc/min.

People often forget this, and take the reading from the tester as the leak rate, later discovering leaking parts have escaped the process.

15.2.5 Homogeneous Gas Mixtures

One thing to be very aware of is how we pressurise our component with the trace gas, as we must ensure that any leakage path has the correct concentration passing through it, by ensuring a completely homogeneous mixture inside the part/assembly. Simply pressurising with the gas may cause part of the component to contain only air (Figure 15-8), whilst the rest contains the trace gas mixture.

Figure 15-8

This is normally achieved by evacuating (pulling a vacuum on) the part before pressurising it with the trace gas, as in this way trace gas is 'pulled' to all parts of the com[ponent, ensuring trace gas is present at all potential leak sites.

Other techniques are sometimes employed, such as:

- Filling/pressurising from multiple points
- Air mixing fans to stir up the gases within the part

But neither of these can guarantee that all parts of the component under test contain the correct gas mixture, as an large assemblies such as automotive engine assemblies have many pathways where just air could be trapped, and no or little tracer gas is present behind the leak path.

15.2.6 Transition Times

Essentially, the 'Transition Time' is the time it takes for the helium/trace gas to go from the inside of the component, to the outside of the component (where it is detected) through the leak path.

Typical examples of this include the passage of the trace gas up the thread of a bolt/screw (Figure 15-9), or through porosity in a casting.

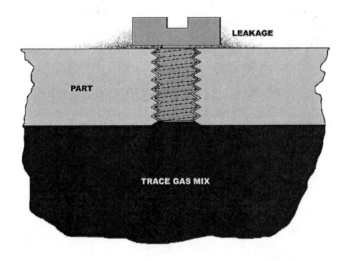

Figure 15-9

In this diagram, the Helium (RED) is at the end of the bolt. The bolt has not been correctly 'sealed' in place, and so there is a leak path up through the threads. Clearly, it will take some time for the helium gas to travel the full length of the bolt thread, and begin escaping at the head of the bolt.

Example:

- *If the diameter of the bolt thread is 8mm and there are 10 threads engaged, then the length of the path can be calculated to be 25 cm.*
- *If the gap has a cross sectional area of the channel is 1mm2 then the total volume of this channel is approximately 2.5cc.*

507

- *Now if the leak we are searching for is 20cc/min (0.33cc/sec) then clearly it will take a Transition Time of at least 7.5 seconds before any helium appears at the top of the bolt.*

The way to ensure that this is not an issue for you is to review the design of the part, and look for examples where there could be long transition times and ensure our test cycles are long enough to be able to adequately detect such a leak path.

Porosity is created by gas bubbles within our casting building up to form chains through the casting, most often only apparent when the surface is machined. Such chains can be quite long (Figure 15-10), and as such it can take similar amounts of time as that shown in our threaded bolt example for the trace gas to pass through the full length of the porous chain.

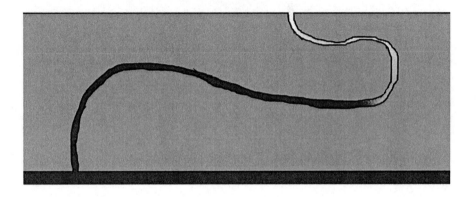

Figure 15-10

The best solution for porosity is simply to ensure your casting process is effective in minimising the risk of creating porosity in the first place, as it is very difficult to predict the length of porous chains, and design our leak test to be sure to detect them.

As we can see, the majority of issues relate to temperature, volume and trace gas clouds and travel, but always do consider these potential problems when developing your leak test solution.

16. Problems and How to Identify/Recognise Them

Of course, there are many issues that we may well be able to identify, and put solutions for in advance, however, as with all best laid plans, things can go wrong after we have set up and begun operating our leak test for the part, so how do we recognise when such problems occur, and what can we do about them?

I will go through some of the common issues that might occur, and the process we can take to identify the potential root cause, with a view to putting some corrective actions in place.

You will no doubt see from the details that follow, that I will constantly refer to test result analysis, and I want to point out once again, the importance of collecting test result data wherever possible. You will find some fault-finding charts in the Appendix of this book to aid in your own investigations.

It is important to remember that I cannot include all eventualities, but if you keep in mind what the equipment is doing you can use these guidelines and work through your own fault finding in a perfectly logical way to draw your own conclusions.

16.1 Failing Everything

Not that common with modern leak testers, but nonetheless worth reviewing the issue, and looking at how we will identify the root cause.

16.1.1 Air Testing (Pressure Drop and Flow measurement)

Remember at all times, that the measurement device is simply measuring pressure (or flow, which by its nature depends on pressure), from the measuring instrument itself (Figure 16-1).

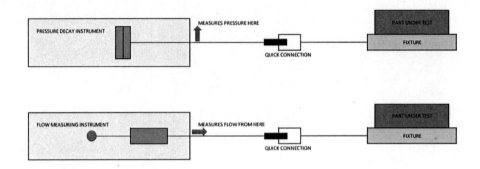

Figure 16-1

So if we are failing everything, it is possible that we have developed a leak somewhere beyond the connection to the instrument, although this maybe not the case as we will see below.

1. The first and easiest step is to utilise/test our master good part to test the complete system and review the result in relation to our leak test limit (Figure 16-2).

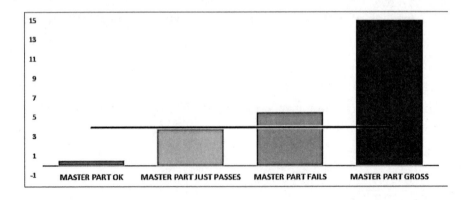

Figure 16-2

a. Master part passes with expected result – Machine is functioning correctly, and there is likely a difference between our Master, and our production parts
b. Master part only just passes – Possible leak in our system, or maybe incorrect test parameters

c. Master part fails – Possible leak in our system, or maybe incorrect test parameters

d. Master part gross leaks – Highly likely that our system has developed a leak

2. The second option is to reverse check the system by following the fault finding steps below (see fault finding chart in Figure 16-3 below):

a. First of all, blank off the rear of the leak tester and check that we can get a pass result for the leak test instrument in isolation. (If this fails, then we may need support from our leak test instrument supplier.)

b. If the instrument passes, then blank off at the next available joint; this may be the quick connector to our interchangeable fixtures, or at the fixture itself. This checks for leaks in the pipework, connecting the fixture to the leak tester Or try a different fixture if you have interchangeability.

c. If we can achieve a pass all the way to the fixture, then we are potentially going to be looking at possible seal or clamping issues.

d. If the seals and clamping are OK, then only a master part can then be used to check to see if it just our production parts or not.

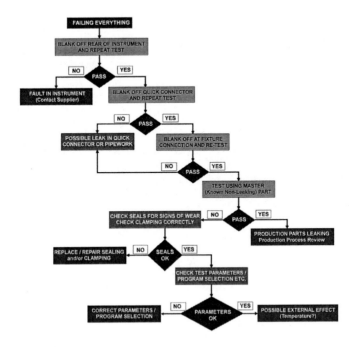

Figure 16-3

511

16.1.2 Tracer Gas Testing

Again, the first thing to remember about the actual gas detectors, is that they only respond to the tracer gas being present in the instrument detection device. so if we are getting a failure, the most likely cause is that gas has been detected.

16.1.3 Direct Sniffing Method

When we are directly sniffing for leaks, the most likely cause of constantly detecting trace gas are two-fold:

1. Background contamination – this can easily be confirmed by utilising a clean air supply to blow across/around the area being sniffed, or alternatively taking the detector to a different area.
a. If background levels of gas are proved, look for alternative sources, particularly if a non-specific detector is being used. (I personally have had experience of perfumes, and aftershaves being detected!)
2. Alternatively there may be a leak in our fixturing, or gas supply system
a. My advice is to use soap solution to see if you can detect any signs of leakage.

16.1.4 Trace Gas Systems

In the case of leak test machines, then it is very likely that something in our machine has developed a leak, or that there are alternative sources of the trace gas.

As always a master known non leaking part is often the simplest way to check. If the master part passes, then we should look at our production parts to see if we can identify the root cause, due to a manufacturing process change, or even a design change that we have not been alerted to. (Yes, it does happen!)

16.1.4.1 Leaks in the System

Finding leaks in tracer systems is far more difficult than with air test machines, as often we do not have access to the parts that can leak during our test, and often it is a case of replacing parts one by one to see if the leak can be stopped. My advice is to follow these steps, which are a guide to the most likely causes in order:

1. Replace seals on fixturing, or quick inflating sealing units (that connect the part)—this is the most common source of leaks developing.
2. Replace quick connectors in the test line – these are constantly being connected/disconnected, and will wear in time.
3. Check other joints in our trace gas supply pipework to the part. I would suggest pressurising these with air and use soap solution to identify possible leaks.
4. Check the pipework itself for leakage (using air and soap solution). Believe it or not, I was once called out to a machine that was failing everything, and after a long investigation, I traced the leak to a pinhole in a piece of nylon tube. Examining the tube under strong magnification later it was apparent that a pin had been used to make the leak…I will leave you to consider how!

If all of the above fails to locate the source of leakage, then it may be that the gas we are detecting is from another source.

16.1.4.2 Alternative Leak Sources

Very much as for direct sniffing, the source of the trace gas may be from another source. The most likely sources are:

1. **Outgassing**
    Particularly with vacuum systems, dirty fixtures or chambers can retain gas and release during our measurement phase. The simple solution is to thoroughly clean down the machine (ensuring it is dry) and finally blow-down the machine with a clean air supply.
2. **Background Contamination**
    This would be found in the surrounding area, so I often recommend that if you do have a trace gas system, also by a cheap hand sniffer to as you can use this by zeroing in a clean environment (possibly outside), and then go back to the machine area to see if background levels can be detected.
    a. A possible source of this background contamination can come from the exhaust of our machine, which safely removes the trace gas after test. check for leaks in this also using soap solution, but ensure all unused

trace gas is safely piped away from the area, preferably to the outside of the building.

One very unexpected source of background contamination I came across was from the exhaust of the machine which was piped away. However, the factory was based in the bottom of a valley, and unfortunately the trace gas we were using (Sulphur Hexafluoride) was heavier than air, and we found that the we held our hand sniffer, the greater the response, indicating that the gas was gathering around the base of the machine. The solution was simply to dig a hole below the test machine (Figure 16-4), and then include a fan to draw the gas which was settling around the machine out of the area with a fan.

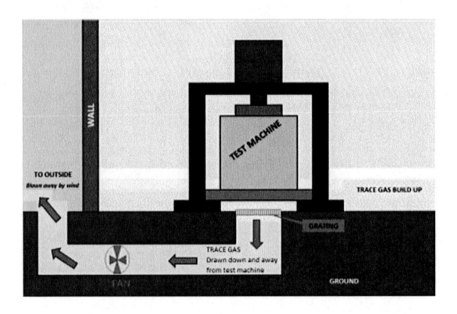

Figure 16-4

16.2 Passing Everything

This is in fact very rare, as leak test systems are relatively fail-safe, failing rather than passing in the event of problems. Also, if you follow my advice and carry out regular calibration checks, then you will be aware of any changes happening before they reach the point of no detection!

However, it does sometimes happen, that you seem to not be detecting leaking parts, when you are confident that leaks, so let us consider some of the root causes. Always remember the basic fact about any measuring device, and think about what it is actually measuring:

- In the case of air systems pressure or flow of air
- In tracer systems it is simply how much trace gas is entering the detector

16.2.1 Air Testing (Pressure Drop and Flow measurement)

If no pressure change is being measured by the detection device, then either no pressure change is happening, or the detector isn't connected to the area where the pressure is changing.

Again, the use of masters is the simplest way we cha check things, in this case our master is the master calibrated leak, as this should give us an actual amount of pressure change (or flow) that we can expect, and can be a good indication as to why we are not detecting leaking parts.

If you recall, my recommendation is ideal to locate the calibration port (into which you connect your master leak) as close to (or if possible built into) the part under test as possible. However, I do understand that it is often more practical to utilise the calibration port built into the leak tester itself, so I will consider both options as we go through these following fault finding regimes, so that hopefully I can show the benefit of having our calibration port as near the part under test as possible.

As always, to confirm the operation of your tester, make a test on a known good part, followed by a test with the same good part, plus the addition of the calibrated master leak. The diagram below (Figure 16-5) shows our good part test result, followed by four different options for our result with the master leak. But what do these tell us?

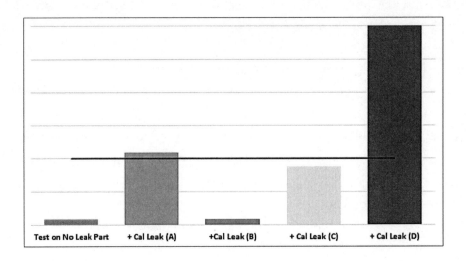

Figure 16-5

First of all, let us consider a leak test, where our calibration port is near to (or connected directly to) the part.

1. Cal Leak Result (A)
    This shows that our system is working fine, as the with leak result is the same as the calibrated master leak, plus our no leak result.
a. However, if you are still not failing known leaking parts, consider other effect such as temperature of production parts being tested (are they much warmer, and creating a pressure rise during the measurement phase?)

2. Cal Leak Result (B)
    This shows virtually no change to our reading when we introduce a leak. This immediately tells us that there is no connection between the leak test measuring device and the calibration port/ part under test.
a. The first thing to check is that you have correctly installed (fully pushed home) the master calibrated leak into the calibration port.
i. Calibrated master leaks can become blocked so do verify with open tube connected to calibration port
b. This could be due to a blockage in the test line between our tester and the calibration port/part under test.

c. But it could be even simpler, in that the instrument may simply not be connected, and if you have used self-sealing quick connectors to connect the fixture/part, then maybe this is the root cause.

d. Or maybe after having your leak tester maintained, or you have been investigating a fails everything scenario you have inadvertently left the blanking of the test instrument in place. (Yes, I did do this on more than one occasion!)

3. Cal Leak Result (C)

This result indicates that the calibration value is almost correct, but just a little low—it does however show that the leak tester is connected to the calibration port/part under test.

a. The root cause of such a result may be that you are not running the correct set of test parameters (incorrect program selected) for this particular part

b. Or it could mean that the calibration of the instrument may require adjustment

4. Cal Leak Result (D)

A very much larger reading than expected on the instrument indicates that the incorrect volume is being tested, but that the instrument is measuring leaks at the calibration port/part under test.

a. The most likely cause is that you are simply using the wrong test program (parameters) for this part.

b. There is another possibility (although most unlikely) that the instrument is faulty, in which case you would need to consult the instrument supplier.

Let us now consider the same results when we are utilising the calibration port on the instrument.

1. Cal Leak Result (A)

This shows that our system is working fine, as the with leak result is the same as the calibrated master leak, plus our no leak result.

a. However if our component under test is very, very small, then it does not help us at all, as the total volume under test is virtually the same with, and without the part connected! –

i. In this situation, the only real way you can confirm the test is operating correctly, is to run a test with no part connected (or a part having a gross leak) to see if we get any readings at all.

2. Cal Leak Result (B)

This shows virtually no change to our reading when we introduce a leak. This tells us that the instrument t is simply not measuring the calibrated master leak.

a. This could simply be that you have not correctly/fully pushed home the master leak into the calibration port

i. Calibrated master leaks can become blocked so do verify with open tube connected to calibration port

b. Less likely is that the calibration port on the instrument is not connected to the internal test circuit on the test instrument, in which case you would need to contact the supplier

3. Cal Leak Result (C)

This result indicates that the calibration value is almost correct, but just a little low– it does however show that the leak tester is measuring leakage.

a. The root cause of such a result may be that you are not running the correct set of test parameters (incorrect program selected) for this particular part

b. Or it could mean that the calibration of the instrument may require adjustment

4. Cal Leak Result (D)

A very much larger reading than expected on the instrument indicates that the incorrect volume is being tested, but that the instrument is measuring leaks at the calibration port/part under test.

a. The most likely cause is that the part is simply not connected (and quick connectors if used are self-sealing).

b. It could however indicate a blockage in the test line between the instrument and the part. This can be checked by introducing a gross leaking part and testing this without the master leak to confirm that the leak tester does detect a leak in the part.

c. Of course it could also mean that you are using the wrong test program (parameters) for this part.

d. Of course it could be (although very unlikely) that the instrument is faulty, in which case you would need to consult the instrument supplier.

16.2.2 Tracer Gas Testing

Again, keeping in mind that the detector will only respond when a trace gas enters the detection device itself, you can work through potential causes in a quite logical manner

Whatever technique (sniffing or within a complete test machine) you are using, the most obvious root cause of passing everything is quite simply that there is no trace gas to be detected.

So before you go looking for a fault in your instrument or test machine, please do check that the trace gas is connected and turned on. I appreciate that with most machine builds, there will be a check that test pressure is being applied to the part, but if this pressure sensor/transducer is located prior to (in between the supply and the part) the part itself, then it does not mean the gas is reaching the part, as we will see below.

Again, the simplest test is to make use of a calibrated master leak (that you will have purchased with your equipment), and to carry out a test using this to confirm detection.

16.2.3 Direct Sniffing Method

It is very likely that your master calibrated leak will be a separate unit, and not connected to the same trace gas supply as you part. If this is the case then consider the following:

1. Result is as expected then your detector is working OK and the reason you are not detecting leaks in the part is because the trace gas is not reaching the leak path because:

a. Your trace gas supply to the part is not turned on, or is disconnected.

b. There is a blockage in the connection between the supply and the part, so no trace gas is entering your part.

c. The trace gas mix inside the part is not mixing correctly and only air (or an incorrect concentration of trace gas) is present at the site of the leak.

2. Result is a little lower than expected

This shows the detector is functioning, but one of the following may be possible:

a. The detector requires recalibration/adjustment.
b. The gas in your master leak device is not at the correct pressure.
c. The leak may be partially blocked.
3. No response to leak

(*Note: This is less likely if you regularly carry out calibration checks as you will notices a steady decline over time.*)

Definite fault with any of the following being the possible root cause:

a. The gas in your master leak device has run out.
b. The master leak may be completely blocked.
c. The detector is faulty—seek advice from the supplier.

However, if your master leak is connected directly to the same source as your part under test:

1. Result is as expected then all is OK and you are leak testing OK
a. Just may be that your parts do not leak
b. The reason you are not detecting leaks in the parts is because the trace gas is not reaching the leak path because:
i. There is a blockage in the connection between the supply and the part, so no trace gas is entering your part.
ii. The trace gas mix inside the part is not mixing correctly and only air (or an incorrect concentration of trace gas) is present at the site of the leak.
2. Result is a little lower than expected

This shows the detector is functioning, but one of the following may be possible:

a. The detector requires recalibration/adjustment.
b. The gas in your master leak device is not at the correct pressure.
c. The leak may be partially blocked.
3. No response to leak

Definite fault with any of the following being the possible root cause:

a. Your trace gas supply to the part is not turned on, or is disconnected.
b. The master leak may be completely blocked.
c. The detector is faulty—seek advice from the supplier.

16.2.4 Not Detecting Leaking Parts in a Machine Test

In trace gas machines, again, it would be best to utilise a master calibrated leak to help determine the root cause for not detecting leaks in your parts. However, it does depend on the location of the master leak, and also the supply to the master leak. There are a wide range of options as can be seen (Figure 16-6). The leak could be positioned either at the part/chamber, or on the inlet or outlet from the chamber. In addition the gas supply to the master leak may be from the same source as the part, or a different source all together.

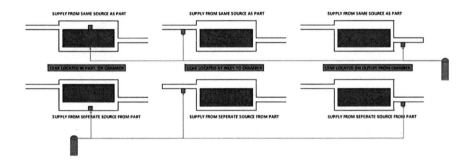

Figure 16-6

Let us look at the different potential results and try and make some sense of their meaning for each scenario.

16.2.4.1 Master Leak Gives Expected Result

1. Leak Located in Part/Chamber
a. If the master leak is located within the part itself, then this replicates the normal test, and if we get an expected result, then it indicates that all of our system is working correctly, and the fault lies within the production

521

parts; maybe there has been a design change, so the trace gas can no longer reach the leaking area?

b. However if the master leak is located in the chamber, then it is very likely that separate valve systems are employed to install the trace gas behind the leak and the part when required.

    i. In either case check the valves controlling the supply to the part, as it is likely that they are not operating. Clearly, with an expected result on the master leak, the trace gas is getting to the master leak.

    ii. If valves are operating ok, then it is very likely that the fixture/part under test may not be correctly connected to the trace supply, or maybe there is a blockage in the supply lines to the part.

    iii. Where gas mixing is concerned (where you are controlling the trace gas concentration to the part on board the machine), you will also need to check the mixing system to ensure it is correctly mixing the trace gas to the correct concentration for the part under test.

2. Leak Located at Inlet to the Chamber

This indicates that the chamber, and flows around the chamber are satisfactory, as we can detect a leak that occurs at the furthest point from the detector. However, it tells us nothing about the gas supplies to the part, and the same rules apply to this as to the leak being in the part/chamber.

a. Again check the valves controlling the supply to the part, as it is possible that they are not operating.

b. If valves are operating ok, then it is also possible that the fixture/part under test may not be correctly connected to the trace supply, or maybe there is a blockage in the supply lines to the part.

c. Check that on-board mixing systems are operating correctly, and that the gas concentration is reaching the part.

3. Leak located on outlet from the chamber, or at the inlet to the detector

This is the normal type of calibration check when the calibrated master is located within the detector itself. And it only really tells us that the detector itself is detecting correctly in which case the root fault could be many fold, and all of the following would ned to be confirmed.

a. Tracer gas source supply to the part is correct and at the right pressure, and concentration (particularly for on-board mixing).

b. The part/fixture is correctly connected to the trace supply, with no blockages
c. Valves connecting the tracer supply to the part are operating correctly
d. The air flow through the chamber is operating and at the correct rate of flow.
e. Maybe the part design has changed, and the trace gas cannot reach the leak path.

My recommendation is to force a small amount of trace gas into the inlet to the chamber and see if this is detected.

16.2.4.2 Master Leak Gives Low Result (just below expected level)

There are as always, a number of reasons that this could happen.

1. In the majority of cases this is a good indication that the detector calibration may require adjustment, so this is the very first thing to check.
2. However it could also mean that the trace supply is at the incorrect pressure or concentration.
3. In purge flow measurement systems it could also mean that the Low Purge Flow is higher than it should be (thus reducing the concentration of the master leak within the flow to the detector).

16.2.4.3 Master Leak Gives High Result (above the expected level)

This again is very similar to a low result in that:

1. The detector calibration may require adjustment.
2. Alternatively it could be that the trace supply is at the incorrect pressure or concentration.
3. In purge flow measurement systems it could also mean that the low purge flow is lower than it should be (thus increasing the concentration of the master leak within the flow to the detector).

16.2.4.4 Master Leak Gives No Leak Result

This generally tells us that no trace gas is getting to either the part, or the master leak.

a. Check first that the trace supply(s) are on and at the correct pressure.
b. Also check that the fixture is correctly connected (quick connectors etc.) to the trace supply.
c. Check that the valves within the trace supplies are operating correctly and that there are no blockages in any of the supply lines.
d. If the leak is at the outlet of the chamber (inlet to or within the detector), then this could indicate that the detector is no longer measuring correctly, and may be in need of maintenance or repair.

16.3 My Customer Fails Parts that Pass on My Tester

Not surprisingly, this is one of the most common complaints I have been asked to advise on throughout my career in leak testing. Invariably, when this problem arises, we must go right back to basics to start with and understand everything from the basic specification, right through to how the customer is defining the leak.

My own personal training and experience with this fault finding such issues, allows me to apply the correct principals to my investigations into understanding the root cause and subsequently some form of solution.

Whilst I cannot go through every possible situation, let me start by taking you through the steps I normally take in investigating such issues, and give you just a few examples of how these steps were so helpful.

16.3.1 Understand the Problem

The first thing we need to do is really understand everything about the leak that the customer is reporting. The following questions will help:

1. Where is the leak (within my part)?
a. This is very important in that we may not even be testing this area of the part?

Example (Figure 16-7): one leak test machine I worked on had inflatable sealing connectors. These actually masked the leak path being reported by the customer, so we had to redesign the connection to the part under test!

Figure 16-7

b.   I have often discovered that the leak is where the customer is connecting to the component, and that the leak is in the connection to the part.

Example (Figure 16-8): one of my suppliers was testing using a large soft seal to connect to the component. This seal masked the scratch that my company was finding when we used the correct thin gasket!

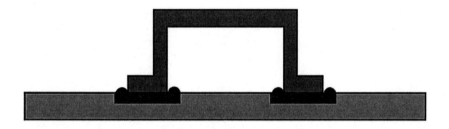

Figure 16-8

c.   I have also seen instances where the component is incorrectly designed (such as thin wall thicknesses in castings, or incorrect O-Rings specified in joints).

Example: One company I worked for had to redesign the casting body of a component to remove sharp corners that became stressed when bolted to the assembly.

2.   How and when does the leak appear?

a. Quite often we are carrying out our leak test with air, or trace gas, but the leak appears to the customer as an escape of fluid.

Example: A filter manufacturer was using an O-Ring that sealed in the part ok for the duration of the leak test producing an OK result, but once the liquid came in contact with the O-Ring, it lubricated it sufficiently to allow it more movement, and so allowing the fluid to pass by.
This may give rise to changes and/or adjustments in specification

b. In many cases the leak only appears after the part has been attached to a larger assembly and run for a period of time.

Example: This is common with automotive products that get heated during operation (whilst we can really only test the part under ambient conditions), and the component expanded slightly when warm causing it to leak at a greater rate than the specification.

c. Similarly, the component may see different pressures/forces during operation that we are not mimicking on our leak test of the part.

Example: One of the best examples of this is the automotive radiator manufacturer, who had to add a vacuum leak test as well as the normal operating pressure leak test, to be able to detect leaks created by the customers filling system that evacuated the radiator prior to allowing fluid in during the rapid fill

d. Finally, is the customer finding the leak when in operation or during their leak test on the part when it is attached to a larger/complete assembly.

Example: I worked for a company that carried out air leak testing on engines, but these leak tests had to be carried out at one specific pressure for each individual circuit, even though different parts of that circuit might see different pressures during normal operation.

3. How big is the leak?
a. Is the customer able to advise how much leakage there is (remember our Fit For Purpose Rule—maybe the part can leak a small amount in operation without detriment to its operation.

Example (Figure 16-9): One exhaust system manufacturer was failing parts as they were testing them using a bubbles underwater test, and failing all parts that exhibited any sign of bubbles. Even though in practice it didn't matter if the exhaust system leaked a small amount of gas when in normal use.

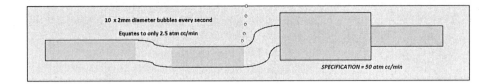

Figure 16-9

i.   Again this may give rise to questions surrounding the specification levels/limits and adjustments being required.

16.3.2 Review/Understand the Specification

Quite often, the leakage limit for the component is determined by the customer, and although we are working to this specification, it may not reflect the in operation use of the component.

The following questions should all be asked at the outset of the part development, and the leak test equipment development, but in any case, it is always worth reviewing these.

1.   What precisely are we leak testing for?
a.   Are we looking for escape or ingress—this will determine the pressure gradient across the component and will help us employ the correct test.
b.   Are we looking for liquid leakage, vapours, or gases?
c.   Is there a level of leakage allowed?
2.   What pressures does the part see in operation at the customer?
a.   We must be sure to be able to test the part so that it does not leak in normal operation.
b.   However, the customer may be performing their own leak test on the complete assembly to which the part is attached.
i.   Maybe this (customer leak test) differs from ours, and/or from the in-operation conditions.

16.3.3 Review Leak Test Results

One of the most important actions to carry out when questions arise about our parts (this again shows the benefit of recording leak test result data in our leak test machine, as this can save so much time). Consider the following when reviewing test results:

1. Reviewing our normal test results
   review a set of test results from the leak test machine to assess its general performance.
   a. Are my results repeatable and stable?
   Or do they contain -ve values that may subtract from potential leakers that are beyond my limit? (Figure 16-10)
   i. This is a good check of the machine parameter set up.

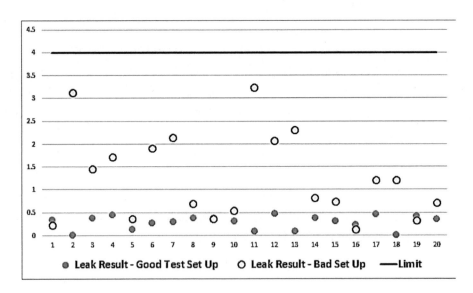

Figure 16-10

   b. Do my calibration check results show good repeatability, and confirm that our system is leak testing correctly? (Figure 16-11)
   i. These confirm the accuracy and repeatability of your leak test.

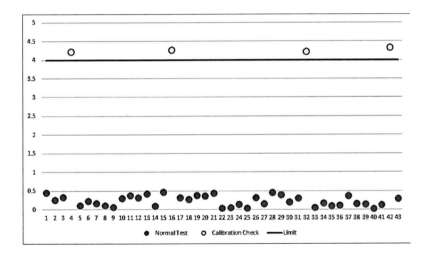

Figure 16-11

c. Does my limit meet the required specification?

i. Try to employ a master leak that is slightly above the limit to confirm failure results, as I have shown in the calibration check results above.

d. Do I have good signal to noise ratio for my good part results compared to my known leakage limit (Figure 16-12). Observing our regular day to day results may show a considerable amount of freedom to move our limit?

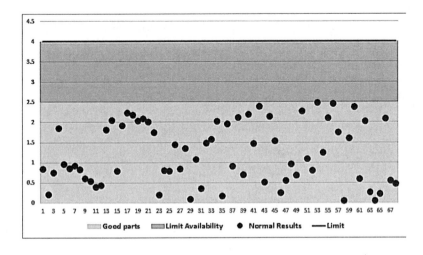

Figure 16-12

e. And can I see any potential outliers that may be the source of the failed parts? (Figure 16-13)

i. This would allow for adjustments if it is found to be beneficial.

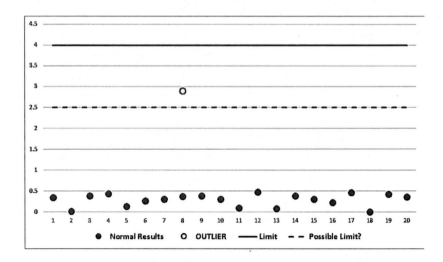

Figure 16-13

f. Can I see any drift or unwanted results that may be caused by external effects such as temperature changes, or shift changes etc.

2. Recover the failed parts if possible and repeat the leak test on these specific parts. This can be really useful to understand the leaks being reported by the customer.

a. Do the parts have signs of being leak tested, such as a pass ink mark, or an etched pass indication etc.

i. If not then how did they reach the customer—maybe time to review our processes.

b. Do these parts pass my test now?

i. Do we have the test results from the first time they were tested (e.g., a date code, or serial number that we can trace).

ii. If they now fail, has the process used by the customer affected them in some way?

Example: I once visited the customer of a fuel filter manufacturer, and discovered that the customer was clamping the parts in a vice to fit an additional fitting—this clamping of the parts was causing fine cracks in the casing!

c. What leak value do these failed parts give?

Hopefully, you will see from the charts the benefit of keeping a record of test results, and how they can help diagnose problems that may arise. Or better still track them yourself regularly to help identify and root cause any concerns, or potential improvements that can be made.

16.4 Calibration Check Results Varying

Quite simply, there are only two real causes of this condition:

1. Leak test set up incorrect
    Invariably, the root cause is simply due to incorrect test parameters. Either they have been altered for some reason, or they were just not set up properly during the initial commissioning stage. The only solution is to review all test parameters.
2. External effect
    Usually, a temperature effect caused by someone putting a heater or fan nearby due to changeable weather conditions. Or as in one case I discovered just the fact that the roller doors at the end of the factory were opened from time to time, creating a draught across the part during testing.

Such events can usually be identified by reviewing normal test results, which will likely vary along with the calibration check results.

16.5 Occasional Failure for no Apparent Reason (Part Passes when Retested)

This is a common theme for complaints about leak testers, and I was aften called out to look at a faulty leak tester(?) for this very reason. In fact the leak tester was always operating correctly, and the root cause was pretty much due to an external or other reason. I will just briefly go through some of the root causes I have discovered during my time as a leak test engineer.

Again, it is so important to completely understand the nature of the failures, and to review the test results, as it may be that you can establish a reason for the results by noticing a pattern in the results. Here are just a couple of examples that I have seen.

16.5.1 Seems to Get More Failures at a Particular Time of Day (Or Particular Months During the Year)

This could be a number of reasons, but most examples I have encountered of such reports have generally been related to external effects.

16.5.1.1 Example 1 – More failures at a particular time of day

A supplier (based in Turkey) to my company seemed to get a lot more failures during the late afternoon shift than at any other time. When we reviewed the test results over the course of a 24 hour period we saw a definite shift in results at the time they got their most failures.

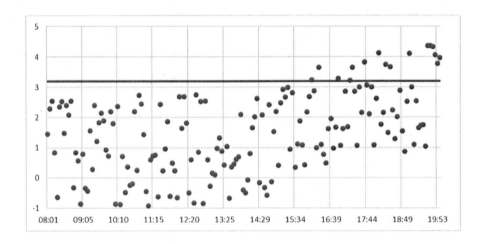

Figure 16-14

*As you can see their results (*Figure 16-14*) were ok, although not ideal during most of the day, but began to shift at around 3:30pm each day till the end of the day's production.*

After some investigation it was established that their seemed to be correlation between their manufacturing times, and their leak testing and that manufacturing was virtually completed for the day at around 3:00pm each day

(Figure 16-15), so the parts they were testing at the end of the day were predominantly stored parts.

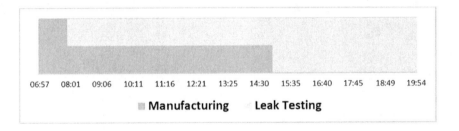

Figure 16-15

This alerted us to the fact that the true results were those during the latter part of the day, as the parts tested then were predominantly at ambient temperature (similar temperature to the surroundings, and leak test machine). The manufacturing included a hot wash, warming the parts, and so when they were tested, the warm parts created a pressure rise in the air under test, causing the "-ve" results.

The solution was to introduce a longer delay between the hot wash and the leak test so that all parts leak tested were at ambient conditions. But this meant that in addition we had to review and revise their test parameters to get better overall results.

16.5.1.2 Example 2 – More failures in the summer months

In this example the manufacturer of small valves noted an increased failure rate on warm days during the summer months.

My visit immediately alerted me to the root cause, as I noticed that they were using differential pressure methods to leak test the valves on open workbenches that all backed on to a basic corridor, at the end of which I noted a door (Figure 16-16), which they told me was opened during warm days to allow a breeze through the factory (making it more comfortable for the operators).

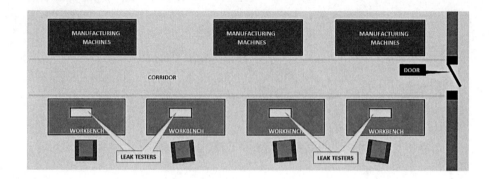

Figure 16-16

On closer examination, I noted that the test connections to the part were via nylon tubes which simply travelled from the rear of the instrument to the fixture on which the valve was placed in front of the instrument.

I soon realised that the cooling breeze was also cooling the test line to the small valves, whist the reference side of the transducer was simply blanked at the instrument and so unaffected.

The solution was simple (Figure 16-17). We added a reference tube, intertwined with the test line connection, so that both sides of the transducer would be affected by the cool breeze, balancing the small pressure changes caused by the breeze on both sides of the transducer.

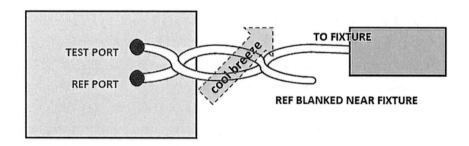

Figure 16-17

16.5.2 Seems to Get More Failures at the Beginning of the Week (Or First Couple of Parts Each Day)

This invariably happens when leak test instruments are idle for a considerable period of time (such as overnight, or at weekends). There are two possible scenarios that I have encountered, but both really relate to the fact that during idle time, seals are not frequently worked, and become slightly set. (after all once they have been compressed once or twice, they warm very slightly, and become more elastic, and tend to flow and seal better. This also happens after maintenance has been completed on a leak test machine, and new/unused seals are installed.

My recommendation to leak test users is always to complete a couple of tests, ignoring the results at the start of any leak test operation after any long period of not being used. This can be a good time to carry out calibration checks, by testing the master OK part initially a couple of times, taking the 2nd test result as the null/good result, and then to add the calibrated master leak to check all OK.

16.5.3 Completely Random Failures

This is the most difficult scenario to root cause, as they are a multitude of reasons. Most often it is simply down to the connection of the part to the test fixture and leak tester that is the cause of the problem. Let me give you three examples of random failures that I have identified.

16.5.3.1 Example 1 – Seal Wear

The first thing to consider as a likely cause is simply seal wear. By this I mean that seals used to connect to (or seal open apertures on) the part are wearing out, and are now on the point of reaching failure (by adding a small amount of leakage to the leakage in the part itself). To establish this as the root cause, we can first of all review our test results, to determine if we can detect a trend (Figure 16-18).

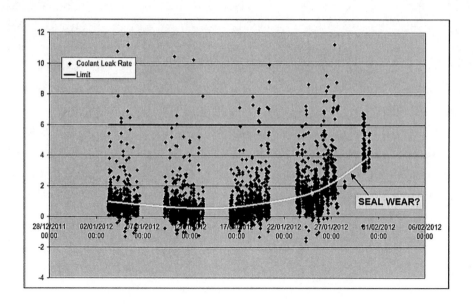

Figure 16-18

(Interesting note: The graph shown here though was not seal wear, but actually an increasing amount of rust being found present behind the seals of this tester—caused by a badly manufactured fixture plate, that had not been correctly anodised before commissioning!)

With or without test results, the task in identifying the actual root cause (or seal that is at fault) can quite arduous (time consuming), as we must inspect each seal to determine if it is fit for purpose or not.

In the appendix, you will find some charts showing examples of typical seal wear.

16.5.3.2 Example 2 – Quick Connector Leak

One great example I had of this was a Quick Connector that was used to connect the part to the leak tester.

Because the connector was built on to the end of a large/heavy hose, and depending on the angle of the hose/connector when it was plugged in, would determine the position of the internal seal within the quick connector. This variation in position caused the occasional fail result, but in most cases the O-Ring inside the connector sealed OK.

But sealing problems are not the only root cause of random failures, as I have discovered during many years of being called out to sort out problems.

16.5.4 Random Failures that Are not Real

In many cases, random failures are not due to a fault in the equipment at all, but are actually leakages measured that are real leaks, although not really the leaks we are looking for.

16.5.4.1 Example 1 - Borderline Leakers

The most common cause of reports of random failures however, are actually not random failures at all, but simply that the part would fail very close to the limit, and on subsequent tests pass, due to the inherent variation in test results (Figure 16-19), or due to some minor external effect.

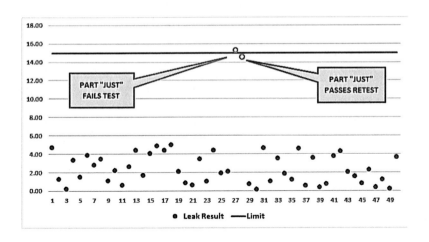

Figure 16-19

As we can clearly see, in this example there is an opportunity to review our limit to ensure we capture both conditions as a leak, however my experience in large assemblies shows that this often points to one particular component within the complete assembly that is always suspect, and in such cases the solution has

537

invariably been to review the leak testing (and manufacturing processes) of the supplier of that particular component.

16.5.4.2 Example 2 – Operator Error / Missed Rigging (Sealing Connection)

This most often occurs when operators are required to place a number of sealing connectors into a large assembly that has many open ports, and the simple fact of the matter is that the operator has missed one of the sealing connectors (often known as rigging) off. This was the case at one engine manufacturer, where they would fail an engine on the production track, but the leak could not be repeated/located in the repair area.

Again, examination of the results (Figure 16-20) gave us a clue, as these random failures would invariably show a very large/gross leak on the first test, which could not be repeated on subsequent tests.

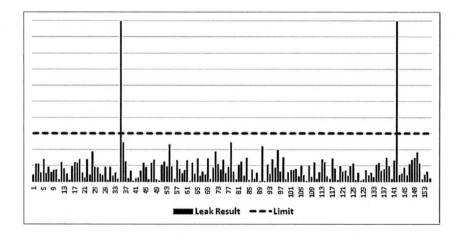

Figure 16-20

The operators were concerned about their jobs, as if they were found to make mistakes, then they could get reported, so they would say that the machine was faulty rather than alerting people to their mistake.

The solution we used was to have an amnesty for a few weeks, where the operators could advise if they had missed off a piece of rigging, as long as they advised which piece of rigging they had forgotten. This proved popular, and very successful, as we were able to identify common missed rigging, and were able to make improvements to this particular piece of rigging to make it easier to fit, and more obvious if missed.

16.5.5 Other External Effects

I have just included this as I have also seen a number of random failures as a result of totally disconnected effects. In the main the type of thing I am talking about is the effects of other equipment in our factory.

16.5.5.1 Air Starvation

I have, in my time, encountered leak test machines being starved of air, by which I mean the supply pressure drops creating fluctuation in our clamp forces, or even our test air supply pressure.

16.5.5.2 Electrical Interference

Some heavy-duty machines with large electric motors, can cause electrical spiking on the mains supply lines. These in turn ripple through to our leak test machine, causing random effects on our electrical control systems. This is not so common these days with good electrical filtration, however some machines also create electrical noise in the air, which then translates to our leak tester causing random fails (or worse still, passes).

17. Maintenance of Leak Test Equipment

So far, we have only considered problems but more importantly, we want to stop any problems occurring, so I just want to include a few lines about regular maintenance (sometimes known as TPM - Total Preventative Maintenance).

As with all equipment (domestic boilers, cars, lawnmowers, etc.), regular maintenance can prevent sudden problems occurring, and not just that, but can prolong the life of the equipment. Think about your family car for instance, if we just continually drive it and do not have it serviced regularly (such as oil changes, tyre wear checks etc.), then at some point a fault could occur that can be disastrous. I know from bitter experience from not getting my car serviced (long ago when I was I was young and carefree), when travelling on holiday, my car came to a grinding halt, as I had not checked my oil level. The result—a very costly repair with a new engine having to be fitted. But this only hurt my wallet, and not me. If my tyres were not regularly checked, the result of a tyre failure could be far worse!

And so it is with leak testing we want our Leak Tester to continue to perform well and for a long time (I know of leak testers that have been running almost continually for over 30 years). So let us briefly review some of the golden rules of maintaining our leak testers to ensure prolonged accurate service.

17.1 Rule #1 – Cleanliness

I cannot stress enough that keeping things clean and tidy is the single most important thing for all leak testing. Keeping our fixtures/machines clean and free from contaminants will greatly reduce the risks of problems going forward long into the future.

Simply wiping fixtures, work surfaces, seas etc. with a soft, clean and dry cloth regularly can reduce downtime considerably.

Where rigging is used, look for ways to keep this in good working condition, by using tooling boards, or purpose made storage trays, so that the seals do not sit in dirty containers, and become contaminated (Figure 17-1).

Figure 17-1

17.2 Rule #2 – Calibration Checks

It is also very important to regularly confirm the performance of your leak test equipment by using calibrated master leaks to confirm the correct response to the leakage rate of the calibrated master. Without this, you could spend many months not actually leak testing at all, and the first you know of issues is from customer complaints.

Calibration check frequency very much depends on the confidence level you have with your equipment, however there are few golden rules I generally apply regarding when to carry out a calibration check, as follows:

17.2.1 Change of Part Fixture

With interchangeable tooling, or where different part types are tested on the machine that may require different program parameters/reject levels etc. it is advisable to carry out a calibration check as confirmation that the new program/parameters have been correctly selected and are satisfactory.

17.2.2 Equipment not Used for a Period of Time

Whenever the leak test equipment has been unused for any length of time (particularly if it has been powered off/down), then performing a calibration check will ensure that all is still operational and correctly set up.

17.2.3 Regular/Routine Checks

These are, as I said, very much dependent on your confidence levels with the leak test equipment, but as a guideline to frequency I use the guidelines below.

17.2.3.1 Every Shift

Recommended for any new leak test system, as it not only builds your confidence in the reliability of the equipment, but also gives all operators a better understanding of the workings of leak testing.

17.2.3.2 Daily

Carry out daily checks for any equipment that is likely to be affected by surrounding conditions, and where the equipment is regularly powered down each night. If you find that the results are repeatable, then you may like to extend to weekly or further.

17.2.3.3 Weekly

As confidence builds, a weekly check may be sufficient. However in circumstances where the production line of larger mixed assemblies (such as I was involved in with automotive engine leak testing), this may be more appropriate than more frequent checks.

17.2.3.4 Monthly

This would be my recommendation for the longest period between calibration checks. It is often used when confidence in the equipment is very high, and product changes are not involved.

17.2.3.5 Annually

Personally, I would not recommend such long periods between calibration checks, however if confidence is extremely high, then I can understand why people might chose this option to reduce non-productive time carrying out calibration checks.

17.3 Rule #3 – Review Results

A great way of continually reviewing the performance of your equipment, and looking for any issues that may be arising from things like seal wear, environmental changes etc. For me the plotting of results on a chart is the best and clearest way to look at all test results as it makes reviewing very easy and obvious (a picture tells a thousand words), whilst just looking at a set of numbers on a spreadsheet is not clear.

17.4 Routine Checks (Table 17-1)

As well as my golden rules, there are a number of things you can do to prevent poor performance from your leak tester. These involve a number or regular checks, and maintenance activities.

Listed below are a few simple regular checks that can be made at frequent intervals:

Frequency	Check	Action	Reason
Every Test	In every leak test application, it is the component that we test that cause many of the problems and issues we have discussed to occur	Visually inspect all components to be tested prior to testing, or placement on the fixture Wipe or ensure that the component is clean before testing	Do not test any components that appear in any way damaged, contain moisture, or contaminants

Frequency	Check	Action	Reason
Every Shift change or fixture/part changeover.	CLEANLINESS: Check Fixturing and all Seals / Seal Faces: They should again be dry and very clean	Wipe Fixtures and seals with a clean dry cloth every day Wipe down/clean any parts of the machine that may come into contact with the part under test, or any area that requires operator observance	Fixturing and Seals are very important to make a non-leak condition General cleanliness is important in all aspects of leak testing.
Daily	Check Seals and Fixturing for Wear	Replace any seals that look worn or damaged in any way Remove any signs of dirt or grit from seal areas, 'O'-Ring grooves Repair and clean any parts of the fixturing that appears damaged	Fixturing and Seals are very important to make a non-leak condition

Frequency	Check	Action	Reason
Weekly	Check the Mains air (and Trace Gas Supplies) that are supplying the equipment: Check that they are Clean and dry, and at sufficient (recommended) pressure levels Also check any other pressures etc. that are important to the leak test performance.	Replace any dirty Filters Remove any moisture within the gas supply filter bowl where fitted	Air and Tracer Gas Leak testers are susceptible to contamination and moisture
Weekly	Check Oil Levels, and other consumables	Top up as required	To ensure reliable operation of the equipment

Table 17-1

17.5 Routine Maintenance Checks (Table 17-2)

Some of the actions above together with a few other checks, should be made at regular intervals to reduce the likelihood of breakdown.

Frequency	Check	Action	Reason
Monthly	Check Seals are in good order	At least once a month the seals should be changed whether or not they appear OK	Reduces down time for seal wear

Frequency	Check	Action	Reason
Monthly	Make a Full Calibration Check *(this is my recommended maximum period between calibration checks)*	Make Zero (non-leak) and Master leak Measurements and record results. Set alarm level, or adjust calibration factors according to procedure used.	Sets the system to accurately measure the leakage to our required specification (Also helps to indicate possible faults)
Yearly	Check operation and function of all parts of the system	General inspection and overhaul to be made on all electrical, pneumatic (pipework), and mechanical parts/components of the complete leak test facility This includes checking the functionality of any sensors, of measurement devices that form part of our leak test machines.	General preventative maintenance.

Table 17-2

17.6 Manufacturers Recommendations

Obviously, maintenance involves a lot more than just routine checks, and often will involve regular replacement of consumables such as oil/water etc. just as the garage completes on your car when you take it in to be serviced. Here are a few that I have encountered during my time, but this list is not fixed, and I strongly advice seeking the equipment supplier's advice in these matters.

- Oil changes

  When using any lubricated system, such as vacuum pumps etc. their reliable performance requires the lubricant to be clean and in very good condition (just as in your own car).

- Pump overhauls

  Many pumps and hydraulic systems do require routine overhaul from time to time. This is really something that should be carried out by the OEM (Original Equipment Manufacturer).

- Water change

  To avoid health issues the water in a water bath system should be completely replaced regularly, and the bath thoroughly cleaned.

- Instrument calibration check

  Not an essential for me as our calibration checks ensure reliable and repeatable performance, however many suppliers will require the sensing/measuring device within their instrument to be calibrated regularly (usually annually).

- Detector overhaul

  Mainly appropriate to Helium Mass Spectrometers, these types of detectors require replacement of key elements such as the ionising filament, to continue to function reliably.

18. Appendix

18.1 Conversion Tables

Here are a few conversion charts that may be helpful.

18.1.1 Length Conversions (Table 18-1)

MULTIPLY BY	TO CONVERT TO THESE UNIT							
	millimetres	centimetres	metres	kilometres	inches	feet	yards	miles
millimetres	1	0.1	0.001	0.000001	0.039370	0.00328084	0.001093613	6.21371E-07
centimetres	10	1	0.01	0.00001	0.393700	0.0328084	0.010936133	6.21371E-06
metres	1000	100	1	0.001	39.37008	3.2808399	1.093613298	0.000621371
kilometres	1000000	100000	1000	1	39370.08	3280.8399	1093.613298	0.621371192
inches	25.4	2.54	0.0254	0.0000254	1	0.08333333	0.027777778	1.57828E-05
feet	304.8	30.48	0.3048	0.0003048	12	1	0.333333333	0.000189394
yards	914.4	91.44	0.9144	0.0009144	36	3	1	0.000568182
miles	1609344	160934.4	1609.344	1.609344	63360	5280	1760	1

(Left side label: TO CONVERT FROM THESE)

Note: Some numbers have been rounded up for ease of reading

Table 18-1

18.1.2 Volume Conversions (Table 18-2)

MULTIPLY BY		TO CONVERT TO THESE UNIT						
		cubic millimetres	cc /cubic centimetres	millilitres (mL)	centilitres (cL)	cubic metres	cubic inches	cubic feet
TO CONVERT FROM THESE UNITS	cubic millimetres	1	0.001	0.001	0.0001	0.000000001	6.10237E-05	3.53147E-08
	cc / cubic centimetres	1000	1	1	0.1	0.000001	0.0610233744	3.53147E-05
	millilitres (mL)	1000	1	1	0.1	0.000001	0.0610233744	3.53147E-05

centilitres (cL)	10000	10	10	1	0.00001	0.610237441	0.000353147
cubic metres	1000000000	1000000	1000000	100000	1	61023.74409	35.31466672
cubic inches	16387.064	16.387064	16.387064	1.6387064	1.63871E-05	1	0.000578704
cubic feet	28316846.59	28316.84659	28316.84659	2831.684659	0.028316847	1728	1

Table 18-2

18.1.3 Pressure Conversions (Table 18-3)

MULTIPLY BY		TO CONVERT TO THESE UNIT							
		Pascal	Kilopascal	Megapascal	millibar	bar	Atmosphere	mm of mercury	inches of Water
TO CONVERT FROM THESE UNITS	Pascal	1	0.001	0.000001	0.01	0.00001	9.86923E-06	0.007501	0.004015
	Kilopascal	1000	1	0.001	10	0.01	0.009869	7.50062	4.01463
	Megapascal	1000000	1000	1	10000	10	9.86923	7500.62	4014.63
	millibar	100	0.1	0.0001	1	0.001	0.000987	0.750062	0.401463
	bar	100000	100	0.1	1000	1	0.986923	750.062	401.463
	Standard Atmosphere	101325	101.325	0.101325	1013.25	1.01325	1	760.000	406.783
	mm of mercury	133.3224	0.133322	0.000133	1.3332	0.001333	0.001316	1	0.535240
	inches of Water	249.0889	0.249089	0.000249	2.49089	0.002491	0.002458	1.86832	1

Note: Some numbers have been rounded up for ease of reading

Table 18-3

18.1.4 Bubbles to Leak Rate Conversions (Table 18-4)

LEAKRATE cc/min		BUBBLE SIZE / DIAMETER (mm)									
		0.1	0.2	0.5	1	2	5	10	20	50	100
Bubble volume (cc)		4.19E-06	3.35E-05	0.00052	0.00419	0.0335	0.524	4.19	33.5	524	4190
NUMBER OF BUBBLES PER SECOND	1	6.98E-08	5.59E-07	8.73E-06	6.98E-05	0.00056	0.0087	0.070	0.559	8.73	69.8
	2	1.40E-07	1.12E-06	1.75E-05	0.00014	0.0011	0.017	0.140	1.12	17.5	140
	3	2.10E-07	1.68E-06	2.62E-05	0.00021	0.0017	0.026	0.210	1.68	26.2	210
	4	2.79E-07	2.23E-06	3.49E-05	0.00028	0.0022	0.035	0.279	2.23	34.9	279
	5	3.49E-07	2.79E-06	4.37E-05	0.00035	0.0028	0.044	0.349	2.79	43.7	349
	6	4.19E-07	3.35E-06	5.24E-05	0.00042	0.0034	0.052	0.419	3.35	52.4	419
	7	4.89E-07	3.91E-06	6.11E-05	0.00049	0.0039	0.061	0.489	3.91	61.1	489
	8	5.59E-07	4.47E-06	6.98E-05	0.00056	0.0045	0.070	0.559	4.47	69.8	559
	9	6.29E-07	5.03E-06	7.86E-05	0.00063	0.0050	0.079	0.629	5.03	78.6	629
	10	6.98E-07	5.59E-06	8.73E-05	0.00070	0.0056	0.087	0.698	5.59	87.3	698

20	1.40E-06	1.12E-05	0.00017	0.00140	0.011	0.175	1.40	11.2	175	1397
30	2.10E-06	1.68E-05	0.00026	0.0021	0.017	0.262	2.10	16.8	262	2095
40	2.79E-06	2.23E-05	0.00035	0.0028	0.022	0.349	2.79	22.3	349	2794
50	3.49E-06	2.79E-05	0.00044	0.0035	0.028	0.437	3.49	27.9	437	3492
100	6.98E-06	5.59E-05	0.00087	0.0070	0.056	0.873	6.98	55.9	873	6984

Note: Some numbers have been rounded up for ease of reading

Table 18-4

18.1.5 Leak Rate to Bubbles (Table 18-5)

Number of Bubbles per unit time	BUBBLE SIZE / DIAMETER (mm)								
	0.1	0.2	0.5	1	2	5	10	20	50
Bubble volume (cc)	4.19E-06	3.35E-05	0.00052	0.0041905	0.0335	0.524	4.19	33.5	524
1	3977	497	31.8	3.98	29.829546	1.909090909	14.31818182	1.789772727	2.749090909
2	7955	994	63.6	7.95	59.659091	3.818181818	28.63636364	3.579545455	5.498181818
3	11932	1491	95.5	11.9	1.49	5.727272727	42.95454545	5.369318182	8.247272727
4	15909	1989	127	15.9	1.99	7.636363636	57.27272727	7.159090909	10.99636364
5	19886	2486	159	19.9	2.49	9.545454545	1.193181818	8.948863636	13.74545455
6	23864	2983	191	23.9	2.98	11.45454545	1.431818182	10.73863636	16.49454545
7	27841	3480	223	27.8	3.48	13.36363636	1.670454545	12.52840909	19.24363636
8	31818	3977	255	31.8	3.98	15.27272727	1.909090909	14.31818182	21.99272727
9	35795	4474	286	35.8	4.47	17.18181818	2.147727273	16.10795455	1.030909091
10	39773	4972	318	39.8	4.97	19.09090909	2.386363636	17.89772727	1.145454545
20	79545	9943	636	79.5	9.94	38.18181818	4.77272727	35.79545455	2.290909091
30	119318	14915	955	119	14.9	57.27272727	7.159090909	53.69318182	3.436363636
40	159091	19886	1273	159	19.9	1.27	9.545454545	1.193181818	4.581818182
50	198864	24858	1591	199	24.9	1.59	11.9318181	1.491477273	5.727272727
100	397727	49716	3182	398	49.7	3.18	23.86363636	2.982954545	11.45454545

LEAKAGE RATE (cubic centimetres per minute)

Note: Values in Norm Font are Bubbles Per second

Note: Values in italics are bubbles per hour

Note: Grey Boxes = Bubbles per minute

Note: Values in black boxes are bubbles per day

Note: Some numbers have been rounded up for ease of reading

Table 18-5

18.1.6 Weight Loss Conversions (Table 18-6)

To convert for gas	Mol Mass (gm)	TO CONVERT (Multiply by)							
		gm/yr to cc/sec	oz/yr to cc/sec	gm/yr to cc/min	oz/yr to cc/min	cc/sec to gm/yr	cc/sec to oz/yr	cc/sec to gm/yr	cc/sec to oz/yr
Ammonia	17	4.18E-05	1.17E-03	2.51E-03	7.02E-02	23934	855	399	14.2
CO 2	44	1.61E-05	4.52E-04	9.69E-04	2.71E-02	61946	2212	1032	36.9
Methane	16	4.44E-05	1.24E-03	2.66E-03	7.46E-02	22526	804	375	13.4
R12	120.9	5.88E-06	1.65E-04	3.53E-04	9.87E-03	170210	6079	2837	101
Helium	4	1.78E-04	4.97E-03	1.07E-02	2.98E-01	5631	201	93.9	3.35
Argon	39.9	1.78E-05	4.98E-04	1.07E-03	2.99E-02	56174	2006	936	33.4
R134a	102	6.96E-06	1.95E-04	4.18E-04	1.17E-02	143601	5129	2393	85.5

Propane	44	1.61E-05	4.52E-04	9.69E-04	2.71E-02	61946	2212	1032	36.9
Butane	58	1.22E-05	3.43E-04	7.35E-04	2.06E-02	81656	2916	1361	48.6
Air	29.9	2.38E-05	6.65E-04	1.43E-03	3.99E-02	42095	1503	702	25.1
SF 6	144	4.93E-06	1.38E-04	2.96E-04	8.29E-03	202731	7240	3379	121
Note:		I mol =	22400	secs/yr =	31536000	mol/secs	0.000710299		

Table 18-6

18.1.7 Leak Rate Unit Conversions (Table 18-7)

MULTIPLY BY		TO CONVERT TO THESE UNIT							
		cc/sec	mBL/sec	cubic mm/esec	cc/min	litres/min	cubic metres/min	cubic feet per year	torrL/sec
TO CONVERT FROM THESE UNITS	cc/sec	1	0.987167	0.001	0.016667	16.6667	16666.7	0.000896	1.31579
	mBL/sec	1.013	1	0.001013	0.016883	16.8833	16883.3	0.000908	1.33289
	cubic mm/sec	1000	987.167	1	16.6667	16666.66667	16666667	0.895977	1315.79
	cc/min	60	59.23	0.06	1	1000	1000000	0.053759	78.9474
	litres/min	0.06	0.05923	0.00006	0.001	1	1000	5.37586E-05	0.078947
	cubic metres/min	0.00006	5.923E-05	0.00000006	0.000001	0.001	1	5.37586E-08	7.89E-05
	cubic feet per year	1116.1	1101.78	1.1161	18.6017	18601.7	18601667	1	1468.55
	torrL/sec	0.76	0.75024679	0.00076	0.012667	12.6667	12666.7	0.000681	1
Note: Some numbers have been rounded up for ease of reading									

Table 18-7

18.1.8 Leakage Rate to Pressure Decay Rate (Table 18-8)

PRESSURE DECAY (Pascals per sec)	Volume under test (Cubic Centimetres)								
	10	20	50	100	200	500	1000	2000	5000
0.1	16.7	8.3	3.3	1.7	0.8	0.3	0.2	0.1	
0.2	33.3	16.7	6.7	3.3	1.7	0.7	0.3	0.2	0.1
0.5	83.3	41.7	16.7	8.3	4.2	1.7	0.8	0.4	0.2
1	166.7	83.3	33.3	16.7	8.3	3.3	1.7	0.8	0.3
2	333.3	166.7	66.7	33.3	16.7	6.7	3.3	1.7	0.7
3	500.0	250.0	100.0	50.0	25.0	10.0	5.0	2.5	1.0
4	666.7	333.3	133.3	66.7	33.3	13.3	6.7	3.3	1.3
5	833.3	416.7	166.7	83.3	41.7	16.7	8.3	4.2	1.7
6	1000.0	500.0	200.0	100.0	50.0	20.0	10.0	5.0	2.0
7	1166.7	583.3	233.3	116.7	58.3	23.3	11.7	5.8	2.3
8	1333.3	666.7	266.7	133.3	66.7	26.7	13.3	6.7	2.7
9	1500.0	750.0	300.0	150.0	75.0	30.0	15.0	7.5	3.0
10	1666.7	833.3	333.3	166.7	83.3	33.3	16.7	8.3	3.3
20	3333.3	1666.7	666.7	333.3	166.7	66.7	33.3	16.7	6.7

(Leak rate (cc/min) — left vertical axis label)

Note: Some numbers have been rounded up for ease of reading

Table 18-8

This can also be shown graphically (Figure 18-1):

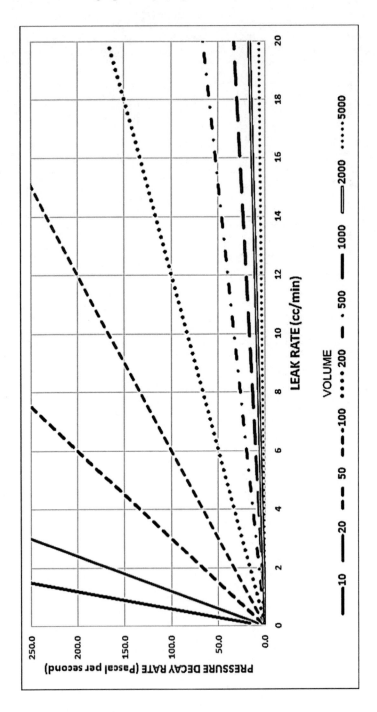

Figure 18-1

18.1.9 Hole Size to Leakage Rate (Table 18-9)

Hole diameters are often known as VLD (Virtual Leak Diameter).

These charts show the approximate leakage rate in atm cm3 min-1 for a given hole diameter depending on the gauge pressure applied. In this particular table I have used a wall thickness, or length of leak hole of 5mm, and assume that the leak path is a perfect tube (Figure 18-2) with a circular cross section.

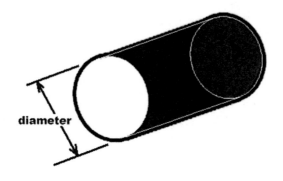

Figure 18-2

cc/min	Gauge Pressure (Bar) - Above Atmospheric										
diameter (micron)	0.01	0.025	0.05	0.1	0.25	0.3	0.5	0.75	1	2	5
1	1.6E-08	3.9E-08	8E-08	1.6E-07	4.4E-07	5.4E-07	9.7E-07	1.6E-06	2.3E-06	6.2E-06	2.7E-05
5	9.8E-06	2.5E-05	5E-05	0.0001	0.00027	0.00033	0.00061	0.001	0.00146	0.00388	0.01699
10	0.00016	0.00039	0.0008	0.00163	0.00437	0.00536	0.00971	0.01602	0.0233	0.06214	0.27185
15	0.00079	0.00199	0.00403	0.00826	0.02212	0.02713	0.04915	0.0811	0.11797	0.31457	1.37626
25	0.0061	0.01536	0.0311	0.06372	0.17067	0.20935	0.37926	0.62578	0.91023	2.42727	10.6193
30	0.01265	0.03185	0.06449	0.13212	0.3539	0.43411	0.78644	1.29762	1.88745	5.03319	22.0202
40	0.03997	0.10066	0.20381	0.41757	1.11849	1.37201	2.48552	4.10112	5.96526	15.9074	69.5947
50	0.09758	0.24576	0.49759	1.01945	2.73068	3.34963	6.06818	10.0125	14.5636	38.8363	169.909
75	0.49398	1.24417	2.51905	5.16098	13.8241	16.9575	30.7201	50.6882	73.7283	196.609	860.164
100	1.56122	3.93218	7.96145	16.3113	43.6909	53.5941	97.0908	160.2	233.018	621.381	2718.54
150	7.90368	19.9066	40.3048	82.5757	221.185	271.32	491.522	811.012	1179.65	3145.74	13762.6
200	24.9795	62.9148	127.383	260.98	699.054	857.506	1553.45	2563.2	3728.29	9942.1	43496.7
250	60.9852	153.601	310.994	637.158	1706.67	2093.52	3792.61	6257.81	9102.26	24272.7	106193
300	126.459	318.506	644.877	1321.21	3538.96	4341.12	7864.35	12976.2	18874.5	50331.9	220202
500	975.763	2457.61	4975.9	10194.5	27306.8	33496.3	60681.8	100125	145636	388363	1699089

Table 18-9

Or Graphically (Figure 18-3):

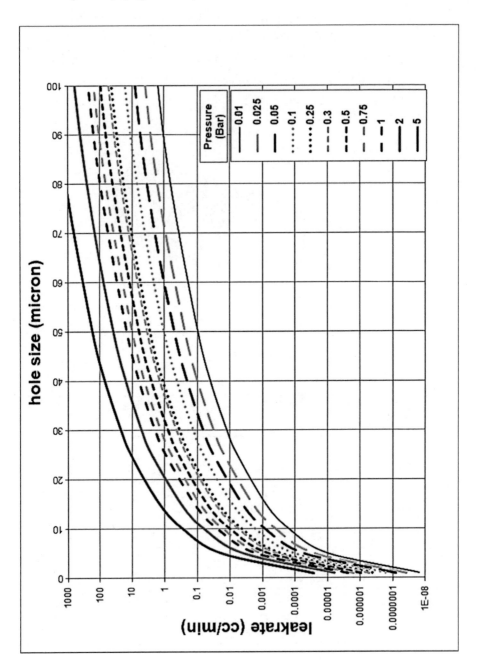

Figure 18-3

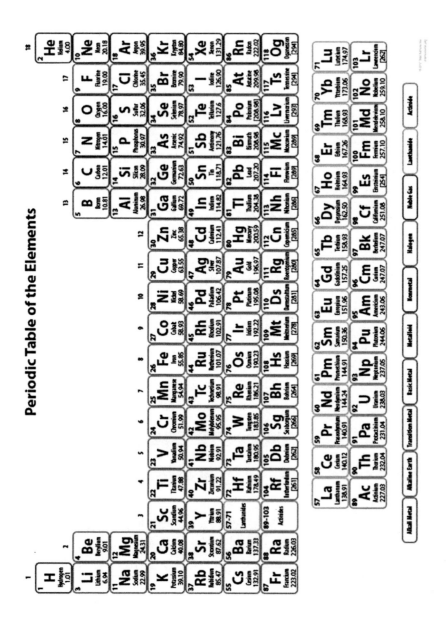

Figure 18-4

18.3 Typical Industry Standard Leakage Rates (Figure 18-4)

Some examples of leak specifications on automotive products

SOME EXAMPLES OF LEAK SPECIFICATIONS ON AUTOMOTIVE PRODUCTS

COMPONENT	TYPICAL TEST PRESSURES	TYPICAL LEAK SPECIFICATION	TEST METHODS EMPLOYED
1. Electrical components			
Windscreen Washer Pump	300 mBar	2 - 4 cc/min	Pressure Decay
2. Shock Absorbing components			
Air Suspension Parts	5 - 6 Bar	0.00001 cc/sec	Trace Gas
3. Power Steering Components			
Power Sttering Pump	5 - 7 Bar	5 - 8 cc/min	Pressure Decay
Steering Gear	5 - 7 Bar	5 - 8 cc/min	Pressure Decay
4. Exhaust components			
Catalytic Converter	0.5 Bar Vacuum	1 - 2 L/min	Flow
Exhaust System	0.5 Bar Vacuum	200 - 1000 cc/min	Flow
Flexible Bellows	0.5 Bar Vacuum	50 - 100 cc/min	Flow
5. Air Conditioning System			
Compressor	200 - 300 psig	0.00001 cc/sec	Trace Gas
Evaporator	200 - 300 psig	0.00001 cc/sec	Trace Gas
Condenser	200 - 300 psig	0.00001 cc/sec	Trace Gas
A/C Hoses	200 - 300 psig	0.00001 cc/sec	Trace Gas
6. Engine Assembly			
Coolant System	1.3 - 2.5 Bar	3 - 4 cc.min	Pressure Decay
Inlet Manifold	0.5 Bar	10 - 20 cc/min	Flow
Exhaust Manifold	0.3 - 0.5 Bar	10 - 20 cc/min	Flow
Oil Pan	0.1 - 0.5 Bar	4 - 10 cc/min	Pressure Decay
7. Transmission			
Transmission Case	0.1 - 0.5 Bar	10 - 20 cc/min	Pressure Decay
Complete Assemblies	0.1 - 0.5 Bar	10 - 20 cc/min	Pressure Decay
8a. Fuel Systems (LIQUID LEAKS)			
Fuel Pumps	0.5 - 10.0 Bar	1 cc/min	Pressure Decay
Injectors	0.5 - 10.0 Bar	1 cc/min	Pressure Decay
Rails	0.5 - 10.0 Bar	1 cc/min	Pressure Decay
8b. Fuel Systems (VAPOUR LEAKS)			
Fuel Pumps	0.5 - 10.0 Bar	0.001 cc/sec	Trace Gas
Injectors	0.5 - 10.0 Bar	0.001 cc/sec	Trace Gas
Rails	0.5 - 10.0 Bar	0.001 cc/sec	Trace Gas
9. Coolant Systems			
Radiator	1.3 - 2.5 Bar	3 - 4 cc.min	Pressure Decay
Water Pumps	1.3 - 2.5 Bar	3 - 4 cc.min	Pressure Decay
Thermostats	1.3 - 2.5 Bar	3 - 4 cc.min	Pressure Decay
Intercoolers	1.3 - 2.5 Bar	3 - 4 cc.min	Pressure Decay
10. Braking Systems			
Master Cylinders	5 - 20 Bar	2 - 3 cc/min	Pressure Decay
Brake Calipers	5 - 20 Bar	2 - 3 cc/min	Pressure Decay
Brake Cylinders	5 - 20 Bar	2 - 3 cc/min	Pressure Decay

Figure 18-5

18.4 Fault Finding Charts

18.4.1 Part Fails Everything – Air Testing (Table 18-10)

Make a test with a known good/master part:

RESULT	REASON	POSSIBLE CAUSE	ACTIONS
Master Part passes with the expected test result	Machine is functioning correctly	Difference between Master Part and Production Parts	Maybe they are not clamping or sealing the same way due to different thickness of material, or maybe the sealing face path is slightly different.
			manufacturing processes need to be reviewed, as we are now making leaking parts?
		maybe the temperature of our parts is not at the same temp as the master	allow a production part to reach the same temperature as the master and retest to assess if it now passes
Master Part only just passes	Maybe our system has developed a partial leak, and that our production parts are taking this background value above the leak limit	Seals worn	Check and replace seals to see if an improvement is noticed
		Connections between machine and part are leaking	Check all connections and pipework for signs of leakage (possibly using soap solution) – I have personally seen quick connectors develop leaks

Table 18-10

557

RESULT	REASON	POSSIBLE CAUSE	ACTIONS
Master Part only just passes	Machine Set Up is incorrect (or changed)	Maybe incorrect test parameters causing adiabatic effects	Check that correct Program is selected for this part
			Check program parameters are correct
			Check repeatability and calibration using master part and calibrated leak master
Master Part Fails (or gross leaks)	System has likely developed a leak	Seals worn	Check and replace seals to see if an improvement is noticed
		Connections between machine and part are leaking	Check all connections and pipework for signs of leakage (possibly using soap solution) – I have personally seen quick connectors develop leaks
	Machine Set Up is incorrect (or changed)	Maybe incorrect test parameters causing adiabatic effects	Check that correct Program is selected for this part
			Check program parameters are correct
			Check repeatability and calibration using master part and calibrated leak master

Table 18-11

18.4.2 Part Passes Everything – Air Testing (Table 18-12)

Utilise master part and calibrated master leak to make tests and determine response to calibrated master leak. Depending on the result for the master leak, follow the guidelines below:

RESULT	REASON	POSSIBLE CAUSE	ACTIONS
Cal Leak Result is as expected	If Calibration Port located at Part	No issues	No Actions
	If Cal Leak is in instrument and part is very, very small	Confirm part connection	Test gross leaking part to confirm connection between instrument and part
No change when Master Leak Introduced	Calibrated Master Leak not detected	Calibrated Master Leak not correctly installed	Ensure Calibrated Master Leak fully pushed home
		Calibrated Master Leak blocked	Try testing with open tube connected to calibration port to confirm leak detected
	If Calibration Port on/close to part	Blockage in test line	Check for blockages and re test master leak
			Is quick connector self-sealing
			Is leak tester blanked off from previous investigations
	If Calibration port in instrument is used	Potential fault in instrument	Consult Supplier

Table 18-12

18.4.2.1 Part Passes Everything – Air Testing (Continued) (Table 18-13)

RESULT	REASON	POSSIBLE CAUSE	ACTIONS
Lower than expected reading for Master Calibrated Leak	Incorrect Test Program Parameter	Incorrect program being used	Check program selection system
		Incorrect Parameters	Check Parameters in instrument
	Incorrect measurement of leak	Instrument out of Calibration	Carry out full Calibration check and adjust volume factors etc. as necessary
Much larger reading than expected for Master Calibrated Leak	If using Calibration port on instrument	Part Not Connected / Blockage in Test Line	Check Self Sealing Quick Connectors between instrument and part
			Check for blockages by testing gross leaking part and ensuring it is detected
	Incorrect Test Program Parameter	Incorrect program being used	Check program selection system
		Incorrect Parameters	Check Parameters in instrument
	Instrument not measuring leaks	Instrument fault	Consult / Contact equipment or instrument supplier

Table 18-13

19. Seal Examples
(Figure 19-1 to Figure 19-4)

Although by no means all possibilities, the following tables show typical seal issues, compared with the description of the requirements for a good seal.

Figure 19-1

FLAT / FACE SEALS

GOOD	BAD
	Flat Seal is contaminated (Swarf/dirt etc. can cause small leaks)
Flat Seal that is Fit For Purpose: Clean, and free of contamination, with no/very little signs of wear	Flat Seals showing signs of damage
	Flat Seal is badly manufactured (Cut lines cause small leaks)

Figure 19-2

Figure 19-3

THREADED PART SEALING	
GOOD	**BAD**
 Where a piece of "rigging" is bolted/screwed in place the threads should be clean, free of swarf, and should show no signs of damage	 Damaged Threads – A good indication of damage is when it is difficult to tighten correctly (may cause incorrect location and create leaks)
	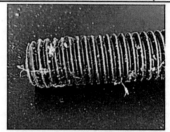 Dirty/Contaminated Thread – This example shows swarf on the thread (will cause eventual damage to the thread, causing leaks)

Figure 19-4

20. Exercise Answers

20.1.1 Mathematics Exercises

1. Monday, I bought 3 oranges and 4 pears for 66p, Wednesday I paid £1.10 for 10 apples and 3 oranges. Today 6 pears and 4 apples cost me 86p. How much do I need to take with me at the weekend to buy 5 oranges?

a. First, write down the equations as follows:

$$3 \times O + 4 \times P = 66$$
$$10 \times A + 3 \times O = 110$$
$$6 \times P + 4 \times A = 86$$

(O = Oranges, P = Pears, A = Apples)

Now by rearranging the first equation (subtracting the -4P from both sides) we can see:

$$3 \times O = 66 - 4 \times P$$

and rearranging the second equation (subtracting 10 x A from both sides) we can see that:

$$3 \times O = 110 - 10 \times A$$

so combining these equations we get:

$3 \times O = 110 - 10 \times A = 66 - 4 \times P$

$10 \times A = 110 - 66 + 4 \times P$

now $110 - 66 = 44$, so:

$10 \times A = 44 + 4 \times P$

and if we now divide both sides of the equation by 10 we get:

$A = 4.4 + 0.4 \times P$

If we now put this into the 3rd equation:

$6 \times P + 4 \times (4.4 + 0.4 \times P) = 86$

which becomes:

$6 \times P + 17.6 + 1.6 \times P = 86$

so $6 \times P + 1.6 \times P = 86 - 17.6$

or $7.6 \times P = 68.4$

we can work out a value for P by dividing both sides of the equation by 7.6:

$$P = \frac{68.4}{7.6}$$

so $P = 9$

putting this value into the first equation we can work out a value for O:

$3 \times O + 4 \times 9 = 66$

so $O = \dfrac{66 - 36}{3} = 10$

Answer = 5 oranges = 50p

2.   Simplify the fraction $\dfrac{12 \times 10^6}{-6 \times 10^{-2}}$

First divide top and bottom by 6:

$$= \frac{2 \times 10^6}{-1 \times 10^{-2}}$$

Now multiply top and bottom by 102

$$= \frac{2 \times 10^6 \times 10^2}{-1 \times 10^{-2} \times 10^2}$$

Now we can add the indices on the top of the fraction (6 + 2 = 8 so 106 X 102 = 108) and we could do the same for the bottom line (-2 + +2 = 0), and so the 10-2 and 10+2 cancel each other

$$= \frac{2 \times 10^8}{-1}$$

And +2 divided by -1 becomes -2

Answer = -2 x 108

3. Year 8 at the school has 3 classes as follows:
   Class 8A there are 8 girls and 11 boys
   Class 8B there are 16 children and 25% of them are girls
   Class 8C only five of the 19 children are boys
   Work out the % of boys in the year, and the average class size

a. First of all work out the total numbers of boys and girls in each class
   From this simply add up all the totals, and calculate the percentage of boys in the total (100 x # Boy/total pupils)

	Boys	**Girls**	**Total**
A	11	8	19
B	12	4	16
C	5	14	19
TOTALS	28	26	54
% Each	52%	48%	100%

Answer = 52% of year are boys

(28 divided by 54 and then times 100 for %)

b. To get the average class size, simply add up the total number in each class, then divide by the number of classes

	Boys	Girls	Total
A	11	8	19
B	12	4	16
C	5	14	19
TOTALS	28	26	54
Average	9.3333	8.6667	18

(average 18 in each class)

Answer = Average of 18 children in each class

(add up all the children 19 + 16 + 19 = 54 divided by the number of classes 54/3)

4. In a field there are 3 horses, 197 geese, 2,000 cows, and 7,800 sheep: Work out the ppm of horses in the field

a. First of all work out how many animals in the field all together 7,800 + 2000 + 197 + 3 = 10000

b. Now 3 of these are horses

c. so in the same way as we did our percent calculation, per million, is worked out by the number of horses x 1million divided by the total number of animals

$$= \frac{3 \times 1000000}{10000} \quad or \ we \ could \ write \quad \frac{3 \times 10^6}{1 \times 10^4}$$

Answer = 300 ppm *or 3 x 102 ppm*

20.1.2 Geometry Exercises

1. Our water bath is 0.5m long, 25 cm wide, and 160mm deep. How many litres of water do we need to fill the bath to the top?

a. Convert all to cm first (0.5m = 500cm, 160mm = 16cm).
   now multiply all together (500 x 25 x 16), to get the number of cm3, then divide by 1000 to get litres

Answer = 200 Litres

2. Holding our bicycle tyre under water, we see 50 bubbles appear over a period of 85 seconds. Each bubble is 3mm across. How many cm3 of air is escaping every minute to one decimal place?

a. First work out the volume of each bubble (4/3 π d^3/8) = 4/3 x π x 3 x 3 x 3/8), in mm3.
   Then multiply this by the number of bubbles (14.143 x 50) to get the total air leaked (707.15) and divide that by the time taken for these bubbles to get how many mm3 sec-1 (8.32).
   Now multiply this by 60 to get mm3/min (499.2), and finally divide this by 1000 to get cm3 min-1
   Answer = 0.5 cc/min

20.1.3. Notation Exercises

1. *Express 1 x 10-3 cm3sec-1 as mm3min-1*

a. *1 x 10-3 cm3 = 0.001cm3, = 1mm3*

if we have this amount in 1 second (sec-1 means per second) then we will have 60 times this in one minute
Answer = 60 mm3 min-1

2. *Three parts are bolted together, they measure 0.217m, 75mm, and 3000μm. How many cm is the total length*

a. *0.217m = 21.7cm, 75mm = 7.5cm, and 3000 = 3mm = 0.3cm.*

Adding them all together
Answer = 29.5 cm

3. We want to set our pressure to 5psig, but our gauge is in millibar—what value should we set on the gauge (to the nearest whole number)

a. 1 Bar is 14.504psi, so simply divide 5 by 14.504 to get the value in Bar (=0.345) and then multiply by 1000 (as there are 1000 mB in 1 Bar)

b.

Answer = 345 mB

20.1.4 Science Exercises

1. For our leak test on an engine fuel circuit, we have pressurised our engine fuel circuit to 1 Bar wrt atmosphere (*assume 2 Bar Absolute*). There is a single fuel filter with a 1 Litre volume, and the fuel circuit pipework is 5mm internal diameter and is 102cm long. All other volumes (pump/ common rail etc.) add up to a total volume of 15cm3) Calculate the temperature change (to 2 decimal places) that would cause the pressure to drop by 13.6 Pascals, if the temperature at the start of the measurement is 20 oC (293oK).

a. First of all convert all our values into the same units (Pressure in Pascal):

Volume in cm3, and temperature in oK)

Start Pressure (P1) = 2 Bar = 200000 Pa

Finish Pressure (P2) = 200000 – 13.6 = 199986.4 Pa

Start Temp (T1) = 293 oK

Using $P1/T1 = P2/T2$

T2 = T1 P2/P1

= 293 x 199986.4/200000

= 292.98 oK

The Temp Change is then T1 – T2

Answer = 0.02oK

2. During our test on a 1 litre plastic container, we notice that the container swells/expands a little when we apply our 1 Bar Test Pressure. Our test result showed a 12 Pascal drop in pressure. What was the volume change in cubic millimetres caused by the expansion of the container?

a. Again using same units throughout,

Start Pressure (P1) = 2 Bar = 200000 Pa

Finish Pressure = 200000 – 22 = 199978 Pa

Start Volume = 1000 cm3 (Volume of container)

Using P1 x V1 = P2 x V2 Calculate V2

V2 = P1 V1/P2

= 200000 x 1000/199988

= 1000.06 cm3

The Volume Change is therefore (V1-V2) 0.06cm3

Answer = 60mm3

21. Final Summary and Recommendations

I really hope you have found the contents of this book both interesting but most of all helpful and useful. Those of you who have met me, will know my passion for this subject, and I will continue to be available (for as long as I can) to help anyone who needs help or advice on my favourite (well almost) subject.

I would like to however just make a few final comments regarding leak testing which I trust will emphasise much of the contents of this volume, and help you too, to become an expert.

1. I strongly advise that all businesses that are utilising leak test equipment appoint an engineer who takes ownership of the leak test facilities within your operation. Although as I hope you now realise leak testing is relatively easy to understand, it nonetheless does require a level of dedication, and where I have worked with companies who have their own in-house leak test engineer, problems (and costs) have been greatly reduced. Ideally, this person will have a good grasp of the basic requirements for a leak test engineer, such as a good grasp of mathematics and an understand basic laws of physics with rudimentary chemistry understanding.

2. Logical thinking is the key to working with leak test equipment. Really focus on what the equipment is actually doing. (Pressure decay just measures pressure, trace gas detectors just measure the concentration of trace gas.) You will find that when issues do occur, they are much simpler to resolve, although they will also be fewer and far between if you understand from the outset.

3. Think about things in simple terms. (I draw pictures in my head, which helps me understand.) It really helps if you can find analogies that you know more about (for me PV/T being a constant was just like V=IR from my electronics training), and think of things in simple to picture

models—like gases being made up of rubber marbles, and pressures and volumes like buckets of water.

a. Think about leaks as something you can see, such as bubbles under water, or rubber balls bouncing about.

4. Remember the golden rules:

a. *Fitness for purpose*, when considering your test pressures, and leak specifications.

b. Testing should wherever possible directly *Mimic the part in use*, particularly, in clamping, sealing and pressure differentials. (We cannot account for thermal differences, etc.)

c. *Signal to noise*—we don't want to be looking for a needle in a haystack.

d. Pressurise parts before immersion to avoid liquid ingress into the leak path.

5. Remember key formulae:

a. Universal Gas Law (PV/T = Constant) is so important– from this you can work out everything you need to know about the effects of Pressure, Temperature and Volume. From this you can establish the pressure decay to flow (and vice-versa conversions)

b. Calculating Leak Rates in Bubble format (although I have provided what I hope is a useful table in the Appendix)

6. Regular performance Checking. This will save you time (spotting issues before they become a problem) and money (no need to have the supplier visit every year?) in the long run.

a. Maintain a master part wherever possible (or a reference volume)

b. Purchase/Use a Master Calibrated Leak.

c. Regularly perform calibration checks on your leak test equipment

7. Result Recording is so useful, as it offers many advantages.

a. Regular review of results can help identify trends

b. Can help identify optimisation and improvements that could benefit you and your customer (win/win)

c. Will help you with fault finding on the equipment, or root causing an issue.

8. Wherever possible, avoid the things that might give you problems (temperature effects, background contamination, etc.) and you will mostly have trouble-free leak testing for many years. Don't try and

compensate for something that can be avoided. However, there are special options available that can be of assistance.

9. Finally, remember that you are not alone: Seek help from the experts. Speak to experts on helium testing when discussing helium test systems, and experts in pressure decay and flow measurement testing for air systems. (I still do this myself.)

Now it is over to you...

THE END